THE WRITING OF THE WALLS

ARCHITECTURAL THEORY IN THE LATE ENLIGHTENMENT

ANTHONY VIDLER

BUTTERWORTH ARCHITECTURE
London Boston Singapore Sydney Toronto Wellington

First Published in Great Britain in 1989 by Butterworth Architecture
an Imprint of Butterworth Scientific

ISBN 0 408 50053 0

For Emily

CONTENTS

ACKNOWLEDGMENTS

The research for this book has been conducted over a number of years in libraries and archives in both Europe and the United States. Its themes have been discussed in seminars and lectures and, in some cases, they have been partially advanced in published articles. During this process, I have incurred many intellectual debts, which I gratefully acknowledge. Here, however, I am able to mention by name only those whose interest and support have been essential in the framing and development of my work. Manfredo Tafuri and Georges Teyssot in Venice, Bruno Fortier and Françoise Choay in Paris, Joseph Rykwert and Robin Middleton in London, Carl Schorske and Alan Colquhoun in Princeton, have all contributed by example and discussion; Monique Mosser has always been ready to offer practical advice and critical expertise; Antoine Grumbach has from the beginning made Paris a second home for me. Lectures at the School of Architecture in Princeton, at the Architectural Association School of Architecture in London, at the Dipartimento di Storia dell'architettura in Venice, and at the Institute for Architecture and Urban Studies in New York, have allowed the presentation of ideas in formation. The editors of *Oppositions, AA Files,* and *Lotus International* have provided more than technical advice in the preparation of earlier versions of some of the chapters, portions of which have appeared in their journals. The editorial skills of Judy McClain-Twombly and Robert Wechsler and the insistent optimism of Kevin Lippert of the Princeton Architectural Press have, finally, succeeded in prying the text from its author.

Paris, June 1986

INTRODUCTION

Recent studies of late-eighteenth-century French architecture have contributed much to reformulating the somewhat oversimplified categories debated in art history since Emil Kaufmann's idiosyncratic definition of "neo-classicism" rescued the period from an all-embracing "classicism." Kaufmann's subsequent modifications of this characterization—"architecture in the age of reason," "autonomous architecture," "revolutionary architecture"—have also been questioned by those who contest the too easy relationships between abstract form and philosophy, between architectural composition and social individualism, implied by his "spirit of the age" approach.[1] In the last fifteen years, a series of monographs and thematic works has revealed an architectural practice less "theoretical" and more tied to classical conventions than was assumed by Kaufmann and other proponents of a hypothetical "architecture of the Enlightenment."[2]

Cultural, intellectual, and social history, in their methods and in their subject matter, have been equally subject to radical revision over the past fifty years; the assumptions on which Kaufmann, Ernst Cassirer, and their contemporaries based their unitary concept of the Enlightenment have been undermined. The influence of the Annales school and, more recently, of a broadly conceived "histoire des mentalités" has led to the reexamination of traditional disciplinary boundaries. The history of ideas and the history of artistic styles have been subsumed under larger questions: the dissemination of knowledge, the distribution of power, and the representation of status. The history of architecture has thereby been enriched: building-type studies have been extended into institutional analyses; town planning has been viewed in the framework of territorial and colonial expansion; architectural expression has been interpreted as part of a larger social discourse of signs; and architectural theory has been construed as a means of professional formation.[3]

Many of these histories have looked at events within the context of the sociocultural changes that occurred at the end of the Old Regime and during the Revolution. The complicated shift from feudalism to modernism has been viewed in terms of continuity and gradual innovation instead of rupture and complete renewal. Many scholars have seen architecture as implicit or explicit evidence of political or cultural tendencies. Their contributions have made it possible to consider architecture as one among a number of professional practices involved in the representation and construction of an emerging social order. Architectural education, patronage circles, the professional press, design techniques, new building types, new sources of expression, transformations in taste, may all be seen as part of the general institutionalization of society, with its attendant political and economic strains.

To take one example: even as the monolithic idea of an intellectual Enlightenment has been recast in terms that include a consideration of literacy, book production and distribution, and Grub Street "philosophers," so the apparently effortless "invention" of new architectural forms heralded by Kaufmann has been rethought in terms of urban conflict, the reform of poor-relief, sumptuary codes, social symbolism, and techniques of graphic reproduction. An "autonomous" and "Revolutionary" architecture has been resituated at the heart of the crisis of the Old Regime.

Accompanying this interdisciplinary research, there has emerged a distinct self-consciousness about the nature of history itself, a reflection on the status of the questions, evidence, limits of explanation, and narrative forms of the discipline. This has opened the way for a rewriting of the history of historical thought: the contributions of antiquarians, collectors, travelers, and textual scholars have been assessed with respect to the formation of cultural and artistic history in the seventeenth and eighteenth centuries. The commonplaces of an "ahistorical Enlightenment" and a "historicist" nineteenth century have been modified.[4]

In the frame of reference provided by these initiatives, I have identified two domains where, toward the end of the eighteenth century, architectural thought and social change intersected. Both these domains seem to me essential for the understanding of artistic symptoms recognized but not wholly explained by previous hypotheses. The first, the realm of institutional reform, was a response to social and political necessity. The second, the domain of historiography, was the product of widening geographical horizons and increasing precision in scholarly methods.

Apparently separate fields, institutional reform and historiography were in fact strongly linked and complementary in their influence on architectural theory and practice. Both engaged the interest of academicians and professionals in a number of disciplines; both were influenced by Encyclopedist and philosophic currents; and, most importantly, both were concerned with the visual codes and symbols by which architecture represented its social purposes, "the language of monuments," as it was familiarly called.

The reform of social institutions increasingly became a preoccupation of successive administrations after the end of the Seven Years War in 1763. Pressures for poor-law reform, for the reconstitution of the Hospital-general system, for the improvement of medical care, and for the overhaul of judicial codes and penal establishments, together with a heightened sense of industrial competition from England, contributed to the development of a veritable "discourse on institutions." Informed by the social philosophy and economic theory of the Encyclopedists and their circles, benefiting from academic research in medicine and the physical sciences as well as from the increasing professionalization of architects and engineers, the debates touched on the redefinition of the factory, the hospital, the prison, the workhouse, and the whole gamut of public constructions serving and servicing the city and the country, from markets to cemeteries.

Encouraged by State sponsorship and private entrepreneurship, and with not a little disciplinary rivalry with engineers, doctors, and lawyers, architects gradually defined their role as designers for the public realm. Traditional ideas of embellishment and monumentality, the classical repertory of building types and representational forms, these no longer seemed adequate to satisfy the criteria of economy, utility, and programmatic nicety demanded by administrators. Economists, doctors, lawyers, and engineers were, for their part, only too ready to demonstrate by example that architecture was an unnecessary art, an inappropriate decoration of *besoin*, or need.

Out of these debates a new understanding of architecture emerged, one that absorbed or transformed classical wisdom on at least two fronts. First, the traditional sense of a building that embodied "beauty" in its proportions and its three-dimensional geometries was gradually subordinated to the idea of a geometrical order that followed the dictates of social or environmental needs. Second, the classical theory of representation, in which a strict hierarchy of embellishment responded to social *convenance*, was extended into a theory of architectural communication that would be readily accessible to the public. In this "primitive functionalism," the organization of the plan, the division of built space, was isolated as a tool of social control and reform, while the characteristics of the legible facade were identified in order to make of the building a school of sensations and morals.

This reexamination of the social practice of architecture was supported by the tendency of philosophic thought, following the investigations of Etienne Bonnot de Condillac into language and Jean-Jacques Rousseau into society, to return all subjects to their "natural" and therefore principled "origins." By this was meant the institution of single causes and their rational consequences, according to a coherent model, rather like that provided by Newton for the physical sciences. In architecture, this process involved rewriting the Vitruvian myth of the origins of building, a task accomplished with elegance by the abbé Laugier. His hypothetical "primitive hut" offered a criterion of judgment by which all subsequent inventions were to be measured; it also reduced architecture to the rational combination of three structurally defined elements according to the rules of simple geometries, in the service of social need.

But architecture, as both philosophes and architects agreed, was more than pure structure; it was also a kind of language, endowed with an ability to signify by means of the classical conventions and the history of their use and reuse. Architecture might indicate proprieties of rank and use as well as represent the nature of different building types. It might also, in the light of John Locke's theory of sensations, evoke emotions and moods, passions and ideas, by means of the qualities of its forms in light and shade. Edmund Burke's sketch of the possible effects aroused by an architecture of the sublime thus complemented the many enquiries into the modern iconologies and Orders that sought to renew classical codes. Cultural signs and natural sensations were examined for their ability to characterize, unambiguously, hitherto unknown or nonarchitectural building types.

On another level, this sense of architecture as cultural sign informed the research of historians, antiquarians, and anthropologists who, from early in the century, adopted the premise that architecture might be studied as an indication of the social mores and cultural identity of a people. At first conducted according to the rules of a static, systematic, and comparative institutional history outlined by Montesquieu, this research was slowly invaded by a sense of cultural relativity. The need to explain a culture on its own terms, to relate its artifacts to its laws and its language, its politics and its social order, began to override the traditional demands of religious, moral, and aesthetic judgment. The architecture of cultures outside the classical canon, for example Egypt or the Middle Ages, was gradually assimilated by way of research into, respectively, the origins of religion and the forms of chivalry. Gradually, historical explanation accepted the evidence of coins, urns, inscriptions, and nonliterary remains of every kind, including the evidence provided by sculpture, painting, and architecture. Historians began to confront the difficult methodological questions of combining aesthetic appreciation with historical description and writing the history of epochs during which art seemed in decline or decadence.

By the end of the century, they had sketched the outlines of an art historical method that joined a style of art to a form of culture and society. Naturally enough, this broadening history, with its range of examples drawn from nonclassical cultures, was pillaged by architects, who were seeking different motifs and types and were attracted by what seemed to be a universal language of symbolic forms common to all primitive societies.

The order of this book roughly follows these two concerns: institutional and historiographical. The first part, dedicated to theories of institutional form, opens with a consideration of ideas of "institution" in architecture and society from the early theses of the anthropologist Joseph-François Lafitau, through the experiments of Robinson Crusoe, to the developed theses of origins proposed by Rousseau and the abbé Laugier. I go on to discuss a parallel "return to origins" attempted by Diderot and his collaborators in the *Encyclopédie*: the principled analysis of manufacturing techniques and their implied spatial definition. The extension of this concern to the planning of entire factories, together with the social organization entailed by the *manufacture réunie*, is then discussed in relation to the industrial and rural architecture of Claude-Nicolas Ledoux, his building of the Saltworks of Chaux, and his projects for the forest *métiers* in the surrounding region. His attempt to develop a form of architectural expression for the factory was paralleled by similar propositions for the reform of hospitals. The debate that ensued is outlined in a chapter that contrasts the protofunctionalist schemes of doctors with the still monumental expressions of architects, pointing to the yet unresolved division between forms based on criteria of use, however fanciful, and those derived from an architectural tradition. A note on the various proposals for prison architecture before the Revolution underlines this distinction.

I conclude this part with two chapters on the extension of the idea of institutional reform to society as a whole. The first, describing the architecture of Freemasonic lodges and the rituals of sociability it framed, points to the way in which a theory of social perfectibility was joined to a set of symbolic forms that were, for a number of architects in the last two decades of the century, to serve as icons for ideal projects. The second, delineating the "alternative" societies and architectures invented by three thinkers, the Marquis de Sade, Charles Fourier, and Jean-Jacques Lequeu, themselves victims of institutional confinement and exclusion, emphasizes the power of the metaphor that linked architecture to society even in the imaginations of those who criticized and transgressed the existing order.

In the second part of the book, devoted to theories of historical interpretation, I have chosen to concentrate on a number of scholars whose texts reveal the variety of historiographical positions taken towards the end of the eighteenth century. I begin with a discussion of Johann-Joachim Winckelmann, whose powerful combination of aesthetic appreciation and chronological narrative was as influential in France as in Germany and Italy. I then contrast Winckelmann's idealist aesthetics with the iconographical approaches explored by antiquarians and linguists in the 1770s and 1780s, notably the theories of allegorical interpretation advanced by Court de Gébelin and the global reading of antiquity as "symbolic form" proposed by Viel de Saint-Maux, architectural critic, man of letters, and fellow Freemason in de Gébelin's lodge. Out of these two, apparently diverse decodings of the past, the Greek idealist and the antiquarian symbolic, Quatremère de Quincy forged his individual definition of "type" in architecture. Combining traditional attitudes towards characterization and representation with a normative vision of historical development, this notion forms the subject of a chapter that examines Quatremère's theory in the context of his early attempts to write a scholarly history of architecture from Egypt to Rome.

These historical researches were, at the end of the century, focused and institutionalized in the debate over the nature of museums, that is, whether they were "temples" that would symbolically bring together knowledge in a universalizing "pantheon" or, more originally, carefully designed stage sets for the exposition of a history divided into epochs and characterized by styles. I study this conflict of models in the context of Alexandre Lenoir's Musée des monuments français, which, self-consciously established according to Winckelmann's principles, displayed its contents in chronological order, century by century. The stylistic mise en scène provided by Lenoir dramatically, if not entirely accurately, illustrated the tenets of an emerging relativism that emphasized national history, the Gothic, and the identification of a particular language of forms corresponding to clearly marked periods. I conclude the book with an exposition of these principles of relativism as developed by the patron and collector Séroux d'Agincourt, who, in his monumental history of art, employed the carefully measured drawings of his collaborators to gather as many examples of each century as would make possible an objective assessment of style. Following Edward Gibbon's presentation of the "decline and fall" of Roman civilization, Séroux had to overcome his own classicizing taste in order to confront the styles of medievalism. His mixture of relativism and comparative method perfectly summarized the historiographical problems of the late eighteenth century even as it anticipated the more developed historicism of the nineteenth.

REBUILDING THE PRIMITIVE HUT

THE RETURN TO ORIGINS FROM LAFITAU TO LAUGIER

7

The first inventor of the arts was need, the most ingenious of all masters and one whose lessons are the best learned. Thrown down at birth, as Lucretius and Pliny said, naked on the bare earth, submitted from the outside to cold, humidity, the blows of other bodies, suffering on the inside from hunger and thirst, all of which strongly impelled him to search for remedies, man could not remain inactive for long. He felt himself forced to seek means of escape, which he found and then perfected in order to make their use more certain, easier, and complete when the need arose again. Thus, for example, when he felt the inconvenience of rain, he searched for a tree. If it was young and thin, he immediately found a way to ensure himself a better covering by bringing the branches together and intertwining and joining them to those of other trees in order to procure a more extended, secure, and useful roof for his family, provisions, and flocks. Finally, these observations having been multiplied, industry and taste having added something new day by day to these first experiments, either on behalf of embellishment or solidity, there emerged with time that series of precepts we call Architecture, which is the art of making dwellings firm, convenient, and decent.

Abbé Batteux, *Les Beaux-arts réduits à un même principe*, 1776[1]

THE COMPLEX ALLIANCE between antiquity and modernism that underlay the political and social idealism of the Enlightenment and supported the emerging disciplines of anthropology, natural history, and history, also informed the so-called primitivism of the eighteenth century and, especially, the understanding of architectural origins.[2] In the zealous discovery of contemporary savagery, whether in the Americas or Europe; in the enquiries into the structural and spatial beginnings of dwellings and monuments; in the formation of an architectural ethics that saw building and society intimately linked by functional and symbolic necessity; in the refusal of ideas of civilized progress in favor of a return to natural mores, the fragmentary texts of Hesiod, Lucretius, Posidonius, Seneca, and above all, of Vitruvius, played a formative role. These texts were valued not so much for their narrative forms, which described the origins of building according to a formula often repeated since the Renaissance, nor simply for their content, which seemed mythical enough to a materialist philosophe, but for the authority with which an antique notion of commencement might invest a modern idea of improvement. For the generations that followed Claude Perrault, and increasingly after 1700, the quarrel between the ancients and the moderns was less a debate to be won than a relationship to be made.[3]

VITRUVIUS AMONG THE INDIANS: LAFITAU

This didactic contract between ancient and modern had, in the first place, been pointed out by Vitruvius himself as he drew lessons on primitive construction methods from those of his contemporaries in Gaul, Spain, Portugal, Aquitaine, the Crimea, and northern Turkey, from, that is, the peasant cultures of the late Roman Empire. By these examples, the myth of origins, which described the building of the first huts as a result of the discovery of fire, the invention of language, and the establishment of society, was endowed with verisimilitude.[4] Similar details of primitive building techniques still in use by the inhabitants of Marseilles and Athens demonstrated the relationship between different materials and different regions; they also emphasized the progressive improvement, stimulated by competition and emulation, that had led to the perfecting of building and its gradual transformation into architecture by the application of the rules of proportion.

Vitruvius's account was of interest to early-eighteenth-century writers on a number of levels. It conveniently joined the origins of language and building to that of society, providing a model of language-origin alternative to that of the book of *Genesis;* it outlined a stadial model of civilized progress, based on the impetus given to intelligent activity by need, or *besoin;* its careful descriptions of the primitive forms of habitation—conical huts and square log cabins with pyramidal roofs, both realistically illustrated by Perrault (plate 1)—established the terms in which the geometries of dwelling, primitive and modern, might be analyzed and compared. Finally, and perhaps most importantly for the formation of eighteenth-century primitivism, the comparison of moderns with ancients was readily reversed. "If," wrote the Jesuit missionary Joseph-François Lafitau on his return from Canada, "the ancient authors have given me the understanding to support some apt conclusions regarding the savages, the customs of the savages have given me the understanding . . . to explain many things that are in the ancient authors."[5] This realization that, as the historian Arnaldo Momigliano has put it, "the Greeks were also once savages," gradually invested the classical world with a less shadowy pre-history. In this way, the antiquarian became the benificiary of the explorer, able to interpret the origins of mythology, religion, customs, morals, and languages according to a more or less systematic comparison of ancient texts and modern observation. The parallel was made less arbitrary by the general belief that the American tribes were in any case the descendants of the original inhabitants of Greece.

Lafitau illustrated the method in the frontispiece to his *Moeurs des sauvages américains comparées aux moeurs des premiers temps* (plate 2). According to his own description, the frontispiece represented a person in the attitude of writing, occupied in comparing many monuments of antiquity, pyramids, obelisks, pantheistic figures, medals, and ancient authors, with many accounts, maps, voyages, and other curiosities of America, among which she is sitting.[6]

To her left, two genii approach, the one carrying a caduceus of Hermes and an Indian peace-pipe, the other a symbolic Iroquois tortoise and an oriental sistrum, thus dramatizing the comparison between the New World and the Old; in front of her, a figure of Time, "whose function is to know all things and discover them at length," directs her gaze toward an allegorical vision that appears on the rear wall of the study. Here, floating in the clouds, are Adam and Eve with the serpent and, above, surrounded by angels and prophets, the images of Christ and the Virgin on either side of an altar. Time, explained Lafitau, gestures as if "to touch with his finger the connection all these monuments have with the first origin of men, with the basis of our religion, and with the entire system of revelation created for our first parents after their fall."[7]

Beyond the evident religious message of this engraving, the common descent of mankind from Adam and Eve, the destiny of all primitive religions, antique or modern, in Christianity, there is perceptible another, more philosophical meaning. Lafitau, transforming the traditional, Renaissance image of History from one who writes on the back of Time to one who confronts Time and his effects, has recognized the active role of the historian interpreting antiquity. In depicting Time referring the writer back to a single primary "origin," he stressed the systematic and static nature of the comparison he wanted to make. As Vidal-Nacquet has remarked, Lafitau found no contradiction between "the action of Time and that of comparison or, as we would say today, between 'diachrony' and 'synchrony'."[8]

This suspension of history is consistently managed throughout Lafitau's study, which methodically treats of the origins of the American tribes in Europe, their character, government, politics, marriages, education, pastimes, villages, domestic occupations, warfare, illnesses, medicine, death and burial, and, of course, religions (plate 3). In this sense, the Jesuit missionary has often been characterized as the father of an ahistorical ethnology or anthropology. The spirit of comparison that allowed him, in the words of Marcel Detienne, "to walk the Lacedemonians through the Iroquois villages and the Hurons through the Athens of Cecrops or Plutarch with an equal indifference, without wishing in any way at all to ensavage the Greeks or to hellenize the American savages," also allowed him to study rituals, customs, and forms as systems of signs to be interpreted culturally and socially.[9] His analysis of initiation ceremonies, for example, besides authorizing many eighteenth-century experiments in the foundation of new societies, anticipated many subsequent typological surveys of ritual and rites of passage (plate 4).

Central to this comparative analysis of cultures, and participating in their formation on every level, was architecture. In long chapters on the forms of Indian villages, the construction of their huts, their temples, and their religious symbolism, Lafitau inserted the received history of antique architecture—the Vitruvian account of origins, the Greek and Roman monuments as described in Pausanius and Denys of Hallicarnassus—into the detailed observation of the huts and ceremonial buildings of the American Indians. Both sets of monuments were interpreted, not simply as expressive of particular religious beliefs or social habits, but as signs of the nature of the different cultures as a whole, like speech and writing. The result of Lafitau's enquiries, for the understanding of architecture both primitive and developed, was its integration as one form among a culture of forms, a specific kind of sign within a system of related visual and social signs.

Lafitau's cultural history of shelter thus quickly went beyond the rudimentary descriptions of Vitruvius. Authors who, he wrote, "describe for us the first men as having only the trunks of trees and cavities in rocks for shelter," might well have added that the Eskimos, the savages of Detroit, the inhabitants of California all "retreated into caverns prepared by nature" in the winter or "slept in the open beneath the trees" in the summer.[10] Others, like the tribes of the Orinoco, interweaved the tops of high palms to form a kind of roof and built themselves tree-houses, "which seem made more for vultures than for man." These "nests" were necessitated by floods, crocodiles, enemies, and the perpetual harassment of mosquitoes.[11] Half natural, half artificial, such shelters represented a state of savagery only one step above nature.

It was among more sedentary peoples that the building of huts became a more regular practice. "Wandering nations" who, like the Algonquins, spent little time in one place, "contented themselves by making extremely low huts," (plate 5) while more stable nations had "dwellings a little more spatious and solid."[12] Even as the ancient Egyptians, as recorded by Diodorus of Sicily, built their houses out of sticks and reeds, so the Floridans, the Caribs, the Brazilians, and the Iroquois used "canes, reeds, the wood and leaves of cabbage-palms and bourbon-palms, the bark of birches and elms."[13] The forms of these huts were equally assimilable to those of antiquity: the Floridans and the peoples of Natchez in Louisiana built round houses, "like the tabernacles or tents of the ancients," or like those of the Gauls as described by Vitruvius. Others, like the Caribs, built oval houses, shaped according to the needs of their communal living habits, some sixty to eighty feet long, their pyramidal roofs sloping to the ground from a central ridge pole. The Brazilians similarly constructed large sixty-person houses in the form of arbors.[14]

Of all the tribes studied by Lafitau, the Iroquois were the most comfortably housed: a long bower or arbor-like shelter, a kind of tunnel, along which were ranged the fireplaces of the families, each marked by a square of four posts that held up the roof and lined on each side by seating and sleeping platforms. These also carried resonances of antiquity, as, "having no windows, they were only lit from above, in the same way as the celebrated temple of the Rotunda, the Pantheon built by Agrippa, which can still be seen standing in Rome."[15] Lafitau's descriptions thus moved between archaeological comparison and anthropology. Meticulously recording building techniques and parallels between ancient and modern, he also established a spatial phenomenology of dwelling that corresponded to his understanding of the mores and customs of different peoples. The relation between geometry and living patterns was clearly drawn, as was the comparison to the rustic constructions of contemporary Europe—the bower and the conical ice-house (plate 6).

Side by side with his inventory of the types of domestic construction, Lafitau observed the more ceremonial buildings of religious ritual and the symbolic representations of divinities. His history of the "origins and progress of idolatry" traced the emergence of symbolic forms, from the simple designation of a mountain or sacred wood, the erection of a standing stone or altar, the shaping of stones into cones, pyramids, and cylinders as memorials, to the sculpting of images and simulacra, as a parallel process in antiquity, in Biblical times, and in America.[16] The sacred symbols of the Lycians and the Druids were matched by those of the Appalachians in Florida, who dedicated a "perfectly round" mountain to the sun. The tribes of Natchez erected conical stones in their temples like the Amazons and Orientals or the Egyptians, whose obelisks and pyramids "no doubt represented the divinity" (plate 7).[17] And where he could find no temples or symbols among the Indians, Lafitau compared their reverence for fire to that of the Persians, who refused all signs but fire itself.[18] The temples of the Natchez even, like that of Vesta in Rome, harbored a perpetual fire, sustained by appointed acolytes (plate 8).[19] In an illustration that prefigured later histories of "symbolic" architecture, Lafitau depicted this history of representation in stone, from the first cubic stone to the pyramids, *conces,* and *hermes* of later religions.[20]

But Lafitau's assumption of precise correspondence between the ancients and the savage moderns was, like much early-eighteenth-century primitivism, mediated by a strong sense of contemporaneity and progress. To the French missionary, the contrast between the Americans and the Europeans was salutary: the savages of America, he wrote, "make a virtue of their idleness; laziness, indolence, and sloth are their taste and the basis of their character"; in Europe, on the other hand, "man, born for work, languishes and is bored in repose."[21] The Californians slept in caves to save them the trouble of building shelters; the Iroquois were "always sitting or lying and never walk about"; most primitive peoples were seen "always with folded arms, doing nothing else but holding meetings, singing, eating, playing, sleeping, and doing nothing."[22]

Thus, with the Golden Age of Hesiod, the Biblical Eden, and the legend of the Lotus Eaters situated geographically, the modern work-ethic was ratified by anthropology. In this guise, primitivism might have been interesting to the scholar, but it was hardly a state to be envied. The hut, a sign of savagery, was also a mark of deprivation and poverty: "the huts of every nation still show the poverty and frugality of those born in the infancy of the world . . . the savage nations have only miserable hovels and thatched huts, known in Antiquity as *mapalia* or *tuguria,* names entirely appropriate to give an idea of poverty."[23]

Voltaire, in his *Essai sur les moeurs,* extended this implication, commenting ironically on Lafitau's confinement of "savagery" to the Americas: "do you mean by savages, churls living in huts with their women and animals exposed unceasingly to the inclemency of the seasons? . . . There are savages like this all over Europe."[24] This sentiment was echoed by the Marquis de Sade, much later. He summarized the civilized world's disgust with the *chaumières* of the poor:

> The rustic hovel to which I repair for shelter when, during the hunt, the excessive heat of the sun's rays falls perpendicularly upon me, that hut is certainly not to be mistaken for a superior building; its worth is merely circumstantial: I am exposed to some sort of danger; I find something which affords protection; I use it; but is it something the grander on that account? Can it be the less contemptible?[25]

In Lafitau's idea of the primitive there was little sense of that principled "return to origins" espoused by philosophes later in the century. As he confessed to the Duc d'Orléans in the dedication to his book, "a depiction of the mores of the peoples of the New World. . . presents only savage exteriors and barbarous customs," interesting to the modern reader by virtue of their "contrast" to those of the advanced nations of Europe.[26] Lafitau's vision of savagery was as picturesque as it was anthropological. He saw the pagan Indians through an aesthetic of the sublime, as so many "shadows in a picture" or like the sight of "certain landscapes in which whatever is frightening in nature is sweetened by a pleasure that extends to horror itself."[27] In the last analysis, his studies were integrally bound to the strategies of his mission: how to turn religion to its true path by means of an intimate knowledge of its errors.

The careful collation of ancient and modern examples of primitive life became, in the first half of the eighteenth century, a commonplace of scholarly enquiry, from Samuel Pufendorf, whose descriptions of the state of primitive man were drawn equally from Lucretius and travelers' tales, to those who, like Antoine-Yves Goguet and Cornelius De Pauw, extended the implications of Lafitau's method to the detailed discussion of Eastern and Middle Eastern societies.[28] While the mass of "evidence" thus assembled was less than enlightening with respect to the historical conditions of primitive society, it had the effect, important for the history and theory of architecture, of establishing a belief in the intimate, if not instrumental, relationship between social customs and the forms of dwelling, between religious rituals and the iconography of monuments. When endowed with the status of principle by the mid-century philosophes, such a belief was to inform not only the rewriting of architectural history in terms of its symbolic form and embedded cultural meaning, but also the invention of new building types, domestic and public.

FROM THE TREE TO THE CAVE: ROBINSON CRUSOE

The idea of beginning at the beginning was given its paradigmatic expression for the eighteenth and much of the nineteenth century in a work published in the year of Lafitau's departure for Canada, *The Life and Strange Surprizing Adventures of Robinson Crusoe, of York, Mariner.*[29] In this tale of isolated man, deprived of civilized comforts, struggling to subject nature to his needs, and, in the process, reestablishing on more principled grounds the modern forms of production, Daniel Defoe essentially turned a century of missionary exploration to practical account. By reenacting the story of origins, with all the acquired experience of life in the wild provided by travelers' tales, Defoe sought, so to speak, to correct the errors, moral and economic, committed by savages and civilizees alike. As Marx pointed out, Crusoe, despite Defoe's knowing references to the classical tradition of primitivism, was a paradigm of economic man, mercantile and colonialist. He was also a moral determininst, who, out of the conditions of a kind of solitary confinement, managed to reinstate a rational and technological order of the soul as well as of nature. For Crusoe, as Rousseau understood, was in no way a "natural man." Imbued with Protestant mores, educated and completely civilized, he had simply been deprived of the "strange multitude of little things necessary" for daily life, from bread to tools. He was, in other words, like the colonial administrator or the tourist, forced to make do, to improvise in his new surroundings a fair imitation of the home he had temporarily left.

This sense of transience, of modern nomadism, in an era of agrarian displacements, geographical exploration, and conquest, was especially marked in the form of Crusoe's dwelling: a heterogeneous amalgam of found and natural objects. And yet, even here, Crusoe exhibited a desire to improve on his predecessors by means of a careful application of experientially tested principle. Indeed it would seem from Defoe's narrative that Crusoe had had a thorough grounding in the literature of architecture, notably in Vitruvius and in Sir Henry Wotton's commentary on the ancient architect, *The Elements of Architecture,* first published in 1624. From Vitruvius, Crusoe derived his understanding that architecture had a specific origin and development; from Henry Wotton, who incorporated the tenets of Alberti and other Renaissance theoreticians into his own brand of common-sense empiricism, Crusoe absorbed the principles of selecting a site for reasons of health and defense.[30]

Having spent his first night perched uncomfortably in a tree and realizing the fragility of his makeshift tent, he began to study the problem of "what kind of Dwelling to make, whether I should make me a Cave in the Earth, or a Tent upon the Earth."[31] His solution to this dilemma—to build both a cave and a tent—already incorporated the historical hindsight of improving on Vitruvius's narrative of origins, according to which it had taken countless generations to evolve from the cave and the bower to the hut. Crusoe's criteria for the situation of this hybrid dwelling were entirely modern, directly paraphrasing Wotton's "physical," "economic," and "optical" conditions for siting buildings.[32] The "moorish ground" by the sea was neither wholesome nor provided with fresh water; a "more healthy and more convenient spot of ground" would naturally supply the needs of health and security. As if following Wotton step by step, he looked for a site supplied with fresh water, ventilated by breezes, sheltered from the heat of the sun, secure from ravenous creatures, and provided with a view toward the sea. The plateau he found, on the side of a steeply rising hill, the beginnings of a cave already hollowed into the cliff below, satisfied all these requirements. On this flat greensward, directly in front of the cave-cellar he had dug out of the hill, Crusoe pitched his tent and surrounded it with a semicircular stockade some thirty feet in diameter and five-and-a-half-feet high. Gradually, he turned this defensive wall into the wall of a much expanded house and laid branches from it to the cliffside, covering them with thatch. As he enlarged the cave, he supported it with posts and partitions.[33]

Thus Crusoe's primitive hut was a decidedly sophisticated building, relying on a sense of progress in architecture and a developed history of that progress; indeed, it encapsulated all the stages through which natural man was thought to have developed, as Vitruvius himself had it, constructing "better and better kinds of huts as time went on . . . by observing the shelters of others and adding new details to their own inceptions."[34] Not incidentally, Crusoe also provided for the exercise of what Wotton had called "the Royaltie of Sight," a pleasure parallel to that "lordship of the feet"—the joy of walking over one's possessions—that was the first condition of an aesthetics of property, one that "can endure no narrow circumscription" and "must be fedde with extent and variety."[35] A century after Wotton's territorial vision, the sensibility for economic landscape was embedded in Crusoe's improving gaze.

Defoe's materialist account of architectural origins, then, was both progressive and principled, embodying the simple and fundamental precepts of all good building, joined inextricably to economic and social development. Robert Morris, neo-Palladian popularizer and younger contemporary of Defoe, enshrined similar building codes in the less utopian practice of English landlords between 1725 and 1750. Morris developed Wotton's laws of lordly sight into one of the first theories of picturesque landscape design and found support for Vitruvius's myth of beginnings in rural England and Wales, where, he noted, one could see "huts and cottages built in the same manner [out of mud wall and thatch], just as if the inhabitants had newly started into being and were led, by Nature and Necessity, to form a Fabric for their own preservation from the inclemencies of the season or other, more prevalent motive."[36] Out of such experiences, Morris concluded, developed the Cottage, and then the Villa and the Palace, all rooted in the soil that gave their owners wealth.

Crusoe's hut, however, only partially fulfilled the terms of this progressive development; still tied to the cave, the tree, and the movable tent, it represented a half-way stage to independent building. Deprived of a sociability that, Vitruvius held, was essential to the spirit of emulation, communication, and competition that impelled the building of better houses, Crusoe sustained his position as a civilized being in nature by much effort and often slender margins. The line between savagery and humanity was tenuous and held more by moral determination than by forms of art. His house had a defensive rather than a domestic posture and, unlike the advanced, bourgeois house, it refrained from displaying its contents on the outside.[37] Rather, it dissembled behind a facade of thickly interlaced trees, achieving in nature the anonymity later to be sought by prisons and asylums, those other machines of perfect isolation and security. This double character of isolation—freedom and imprisonment—found its architectural figure in what Crusoe was pleased to call his "Castle." Certainly, there was no room either for a free-standing hut or for its symbolic embellishment in a world ruled more by fear than by optimism.

SHELTERS OF SOCIABILITY: ROUSSEAU

When, in 1762, Rousseau looked for a work that he might entrust to the young Emile as an introduction to the "solitary state" of man in nature and, thereby, a "touchstone of all others," he selected Defoe's narrative of *Robinson Crusoe,* which, as he noted, provided "the happiest introduction to natural education," a preface to the principled behavior of man in a social state.[38] Rousseau, however, impatient with the moralistic and religious overtones of Defoe's first chapters, wanted to reduce even this essentialist story to its essentials, stripping it of its "nonsense" in order to concentrate Emile's attention on the central history of Crusoe, beginning with the wreck and ending with the arrival of the rescue ship. Crusoe's tale might then be read as an object lesson in instruction for all the needs of a single man at large in the wild. Rousseau advises Emile to check each of the mariner's practical efforts by emulation, thereby embodying the experience of reading in the building of his life. Thus we might imagine Emile recreating Crusoe's fearful exploration of his territory, his first experiments in baking bread, his manufacture of primitive tools, and, finally, the building of his dwelling. Pressed to their logical conclusions, and no doubt against Rousseau's best instincts, Emile's experiments would have turned him, like Crusoe, into an agrarian improver, a colonial capitalist, and a rich man.

With these consequences in mind, Rousseau might have put a stop to Emile's innocent games, for with the development of architecture came that of civilization, a state Rousseau had criticized sharply in his *Discours sur les Sciences et les Arts* (1750), which describes in architectural terms the fatal difference between natural and civilized man, portraying the growth of luxury and embellishment as supported, if not caused, by the development of building:

> One cannot reflect on mores without taking pleasure in recalling the image of the simplicity of earlier times. It is a beautiful river bank, adorned by the hands of nature alone, toward which we incessantly turn our eyes and from which we feel ourselves distanced with regret. When men, innocent and virtuous, loved to have the gods as witnesses of their actions, they lived together with them in the same huts; but soon becoming evil, they wearied of these inconvenient spectators and relegated them to magnificent Temples. They chased them out, finally, in order to establish themselves therein or, at least, the Temples of the gods were no longer distinguishable from the houses of citizens. This was then the height of depravation; vices were never pressed further than when one saw them, so to speak, holding up the entries of the Palaces of the Great on columns of marble as well as engraved on Corinthian capitals.[39]

Rousseau did not, it should be noted, dispute the received history of architectural development, but rather its supposed beneficent effects. The simple life on the flowered river bank became an emblem of rustic and natural mores, which were to be contrasted to the attributes of high architecture displayed in temples and palaces, signs of luxury and decadence. And yet, as Rousseau admitted in the second of his two celebrated discources, the *Discours sur l'origine de l'inégalité* (1755), even this apparently simple hut had an ambiguous status in the history of morals. Modifying the Vitruvian narrative, Rousseau traced the emergence of man from his original, savage state, "alone, idle, and always close to danger," gradually forced by necessity and experience to distinguish himself from the animals, to develop self-consciousness, to invent tools and thereby dwellings:

> The more the mind was enlightened, the more industry was perfected. Soon, ceasing to sleep beneath the first tree or to retire into the caves, they found some kinds of hatchets made of hard and sharp stones, which served to cut wood, to dig the earth, and to make huts of branches, which they then thought of covering with clay and mud.[40]

This advance, however, had a double and morally contradictory effect. On the one hand, bringing husbands and wives, fathers and children together in a common habitation engendered "the sweetest sentiments known to man, conjugal and paternal love." On the other hand, the building of huts immediately introduced "a kind of property," from which originated quarrels and combat.[41] Thus, while in the first discourse we are led to see the primitive hut as an alternative to civilization, in the second we find that the first hut, product of the inevitable process of *perfectibility,* is morally necessary for awakening the best of human sentiments, but it is also the cause of the worst. The "state of nature" depicted by Rousseau was precarious and always threatened by its opposites, savagery and civilization. Only while men "were content with their rustic cabins" did they live "free, healthy, good, and as happy as they could be by their nature." The instant they discovered the possibilities of the accumulation of property and wealth, slavery and misery were born.[42] Rousseau saw the "smiling countryside" of agricultural man watered by the sweat of unhappy labor and "the walls of cities built out of the ruins of country cottages."[43] Hence Rousseau's censorship of Defoe, bracketing Emile's reading between the shipwreck and the rescue, withholding the revelation of the consequences of natural experience, and suspending Emile-Crusoe in a moment held outside time and history.

The site of Rousseau's natural society might thus be envisaged as somewhere between the savage forest and the civilized town; its form was comprised of a circle of simple huts surrounding a communal fire; its rustic festivals took place around an old tree, the first maypole. In the *Essai sur l'origine des langues,* Rousseau depicted this *société du bonheur.*

> In this happy age where nothing marked the hours, nothing obliged them to be counted: time had no other measure than amusement and boredom. Under old oak trees, conquerors of the years, an ardent youth by degrees forgot its ferocity: little by little it became sociable; in being forced to make itself understood, it learned to explain itself. There the first festivals were created: feet bounding with joy, eager gestures no longer sufficing, the voice accompanied them with passionate accents; pleasure and desire mingled together, made themselves felt at the same time.[44]

From this bucolic vision sprang a host of more or less sentimental, naturalist utopias at the end of the century, sometimes mixed with oriental or savage exoticism, sometimes, as in de Sade, defining "nature" as a state of unfettered eroticism. Architects in turn seized quickly on the imagery of rusticity for the *fabriques* and *hameaux* of *jardins anglais* and cottage architecture, following the tone set by Rousseau himself in *La Nouvelle Héloise.*

> We who consider ourselves informed often need to go to the most ignorant of peoples in order to learn from them the origin of our knowledge; for we need this origin above all; we are ignorant of it because it has been a long time since we were disciples of nature.
>
> E. B. de Condillac, *La langue des calculs* (1798)[45]

While Defoe provided an exemplary illustration of the moral, in the words of Richard Steele, "that he is happiest who confines his wants to natural necessities," and while Rousseau drew a convincing enough picture of the life of savage man and the ensuing corruptions of civilization, neither writer fully subscribed to the absolute empiricism of origins proposed by Condillac and adopted by d'Alembert as the sign of Encyclopedic method. In philosophical terms, "origins" referred neither to anthropological nor to historical truth, but to a logical analysis of the principles and development of knowledge. "The first step we have to make," wrote d'Alembert in the *Discours préliminaire* to the *Encyclopédie*, "is to examine, if we are allowed the term, the genealogy and filiation of our ideas, the causes that have given rise to them, and the characteristics that distinguish them; in a word, to return to the origin and generation of our knowledge."[46]

According to these criteria, a return to origins would serve to define the specificity and limits of an area of knowledge, a social institution, or an art. It would also provide rules of conduct and judgment, principles by which existing practice might be reformed. A general "genealogy of knowledge," as proposed by d'Alembert, would establish the nature of and the interrelations among different branches of learning: the etymology of words would write the history of the human mind as it sought to name and reflect on experience; a model of language origin would clarify the nature of grammar and provide clues to a reasonable and moral rhetoric; a study of the origins of sociability, of laws and mores, would guide legislators and indicate the conditions of a natural social contract.[47] Condillac had posited the "origin of human knowledge," drawing a picture of the birth of language from experience and developing what was to become a paradigmatic narrative of beginnings as he traced the slow evolution of speech from the first cries of fear and pain to their institutionalization as words and their depiction first as pictographs, then as written signs.[48] It seemed to him that "primitive languages, although limited, were better made than ours, and they had the advantage of showing clearly the origin and development of acquired knowledge."[49]

The origin of the arts, seemingly more concerned with pleasure than with the severe dictates of need, posed a more complicated problem. The abbé Batteux, unwilling to jettison centuries of classical imitation theory, simply returned the *beaux-arts* to a single principle of natural imitation; Condillac himself was more inclined toward an origin in use than in pleasure, stemming from the same root as language.[50] Primitive man, he claimed, was unable to experience "things of pure pleasure," bound as he was to what was either useful or necessary:

> Poetry and music were thus only cultivated in order to make known religion and the laws, and to conserve the memory of great men. . . . All the monuments of antiquity prove that the arts, at their birth, were intended for the instruction of peoples.[51]

Only later, with the development of wealth and leisure, was this moral and didactic function transformed under the combined influence of climate and society into the rules for artistic imitation. Condillac's relativistic materialism saw even these rules as ultimately stemming from nature, imitating not the outer forms of the world but its inner processes. "The fine arts," he concluded, "seem to precede observation, and they must have developed to a certain extent to have been reducible to a system. The fact is, they are less our work than nature's."[52]

In this context, the model of architectural origins described by the historian and philosophe Marc-Antoine Laugier might be interpreted strictly within the terms of Condillac's method. Writing some seven years after the publication of Condillac's *Essai,* Laugier, in his *Essai sur l'architecture*, pressed the reductive logic of origins to its extreme.[53] Under the unambiguous heading, "General Principles of Architecture," Laugier turned the narrative of origins into a manifesto for aesthetic judgment. Utilizing fragments of the traditional accounts from Vitruvius to Rousseau, he systematically eliminated any references to social or material causes beyond those of what he called "simple nature," within the powers of man "in his first origin, with no other assistance or guide than the natural instincts of his needs."[54] His picture of this first man, stretched out on a soft greensward beside a tranquil stream, might have echoed that of Rousseau's "beautiful river bank, adorned by the hands of nature alone," but Laugier's primitive, unlike Rousseau's, remained in a state of savage isolation throughout the building of the hut.[55] There were no other beings in his world, human or animal; only nature exercised an influence. First the burning sun, then the torrential rain, drove Laugier's savage into the coolness of the forest and then into the shelter of the cave. It was the cave, with its unhealthy air and its darkness, which deprived him of sight, that forced him finally to invent a dwelling: "the man wishes to make himself a dwelling that covers him without burying him."[56] Thoroughly imbued with the precepts of Condillac, Laugier proposed an origin entirely derived from the action of natural phenomena on the senses. Even the hut itself was a quasi-natural construction, its elements provided pre-cut, so to speak, by nature, for the use of a man without tools or fellow-helpers:

> Some fallen branches in the forest are the materials suitable for his design. He chooses four of the strongest, which he erects vertically, disposing them in a square. On these, he places four others horizontally and, above these, he raises some more that are sloped and that come together at a point on two sides. This kind of roof is covered with leaves, thickly enough so that neither sun nor rain can penetrate; and thus man is housed.[57]

Like Condillac's natural man, he brought to nature's materials a rational faculty of reflection, quite naturally thinking in terms of pure geometry as the rule for assembling his structure. He also provided an "industry" that "supplements the carelessness and oversights of nature."

In this way, Laugier reduced the origins of architecture to a "single principle," following Condillac's *Essai sur l'origine des connaissances humaines,* "a work in which everything that concerns the understanding is reduced to a single principle," and perhaps responding to the abbé Batteux, who, himself a friend of Condillac, had attempted to reduce the fine arts "to a single principle," but had excluded architecture in the process.[58] For Laugier, the hut as origin assumed a paradigmatic status for all architecture: if art, in general, "imitated" nature, then architecture might be demonstrated to imitate in its turn not the outer appearances but the inner procedures of nature—the cause and effect of physical sensation and need. "It is the same in architecture as in all the other arts," wrote Laugier; "its principles are founded on simple nature, and in the procedures of the latter are clearly marked the rules of the former."[59] Thus the hut was a "model" for the succeeding "magnificences of architecture." The vertical branches gave the idea of columns; the horizontal members inspired the invention of entablatures; the inclined roof beams formed the first pediments. As such, the memory of the hut would act as a salutary corrective to all subsequent additions:

> It is by bringing them closer, in practice, to the simplicity of this first model, that one avoids essential faults, that one grasps the true perfections.[60]

The "little rustic hut" dramatized the fundamental distinction between three levels of architectural invention: those parts of the building essential to the composition of the Orders, those introduced subsequently according to need, and those added simply by caprice. Laugier made it clear that only the first category was in his sense true: the columns, the entablature, and the roof forming a pediment on two sides of the building. "If each of these three parts is found to be placed in the situation and in the form suitable to it, there will be nothing to add for the work to be perfect."[61]

Laugier and his neoclassical followers were well aware of the "severity of the rules" he had outlined; responding to Frézier, his first serious critic, Laugier denied that he had "reduced architecture to almost nothing."[62] Rather, he had taken away the superfluous, leaving only the natural in all its simplicity; the architect was thereby encouraged to work with more precision and discipline. Like the musician, who had for centuries been content to combine seven tones in different ways without exhausting their potential, the architect, with Laugier's three basic elements "and with a light smattering of geometry," would "find the secret of varying his plans infinitely and of regaining by the diversity of his forms what he has lost by virtue of the superfluities denied to him."[63]

A reduced lexicon of structural elements, their combination and recombination according to geometrical permutations "to infinity," and the natural "variety" of the result, would become the methodological and aesthetic premises of late-eighteenth-century design. Despite J.-N.-L. Durand's later scorn for the obvious impracticality of a model hut without walls, his own diagrammatic design method owed much to this combinative system, with the added influence of the posthumous publication of Condillac's own *Langue des calculs.*

But Laugier, even according to the logical premises of Encyclopedists and philosophes, had left out a great deal. In the first place, he had ignored, or passed over, the central problem of classical aesthetics when confronted with a single origin: how to account for the introduction or emergence of the "art" of architecture out of a response to pure need? According to the abbé Batteux, it was for this reason that architecture could not be reduced to a single origin; it was and would remain a "mixed" art, an "art of necessity."[64] D'Alembert had agreed, defining it as "the embellished mask of need," indicating his prejudice in favor of necessity as opposed to embellishment.[65] Another critic of Laugier, Guillaumot, concluded that "the whole system is carried on a hollow foundation that he likes to call nature, because his rustic hut is in no way a work of nature. Every work by the hand of man is a work of art."[66] Debates over the specific relations of art to need would become commonplace in the late eighteenth century, establishing the groundwork for similar arguments in the nineteenth century over form and function.

Secondly, Laugier, in contradistinction to Rousseau, had chosen to eliminate altogether the *social* roots of dwelling, preferring architectural criteria derived from the internal logic of architecture to the external influences of customs or mores. The difference was emphasized dramatically in the two frontispieces prepared by the engraver Charles Eisen for the second edition of Laugier's *Essai* and for Rousseau's *Discours sur l'origine de l'inégalité*, designed no doubt in tandem and published in the same year, 1755. Laugier's frontispiece was entirely allegorical, illustrating the hut as a literal outgrowth of nature (plate 9). The four branches had become four trees, rooted, according to the underlying principles of natural form, at the corners of a perfect square; they had grown to twice the height of their spacing and, again quite naturally, their branches had crossed and joined together to form gables in the shape of equilateral triangles. In front of this miraculous work of nature, the Muse of Architecture pointed out its virtues to a young Cupid, student of the new principle. As if to reinforce the reductive effect, the Muse was seated on the ruins of classical tradition, fragments of capitals and decorative devices indicating the arbitrary and the capricious in the face of the true. No human form disturbed the birth of this pure principle.

Rousseau's frontispiece, on the other hand, illustrated a story used in the *Discours* as a proof of the incompatability of primitive life with civilized mores (plate 10). It depicted a Hottentot raised by Dutch missionaries on the Cape of Good Hope, demonstrating, to the Governor of the Cape and his aides seated outside the walls of their fort, his desire to "return to his fellows," gesturing toward a group of huts on the shore, his true home. "Nothing," noted Rousseau with delight, "can overcome the invincible repugnance they have in assuming our mores and living in our way." The hut, however rudely built, here became a principle of social happiness, not of architecture.

Thirdly, as evinced by the ruins of architectural decoration in his frontispiece, Laugier had eliminated all reference to the traditional symbolic and allegorical meanings of architecture, religious and secular. The geometry of the circle held no cosmological overtones, the verticality of the column no echo of a standing stone erected for primitive worship. The origins of religious symbolism, traced by Lafitau, had no place in Laugier's understanding. For Laugier, if architecture expressed or communicated anything, it was simply by means of an appropriate measure of simplicity or luxury for the task at hand: the elements of building were first and foremost constructional and logical; their assembly followed a law of geometry; architecture was not a language but a construct.

Some twenty years later, Jean-François Viel de Saint-Maux, arguing for the recognition of a continuous symbolic tradition as the true origin of architectural form, would scoff at Laugier's simplification: to trace architecture to such a barbaric origin was, he claimed, similar to conceiving the origins of music in "the first noise heard by men, whether of the Cuckoo, the Owl, the Cock, the Bull, or the Ass."[67] A similar objection was to be raised to Condillac. Laugier's model, it seemed, for all its later influence, was to be more a point of reference than a formal principle; architecture manifestly could not survive in isolation from its social roots or detached from its codes of representation.

In this regard it is significant that the frontispiece to the English edition of the *Essai,* also published in 1755, showed, in contrast to Eisen's engraving, a company of nine builders actively engaged in cutting wood, mixing clay and roofing, returning to the traditional iconography of editions of Vitruvius after Cesariano. Similarly, Charles Delagardette's depiction of "The Origin of Architecture," added to his publication of Vignola in 1786, left out the builders, but showed a hut clearly the work of men, not of nature: a rural population stood before it in admiration and, in the background, a cave and other more primitive huts demonstrated the stages of perfection outlined by Vitruvius (plate 11).[68] Departing from Laugier, Delagardette emphasized in his text the necessity for tools, and he even found an origin for the column base in the "hospitable bench that our forefathers sometimes placed outside their dwelling and that hid the lower part of the tree."[69] Quatremère de Quincy, in his turn, was to admit the necessity of the hut as principle, but he reinserted it into the canonical theory of imitation, returning the art of architecture to a sculptural origin, *à la* Winckelmann. In this way, for much of the later eighteenth century, despite the attempts of antiquarians and philosophes to replace it with better founded texts, the Vitruvian account of origins continued to assert a quiet supremacy, often under the disguise of the entirely new.

SPACES OF PRODUCTION

FACTORIES AND WORKSHOPS IN THE ENCYCLOPEDIE

Each kind of factory requires an individual treatment that determines its appearance, its siting, and the distribution of its different buildings. These buildings should comprise housing for the directors and the inspectors charged with overseeing the good order, economy, and perfection of each object relative to its fabrication; according to the nature of these objects, the buildings should be furnished with large halls, workshops, laboratories, storerooms, courts, and outbuildings. . . . The ordering of their architecture should be simple, without in any way presenting a martial character.

J.-F. Blondel, *Cours d'architecture*, 1771.[1]

IN THE NUMEROUS descriptions of manufacturing processes, craft practices, machines, and tools that made up that portion of the *Encyclopédie* dedicated to the *Description des arts et métiers*, there was little or no reference made to the architecture of workshops and factories.[2] Machines were meticulously analyzed and disassembled; tools were classified like so many zoological species; terminology was collected and compared like some rare language; processes were returned to first principles; but the space within which so much activity took place was virtually ignored.

From the point of view of the editors, this apparent omission seemed explicable. Concerned from the first with production and the painstaking collection and verification of undocumented procedures, with the dissemination as knowledge of what had been tradition, Diderot and his collaborators were content to delineate the trajectory that joined the raw material to the finished product. The philosophe was quite naturally drawn to the problems of language and method this presented and to the exciting complexities of machines such as the stocking-loom and the blast furnace.[3]

From the point of view of the mid-eighteenth-century architect, lack of discussion regarding factory buildings was even more understandable. The classical tradition, with its strict hierarchy of genres and building types, relegated the workshop and the factory to the lowest of problems with the commonplace admonition, echoed by Jacques-François Blondel, that they should be correctly sited, soundly constructed, and practically laid out.[4] "High Architecture," properly speaking, with its orders and attributes, had no place in such utilitarian buildings. With the exception of the relatively few large establishments—such as a royal foundation or Colbertian sponsorship, where the orders were used in a reduced way to identify the entrance or owner's residence—decoration was strictly out of place in a factory. On this, the materialist Diderot and the classicist Blondel agreed.

But this apparent blindness of the Encyclopedists to the work space was manifested only in writing; in the hundreds of plates illustrating the *arts et métiers* that were published between 1762 and 1777, there emerged a veritable discourse on the architecture of factories, self-conscious and calculated according to the same rational premises that guided the authors, and displayed, appropriately enough, through the rhetoric of the image rather than in that of the text.[5] It is true that these images, depicting every kind of *atelier* from the rustic shed to the *grande-manufacture,* did not represent architecture in a monumental sense; plans were rarely in evidence, and the motifs of high design were conspicuously absent. Indeed, it was the absence of such embellishment that was most striking, as it seemed to imply a lack of attention to design. What was presented, however, was entirely consistent with both a concern for every aspect of production and its rationalization, and with the incorporation of this concern into architecture; that is, the precise calculation of a space, geometrically and compositionally, for the processes, machines, and laborers it sheltered. As, in Diderot's terms, "each worker, each science, each art, each article, each subject, has its language and its style," so each *métier* had its space, at once an extension and completion of its machines and activities and a kind of machine on its own terms.[6]

DEPICTING THE ARTS ET METIERS

The permutations of this space were illustrated simply and systematically, trade by trade. A square room with plain walls, clean-cut openings for doors and windows, furnished with the plainest benches and steps, was exhibited in one-point perspective as if the viewer were looking through the aperture of a camera obscura, observing room and occupants, like a naturalist, without being observed.[7] This "scene," didactically staged for the Encyclopedic audience, remained more or less constant for most of the crafts, save for the occasional shift in point of view to reveal different aspects of a process by a panoramic, bird's eye, or diagonal gaze. What changed in every scene was the position of the windows, the size of the doors, the opening of one or more walls to the exterior, the particular structure of beams and posts required for certain machines. Nothing else intruded on the understanding of the order of work; no indications of materials, no unnecessary details, no more people in the room than were needed to demonstrate the stages of production, no proliferation of goods or residues. This "aesthetic of nudity," as Roland Barthes has called it, was an abstract system of primary geometries as pure as the logic that dismembered the machines and the tasks; in a real sense, it was transparent to those tasks, confirming and shaping the movements of men and wheels, water and smoke.[8]

A typical plan of this ideal workshop was that illustrating the workshop of the Hungarian leather worker: an exactly square room, two windows with square, gridded lights on the left, an opening at the rear, a bench on each side, and a stove at the precise center (plate 12). This type was modified and transformed for the small workshops of gunsmiths, jewelers, and cabinetmakers, for the large establishments of tobacco manufacture, silk, glass, and iron working, and for the urban boutiques of fashion and necessity.[9] Sometimes it was an open room, with benches and windows on all sides, as in the gold-wire drawing-mill; sometimes it was filled with machines, as in the turnery (plate 13); sometimes it was opened to the street, as in the dress shop, the corkmaker's, and the rug merchant's.[10] On occasion, for complex sequences of production, as in the forging of anchors (plate 14), the same *atelier* was viewed from different positions to illustrate the sequence of the work, like a series of *tableaux vivants* through which the observer moved, giving the illusion of a flickering dioptric box.[11] This typical *atelier* was then assembled in series, forming the nucleus of an entire factory: the Gobelins tapestry works in Paris was depicted in this way, one room leading to another as the process unfolded.[12] In every case, it would be possible, given the careful placement of apertures and furniture, to draw up the ideal plan of a particular workshop, noting the exact positioning of men and machines. Following the rhetoric of gestures, it would also be possible to reconstruct the economic movements of hands, arms, and bodies deployed in space, like the intricate patterns described by dancers, horses, and armies, delineated elsewhere in the *Encyclopédie*.[13]

The criteria that governed the depiction of the *arts et métiers* were the same as those that controlled their description: didactic clarity and economy of representation. In the first place, as Diderot noted, pictures explain a complicated process more clearly than would a long description:

> But the lack of practice that one has, both in writing and reading about the arts, makes things difficult to explain in an intelligible way. From this is born the need for illustrations. One could demonstrate by means of a thousand examples that a pure and simple dictionary of language cannot rival pictures without falling into obscure or vague definitions. . . . A view [*un coup d'oeil*] of the object or of its representation says more than a page of discourse.[14]

When approaching a *métier* or industrial procedure, there was no better way to describe and analyze it than by means of graphic techniques. Diderot himself spoke of sending draftsmen to workshops to sketch the machines and the tools; his editor recalled that the philosophe was often seen trying to reconstruct some machine by drawing or playing with a scale model of it on his desk.[15] But however it might have surpassed discursive language, the method of drawing followed the rules of linguistic representation that Diderot had derived from Locke: the machine, however complex, was reduced to its simplest form or its initial element; then other elements were added, as if the viewer were himself assembling the object from a kit of parts; finally the entire object rested complete, in its own space, used and naturalized as a means of production.

> Nothing has been omitted that could be shown distinctively to the eyes. In the case where a machine warranted detailed exposition by virtue of the importance of its use or the number of its parts, one has passed from the simple to the composite. One has begun by assembling, in a first illustration, as many elements as one could perceive without confusion. In a second figure, one sees the same elements with some others. Thus one builds up the most complicated machine without difficulty either for the mind or for the eye.[16]

Here, however, a second criterion came into play, that of common sense and economy. If every sequence of technique and work were to be depicted, a single *métier* would require hundreds of plates; thus a principle of selection was demanded that isolated only the most "important movements of the worker and those single moments of the operation that it is very easy to depict and very difficult to explain." "We have," claimed Diderot, "restricted ourselves to the essentials, to those whose representation, when it is well done, necessarily leads to knowledge of those things that are not seen."[17]

This essentialist and didactic method of representation was effective, indeed, only because it was also the method of the *arts et métiers* themselves. Similar principles guided the invention and construction of machines, the step-by-step articulation of craft procedures, and, by implication, the design of the workshop. Speaking of the proliferation of technical terms in each of the arts, and of the methodological difficulties encountered in reducing them to "a small number of terms, familiar and known," Diderot compared the problem of language to that of production; the sign should take its principle from the thing signified:

> Composite machines are only combinations of simple machines; simple machines are few in number; in the exposition of any procedure whatever, all movements are reducible, without any considerable error, to the rectilinear and the circular. . . .[18]

Thus the philosophe should search for a few, simple constants, "a constant measure in nature" by which to classify, compare, and understand the most complex of things.

We can easily see this movement from the simple to the composite reflected in the way that entire factories were built up in the plates of the *Encyclopédie* out of combinations of the primary square cell. First, the cell itself was transformed into a complicated machine, as in the plate-glass works. Here the *atelier* remained square, but the center became the privileged site of the ovens, and its structure was calculated around them. Then, always retaining the central square, side bays were deployed for ancillary services, as in the bottle-glass works, where a central, circular oven surrounded by six or seven work stations was joined diagonally to subsidiary heating rooms along the side. The structure of the shed was modified accordingly. Finally, the *ateliers* were shown to be parts of a continuous system of work spaces linked together to form a complete factory, as in the royal bottle-glass factory at Sèvres, where the plan and section represented one of four furnace rooms.[19] In this way, with some artistic license, an actual *manufacture* was shown to follow the laws established in the more idealized, hypothetical *ateliers* of the earlier plates. Similar sequences were to be found in the depiction of forges, foundries, sugar refineries, tobacco factories, tapestry works, and paper mills. Even when, in some of the more traditional and rural *métiers,* workshops were presented in a picturesque way, as if painted by Antoine Watteau or Jean Honoré Fragonard (appropriate enough to their "character," as Diderot would demand, but seemingly indifferent to their abstract principles of organization), every articulation of roof lines and structure in fact responded to a precise analysis of an ideal plan (plates 15–16).[20] The rural plate-glass works, plumes of smoke rising from its thatched roof, stood like some rustic *fabrique* in a forest clearing; but each of its major and secondary spaces was labeled, its connection to the outside carefully described (plate 19).[21] Depicted in the drawing of the plate-glass works was a special covered arbor that protected the glass-workers while they rested from their work—as if Laugier's primitive hut had now found its essential function. Nearby, the finished products, the wheels of plate glass, were shown packed in straw and ready for export.

The overriding presence in each of these representations was that of geometry. Showing itself in explicit ways, in the square of a plan, in the circular movement of a wheel traced in dotted lines on a section, in the multiple combinations of the primary forms that made up different forges and furnaces, in the elemental parts of a bench or a loom; or, more subtly, by implicitly guiding the gestures of a weaver, in the curved arcs of glass-blowers' pipes, in the placement of tools on a table, of tables in a room, this geometry was at once natural form and principle. Derived from centuries of practical experience, it was also a wise geometry, more flexible and organic than that of the academicians. The experiential "geometry of the arts," as Diderot argued, grounded the intellectual geometry of mathematicians; combined, the two geometries would lead to the perfection of every machine and *métier:*

> What is the true and absolute dimension of an excellent watch, of a perfect mill, of a ship built in the best possible way? It is for the experimental and operational geometry of many centuries, aided by the most agile intellectual geometry, to give an approximate solution to these problems.[22]

Together with this analytical geometry, another kind may be identified, one that had an equal, if not greater influence on the architects of industry: the universe of primary geometric forms that, like a collection of mineralogical specimens, was exhibited in the actual shapes of furnaces, forges, mills, and laboratories. Cylinders, cones, pyramids, cubes, and spheres were all displayed, pure and naked, in every conceivable simple and complex permutation and combination, as the essential forms of industry. And while the abstract stereometry of the engravers enhanced their primitive and clean effect, revealing in cutaway perspectives hidden forms within forms, these geometries were themselves increasingly evident in the landscape, as blast furnaces, tile kilns, and chemical works proliferated in the forests (plates 20–21).[23]

What the *Encyclopédie* plates accomplished was not so much a radical innovation as a naturalization, presenting industrial geometry as one among others and confirming a way of seeing that hardly distinguished, practically or aesthetically, between the forms of high art and those of useful craft. Later, so-called "visionary" architects might seek to bring a classical and universalizing symbolism, or to apply the aesthetic of the sublime, to these practical signs of industrial progress, but the foundation of their obsession with primary forms was laid in the imagery of Diderot's plates.

Here, however, in his intimation of a cultural absorption of Encyclopedic geometries, in the appearance of a rhetoric of images where only didactic transparency was intended, we may identify a contradiction between what Diderot might have seen as an art of designing factories and what architects might seize on as material for an "architecture" of factories. For Diderot, geometry was the essential form of need, of *besoin;* its procedures governed every natural and artificial action; a factory shed, a machine, a movement, each was subject to its laws. Thus, while space had a grammar and a logical syntax, a shaping and enclosing role, it had no independent rhetoric. Diderot was careful to distinguish the aesthetic quality of a machine from that of a work of art. The former might well, like an animal, have subscribed to the law that nothing may be added or taken away without destroying the working of the whole, but to be art, another level of form had to come into play, relationships based not simply on function, but on the specific characteristics of each art—its "hieroglyphs," as Diderot called them—as it appealed to sound, sight, and touch.[24] While both machines and works of art might share a basis in order and in logical relationships, works of art could not simply follow the logic of utility; they had to possess an expressive—a rhetorical—character.

> The perception of relationships is one of the first steps of our reason. Relationships may be simple or composite. They constitute symmetry. Since the perception of simple relations is easier than that of composite ones, and among all relations that of equality is the most simple, it is natural to prefer it; and that is in fact the case. For this reason, the wings of a building are equal and the sides of windows are parallel. In the arts, for example in architecture, to depart from simple relationships and the symmetries they engender is to make a machine or a labyrinth and not a palace. If reasons of utility, of variety, siting, etc., constrain us to renounce the relationship of equality and the simplest symmetry, it is always to be regretted, and we hasten to return to that relationship by ways that seem entirely arbitrary to superficial men.[25]

Logical relationships might exist, indeed should exist, among the parts of a machine, but their rhetorical expression was considered unnecessary; a work of art, however, designed for perceptible pleasure, had to express the existence of these relationships, thereby demanding the imposition of apparently arbitrary conventions such as symmetry. The question was sharply posed with regard to the architecture of factories: should the artist be content with a space that corresponded to and extended that of the machine in every sense, a building as a *machine à produire,* or should the task of the architect be to take these perfect internal harmonies and express them, dignifying and symbolizing them, embellishing need?

In his explanatory notes to the publication of the plans of the Manufacture royale des Gobelins, published in the second volume of his *Architecture française* in 1752, Blondel, himself an architect of factories, justified the inclusion of so utilitarian a building in a *recueil* of great architecture.[26] The Gobelins, as one of the more splendid of Colbert's foundations, had acquired "a universal reputation throughout Europe by virtue of the magnificent works produced there." It was also one of the more extensive buildings in Paris and entirely representative of the many other factories producing luxury goods for export and, thereby, of the progress, the taste, and the industrial talents of the French. Its architecture, however, was not especially remarkable; indeed, its growth over time and the extensions made to each of its buildings, together with the sheer quantity of its apartments and workshops, gave to "the plan in general, and the courtyards and buildings in particular, an irregular enough form." Like other factories, some built with more regularity, it was sufficiently solid and useful, but entirely "deprived of symmetry and ordering," that is, of architectural character.

The plan, the only one Blondel thought necessary to present, was, as he noted, the product of need: "necessity here prevailed over a more pleasing disposition." Nevertheless, for this reason—that "however irregular, it comprised in its distribution a sufficient quantity of rooms in relation to its purpose"—its representation might serve a didactic role.

> This building, which we admit in truth to be very irregular, could nevertheless be instructive, with the help of these indications [of the various functions], to those entrusted in the future with the composition of buildings for a factory of this type, in teaching them the suitability, the size, and the diversity of the different buildings, courtyards, and gardens it should contain. This is our principal object in this work, [which] treats in general of the distribution and ordering of all the buildings that comprise civil architecture.[27]

The insistence on irregularity, so that there should be no doubt as to Blondel's opinions of the architectural merit of the Gobelins, was overridden by two circumstances: its role in the economy and in the reputation of the nation, and its special complication and size, which made it a lesson for architects. Both of these considerations marked, in Blondel's treatise and more generally, the introduction of the factory not so much as a program for architecture (which had been accepted for a century or more), but as a problem of spatial distribution.

As the few plans of entire factories that were published in the *Encyclopédie* demonstrated, a *grande-manufacture* that had been established as a new enterprise, laid out by an entrepreneur, engineer, or architect, tended to follow a conventional form with workshops, offices, and dwellings distributed symmetrically around a central axis or court. Sometimes, as in the paper mill of l'Anglée near Montargis and in the upper courtyard of Buffon's forges at Montbard, the layout would be that of a château, with a central building and two wings enclosing three sides of a grand forecourt; some factories were more like monastic or palace courtyards; others occupied a single multistory building. In each case, the architecture was restrained; at most a central wing would be marked by pilasters or differentiated rustication, a diagrammatic pediment, or high windows. Blondel's tobacco factory at Morlaix, in Finistère; Perronet and Lindet's Royal Porcelain works at Sèvres; Buffon's forges; the cloth factory of Dijonval at Sedan; and the textile works of Van Robais at Abbéville, all exhibited variations of this simple monumentality, inherited from the classical foundations of Colbert's *manufactures royales.*[28]

The distribution of functions within these factories was also predictably hierarchical, with the central apartments given over to the master or owner, the wings to the workshops, and subsidiary pavilions for housing and workers. Only occasionally was there a complete "substitution" of industrial functions for conventional uses: the plan of the paper works at l'Anglée, significantly the only factory to be shown completely in perspective view in the *Encyclopédie,* was organized around its motive forces: the grand avenue became a canal and the forecourt a basin that was forked in order to feed two waterwheels placed symmetrically on either side of the center (plates 22–23).[29]

The interplay between functional building and architectural representation was nicely exemplified at Buffon's forges, a self-conscious attempt to rationalize production processes according to the Encyclopedic method (plate 24). The factory was established on two levels: one above the river Alençon, where a formal courtyard was surrounded on three sides by dwellings, offices, and workshops; and one at river level, where a canal served as a source of power for the forge itself. The upper courtyard accommodated the chapel, apartments for the workers, housing for the iron-master, his stewards, and wood agents, workshops and stores for the blacksmiths and wheelwrights, as well as stables and barns. On the lower level, the factory was divided into three main buildings, each corresponding to a stage in the process: the blast furnace, the rolling and cutting mill, and, in the center, a finery in the form of a huge barge, its prow pointing upstream. These three workshops, and especially the blast furnace, were laid out as if taken directly from the plates of the *Encyclopédie,* themselves drawn from similar North Burgundian models. Practical, designed as simple containers for their operations, these workshops were joined to the more formal upper courtyard by means of a grand stair that, dividing around a small balcony, acted as a kind of amphitheater from which the experiments in the furnace might be viewed by visitors. Here "architecture" was deployed to make a spectacle out of production as if in anticipation of the more developed theatrical analogy to be used by Ledoux at Chaux.

Nevertheless, the most pressing design problem facing the centralized *manufacture* in the century or so before 1750 was one of technology rather than architecture: the improvement of machines like the stocking-loom; the building of furnaces more reliable in maintaining constant temperatures and conserving wood fuel; the gradual introduction, slow in France, of coke-fired ovens; the development of hydraulic pumps, including the *pompe à feu* introduced in 1756; and the control of chemical processes.[30] This was the burden of the *Encyclopédie,* and it represented a generally accurate perception of the state of industrial arts at midcentury. If the architect had a role beyond that of providing a well-built sequence of rectangular workshops, it was as engineer—reinforcing foundations, spanning large halls, supporting heavy machinery, bridging waterways, specifying materials and methods for forge construction.

In this sense, the work of the architect Germain Boffrand, who built a large, manually turned pump at the prison of Bicêtre in 1733, was indistinguishable from that of the engineer Jean-Rodolphe Perronet at Sèvres.[31] Just as ironmasters became entrepreneurs and scientists became ironmasters, so the lines that divided skills in the eighteenth century were not drawn strictly: technical invention was a generalized preserve of the artisan turned artist or, conversely, the artist turned artisan. Thus Perronet contributed to the *Encyclopédie* a highly technical dissertation on the fabrication of pins, while architects, like Jean-Pierre Ling, took part in experiments in coke-fired furnaces.[32] At least around 1750, there was no realm that might be termed specifically "architectural," in itself concerned with the construction of factories.

But the *grandes-manufactures,* although exceptional enough in a predominately rural economy and certainly technologically behind their British counterparts, were steadily increasing in number, size, and complexity. This expansion was most noticeable in the plate-glass, textile, and iron industries where, by the time of the Revolution, some factories employed up to 1,400 workers.[33] These would often take the form of small communities in their own right, walled round, which, besides their workshops, would comprise machines, storerooms, laboratories, offices, a chapel, dwellings for the master or owner, his assistants, clerks, and workers, together with bakeries, winepresses, and vegetable gardens: veritable ancestors of the factory-village and the industrial town. The royal plate-glass factories at Saint Gobain and Tourlaville, the glass works at Saint-Louis, the textile works of Van Robais at Abbéville and at Sedan, were self-contained villages.[34] Even Buffon's smaller establishment at Montbard, built in 1768, included apartments for the *maître fondeur* and *maître affineur*, and seventeen rooms for workers.[35] In such communities the question of management, not only of materials and machines but of the work force both during and outside the times of work, became a necessary preoccupation of the entrepreneurs; the *social* organization of production began to assume an importance equal to its financial and technological management.[36]

The author of the article "Manufacture" in the *Encyclopédie* had already noticed this fact, expressing a certain amount of nostalgia for the slow disappearance of artisanal, rural, and craft culture.[37] Distinguishing between *manufactures dispersées* and *manufactures réunies,* the article described the relative virtues of each. The *grande-manufacture,* or concentrated industry, led to the perfection of certain kinds of luxury products—the establishment of Van Robais had demonstrated as much—but for the rest, large-scale undertakings were costly and ruinous.

> A *manufacture réunie* could only be established and maintained with an enormous cost of buildings and maintenance, with directors, overseers, bookkeepers, treasurers, clerks, servants, and others, and, finally, with vast provisioning.[38]

Furthermore, and equally as important, the social effects of their management were pernicious.

> At the *grande-manufacture,* everything is done at the stroke of a bell; the workers are more constrained and more rebuked. The overseers, accustomed to have with them a superior and commanding air, which is truly necessary when dealing with a large group, treat them harshly and with scorn.[39]

Against these conditions, which only led to a mobile and impermanent work force, those of the small manufacturer seemed idyllic.

> In the establishment of a small manufacturer, the journeyman is the friend of the master, lives with him, as with his equal, has a place by the fire and the candle, has more liberty, and, finally, prefers to work with him.[40]

Rooted in this way, the rural artisan also contributed to the prosperity of the countryside; as opposed to his itinerant, often pauper, counterparts, shifting from factory to factory, he could employ his leisure hours in cultivation or vice versa.

> A laborer, a day worker in the countryside . . . has in the course of the year a sufficient number of days and hours when he cannot cultivate the land. . . . If this man has a hand-loom at home . . . he can use his time, which otherwise would be lost for him and for the state.[41]

In this utopian vision of a rural France populated by little manufacturers, with an industry operated on a putting-out system, the author was seeking, as Diderot consistently attempted in other articles, to solve the increasing problem of a large population of homeless poor. In the face of a deserted and unprofitable countryside and the anticipated growth of centralized industry, he proposed a return to origins—to the rapidly disappearing craft system, which of course was never so free from social ills—and to an idealized *manufacture,* as depicted in the plates of the *Encyclopédie,* where no signs of social strife, bad working conditions, or constraint were allowed to appear.

However unrealistic the formulation, the article "Manufacture" pointed to a social question that increasingly dominated debates on the proper form of industrial establishments, debates that were couched in terms that, by the end of the century, rivaled the technical discussions of scientists in importance: the discourse on surveillance.[42] Surveillance started, of course, in the *atelier* and was, as many scientists insisted, a vital part of quality control, of economy in fuel and other materials, and in speed of production. But surveillance also involved work hours and, in order to guard against inebriation, ill-health, and absenteeism, the activities and behavior of the worker at leisure. It also involved the families of workers, the upbringing of children, and the education of adults. Such surveillance was less direct than that of an overseer on a workshop floor; it relied on social and symbolic force, by means of housing, recreational facilities, and the substitution of the factory manager or entrepreneur for the traditional authority figures, the lord of the manor and the priest.

This is not to say that such paternalistic initiatives were, in fact, necessary in the eighteenth-century factory. Subject to the strictest disciplinary codes, governing every aspect of his work and behavior in the workshop, paid the most minimal wages, housed for the most part in ill-built barracks, the worker was close to the common criminal in the eyes of the police and the government. Only the most independent artisans, such as the "gentlemen glassblowers," who were indispensable to production, could afford to withdraw their labor or engage in struggles for better conditions. The operating rule in the *grandes-manufactures* was that prescribed by Colbertian law, and the routine was implacably enforced each day, from the first Mass to the last bell, a space of ten or more hours of labor; blasphemy, songs, even speech were forbidden in the shops; punishments were severe for latecomers and for those who defied the ban on cabarets in the hours of rest.[43] In this context, any thoughts of social reform were those of idealists and utopians, but also those of a few pragmatists who saw, as did their British counterparts, that an entirely unwilling and uneducated work force was inimical to improved production.

THE THEATER OF INDUSTRY

CLAUDE-NICOLAS LEDOUX AND THE FACTORY-VILLAGE OF CHAUX

It is for the architect to oversee the principle; he can activate the resources of industry, husband its products, and avoid costly maintenance; he can augment the treasury by means of the prodigal compositions of his art.

C.-N. Ledoux, *L'Architecture*, 1804.[1]

WHILE MANY ARCHITECTS and engineers in the last years of the eighteenth century were fascinated to one degree or another with the processes and potentials of industry—François-Joseph Bélanger sketched the new blast furnaces on his visit to England; François Cointeraux invented new methods of building construction and recorded plans of factories; Pierre Touffaire delineated economical plans of factories as well as shipyards—only Claude-Nicolas Ledoux endowed industry with a central aesthetic role in his work and vision of social progress. His interest in manufacturing, which he owed less to his teacher Blondel than to his fascination with the *Encyclopédie*, his apprenticeship in the Department of Waters and Forests, and his *anglomanie*, which drew him to England rather than Italy, was confirmed early in his career by his appointment to the staff of Jean-Rodolphe Perronet, chief engineer of the Ponts et Chaussées, as a commissioner charged with oversight of the saltworks of Franche-Comté, Lorraine, and the Trois-Evêchés.[2] Ledoux was thereby invested with the duties of an inspector of factories, a member of that elite corps of functionaries originally established by Colbert, which, in the 1770s, acted for the regime as technical, scientific, and economic adviser and supervisor of *manufactures*, under the progressive leadership of Trudaine de Montigny in the Intendancy of Commerce.[3] With Perronet's example as a professional engineer, on the one hand, and with the support of Trudaine, Diderot's friend, on the other, Ledoux was encouraged to propose the establishment of a new saltworks designed to the most advanced principles of technological and social planning. The patronage of the aging Louis XV and his mistress Madame du Barry enabled him to convince the Ferme générale, under whose jurisdiction the *salines* of France were operated, to endorse the project. The initial plans that were drawn up before the death of Louis XV in the spring of 1774 were changed after the accession of Louis XVI and his appointment of a new minister of finance, Turgot, but the enterprise was completed in 1779 and continued to function as a saltworks to the end of the next century.[4]

The new factory was situated in Franche-Comté between the villages of Arc and Senans, south of Besançon and northwest of the oldest saltworks in the region, at Salins, which, by means of a twenty-two-kilometer-long wooden pipeline, supplied Ledoux's works with brine to be evaporated in its boiling-pans. It was also sited near a convenient source of fuel, the Forest of Chaux. The region had been a source of salt from Roman times, with wells supplied by underground springs that ran through rock-salt beds in the Jura and primitive furnaces set over wood fires to crystallize the salt. Its saltworks were thus traditional *manufactures:* their procedures and work rhythms had changed little since the Middle Ages, and local variations throughout Franche-Comté, Lorraine, and Savoy were ingrained.[5] The article "Salines" in the *Encyclopédie* documented every difference in terminology, local custom, and type of salt.[6]

Despite this apparently static character, however, the nature and efficiency of production methods had changed since the 1740s. First, there was an increasing shortage of wood fuel in the centuries-old areas of exploitation, a shortage that involved not only saltworks but also the burgeoning iron industry, not to speak of growing towns and villages. It was such a shortage in the area around Salins that had provoked plans for the new saltworks.[7] Second, there was the value of the product itself, a staple for the salting of cheeses, a vital industry in Franche-Comté, and for the preservation of winter meat and fodder.[8] Third, and perhaps most important, in the 1770s there was the *gabelle,* a tax levied on the sale of salt, a royal monopoly, collected, often with brutality, by the Ferme générale on behalf of a bankrupt state.[9] Thus any economy in the use of wood, improvement in the quality of the product, or increase in the amount produced, would ameliorate social, political, and economic tensions.

Ledoux's initiative was therefore complemented and sustained by economic need; his design reflected these concerns and incorporated a reformist program for industry on two levels: that of physical accommodation, bringing the workers into a social framework of production, and that of architectural expression, systematically developing a language of architecture that would endow industry and its operations with a symbolic code that reinforced both surveillance and community.

Ledoux's first design, prepared some time in 1773, was in some respects perfectly conventional (plate 25). A square courtyard plan with all functions distributed around a space that resembled that of the Hôpital Saint-Louis, or even the Louvre—a memory of Colbertian order—it deployed the boiling-pans and reservoirs to the rear, the administrative offices and director's apartments to the front, and the two essential supporting crafts, the coopers and ironsmiths, in pavilions to either side. Along the sides were also rooms for the workers, casking rooms, and stores for the finished product; in the middle of the open courtyard, which was used for stacking cordwood for the furnaces, was a reservoir for fresh water.

When enlarged from the scale of the engraving, the workshops, equipment, and machines seem to be lifted directly from the plates of the *Encyclopédie:* a rational layout, *en série,* of the *ateliers* prescribed in the illustrations to the article "Salines" (plate 26). Yet a number of innovations emerge on closer inspection. There is the pattern of the workers' dwellings, with a centralized, double-height community space warmed by a common hearth; there is the equivalence established between the chapel and the bakery in corner pavilions to the left and right of the main entrance, destroying completely the conventional dignity of religion; finally, there is the extraordinary proliferation of columns—rusticated pilasters and freestanding Doric orders—framing the gate house, emphasizing the corners of the building, articulating the chapel, and, in their hundreds, supporting the covered galleries that shelter diagonal movement across the courtyard, joining the porches of the central pavilions on each side. Like the Greek stoas so lyrically described by David Le Roy, these porticoes were designed to dignify the worker-citizen while speeding his activity.[10]

In relegating the chapel to a corner, in housing the workers with as much dignity as the overseers, Ledoux certainly flouted architectural convention; but in his liberal use of rustication and provision of columnar arcades, he contradicted all the academic rules of *convenance,* of suitability of genre, of the sumptuary laws themselves. Louis XV noticed it at once: while not laughing as heartily as the assembled contractors after Ledoux had presented his project, the king made it quite clear that he felt personally insulted by the columns. "These views are grand," Ledoux reported him as saying, "but why so many columns; they are only suited to temples and to the palaces of kings."[11] Ledoux's attempts to justify the baseless Doric as a "manufacturing genre" and the rusticated pilasters as a new kind of "industrial order" were brushed aside. Attempting to endow the factory with all the attributes of high architecture, Ledoux encountered the resistance not only of the economically minded, but also of socially conventional patrons.

The debate over the columns, however, only hid what for Ledoux was an equally important notion of the design: its operational and instrumental geometry. Describing the process of design for this first project, "the first thought of the plan," Ledoux exhibited all the attention of an Encyclopedist to the shape of manufacturing space. The plan, he noted, anticipating many future functionalist theories, "derives from the subject and should be adapted to the nature of the site and needs [*les besoins*]"; and for Ledoux, the needs of a factory involved economy of production: "I wanted to dwell on the needs and conveniences of a productive factory where the utilization of time offers the first economy."[12] This was the inspiration for the courtyard galleries, dramatically intersecting the square space: "The diagonal line inscribed in a square seemed to unite all advantages; it accelerated all the services."[13] The worker, "covered by these preserving galleries, can transport the materials without fear of the bad weather that dilutes them; nothing can stop him, nothing can slow down his activity."[14] Thus the plan of the factory was in the first place conceived of as a play of geometries that reduced all movements to their simplest form. Searching for a revised *parti*, Ledoux made this even clearer: "A circle inscribed in a square, would it not produce the same advantages? . . . Ten other plans crowd into [my] thoughts; ten others follow."[15]

On another level, the square, centralized plan also seemed to order the large number of different functions in a legible and convenient way; what functioned well for speed of movement served equally to facilitate surveillance and to ratify social harmony.

> The overseer, placed at the center of the intersecting axes, can embrace in a single glance the details entrusted to him. Nothing escapes the dominating position of the director. The workers are housed healthily, the clerks comfortably; all possess vegetable gardens, which attach them to the soil; all can occupy their leisure time in cultivation, which each day ensures the first needs of life. The furnaces for boiling the salts are removed from communal improvidence; placed at the corners of the building, they bring together the affluence of the waters that flow beneath the preserving galleries.[16]

Technical, social, and managerial needs were all provided for and by the simplest of architectural formulations, a plan.

Despite these advantages of centralization, however, the conception of the factory as a single building drew criticism. Its defects were obvious to those with experience in salt production: foremost was the ever-present danger of fire; then there was the stinging smoke and fumes given off by the boiling-pans, which would pervade the living quarters; finally, there could be no accommodation of future growth.

Ledoux's second plan, which was built between 1775 and 1778, responded to these comments by separating out each of the different functions into different buildings (plate 27).

> The artist felt that he should isolate everything, that the communal and individual dwellings and the furnaces should be prevented from touching—always to be feared when a large number of people are confined. He felt that he should compose his plan according to the winds that ensure health and that he should preserve the enclosing walls from the ruinous activity of the reverberating furnaces, which powder to nothing the thickest masses and compromise the advantages of the public treasury by broken holes that too often require repair.[17]

Accordingly, the salt-workers' apartments, the workshops and apartments of the ironsmiths and coopers, the factory sheds with furnaces and pans, the offices and rooms of the director and his staff, the apartments for the clerk-overseers, were divided up and given freestanding pavilions of their own, each with a distinct three-dimensional order that emphasized the variety of social and technological determinants in the plans and massing. The centralized communal rooms of the workers were emphasized by double-height, mansarded pavilions flanked by single-story apartments; the dwellings of the clerks took on the character of small *hôtels-particuliers;* the factory sheds were fronted by porches for unloading and loading, and were covered with steeply pitched tile roofs whose eaves projected to form sheltered passageways all around the buildings; the director's house, within which was the chapel, was cubic in form, with a tall pyramidal roof and pedimented portico to convey an impression of centralized power.[18] To these spaces—the bare forms of need, so to speak—Ledoux brought a powerful array of architectural motifs, carved in deep bas-relief to dramatize the function of the saltworks: overturned urns poured crystallized water from the smooth walls of the workers' buildings, the gate house, and the factory sheds, the urns sometimes serving also as windows; rusticated colonnades of Palladian derivation dignified the factory sheds; and a giant order of columns formed of alternate square and circular stones fronted the director's house. In perhaps the most dramatic gesture, the gate house was entered through a portico of eight giant, baseless, Doric columns, closely spaced and reminiscent of the Propylea of the Acropolis. Behind this portico was a huge, artificial grotto symbolizing the source of the material of production, the underground salt springs of Salins. To unify these different buildings into a single composition, Ledoux ranged them round the periphery of a broad, semicircular courtyard, with the factory sheds to the rear, flanking the director's house, which stood at the center of the straight diameter; the workers' buildings and the gate house defined the semicircle, which was completed by a ring of vegetable gardens and a high wall.

This semicircular plan functioned at a number of levels. In the first place, it gave the illusion of a built hierarchy of surveillance, the factory community subjected to the continual scrutiny of the director, each worker and all who entered the gate house placed in a position of subservience to an arc of visual oversight. But this image of supervision was more a calculated symbolic effect of the form than a functioning part of the disciplinary apparatus; in reality, the workers were to be hidden from the director's sight by rows of trees, and their own, centralized communal spaces drew them toward a smaller community of hearth and home. Social surveillance was here more implicit and mediated than in the direct instrumental vision of Jeremy Bentham's Panopticon (plate 28); in the almost anthropomorphic massing of the saltworks, the director was equally related to the factory buildings to either side of his residence—his "arms," so to speak—while the workers, in four specialized communities, formed a single community distinct from that of the supervisors and to a certain extent protected from it.[19]

Here a second implication of the semicircular geometry helps to explain Ledoux's intended articulation of these relations; for the plan of the saltworks as a whole was unambiguously derived from that of an antique theater, such as that described by Vitruvius, as reconstructed by Perrault and Patte and illustrated by Diderot in the *Encyclopédie*.[20] Exactly proportioned to follow classical precedent, Ledoux's "theater" substituted factory and director's house for stage and stage-house and replaced the audience with the workers. The "play" was that of production; the difference between a traditional Greek drama and Ledoux's eighteenth-century version was the participation of the audience as actors in the production of social wealth.

The political metaphor implied by Ledoux was, indeed, the same as that described in his engraving of the auditorium of the Theater of Besançon, designed at the same time as the saltworks, seen as reflected in the pupil of an eye (plate 29). In this striking emblem of theatricalized vision, an eye, as if located on center stage, reflects the seats, themselves signifying society and ranged in tiers to emulate a classical amphitheater; the beam of light that illuminates the stage, emanating from the back of the auditorium, is also reflected in the pupil, but is then projected, like the all-seeing eye of Masonic iconography, from inside the orb itself out towards the spectator.[21] If this multireflectional image is transposed to the theater of the saltworks, a reciprocal relationship between the director and the society of workers is implied, somewhat like that imagined by Rousseau in the *Contrat Social:* between a people that elects a lawgiver and his authority over them. In the saltworks, of course, no such election might take place, but the Enlightenment reformer would easily dream of a voluntary acceptance of managerial authority by the workers in return for the benefits of community administered paternally by architect and director. Ledoux was clear on the political significance of his plan:

> One of the great driving forces that binds governments to the beneficial results of the moment is the general disposition of a plan that brings together at an enlightened center all the parts of which it is composed. The eye easily surveys the shortest line; the work follows it with rapid step; the journey's burden is lightened by the hope of a prompt return. Everything obeys this combination, which perfects the law of movement . . . ; placed at the center of the radii, nothing can escape surveillance; it keeps a hundred eyes open as a hundred others sleep, and their burning pupils light up the unquiet night without respite.[22]

Multiplied by a hierarchy of relays that made each worker the *surveillant* of the next, oversight was reinforced and ramified by the multiplication of smaller *centres éclairés,* themselves self-policing in the form of the salt-workers' communal spaces. These, like the overall plan, were conceived according to the geometry of the circle, implicitly in plan and actually in section (plates 30–31). Central fireplaces stood in double-height spaces surrounded by colonnaded galleries giving access on the upper level to bedrooms and stores. In the corners not taken up by the stair were cooking stoves. The section reinforced this communal form: as Ledoux engraved it, the roof was ideally domed with the chimney rising through the center. Again he stated the social implications:

> The section of the workers' building gives a general idea of the beneficial reconciliation that recalls man to the social order, an order drawn from nature; there it is that thriftless opulence asks pardon of the Supreme Being for the offenses the most blameworthy abundance commits in the forests. The communal dwelling *[l'hôtel de la réunion],* heated by a fire that never cools, warms the gratitude of those brought together through beneficence. The galleries of the first floor and the benches along the walls increase the favors of well-being: it is an economic movement without interruption.[23]

Ledoux drew an almost Rousseauesque picture of life in these dwellings, provided by the factory owner with such *bienfaisance.* At once functional and economic, furnishing daily needs with a minimum of fuel, the dwellings were

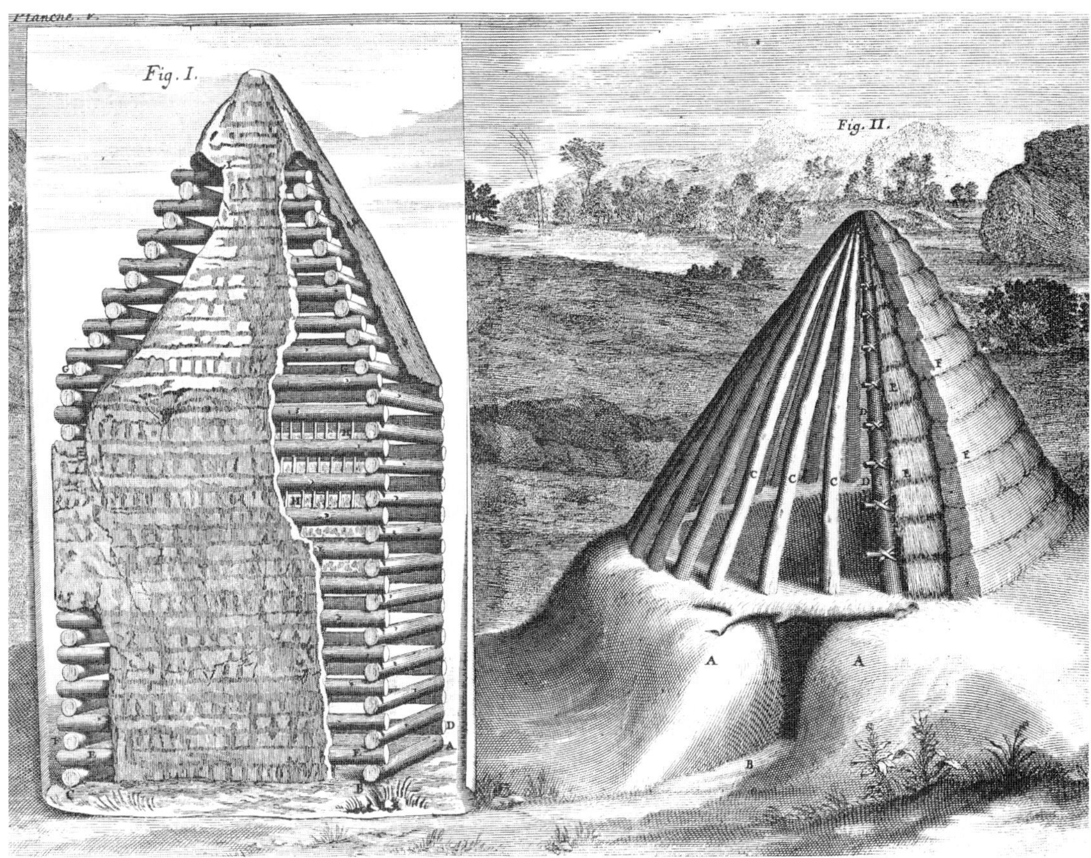

1 Claude Perrault, huts of the Colchians (*left*) and the Phrygians (*right*), illustration to his translation of Vitruvius, 1684.

2 Joseph-François Lafitau, "The Customs of the American Indians Compared to Those of Primitive Times," Frontispiece to his *Moeurs des sauvages américains*, 1724.

3 Lafitau, marriage ceremony.

4 Lafitau, initiation of a Carib.

5 Lafitau, "Journey through the Snow and Winter Encampment."

6 Lafitau, the manufacture of sugar.

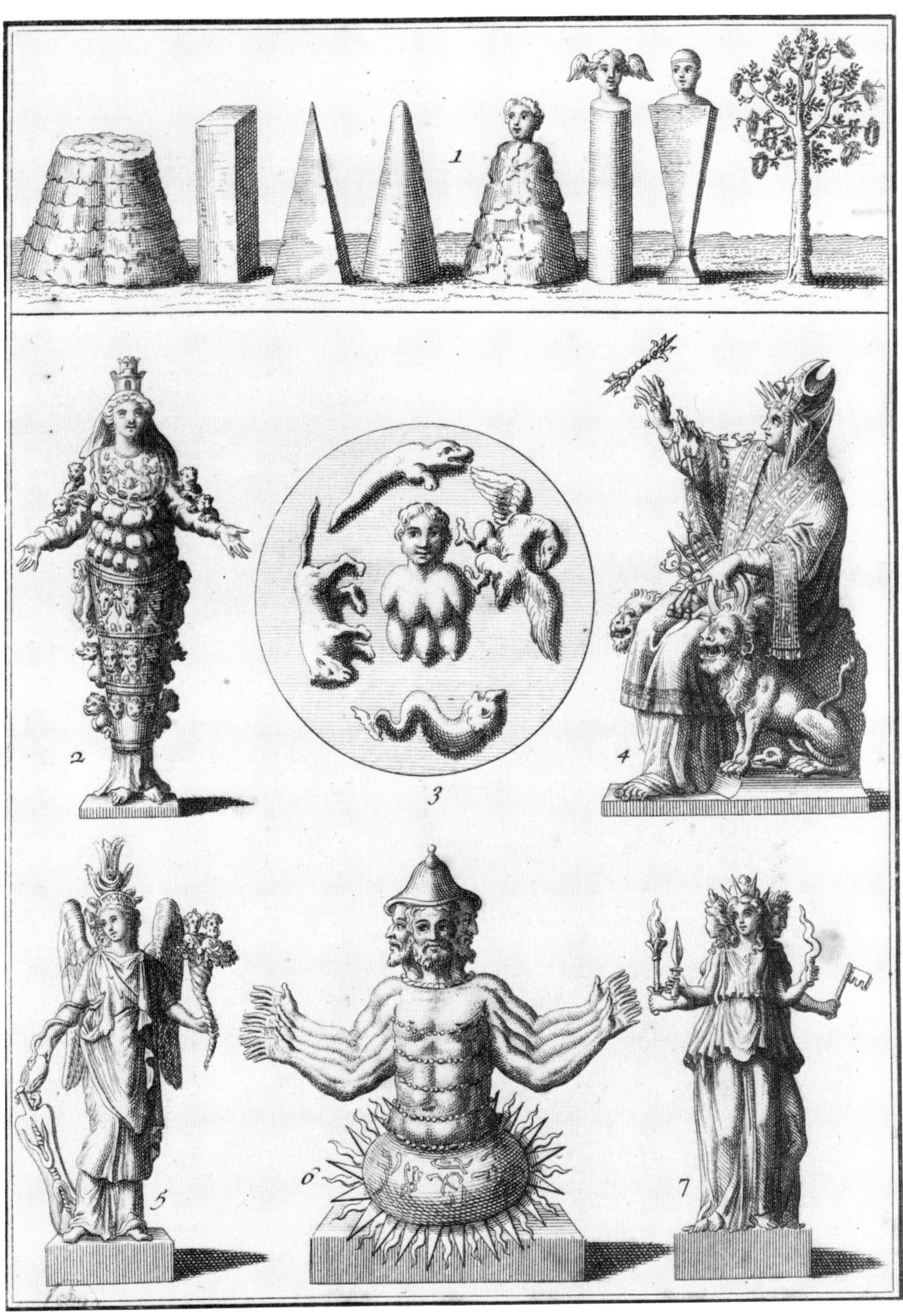

7 Lafitau, "The Origins and Progress of Idolatry."

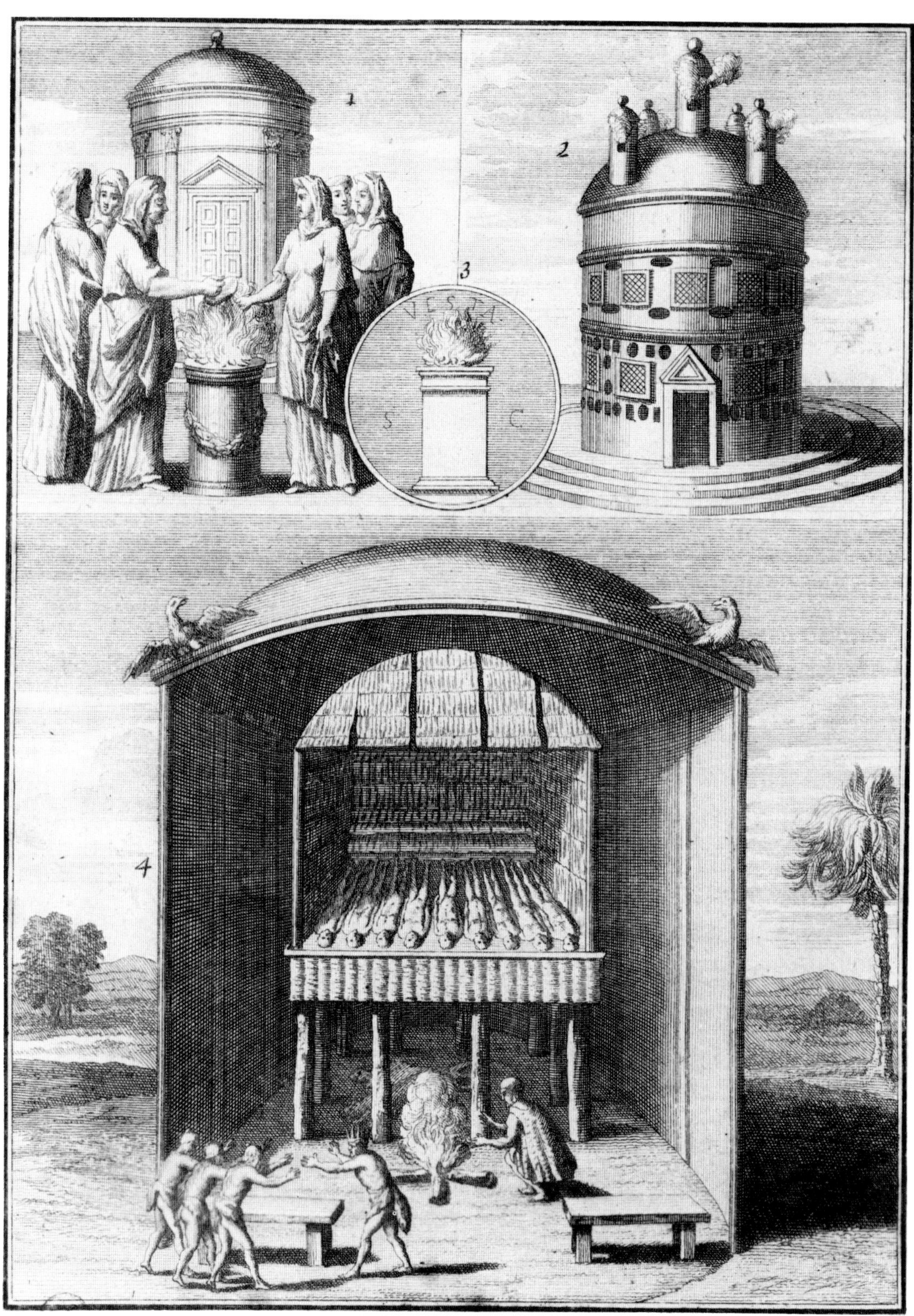

8 Lafitau, "The Cult of Vesta or of the Sacred Fire."
fig. 1, Temple with fire of Vesta on the altar; *fig. 2,* Temple of the Gaures or Guebres, descendants of the ancient Persians; *fig. 3,* Medal of Faustinus, with Vesta represented by the sacred fire that burns on his altar; *fig. 4,* Temple of Natchez in Louisiana.

9 Charles Eisen, "Allegory of Architecture Returning to Its Natural Model." Frontispiece to M.-A. Laugier, *Essai sur l'architecture*, 2nd edition, 1755.

10 Eisen, "[A Hottentot] Returns to His Peers." Frontispiece to J.-J. Rousseau, *Discours sur l'origine de l'inégalité*, 1755.

11 Charles Delagardette, "The Origin of Architecture," 1786.

13 Workshop of a lathe-worker (turnery). From the *Encyclopédie*.

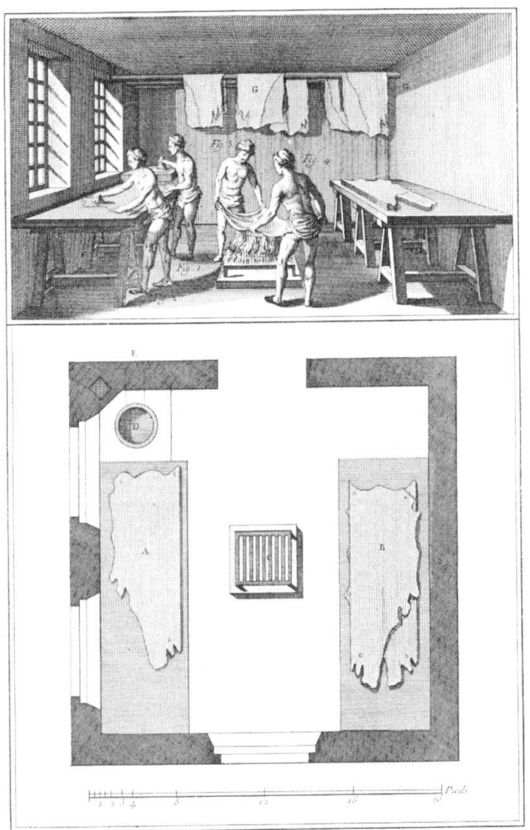

12 Workshop of a Hungarian leather worker, *top*, operations; *bottom*, plan. From the *Encyclopédie, Planches*.

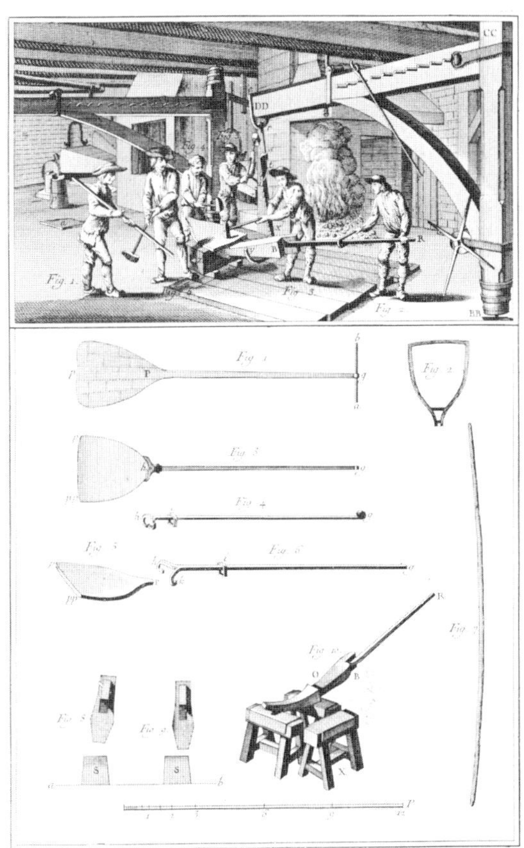

14 Forge for anchors. From the *Encyclopédie*.

15 Workshop for pegs and vine-stakes. From the *Encyclopédie*.

16 Coopers' workshop. From the *Encyclopédie*.

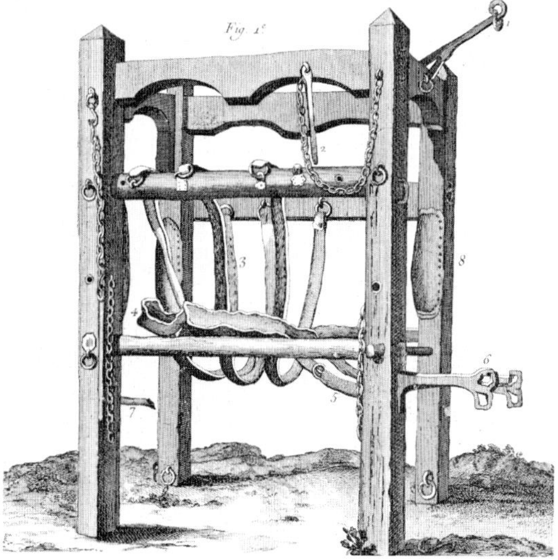

17 Smithy. From the *Encyclopédie*.

18 Smithy. From the *Encyclopédie*.

19 Glass works in the woods. From the *Encyclopédie*.

20 Isaac Ware, "Kiln for Burning Tyle and Brick; Under Ground of the Kiln," 1768.

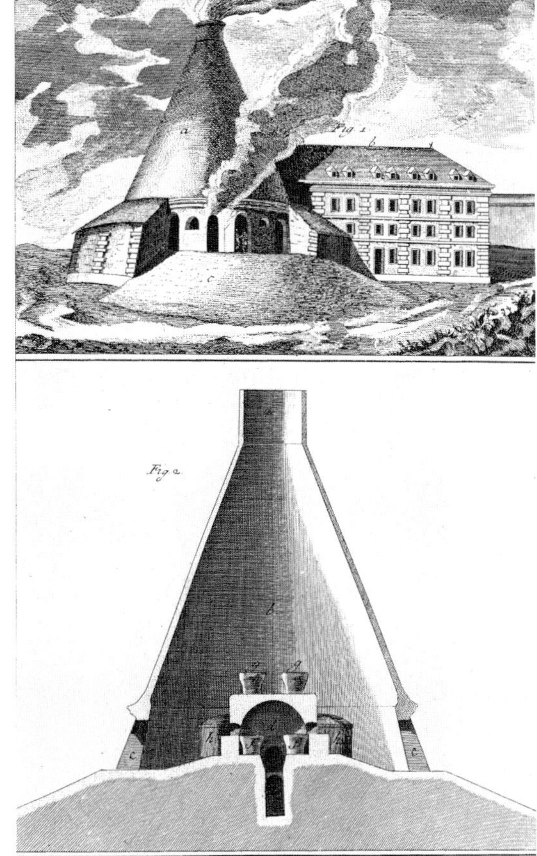

21 English glass works, *top*, perspective; *bottom*, section. From the *Encyclopédie*.

22 Paper factory at l'Anglée, near Montargis, perspective view. From the *Encyclopédie*.

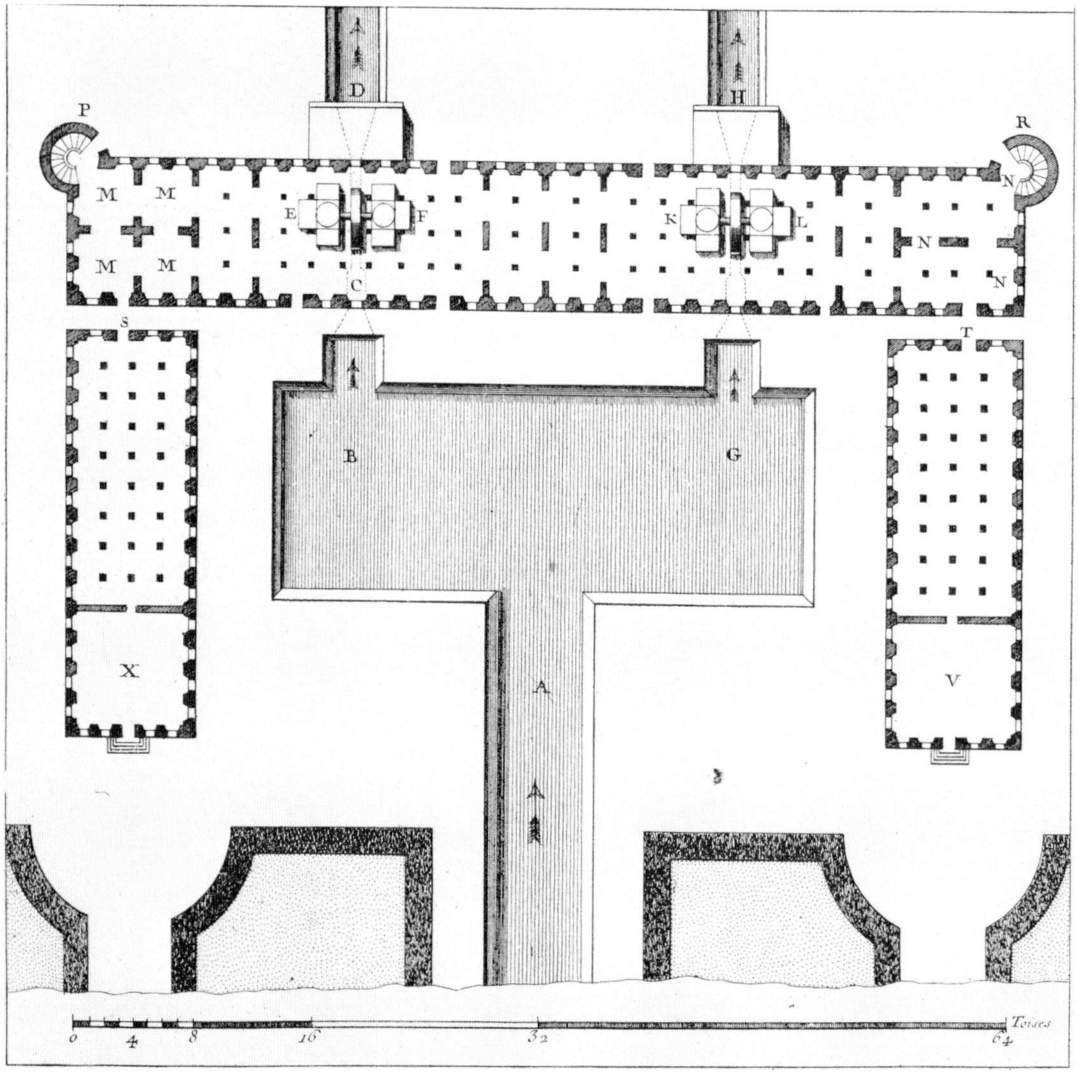

23 Paper factory at l'Anglée, plan. From the *Encyclopédie*.

24 Forge at Buffon, view of grand stair to furnaces.

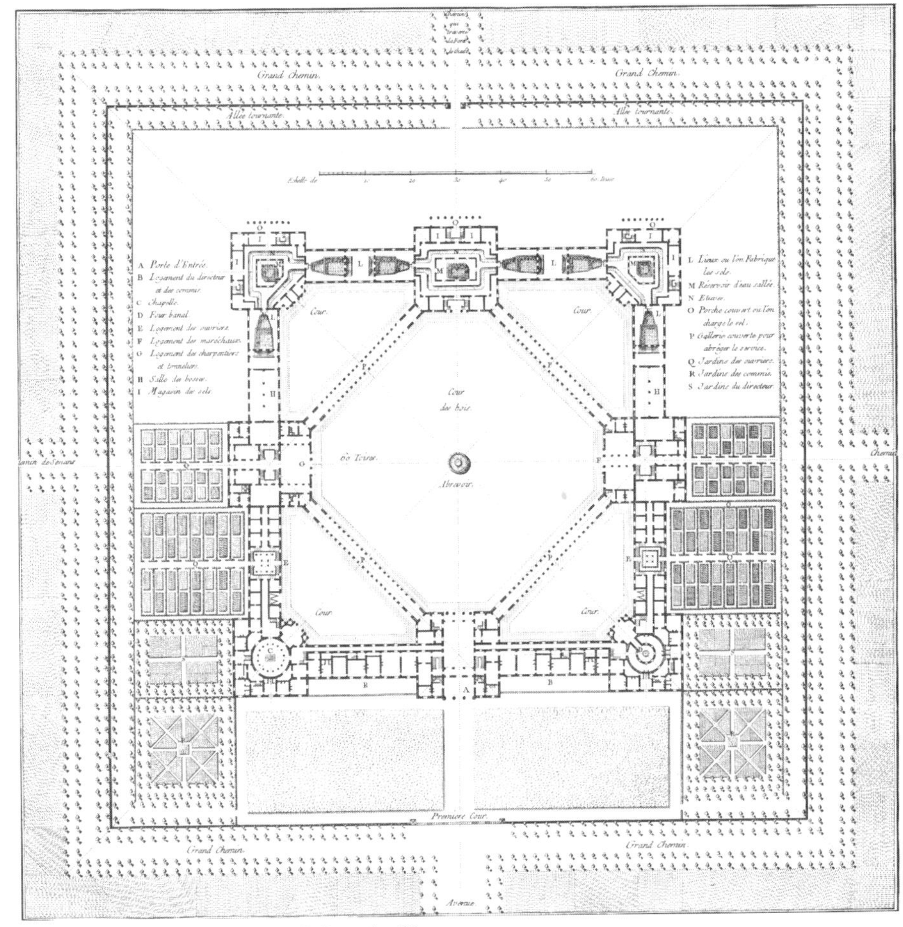

25 Claude-Nicolas Ledoux, Saline de Chaux, first plan, unbuilt project, 1773–1774.

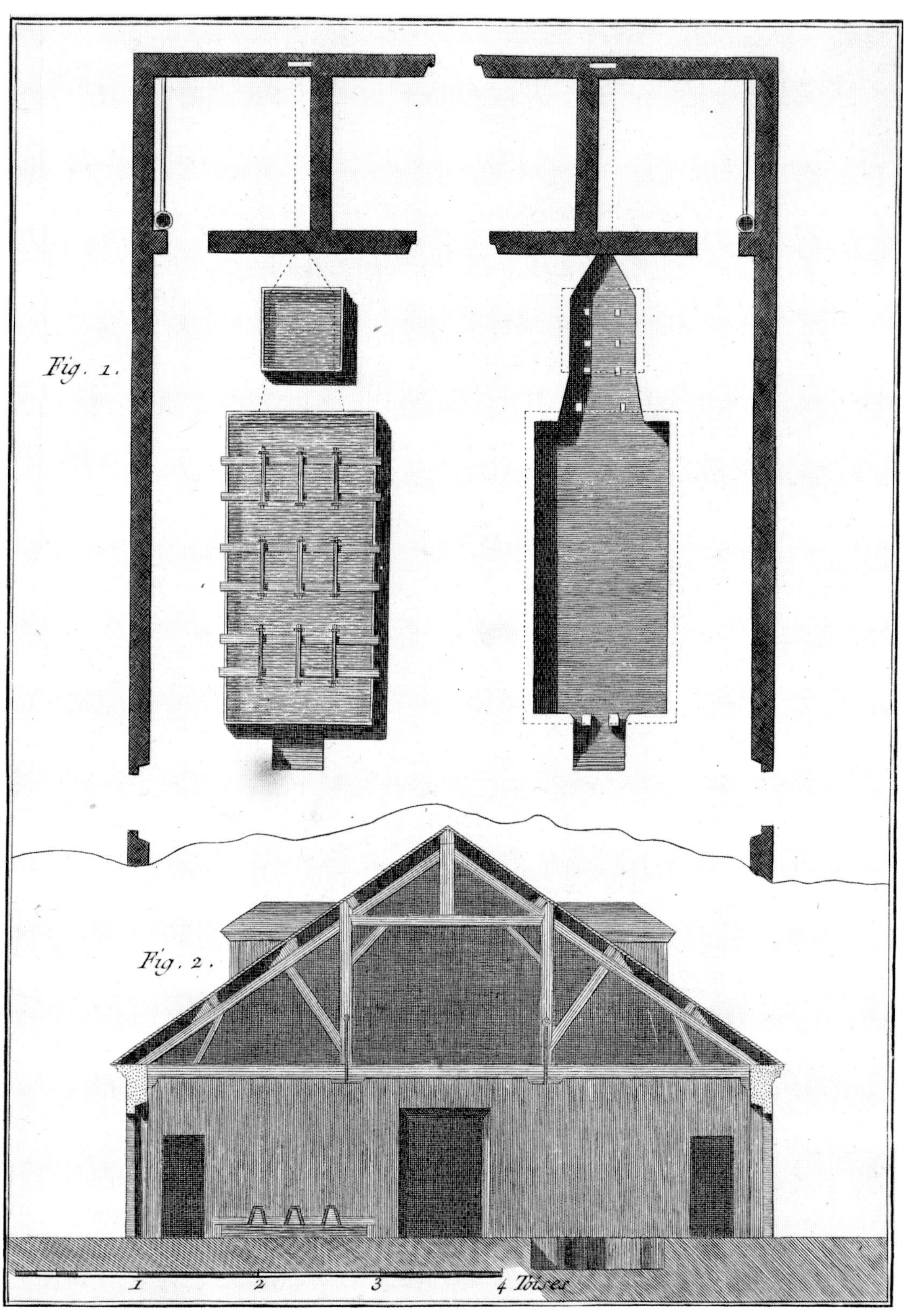

26 Saltworks of Dieuze in Lorraine, *top*, plan; *bottom*, section for new building. From the *Encyclopédie*.

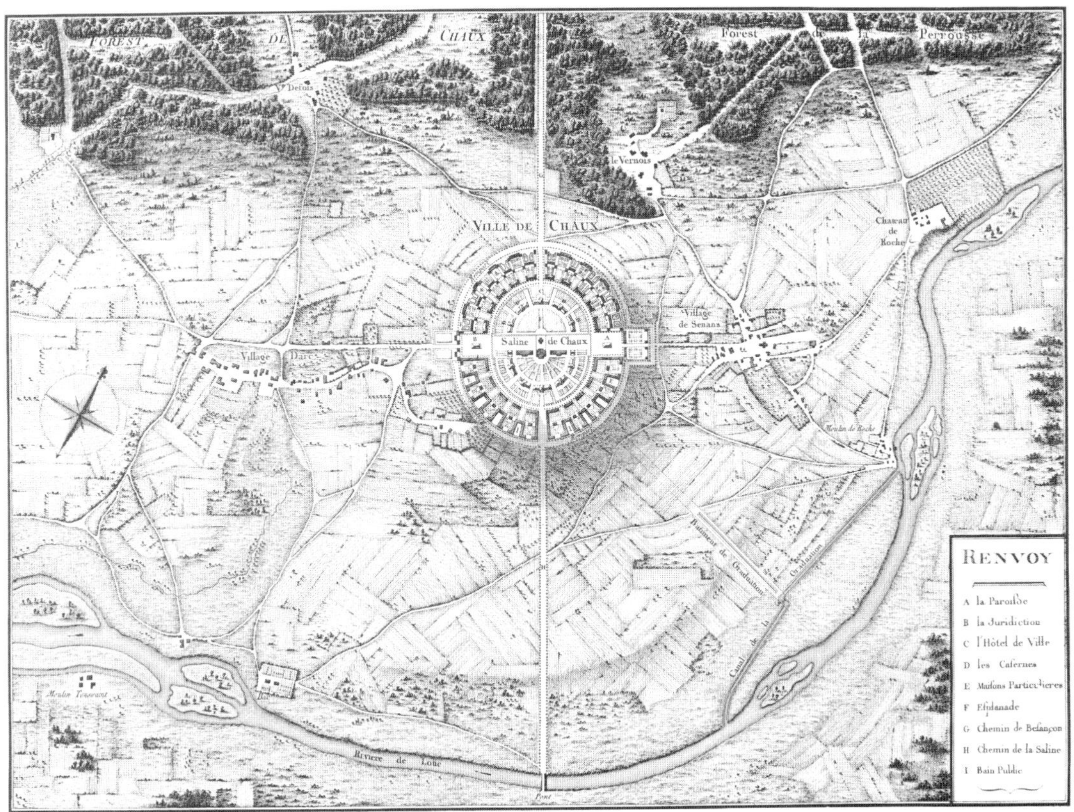

27 Ledoux, Saline de Chaux, general plan as built, 1774–1778.

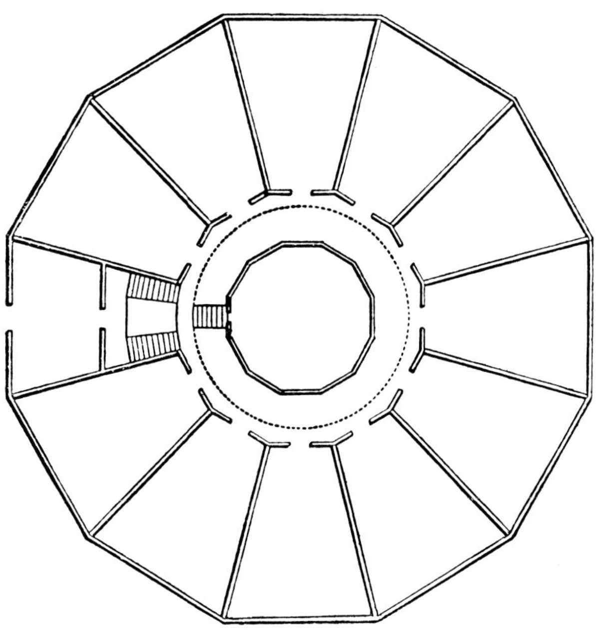

28 Jeremy Bentham, Panopticon Prison, plan of first project, 1797.

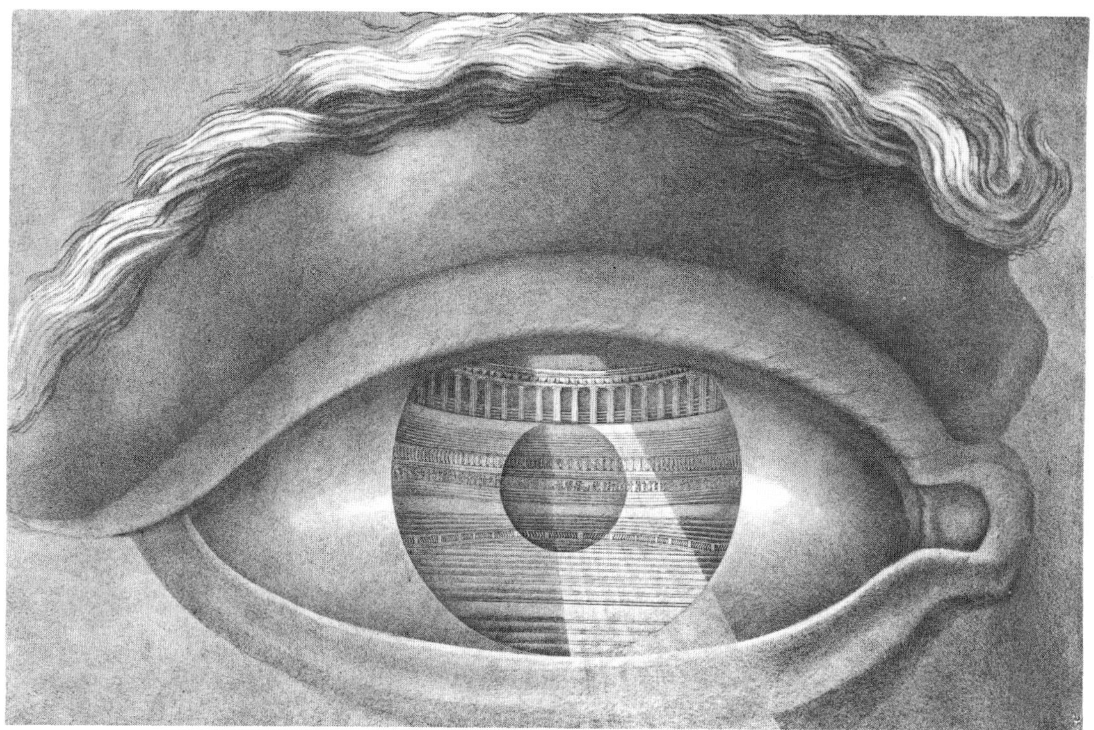

29 Ledoux, auditorium of Theater of Besançon seen as reflected in the pupil of an eye; allegorical representation of the *salle*, which was built between 1779 and 1784.

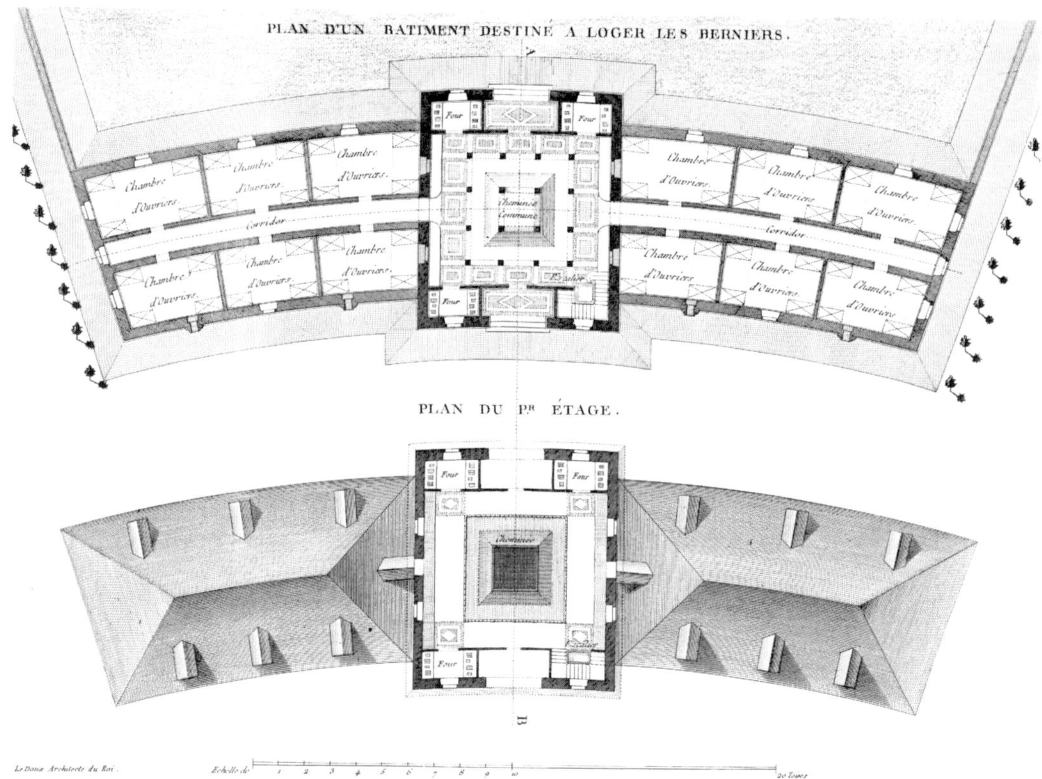

30 Ledoux, Saline de Chaux, workers' building, plans of first and second floors.

31 Ledoux, Saline de Chaux, worker's building, section through central communal space, with fireplace.

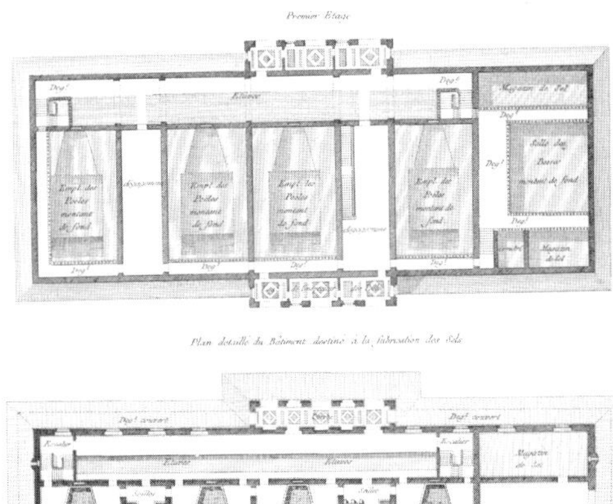

33 Ledoux, Saline de Chaux, factory building, plans of first and second floors.

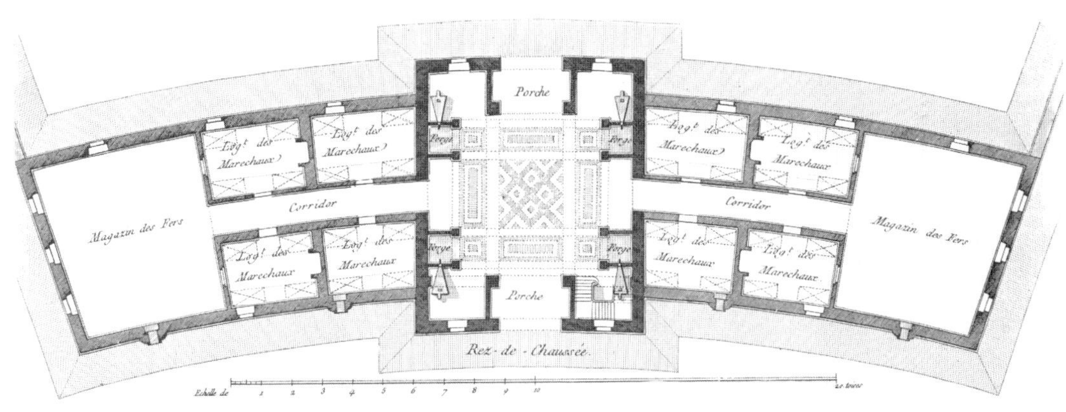

32 Ledoux, Saline de Chaux, blacksmith's building, plan of first floor.

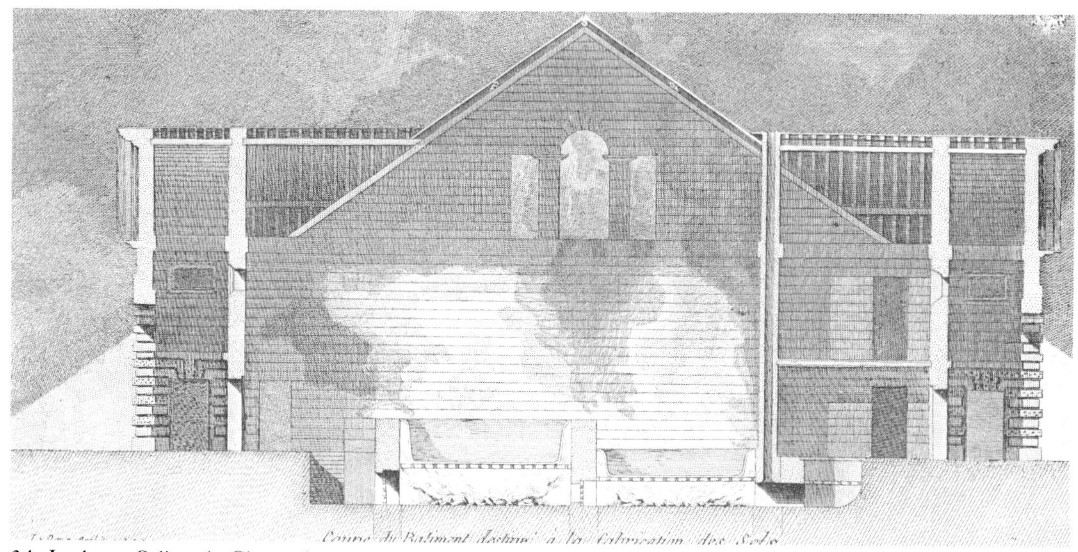

34 Ledoux, Saline de Chaux, factory building, section through evaporating pans.

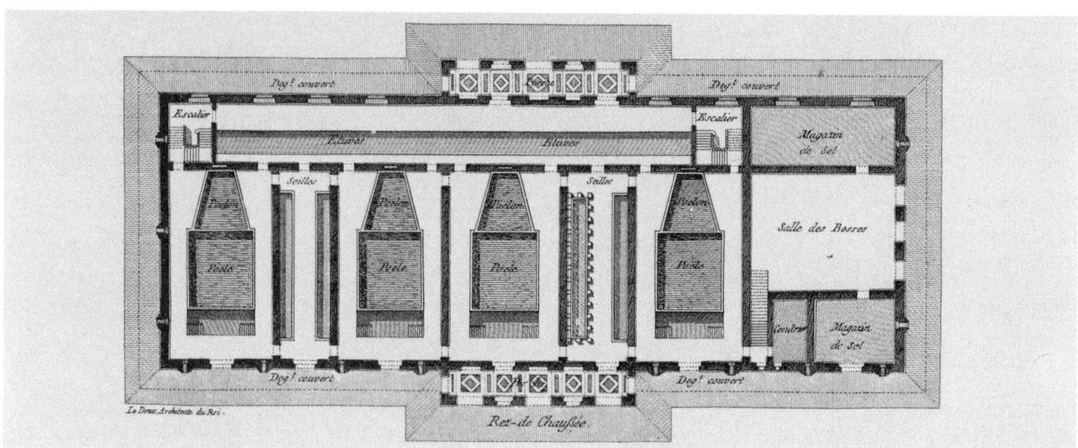

35 Ledoux, Saline de Chaux, blacksmiths' building, plan of first floor.

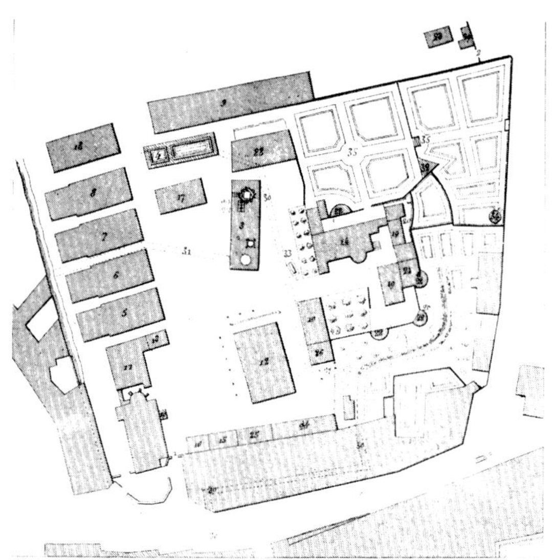

36 Saltworks at Château-Salins, Lorraine, plan, 1787.

also moralizing, acting as "social condensers" that reinstated a balanced mean of pleasure, rest, and labor.

> Each room is occupied by a family; a gallery leads to a common fireplace. This hearth proffers all the means to prepare and watch over food; the clay pots in which it boils cover a hundred burners sustained by a continual flame. These men, concentrated in these preferred places, augment and increase their existence under natural laws; each worker possesses the secret of the gods; surrounded by the sweetest illusions, he is with his wife and children during his hours of rest; he is sheltered from all costly distractions and from the bacchic delirium that could disturb his marriage, tempt or lead him to laziness. He finds, in this reunion with his dearest customs, his pleasures, the consolation for his hardships, the mustering of his needs; nothing obliges him to expose his days to the irregularity of hours that harvests imprudence and indiscretion . . . . If he leaves these cherished retreats, it is to cultivate a productive field, which fills the intervals with labor and amuses his leisure by securing him distractions that shelter him from the errors and desires that shorten the days of those who live in the midst of temptations.[24]

Ledoux thus designed a model of an Enlightenment ideal city, one constructed according to the laws of a geometric system that united the powers of sight with those of spatial order, one that, nevertheless, used all the traditional devices of architecture rhetorically and didactically to reinforce its effects. He also provided a kind of architectural reconciliation of a *manufacture réunie* and a *manufacture dispersée,* maintaining the social benefits of the latter within the necessary concentration of the former.

Ledoux's innovations did not rest at the level of social accommodations. When compared to other saltworks in the region, and especially to that of Montmorot (plate 32) built in 1743 by Jean Querret, an engineer of the Ponts et Chaussées, Ledoux's technical interventions are thrown into clear relief.[25] The rationalized layout of the boiling-pans at Arc-et-Senans and their connection to supply reservoirs; the improved thermal design of the furnaces and the distribution of their heat to drying racks and storage rooms for the finished salt; the supervision of production from elevated walkways; the convenient placement of the packing and storage rooms; all these details mark Ledoux's design as being informed by a systematic vision of the manufacturing process (plates 33–34). Montmorot, built no more than thirty years before, had simply regularized existing practices and, as Trudaine de Montigny found in 1760, offered no improvement in wood economy or quality of product. Equally, where Montmorot had disposed its functions around a rectangular courtyard in a more or less random fashion, Ledoux conceptualized the social relations of production and housed the shift-workers, who operated the boiling-pans and salt-packing rooms, in buildings adjacent to the factory sheds, giving the smiths and coopers their own carefully designed *ateliers* further away. In the smithy (plate 35), the forge occupied the centralized pavilion that for the salt-workers served as a communal space and seemed to regularize and perfect that more picturesque version of the workshop of the *maréchal grossier* illustrated in the

Encyclopédie. Ledoux's description of the "scene of production" in this rural forge at once united the meticulous observation of Diderot and the sublime evocation of light, heat, and domestic drama depicted by such painters as Joseph Wright of Derby.

> Do you hear the hour that sounds? It calls the worker to his necessary center . . . . Here it is that the action commences and the operations develop; glowing coals, ceaselessly stirred and inflamed by the bellows of Vulcan, redden the plates intended for the fabrication of the boiling-pans; they are assembled on a flat, solid level in order to fasten them together; the blacksmiths beat the inflamed iron and subject it to redoubled blows, shaping it in every dimension. The walls are worn out by the sharp sounds they reflect, and their surface is destroyed by the bursts of fire that strike them . . . . A subtle vapor fills the atmosphere, stinging the eye, exciting tears; the thunder rumbles; the sulphurous night disturbs all who approach. You see the timid child arrive, trembling; paternal arms press her close. In vain he tries to calm her fright; she flees and, crying, solicits maternal tenderness, which softens her fears. The vaulted roof is open at the apex and allows the lungs freedom to breathe. There it is that the concentrated fires dilate and the evil vapors dissipate.[26]

And while, dissimulating, Ledoux would agree that "these details hold little interest" for his architectural readers, his own principle was clear and stated again and again throughout his work: from the direct observation of a *métier*, an idea of its natural form should be abstracted, its primitive structure identified, and a design drawn up of a habitat that conforms to its inner laws, reinforces them, and, if necessary, reforms them. "Do not fear," he advised the industrial architect, "to enrich the practice of a trade with a theory that ennobles it."[27]

Ledoux's extravagance in building his "ruinous schemes" later became a legend in prerevolutionary Paris; certainly the contractor for the saltworks and his financial associates did not fail to register complaints about the escalating cost of building his "too sumptuous" designs. The director was to note the humidity of the workers' building and the smoke that filled the workers' apartments whenever the central fire was lit.[28] But as a whole, the operation of the factory compared favorably to others in the region. After the Revolution, a professional and unbiased investigator, one citizen Nicolas, professor of chemistry at Nancy, visited the saltworks of Franche-Comté and Lorraine (plate 36) on behalf of the Committee of Public Health under the Convention and reported that in this, "the most beautiful saltworks of the Republic," the working procedures, similar enough to those of all *salines*, were nevertheless

> executed with more unity and order. . . ; the operations are better attended to there, and the furnaces do not lose as much heat . . . . The smithy is also much better run and the boiling-pans better maintained.[29]

FORGES AND FOUNDRIES

While salt was a traditional industry, more or less receptive to a moderate reshaping of its antiquated processes, the regions in which the *salines de l'est* were situated, from Savoy and the valley of the Isère in the south to Lorraine in the north, were, toward the end of the eighteenth century, expanding rapidly as centers of more modern industries; iron works, glass works, paper mills, and cloth works of all kinds were growing in size and proliferating, if not at the speed or concentration of British industries, at least rapidly enough and in large enough establishments to attract government investment and scientific attention.[30]

The principal reasons for this regional development were, of course, the proximity of water for power, of wood and coal (although this last was used only rarely) for fuel, and of waterways for transport of materials and goods. Franche-Comté seemed an especially favorable and as yet unexploited province; plans for the connection of navigable rivers by canals and for new roads and bridges preoccupied the administration of Ponts et chaussées under Querret, chief engineer for the region.[31] He was aided by engineers such as Philippe Bertrand in Besançon; by the intendant Charles de Lacoré, who like Turgot in Limousin was indefatigable in opening up and developing his department; and, in Paris, by the Trudaines, father and son, and by Turgot himself.

Ledoux, who was close to this cadre of industrial and commercial reformers in the period after the completion of the saltworks, readily imagined a further expansion of industry, perhaps even stimulated by the presence of his own new factory. His relationship with de Lacoré, made firm by the building of the theater at Besançon, for which Bertrand's brother served as local architect, and the later support of the new controller-general of finances in Paris, Charles Alexandre de Calonne, fostered his already grand illusions of a prosperous and populous city that might be dispersed through the Forest of Chaux and the neighboring valleys.[32] As, between 1775 and 1800, he prepared plans for factories, workshops, institutions, and housing of every kind, utopian schemes meant to demonstrate how the architect might aid in the development of a new industrial order, he kept this geographic and economic base in mind.

In this sense, we might interpret Ledoux's otherwise unwieldy publication of real and ideal projects, in 1804, as an architectural completion of the *Encyclopédie;* indeed, a contemporary reviewer characterized it as "a kind of architectural encyclopedia" and compared it to the compendious and systematic "tree of knowledge" constructed by d'Alembert and Diderot.[33] More significant, given the evident lack of such a system in Ledoux's text, is the peculiar layout adopted for most of the plates, which deliberately emulated those of the *Encyclopédie* with their perspective vignettes of each building in context above an analytical presentation of plans, elevations, and sections, even as the workshops depicted by Diderot's engravers surmounted a carefully disassembled machine or a taxonomy of tools.[34] Beyond this, there was the obvious intention to advance the technical and social project implied by Diderot's description of the *arts et métiers,* now set in the active landscape of a newly opened region.

As a setting for his industrial *fabriques,* Ledoux assumed a completion of the highway network and the planned canals of Franche-Comté, Charollais, Nivernais, and Berry, which, joining the Loire, the Rhône, and the Saône, placed the site of the saltworks, at least in his imagination, at the center of European markets.

> The line that intersects the large diameter [of the saltworks] crosses the Loüe, immense plains, the city, the forest, the Doubs, the Geneva canal, the Swiss pastures; to the left, the Meuze, the Mozelle, the Rhine, the port of Antwerp, and the northern seas carry to the deserts of Siberia the precious and sought-after fruits of our commerce and our arts . . . . The small diameter aligns the routes of Arc and Senans, the forges of Roche, the paper mills, the polishing mills: what movement! Some polish the steel, chase the brass, blow the crystal; others cast the molten metal that sustains the rights of nations.[35]

Ledoux envisaged a new port established on the banks of the Doubs, from which goods would be shipped by the Dôle Canal to the Yonne and to the Mediterranean, or by way of the Meuze to the Rhine and to Antwerp. The Rhône and Iverdun Canals led to the lake of Bienne, carrying ship-building timber from Switzerland and Savoy; the Arve Canal allowed for transport from Gex, Bugey, Chatagne, and Chablais. The mines would supply this industrial expansion with raw materials and fuel: "the earth is opened up on all sides, and its fertile flanks produce coal, iron, brass, pyrites."[36]

Ledoux imagined forges for iron and cannons, foundries, steel furnaces, brass works, glass factories, porcelain works, textile factories, the gamut of industries listed in the *Encyclopédie* springing up in the vicinity of Chaux, vying with the clock-making industries of Geneva and the steelworks of Birmingham. At the center of his *cité industrielle* would stand a huge cannon foundry, surrounded by workshops, commercial warehouses, and artisans' dwellings of all kinds; further away, a *manufacture des toiles peintes* modeled on the Oberkampf factory at Jouy spread out by the river Loüe; smaller forges and workshops were distributed throughout the Forest of Chaux.[37] Thus the centralizing geometry of the saltworks expanded radially and along its axes to control an entire territory, as if in the very act of surveying, of mapping and building a network of communication, the earth would be brought under productive cultivation.

The initial incentive for Ledoux's industrial designs after 1780 was the support of the government and, especially, that of the minister of the Navy, Sartines, for the establishment of new cannon foundries at Indret, near Nantes, between 1777 and 1780, and at Le Creusot near Autun in Burgundy, after 1782.[38] The royal foundry of Creusot was set up at the advice of the artillery officer Ignace François de Wendel, with the technical expertise of the English ironmaster William Wilkinson. Supported by Calonne, the foundry built its first blast furnaces in 1784 and started production of cannons the following year. In 1786, another factory was joined to the first, the Queen's Crystal-Glass Factory. By the time of the Revolution, this factory had become the largest and most spectacular in France; using coke instead of wood, employing steam pumps and the latest in English foundry methods, it was, according to one visitor, "one of the wonders of the world."

Le Creusot was built between 1781 and 1784 to the designs of Pierre Touffaire, a naval engineer and architect of the maritime hospital of the Rochefort arsenal (plate 37). The first project included two coke-fired blast furnaces, forges, offices, and dwellings, as well as apartments for the workers; the second project added two more blast furnaces and larger workshops. Both plans followed the same architectural pattern, a central courtyard enclosed on three sides by factory buildings—the palace or château *parti* of earlier *manufactures réunies* and hospitals—but with the essential difference that each pavilion was carefully planned and sited for its respective functions. At the center was a large casting hall with its furnaces; to the front, on either side, were the forges and the boring rooms; and to the front of these were the workers' buildings, housing twenty-four families, with attic rooms for single men. Facing the casting hall at the other end of the main axis was the director's house. To the rear were other workshops and forges in lateral pavilions. Thus, despite the symmetry of the whole layout, it responded perfectly to the symmetry of functions and the flow of the production process, which was virtually described by the supply rails and canals that joined the different buildings.

The glass works designed by Barthélémy Jeanson (plate 38) was similarly planned, but as a continuous building around three sides of a square courtyard, reminiscent of Ledoux's first project for the saltworks, the two conical forges standing at the rear corners. In both buildings the architectural motifs were simple, reduced to a diagrammatic pediment with a clock in the foundry and rustication on the glass works.[39]

Inspired by the projects for both these factories, perhaps even hopefully competing for the commission in 1784–1785, Ledoux designed his own version of a *forge à canons*. The program, he stated, had been "conceived and dictated by a minister of purity [Calonne] who desired to maintain the respect of his country's flag" by setting up a cannon foundry to supply the eastern garrisons.[40] Not surprisingly, Ledoux broke with the traditional plan by centralizing the forges, furnaces, and workshops around a vast square, surrounded by a canal (plate 39). At the four corners stood furnaces, two for brass and two for iron; the outer edges of the square were defined by single-story workshops for polishing, making molds, metalworking, hand-gun manufacture, joinery, and carpentry. The four forge buildings, each two stories high, formed a Greek cross in the center of the plan, joining at the offices and the house of the director. "The dwelling of the director is at the center," noted Ledoux; "those of the clerks are at the extremities." His principal aim, as in the plan of the saltworks, was "to bring together all the necessary services, ensure surveillance, and facilitate the exportation [of products]."[41]

Whether or not this distribution was at all practical, the interest of the design lies in its architectural expression, for here, more than in Chaux, Ledoux reduced the factory to a set of almost pure geometric forms. The blast furnaces, taking their cue from English precedent and from their "primitive" Egyptian forebears—the necropolises of the pharaohs—became pure pyramids, spouting steam and smoke from their summits like industrial volcanoes; the central director's building became a cube with a cylindrical open courtyard inserted at its center; pediments became simple, stepped extensions of the walls, which themselves were neither rusticated nor ornamented but plain with rectangular cuts for windows (plate 40). Here the diagrammatic abstraction of Diderot's plates was allied to an architectural abstraction, referring to historical precedents that endowed the factory with a classical repertoire of signification. Ledoux described a visit to this sublime and terrifying *atelier* as if on a journey through the underworld, the empire of Pluto.[42]

RURAL ATELIERS

Supporting the production of salt and iron was a large work force of rural craftsmen and laborers scattered through the countryside, who depended on the forest for raw materials, building shelters and workshops roughly out of wood and mud, eking out a precarious living between their crafts and seasonal agricultural work.[43] Diderot had illustrated the gamut of these occupations, from clog manufacture to charcoal burning, under the heading "Rustic Economy."[44] Ledoux selected only those tasks directly concerned with the management and exploitation of the forest itself (charcoal burning, woodcutting, sawing, coopering) and designed specific, individual workshops and dwellings for each. Here, as in the earlier designs for the saltworks, the space of production was centralized around a hearth; the type-form that Ledoux seemed to have in mind was the clog and vine-stakes workshop from the *Encyclopédie,* illustrated in perspective section as a hexagonal structure, with a pyramidal roof open at the apex for a chimney, and with benches around the walls for sleep and work (see plate 15). Similar pyramidal huts, less idyllic than this, were described routinely by visitors to country districts throughout the eighteenth century.[45] Taking this natural form as his model, Ledoux then planned architectural versions, each with a particular character suited to the *métier* and each calculated to instill collective and communal values by virtue of its geometries.

This merging of architectural and social program was illustrated most completely in the dwelling of the charcoal-burners (plate 41). The isolation of the work and the independence of the workers, allied to their extreme poverty, made the *charbonniers* appear like savages in the eyes of the forge-owners and entrepreneurs who depended on them for a steady supply of fuel.[46] They lived in forests, in primitive huts similar to those conical shelters delineated by Perrault in his illustrations to Vitruvius's description of the origins of architecture (see plate 1). By investing such huts with architectural attributes and by designing each of them as a small community in its own right, Ledoux evidently hoped to bring their inhabitants into a natural state of harmony in a "communal center."

> Here man learns to support himself; sad amidst his fellows, he inhabits the forests; he passes, in obscurity, days that are inaccessible to the malaise of ambition. Charcoal-burner draws near to charcoal-burner; he develops his activity beneath this compliant arch, which [the architect] has curved within the forest to preserve his asylum from bad weather and the incursions of wild beasts.[47]

The plan was a square divided equally into nine squares; each corner was taken up with two beds, the center with a fireplace, the chimney of which rose to the apex of a ribbed dome. Beneath this dome, on the gallery level, were four more bedrooms and stores, reached by means of a gallery that surrounded the chimney. Ledoux thus repeated with variations the model he had invented for the salt-workers. But this *fabrique* had another function: entered on four sides through open porches, it provided visual oversight along the four *allées* of the forest to which it was aligned. It was, as Ledoux noted, "placed at the center of four routes," and the porches "ensure their surveillance"; Ledoux made the charcoal-burners guardians of the forest in which they worked, turning those who once needed to be policed into policemen themselves.

Deriving his architectural expression from the role of the *métier* and its place in the hierarchy of *métiers,* Ledoux invented first the "dome," reflecting the traditional huts of bent branches, now formalized; then a "pediment" over the porches, formed simply out of a shallow-pitched roof over the entry; finally, a new order—a tree-trunk order, posts placed vertically side by side to form the walls. "The order is simple," Ledoux concluded; "art has still not crossed these deserts, and the luxury that has the initiative over passions that are destructive of austere mores, has still not reached them."[48]

The house of the woodcutters was designed with similar wooden orders, here even more appropriate to the task (plates 42–43):

> The woodcutters' workshop returns us to first ideas. The oaks of the forest are felled, bound closely together, and attached to boards placed edge to edge. . . . This is not the first time architecture has been represented by logs.[49]

The primitive origins of architecture, emblematically set out as principle by the abbé Laugier, were now regained, but in a natural, productive form. As opposed to the decorative *chaumières* that the fashion for rusticity had built in every *jardin ornée,* the rural *métier* had found its proper figuration. But since woodcutters were more prosperous than charcoal-burners, or at least had a more powerful role to play in Ledoux's forest, their dwellings were endowed with more obvious architectural motifs. Their square hut was surrounded on all sides by a covered portico, surmounted by a pediment with each doorway marked by a rounded arch. A cylinder rose from the four central posts and contained the chimney; a full basement accommodated stables, cow shed, chicken run, and meat store.

Another workshop, also labeled a woodcutter's house (plate 44), was illustrated only in perspective. A pyramid in shape, it was made of horizontal logs rising from a square base, with ramped roofs forming a kind of pediment over the porches, and with doorways in a Palladian motif. The resemblance to the pyramidal kilns, or charcoal-burners' pyres, illustrated in the *Encyclopédie* (plate 45) was close, joining it to the "family" of forest shapes even as it asserted its character as architecture with a nod to Egypt and Palladio.[50]

Ledoux integrated the workshops of the sawyers into their dwelling as a semicovered, single-story space (plate 46). The communal room and fireplace was circular, rising as a two-story drum to its shallow, conical roof; from this room three bedroom wings extended radially, and between them were the work benches, outside but covered with a lean-to roof. The entire building was slightly raised on a circular platform and set, in Ledoux's words, "at the center of six *allées* of the forest." Also built of vertical logs and roofed in pantiles, it expressed in an almost typical way the sense of geometric centrality and architectural primitivism appropriate in Ledoux's terms to structures of this genre.

Each of these rural huts was thereby endowed with suitable rustic character. The workshop of the coopers, however, took this idea of proper characterization to another level (plate 47). Square in plan, bedrooms at the corners and a fireplace in the center, as all the others, it nevertheless departed from them radically in elevation. This presented itself as a giant series of inscribed circles, with a circular hole in the center. In three dimensions the intersection of the four circular sides and their attendant roofs generated the form of two intersecting cylinders, the circular bands inscribed on their ends. The circles were easy to explain: this after all was an "*atelier* of workers intended for the fabrication of *cercles,*" that is, the hoops that bound the barrels produced by the coopers (see plate 16). Ledoux's little joke, of a kind that would be repeated in many other figurative designs for his ideal city, was to make the entire house in the form of a double barrel, which remained unrevealed in plan or elevation. Similarly, the curves of the hoops were echoed by the ramps that led from the first-floor *ateliers* to the soaking basins that occupied each of the lower corners and down which the finished barrels were rolled. In this way, the house became a literal confirmation of the work, the workers surrounded by the shape of their product. The workshop was turned into a three-dimensional signboard, advertising in this first age of industry the wares made within. Obviously, Ledoux was restrained in this figurative play by the stern dictates of an abstract geometry; there were few *métiers* susceptible to representation in such simple forms, but the idea of such an *architecture parlante* was seductive and, when adopted by less scrupulous and more literal-minded architects, led to more pictorial caricatures, close to kitsch, the favorite sport of Jean-Jacques Lequeu.

The coopery thus brought the attempt to overlay the geometry of work with that of architecture to its logical but necessarily blocked conclusion; such *capriccii* might be witty diversions or even unique attractions, as commercial architecture has demonstrated, but their forms seriously inhibited, for most processes at least, the movements and operations they "imitated." As chinoiserie in a climate that found the idea of a circular, oriental house faintly exotic and replicated the patterns of Chinese plates in gardens and tapestries, the coopery was, briefly, acceptable. In the same genre must be grouped Ledoux's spherical house for the agricultural guards of Maupertuis (plate 48), the estate of one of his most faithful patrons; the horizontal cyclindrical house for the engineers of the River Loüe, who surveyed the river literally as it ran through their living quarters, planned inside a giant "drain" (plate 49); and the phallic plans of the houses of pleasure, brothels designed for the people of Paris and Chaux. All these designs tried in some way to make "hieroglyphic" signs out of the material of the program, turning architecture, so to speak, into pictographic writing. All of them arrived at a species of caricature by a relentless refusal of traditional architectural attributes and a will to invent, *ex novo,* a new architecture. All left themselves open to the scorn of the nineteenth-century commentator who observed caustically that, following the same principle, Ledoux would no doubt have rendered "the house of a drunkard in the shape of a bottle."[51] And yet, as a collection of three-dimensional transformations of centralized, geometric forms, abstract and crystalline like so many natural specimens, they took their place without difficulty in Ledoux's imaginary landscape of production in Franche-Comté, itself populated by equally bizarre forms since the beginning of industrialization.

CONFINEMENT AND CURE

REFORMING THE HOSPITAL, 1770–1789

I knew, like everyone else, that Bicêtre was at the same time a hospital and a prison, but I was ignorant of the fact that the hospital had been built to breed sickness and the prison to beget crimes.

Comte de Mirabeau, *Observation d'un voyageur. . . sur la Bicêtre*, 1788[1]

THE CLEARLY DIFFERENTIATED social and professional roles, administrative structures, and spatial forms that characterize modern institutions such as the hospital, the prison, the asylum, and the workhouse, were virtually unknown in mid-eighteenth-century France. What by the first decade of the nineteenth century would be regarded as the commonplace instruments of social order and reform, accepted as necessary building types in the architect's repertoire, were, as late as 1770, hardly distinguishable from each other, all absorbed in the generalized system of assistance inherited from the seventeenth century. The hospital, as a specific place for observing and treating illness; the prison, as the designated locale of punishment and, perhaps, reform; the asylum, as the prescribed boundary of insanity; the workhouse, as the moralizing, disciplinary apparatus for the able-bodied poor, these functions and spaces remained unclear in the heterogeneous, part private, part public, framework of the poor-law administration.[2] And yet in a very short period of time—no more than twenty years, between 1770 and 1789—the articulation of professionally and spatially defined realms for each of these institutions was crystallized in theory, if not entirely in practice. Experts found the sprawling and all-encompassing classical institutions of confinement inadequate solutions to the increasing problems of poverty, illness, and criminality; they imagined and sometimes implemented reforms. Economists, jurists, and doctors developed elaborate theories of social order; architects invented plans for new institutions and debated their merits according to criteria established by detailed "programs" drawn up by specialists.[3] Out of a ubiquitous "space of poverty" evolved an idea and project of a space of social order, classified and subdivided into units that were geometrically identified and architecturally reified.

The hospital was the first of these institutions to be defined with any clarity, stimulating fierce debates in the years before the Revolution. A developed idea of the prison, a concept of the asylum, would not emerge until the very end of the century, with corresponding judicial and medical codifications; but the idea of the hospital as the privileged locus of illness was fixed by the late 1780s. This is not to imply that a single, homogeneous idea of the type had been agreed upon by this time, but simply that all experts acknowledged the necessity for such an establishment, however small and localized, or large and centralized, whether for the care of certain diseases and not others, for specialized teaching purposes, or for generalized health care. The precocity of the hospital may be explained from a number of points of view. The existing hospitals harbored atrocious conditions and touched everyone: inside they seemed to promulgate the diseases they were supposed to cure; outside they seemed to be the centers of epidemics, dangerous to surrounding neighborhoods and regions. Specialization in the profession; the development of increasingly rigorous standards of diagnosis, observation, and treatment; the corresponding demand for teaching facilities where the sick might become the object of encyclopedic attention; a rationalist intolerance of the spectacle of so many diseases and conditions mingled together in one institution, these all contributed to the identification of the hospital for detailed study.[4] Finally, the boards of enquiry set up by the Académie des sciences following the fire at the Hôtel-Dieu of Paris in 1772, and the projects, memoranda, inventions, and statistical research that ensued, gave the debate a focus and a point of departure; the policies of all the revolutionary governments ensured its continuity.

THE SPACE OF POVERTY

The space of poverty was national: cities, villages, forests, and wilderness, all had their populations of the poor. Whether vagabonds, escaped criminals, beggars, elderly, transients, or simply indigents, the poor swarmed in the streets of big towns, begged in public places, lurked in the woods, roamed in bands to prey on the traveler, and, above all, moved in continuous streams along the roads and pathways. It has been estimated that more than 200,000 people were on the move at any one time in the France of the Old Regime—returning soldiers, migrant workers, traveling salesmen or *colporteurs,* searching for work or homes in the cities, displaced by famine, drought, war, or the police.[5]

The space of poverty was also institutional, defined by the walls of those fortresses of poverty that had been the result of the effort to confine, stabilize, and immobilize poverty at the end of the seventeenth century. The era of "great confinement," as it has been termed, called for the poor to be removed from sight, put to useful work, healed for the national good, and, finally, moralized.[6] The instruments of this campaign, which lasted fitfully from 1660 to 1770, were a system of interrelated foundations of the Hospital-general, the hospice or workhouse, the charity workshop, and a program of public assistance; that is, a network of institutions of varied function and size that would, once and for all, exterminate poverty from the realm. By these means, the deserving poor, sick, and elderly would find relief from their misery; the undeserving poor—the criminal or idle—would be put to work for the profit of communities; the helpless—orphans, cripples, and chronically diseased—would be cared for according to their needs.

The means were disproportionate to the end: none of the hospitals set up after the middle of the seventeenth century, following the charitable vision of Saint Vincent de Paul, could hold the population that was demanded of it; the charitable alms-giving, soup kitchens, and workshops established in communities for the benefit of the poor could in no way accommodate the needs of the vast mobile crowd. Even the subsidies promised by the state, after the edicts of 1685 and 1724, failed hopelessly to provide for the expansion of the Hospital-general.[7] The simple monastic rule of the Paris Hospital, founded to take care of forty-eight deserving poor selected for their skills and level of sickness, run on conventual lines by the Sisters of Charity—a kind of religious factory—was in every way an inadequate structure to receive the population of two to three thousand poor of every description that filled its wards by the middle of the eighteenth century. Despite edicts that provided for the establishment of such institutions in every town, the ranks of the poor kept swelling. The War of Spanish Succession and the Seven Years War increased drastically the number of demobilized soldiers, out of work and often without fixed homes. Attempts to reestablish them by encouraging the expansion of rural industry outside the tightly controlled guild structure also failed.[8]

By the middle of the eighteenth century, the Hospitals-general had been transformed from the small, peaceable centers of charity and care, work and moralization envisaged at their foundation, into centers of disease, immorality, and crime. In Paris, the Hospital consisted of La Salpetrière, which housed some 4,700 women and employed nearly 2,000 staff members, taking in women, young girls, boys under the age of four, and the poor, the insane, prostitutes, and the sick of all kinds; the Bicêtre, which housed 3,500 men—criminal, sick, and elderly; the Pitié, which housed over 1,000 boy foundlings; and the Saint-Esprit, which housed 100 orphans. The old Hôtel-Dieu, with 3,000–4,000 patients, accommodated all kinds of outcast—the aged, the infirm, foundlings, vagabonds, criminals, the insane—as well as every conceivable disease, while the Incurables held only 300 patients of the better class. Five *dépôts de mendicité*, with over 18,000 inmates by the 1770s, supplemented this overburdened apparatus.[9] All were intolerably overcrowded: the Hospital-General was forced to put five or six to a bed; the Hôtel-Dieu, by the time of the enquiries of the 1780s, sometimes placed ten to twelve on the same mattress. Outside the city proper, the Hospital Saint-Louis, despite its regular plan, was, together with the Hôtel-Dieu, the worst hospital that John Howard had seen on his intensive tours in the early 1780s. Hospitals were regarded widely as places of despair—the "dead end of Hell," Restif de la Bretonne called them—and centers of infection. Philosophers remarked on the irony that such places in fact bred the diseases they were established to cure.

Opposing the conditions within the institutions of confinement and noting that poverty was increasing, reformers suggested two different solutions. On the one hand, physiocrats, liberal mercantilists, and religious conservatives urged a return to the old order, or rather a "natural" form of poor relief, that would dismantle the castles of poverty and sickness in favor of smaller, local charitable institutions. The sick and elderly would be given home care, the able poor put to useful work, and the incorrigible or criminal set to prison labor. On the other hand, there were those who felt that only government intervention on an even larger scale—the building of vast, centralized hospitals, prisons, and workhouses—would serve the burgeoning population with efficiency, as well as with improved surveillance, hygiene, and technical expertise.

In the article "Hôpital" for the *Encyclopédie,* Diderot espoused the conservative position, calling for a solution to poverty not by "multiplying the asylums for the destitute" but by preventing it in the first place. He argued that too much misapplied charity would simply increase the inducements for the able-bodied poor not to work.

> I cannot estimate the number of poor, these lazy and vigorous young men, who, finding in our misunderstood charity easier and more considerable aid than they could secure by work, fill our streets, our churches, our great roads, our towns, our cities, and our countryside. Such vermin can only exist in a state where the value of men is unknown. To render the condition of professional beggars and the true poor equal by mingling them in the same establishments is to forget that there are uncultivated lands to clear, colonies to populate, factories to sustain, public works to continue.[10]

The physiocratic propagandist Nicolas Baudeau advanced a similar argument. He denounced the "palaces of poverty" built and maintained at great expense, those single buildings that served "at the same time as prisons for crime, for libertinage, and for a destitute old age."[11] In their place he proposed a "return" to a decentralized familial charity and home care for the sick, together with a system of small *ateliers* for the employment of those who could work, attached to hospices that would house and care for their inmates with dignity and order. Divided into three separate sections, for men, women, and families,

> these dwellings should be very simple, outside as well as in, but ventilated, clean, decent, and well-ordered; no many-storied palace that breathes luxury on the outside and the most disgusting misery on the inside. We would like large and vast courtyards, much fresh air, water, trees, and shade; all around would be single-story corridors raised above the ground over cellars and stores.[12]

Baudeau's scheme called for rooms of a good size, properly furnished, as well as a workshop. Those who became too old to work would be returned to their old neighborhood to be cared for at home. Even the management of Baudeau's asylum was to be decentralized: the population would be divided into companies of about one hundred, and these into squadrons of ten, a sergeant at the head of each company and a corporal at the head of each squadron. Each company would have its own service kitchens, bathrooms, and workrooms around a courtyard.

The doctors and administrators of the Hôtel-Dieu and the Hospital-general countered this physiocratic, faintly utopian vision of a natural order of work, health, and assistance, echoes of which, as Michel Foucault has pointed out, gained political redolence during the Revolution. After 1772, these professionals expanded their program, which at first they had confined to an overhaul of dilapidated buildings, to include the gamut of health-care institutions.

The history of this discussion is well known and may be summarized as follows. An already heavily criticized Hôtel-Dieu caught fire in 1772; an entire wing was destroyed, drawing public attention to this impossibly overcrowded, unsanitary, sprawling, and badly serviced institution and giving rise to a spate of projects, *mémoires,* and architectural designs for a new hospital or hospitals.[13] Ledoux and Jean-François Chalgrin were among the first architects to address the problem, but a host of other professionals—administrators, lawyers, economists, and doctors—rapidly superseded them in the rush to perfect the technical specifications and urban implications of a new hospital service for Paris. Blueprints drawn up by architects (Pierre Panseron, 1773) were supplemented by those invented by doctors (Jean-Baptiste Le Roy, physician, brother of the architect Julien-David; and Antoine Petit, doctor, professor of anatomy and surgery, both members of the Académie des sciences) and ecclesiastics (Regnier, secretary to the archbishop of Rodez), and they were reinforced by the political pamphlets of journalists and propagandists. The writer Marmontel appointed himself the "voice of the poor," addressed a letter to the king about the fire, and sold it for the benefit of the indigent.

The opposition of the Church, and in particular that of the administration of the Hôtel-Dieu itself, forced all these plans into abeyance. Similarly rejected was the official attempt of the police chief Lenoir to transfer the Hôtel-Dieu to the Hôtel des Invalides. In 1777, Necker put forth a new initiative that sought publicly for a range of ideas—"new and interesting"—toward the amelioration of all the hospitals of France. To judge the proposals, he established a commission that included the administrators of the Hospital-general, the *curés* of Saint Eustache, Saint Roche, and Sainte Marguerite, as well as the director of the Royal Society of Medicine. This commission received upwards of one hundred and fifty *mémoires,* which remained with some exceptions unpublished, in order, the official line went, "not to alarm the Parisian population." In the end, the commission came out solidly in favor of the Hôtel-Dieu administration, declaring all public outcry unfounded and ratifying the position of this center of sickness as the largest, most concentrated, "city of poverty" in the realm.[14]

The stream of *mémoires,* proposals, and projects published by doctors, philosophes, lawyers, and journalists after 1772 pretended to little architectural merit, but instead posed themselves as solutions based on new and scientific knowledge, which inevitably represented these solutions in plan and section. Here the overriding criterion of judgment was not the precise nature of the architectural embellishments but solutions to questions of economy, movement, service, salubrity, and so on.

The architect was thus issued a challenge: faced with these new programmatic requirements and their spatial solutions invented, apparently with ease, by nonarchitects, what was to become of the traditional apparatus of classical precedent, proper characterization, and monumental aesthetics; where indeed might the expertise of the architect be required at all, save for the mundane task of translating doctors' diagrams into building specifications? This, at least, was how many architects and doctors posed the problem, and, certainly during the course of the debate, schemes and counterschemes emphasized one or another professional interest.[15] But, in reality, the question was more complicated, for most of the nonarchitectural plans advanced by other specialists owed their sophistication to the architects they employed to draw up the project; despite the apparent absence of architecture, what was being presented was not an "architecture without architects," but rather another kind of architecture, one that drew on alternative figurative sources for its imagery and that found its means for "embellishment" not in the classical repertory, but in the forms of need. One thing was clear, however: the classical hospital, the form of which had been more or less set by the late seventeenth century, had to be replaced.

The traditional model of the hospital—as in the Hospital Saint-Louis—was at its simplest a square courtyard building and at its most complex a series of interconnected courtyards, defined by separate or connected wings, with a central chapel dominating the composition.[16] Variations on this type were built throughout France in the first half of the eighteenth century as additions or restorations to older conventual foundations or as new institutions. Thus Jacques-Germain Soufflot rebuilt the Hôpital de la Charité at Mâcon as a unified set of wards around a courtyard, with an oval chapel in one corner; in the same city, the architect Melchior Munet built the Hôtel-Dieu with two large courts and a centralized chapel.[17] Soufflot's Hôtel-Dieu at Lyons, built between 1741 and 1764, was the most monumental of such schemes to be designed and built.[18] Blondel reaffirmed the general outlines of the type in his *Cours,* with a central chapel flanked by courtyards, terraces, and promenades. Published in 1771, his long essay on the architecture of hospitals, while reflecting to a remarkable degree the new interest in a comprehensive program for urban health, was nevertheless entirely traditional from an architectural point of view.[19]

Thus it is not surprising that when, in 1771, the Académie d'architecture set the program of a Hôtel-Dieu as a subject for the Grand Prix competition of that year, the responses were entirely predictable. The program itself hardly addressed the scale of the problem; its focus was on the care of "persons of a higher rank than that of the common people" and accommodated only seven hundred beds.[20] Two years later, following the fire, the architect Pierre Panseron reported that the Académie had published a new competition program, this time for a *hospice des malades* of a size that might be built in each of sixteen districts of the city—a proposal already advanced by Blondel—containing facilities for up to fifty patients.[21] Such was the extent of official architectural interest in the question. When architects did respond to the fire of 1772, it was to propose schemes for a new Hôtel-Dieu like that of Panseron, which simply replicated the old type on a grander scale (plate 50).[22] Although Panseron adopted the common strategy of resiting the Hôtel-Dieu on the Ile des Cygnes and rebuilding it to house 5,000 persons, and although his plan paid some attention to the minutiae of administrative and medical functions, in the eyes of the medical reformers Panseron failed to address the principal evil of existing hospitals: their lack of ventilation. Only by responding to the circulation of the air first, and all other requirements second, might a hospital be able to cure a large number of patients otherwise doomed to infect and reinfect each other.

THE FORM OF THE AIR

> Picture to yourself a long row of continuous wards, where sick of every kind are brought together and where they are piled often three, four, five, and six in the same bed, the living beside the dying and dead, the air infected with the exhalations of this multitude of unhealthy bodies, carrying from one to the other the pestilential germs of their sickness and the spectacle of the sadness and agony offered and received on all sides: That is the Hôtel-Dieu.
>
> D. Diderot, "Hôtel-Dieu," *Encyclopédie*[23]

In the middle of the eighteenth century, the spectacle of the horrifying conditions in the overcrowded Hôtel-Dieu of Paris—the patients piled up many to a bed, the foul-smelling and ill-ventilated wards, the badly serviced and ill-maintained buildings, the pollution of the Seine with sewage and rubbish, waters in which the soiled linen of the hospital was washed—was often evoked as a subject of philosophic outrage. Diderot borrowed his description in the *Encyclopédie* from one written by a philanthropist and institutional reformer, Claude Hubert Piarron de Chamousset, whose efforts to reform hospital conditions were lauded by Voltaire and resulted in the foundation of a number of private establishments in the 1750s.[24] De Chamousset outlined his utopia of health care in terms that were to be repeated throughout the century.

> One will construct in fresh air a spacious building divided into clean and comfortable apartments, and composed of many wings, entirely separated and distributed according to the different conditions of the persons for whom they are intended; some for men, some for women. In each, the service will be provided by those of the same sex.[25]

In this pleasant dwelling, doctors and surgeons would work assiduously under the eyes of their supervisors. There would be vigilant and well-directed guards, a scrupulous choice of provisions, and every care to ensure cleanliness and the circulation of air.

The project of another reformer, Claude Chevalier, was similar: his proposed *Maison de Santé* was to be

> well appointed, with a large and magnificent garden, situated in pure air and with a beautiful view . . . ; in a place with a suitable elevation, it presents from all sides the most agreeable site. There the constitution of the air is sweet and tempered, and the influence of the elements is favorable to the nature of those who dwell in it: the site is pure and bracing and in every way suitable to health. Thus, this asylum contains at the same time everything that can contribute to the happiness of life, the useful and the agreeable.[26]

In Chevalier's "Physico-medical dissertation on the causes of many dangerous illnesses," as in the pathology of de Chamousset, the environment was the first cause of both illness and cure. The conditions so dramatically presented by the Hôtel-Dieu might be remedied: the air by the choice of site and by the proper means of ventilation—infected air was, after all, as Duhamel de Monceau observed, lighter than fresh air—and the spatial distribution by proper attention to the arrangement of bodies, things, and walls.[27]

Air had been the object of intensive study since Boyle. It was a mysterious substance with unknown properties, charged with phlogiston, the (hypothetical) caloric element that permitted combustion, calcification, and respiration; it was all-pervasive and therefore all-culpable. Even the purest air, noted the doctor Genneté, "is charged and impregnated like a sponge with everything good and bad"; when this air was exhaled by numerous infected bodies enclosed in a small space, it became poisonous.[28] The "fluid" so necessary to life was converted into an agent of death.

Despite its invisibility, the air had behavior patterns that, observed by scientists and inventors alike, might be susceptible to control. Duhamel de Monceau, who had been called to install ventilators in the laundry of the Hôtel-Dieu in Paris following the plague of 1748, wrote treatises on the proper ventilation of ships, grain stores, hospitals, and rural buildings, borrowing from the experiences of the English inventor Stephen Hales and from observation of Soufflot's Hôtel-Dieu in Lyons. He noted that the high ceilings of certain hospital rooms, the high placement of windows, and, above all, the high dome at the crossing of the Lyons hospital, allowed used air to be drawn out.[29]

Genneté, who described the ventilating system installed by Hales in Newgate Prison—a wooden diaphragm moved by a windmill on the roof—as well as the improvements of Duhamel, supported the argument for high ceilings using the evidence of birds that were found dead in the upper reaches of the Lyons dome. He suggested a combination of mechanical and architectural means. The Lyons academy itself had, in 1761, proposed an essay question on the subject, "What is the destructive quality contracted by the air in hospitals and prisons, and what is the best means of remedying it?" Twenty years later, preoccupied with the same question, the Sociéte royale de médecine asked respondents to "determine by means of a sufficient number of observations and exact experiments if contagious illnesses, principally smallpox, could be transmitted by the air."[30] The prize went to a doctor from Lyons, who confirmed that the transference of germ particles, detached from the sick and received by the healthy body—like a plant spore—was aided by the air.

In the period before the general acceptance of the new chemistry of Lavoisier, before the experiments of the late 1770s demonstrated the nonexistence of phlogiston and the true chemical composition of air, what mattered was its behavior and, more precisely, the form of that behavior.[31] In the imagination of doctors, the fluidity of air allowed it to penetrate the innermost crevices of buildings and expand its influence throughout the city and the countryside. The air was thus one of the first truly urban phenomena to be addressed by scientists; but like other gases and fluids, it might be contained, channeled, drawn, and replaced continuously. The *circulation* of the air, like that of the blood in a healthy organism, might then be stimulated by the shape of the environment. Circulation, here as in other discourses of natural order—economic, biological, and technical—became the watchword for reforming the hospital ward, just as later it was expanded to encompass the entire ventilation of a city.

In a *mémoire* of 1774, Antoine Petit, a distinguished doctor at the University of Paris, member of the Académie des sciences, and professor of anatomy at the Jardin des Plantes, published the first project to unite these concerns for circulation with an architectural form (plates 51–52).[32] He directed his discourse pointedly toward architects: headed by a quotation from Philibert de l'Orme, which admonished the architect to listen first to the wisdom of philosophers and doctors before designing his buildings, and embellished with the attributes of theoretical geometry, his text submitted the common practices of hospital architects to critical scrutiny.

> If one is concerned to build a hospital for the sick, what site should one choose? What form of construction should be preferred? The knowledge provided by the study of architecture is not enough to be able to make so difficult a choice; one must still know what effect external agents such as the air, the water, exhalations, etc., can have on the sick, and in what way they can serve or hinder their cure. Magnificence and solidity are not enough for such a building; essentially it requires salubrity. This last concern can be treated properly only by a doctor.[33]

Thus Petit argued for the removal of hospitals from the center of the city as "the air of large cities is, in general, charged with vapors and with acrid and putrid exhalations and consequently is impure and unhealthy." In Paris, he preferred the site between the old Hospital Saint-Louis and the hill of Belleville where, protected as it would not be on the Ile des Cygnes from the ill-effects of the north wind (which "retards the crises, renders them imperfect, augments pain, excessively tires those with sensitive and delicate chests, harms the gouty and those with scurvy"), a new hospital would stand as a symbol of health overlooking the city.[34]

Equally important were the principles on which its plan would be developed: first the circulation of the air; then the speed of service to each patient; then the accommodation of the greatest number of patients in a bounded space without impairing their health. On all three counts Petit found the traditional plan severely wanting.

> This form is generally square, and the rooms for the sick comprise large, high blocks, on the floor of which are placed many rows of beds. It is certain that this kind of construction teems with inconveniences, of which the least is to increase the cost of service. . . . Another point of greater consequence still is that the air, confined between the four walls, stagnates without being agitated and blown by the winds; it does not renew itself at all; it becomes infected above all when it heats up. . . . This air, nevertheless, is what the sick breathe.[35]

For these and other reasons, Petit rejected the square courtyard as "of all [plans] the most vicious." In its place he substituted another geometry, that of the circle, the radials of which, as many as required, become the ward blocks, joined at the center in a circular chapel and connected at the periphery by covered service arcades, a disposition that had already been sketched by Desgodets in his 1727 plan for a Hôtel-Dieu (plate 53). In this way, the chapel would be visually accessible to all the patients; the necessary services placed around it (the pharmacy, the surgeons' and doctors' rooms, the kitchens, the bakery) would allow for economic and quick delivery; the nurses, also at the center, would be able to survey at a glance the state of the wards.

On this level, with his insistence on visual order and access, Petit seemed to anticipate the panoptical discourse brought to perfection by Bentham some decades later, but with the significant difference of a reciprocal observation by the patient toward the chapel and by the nurse toward the patients' immediate needs. Petit's radial plan, while indeed increasing the efficiency of the establishment, was devised less for the power of sight than for the circulation of air. To this end, the radial plan brought together two hitherto separate precedents, the one ancient and deeply embedded in the lore of architecture, the other modern and only recently imported as a "form" into France. The first precedent was the Vitruvian "city of the winds," a city with streets carefully aligned according to the prevailing breezes, which Petit turned into an institution—a "city within a city." The second precedent, which informed the peculiar and original shape of the dome over the central chapel, was drawn from industry; for what Petit called "a dome made in the shape of an inverted funnel" was in fact an almost perfect replication of the English glass-furnace illustrated in the *Encyclopédie* (see plate 21). Petit deliberately chose this source, for the conical form of the furnace had been invented to increase the draft and thus the temperature in the melting furnace, and at the same time to draw off coke fumes and smoke through the aperture in the roof.[36] It was, therefore, a form of ventilation par excellence, one readily adopted by a doctor versed in experimental science.

> The dome placed at the center of the building . . . will serve as a ventilator and continuously renew the air of all the wards. In order to help accomplish this task more perfectly, I have vented the flues of all the stoves into the dome and have backed up to it the chimneys of the kitchens and pharmacy. Thus the air of the wards, renewed night and day without interruption, will not be corrupted anymore. . . .[37]

In this context, it was perhaps no accident that Petit's radial plan as a whole seemed to emulate a giant windmill.

While Petit ended his memorandum by deferring to an architect to whom he was prepared to "abandon all the details" of execution, it was clear throughout his text that the doctor was claiming primacy in the art of "sketching the plan," that the task of invention, of creating a form with respect to a complicated and technical program, belonged first to the medical profession and only second to that of the architect. Like the industrial entrepreneur Perier at Le Creusot, who boasted of needing no help from architects or engineers in building his factory, Petit preferred to pose as a designer himself.[38] Only professional etiquette forced him to disclose, and this elliptically, that the professionalism of the engraved designs that illustrate his treatise was due to the example of an architect: "I think of it as a duty and a pleasure," he wrote in a footnote, "to make it known that regarding this form of radial building I have found myself of a like mind to M. Prunneau de Monlouis, architect of Paris. I think that this coincidence is the greatest praise that could be made of my idea."[39]

One of Petit's professional colleagues in the Académie des sciences prepared a second project for the new Hôtel-Dieu, conceived in 1773 but not presented to the Académie until 1777, and not published until twelve years after this. Jean-Baptiste Le Roy offered an alternative solution to the question of ventilation (plates 54–55). Le Roy came from a noted family of inventors and physicians: his father was a celebrated clock maker to the king, and of his three brothers, one was also a doctor, another a clock maker, and the third an architect-antiquarian, Julien-David Le Roy, who besides publishing the first measured drawings of the Acropolis was an expert on the design and building of ancient ships.[40] Accordingly, the problem of ventilation, as for Petit, became for Jean-Baptiste a problem of invention. Finding in his research no treatise on the building of hospitals that "profited from the observations of physics and modern medicine," Le Roy developed the principles for such a building according to the overriding criteria of air circulation. But rather than transform the entire hospital into a ventilator, he concentrated on a mechanism for the individual ward; conscious of the need to isolate the different wards, each containing different species of disease, he

> ranged them like tents in a camp or pavilions in the garden of Marly. . . . By means of this disposition, each ward is like a kind of island in the air, surrounded by a considerable volume of this fluid so that the winds can carry off and renew it easily by the free access between them.[41]

Bathed thus in pure air, separated by greenery and set apart from adjacent wards, the ward became the elementary building block of the hospital, which could thereby expand according to need along the military lines suggested by Le Roy. He treated each ward block as a complete system, ventilated by a series of ceiling vents, which were of ogival form, derived from his studies of mine-shaft chimneys. Like a linear chain of Gothic vaults, these chimneys were topped by weather vanes; a second series of vents, cut into the floor of the ward, allowed hot air from the first-floor furnaces to create a draft rising to the ceiling. These "air-wells," as Le Roy called them, completed the circular system of ventilation, making the ward a kind of architectural lung, a breathing building.

> A hospital ward is, if one can say it thus, a veritable machine to treat the sick, and should be considered from this point of view . . . ; every machine has only been developed to perfection after a large number of attempts and experiments.[42]

Le Roy, as Bruno Fortier has noted, here anticipated the characterization of the hospital as a *machine à guérir,* rejecting an architectural patrimony in favor of uninhibited empiricism and a rational layout. Le Roy himself stated that "the true and only magnificence" appropriate to such buildings was an "extreme cleanliness, as pure an air as possible"; decoration was only the smallest part of a building in which everything accessory should be sacrificed to principle.[43]

And yet Le Roy, like Petit, dissimulated in his eagerness to demonstrate freedom from convention; for the ward blocks depicted in the engravings accompanying the *Mémoires* of the Académie des sciences are far from denuded, machinelike sheds. Each of the long, narrow, vaulted halls referred to its conventual origins; the floor was supported by a central row of short, thick "Doric" columns on the first level; and the entire block was surrounded by an arcade of over sixty baseless Doric columns, such as David Le Roy had described in his accounts of the Greek stoas—more "architecture" than might be thought necessary by an experimental doctor. In the overall plan, moreover, these wards were ranged on either side of a grand avenue leading to a chapel, itself set at the rear of a stepped hemicycle, the entire composition emulating the Invalides and following all the rules of academic planning.

It was only in 1814 that these engravings were revealed to be the work not of Le Roy but of an architect, himself a designer of hospitals, Charles-François Viel. Complaining that, having sold the plates to Le Roy in 1780, he was unable to sign them as his own, Viel described in detail the specific boundaries of each professional's contribution.[44] He did not deny that Le Roy had invented the entire scheme of ventilation, the separation of the wards, and the distribution of beds and services, but the "general and particular disposition of this plan," including the concept of the grand court, all the parts that, as he noted, "belong to art, as a composition of architecture," were of his own design. As architect, Viel thus claimed paternity for all the "imitations" of separate ward block plans that had followed those of Le Roy:

> This explanation became necessary in order to clarify what constitutes a work of architecture, which never belongs as a composition to the author of the program, because the arts of design do not express themselves in any way by words. Certainly, the professors in art schools who give programs for pictures, sculptures, and buildings to be composed by their students do not have the pretension of the intellectuals who have written on hospitals, who dare to call the invention of plans, elevations, and sections: their projects![45]

Viel's outrage, fueled by decades of resentment against the proprietary knowledge of the specialist, was in microcosm a map of the boundary disputes to be waged in the modern age of programs between architect and surrogate patron. But it should not conceal the fact that, in both Petit's and Le Roy's schemes, what was inventive architecturally, and what introduced a new range of forms into a traditional catalogue, was the product of the doctor, by his patronage forcing the designer to domesticate them as the forms of function.

In the context of the hospital, this process of mediation between architect and doctor was taken to its formal conclusion in another project outlined programmatically by a doctor and delineated by an architect: the scheme for a perfectly ventilated ward block, presented by a celebrated physician from Dijon, Hugues Maret, and, through correspondence, given architectural form by the elderly Jacques Soufflot in the last months of his life.[46] (plate 56). A contributor to the *Encyclopédie* and editor of the volumes on pharmacy for the *Encyclopédie méthodique,* Maret specialized in epidemic fevers as well as chemistry; his observations on the movement and nature of the air stemmed directly from these more general interests. For Maret, the problem of ventilation in hospitals reduced itself to a simple question: What is the form taken by the air in motion? Once the answer to this was known, a ward block might be designed following such a form. Everything consisted in this, he claimed: "to construct the rooms of infirmaries in such a way that the mass of air enclosed by them may be renewed entirely and at will."

For Maret, air was a mutable substance; it was a fluid that assumed different combinations according to the foreign substances it supported and dissolved. It thereby lost elasticity and took on the qualities of its own impurities, and nowhere more seriously than in hospitals, where it made contact with the bodies of the sick. But if the form of air currents was properly understood, these mutations might be controlled. According to Maret, air possessed a distinct geometry: composed of tiny particles that rub against each other, air dispersed its currents like visual rays. A current was therefore "composed of rays that converge at the point of penetration."[47] That is, air currents were shaped like cones, more or less deformed, flattened, or elongated by the resistance of objects. If a current was directed toward a solid body, the rays were deflected, and hundreds of new cones were set up, varying in direction as the shape of the body. Like light or water, air flowed in precise shapes.

Maret thought he had thus discovered the "primitive types," as it were, of air flow; the form of these types in some way had to generate the form of a well-ventilated room. The ward should be designed so that in every case the old, used, and impure air is faced with the full mass of the cone's base. For this the cone should remain as undistorted as possible in its trajectory through the room. Square or rectangular shapes would allow old air to lurk in the corners. According to Maret's logic,

> infirmaries should take on the form of an ellipse, more or less elongated and truncated at each end; their ceiling should be equally elliptical, and the upper part of the walls should join this vault by means of a curve of the same type, so that the room has the form of an egg, cut by a plane parallel to its long axis.[48]

At each end, outside the doors of the ward, the walls should continue to fan outwards and upwards; the air would thus be offered little resistance during its entry and exit. This streamlined profile would turn the ward into a veritable wind tunnel: the furniture cleared to either side, the twin doors at each end opened at the same time, a single strong current of wind would rush through the room, evacuating the old air and bringing new air behind it. The contours of the walls would preserve the natural force of the cone.

> The properties of the ellipse being that the rays starting at one end of this curve will come together again at the other end after having been reflected by the different points along the line, and the cone being formed by the expansion of the current, having its point at the end of the ellipse, it is evident that all the rays of which it is comprised will come together at the other end, that there will as a result be two cones, each with its point at one end.[49]

No air would be left undisturbed by such a massive, geometrically calculated assault. Maret recommended that those patients who could, stand beside their beds, clutching their bedding, while this powerful draft blew.

Maret's observations were published in the *Journal de Paris*. He suggested that while it was the doctor's task to discover what might be useful, it was up to the architect and the politician to calculate how to undertake the job. Soufflot, himself interested in improving on the somewhat unscientific dome at Lyons, responded with a plan and section of the doctor's proposal.[50]

Soufflot's scheme, as eccentric as it was, represented the extreme pole of a dialogue that, on the one hand, insisted the hospital was a building subject to all the decorum of a great public monument, and that, on the other hand, claimed the hospital was, as Jacques Tenon was to claim, a "tool, a factory for treating patients."[51] Tenon's metaphor, however, was just that: an analogy that allowed the complexity of programmatic demands to be understood as an interdependent whole; Maret/Soufflot's project remained an astonishing prefiguration of a functionalism applied literally in form, in the manner of a nineteenth-century machine or a twentieth-century flow diagram. Even the vestigial Doric columns marking the entrance to the ward block were absorbed in the continuous streamlined contour of the plan.

MONUMENTAL AESTHETICS

> A hospital for the sick is a building where the architect should subordinate his art to the views of the doctor.
>
> Diderot, "Hôpital," *Encyclopédie*.[52]

The discussion between programmatic form and architectural tradition was not resolved by the simple omission of one or the other; the claims of classical representation were too ingrained to be dismissed in favor of a bizarre, anti-architectural "invention." Architects in the 1780s still searched for that delicate balance of monumentality, character, and programmatic clarity that might at once evoke "hospital" to the observer and renew the classical lexicon in its application to a new type.

Of all the hospital proposals advanced before the Revolution, that designed by the architect Bernard Poyet, with the help of Claude Philibert Coquéau and the support of the secretary of state, the Baron de Breteuil, gained the most notoriety precisely because of its attempt to weld medical wisdom and antique precedent.[53] Poyet's scheme was much debated during the years following its presentation to the Académie des sciences in December of 1785, and to this day it remains the scheme most often cited by art historians as representative of the social projects in late-eighteenth-century France. The reasons for its contemporary and posthumous popularity are clear: designed by a "high" architect, student of Charles De Wailly and member of the salons in the Chartres circle, the project tried to tie the question of the program as articulated in the first spate of *mémoires* after 1772 to a suitable expression or character, as defined by academic architectural theory. Even though it was not built, it stood in the same relation to the architecture of hospitals as Ledoux's Saline de Chaux to the architecture of factories: it stemmed from the same interest in reconciling programmatic demands and architectural characterization, and it responded to the conflicting demands of distribution and decoration in a similar way. It was also well-publicized: long after the Revolution, Poyet and his supporters still agitated for construction of the scheme.

Circular with radial ward blocks joined at the periphery by enclosed service passages and focused on a circular chapel at the center, its overall form revealed Petit's influence (plates 57–59). But where the doctor had been content to delineate the outline of a typical plan, "leaving the details to the architect," and to present his scheme independent of any site, Poyet inserted his plan directly into the context of Paris. While "typical" in all its aspects, it was designed to act as one of a number of service-monuments, placed at strategic points throughout the city. Charles De Wailly himself recognized this when preparing his *Projet d'utilité et d'embellissement pour la ville de Paris* for de Breteuil and the Académie des sciences in 1788.[54] Here De Wailly used Poyet's plan for the hospital on the Ile des Cygnes as the starting point for the development of the entire area around the Invalides. In fact, De Wailly doubled the plan, indicating another circular institution on the river to the west, symmetrically placed across the axis of the Invalides; this would have accommodated a new Halle au blé and a public bath.

The Ile des Cygnes was entirely appropriate for the vast institution that Poyet planned. Isolated from nearby dwellings by much open space, it was also surrounded by the river on all sides; Poyet thereby met the criteria of ventilation and rapid service by riverboat. Coquéau wrote,

> On this island the mobile atmosphere into which the Hôtel-Dieu will be plunged will envelop it on every side, and its continual movement, penetrating all the openings facing in every direction, which Poyet has multiplied to the greatest possible degree, will be propagated throughout the extent of the building.[55]

Poyet took the demand for ventilation, like Petit before him, as a call for a "city of the winds" in plan, the large ward blocks radially pointing along the path of each of the winds. He increased the number of radials from Petit's six to sixteen, thus doubling the number of wards on three stories from twenty-four to forty-eight. Instead of a central conical volume, the primitive ventilator used by Petit, Poyet opened a circular courtyard, surrounded by a ring of service galleries joining the inner ends of the wards. At the center of this court stood a chapel.

It was common medical wisdom that winds from different directions held different qualities, good or bad; an article on good health in the *Journal Encyclopédique* of 1763 outlined this theory, one that Ledoux considered in the planning of Chaux. "The North Wind contains nitrates; it is cold and acidic. The East brings in its flow sand from Asia. The South is warm with sulphur, and the West Wind, blowing from the sea, is damp and humid."[56] Poyet suggested that his radial plan, with so many directions, allowed for the proper arrangement of illnesses, each classified with respect to the benefits or dangers of a particular wind: "They will be distributed in these wards by reason of the properties that experience has assigned to each of the winds that disturb and purify the atmosphere."[57]

The rest of the project followed what had already become the commonplaces of hospital design. The wards themselves were isolated by green courtyards, each provided with its own services, bathrooms, offices, kitchens, pharmacies, and so on; these, however, were linked by encircling galleries inside and out to allow rapid movement through and around the complex. The chapel at the center allowed all the patients visually to take part in the religious services. Such conveniences, Coquéau argued, made this hospital for 5,000 beds as easy to run as a small hospice. It was open to surveillance, flexible in accommodation, and economic in the provision of care.

> The independence of all the parts will ensure all the advantages that are attributed to the system of Hospices; the communications and the food service will be so conveniently situated and linked so well to all the wards that the service, for the whole complex, will be as simple, as easy to oversee, as in the smallest hospital. Its extent will allow the multiplication and arrangement at will of central gathering points for this service; being no longer mixed up together, the departments will not get in each other's way.[58]

These advantages, argued Coquéau, resulted from the circular plan. The case for the geometric order of the project was similar to that of Petit ten years before: the existing Hôtel-Dieu was a "kind of labyrinth" where every department was mixed with the next and the service complicated beyond measure. Order itself, "so necessary in establishments of this kind," could not be maintained. How, Coquéau asked, would it be possible to "establish collection points for service, to classify and isolate departments suitably, to arrange rapid and independent communications throughout all parts of the building, in a labyrinth?"[59] Against the labyrinth, the architect proposed a clear and simple order that corresponded in every way with the need for simplicity, rapidity, and regularity of service: "Once this disposition is established by the architect," Coquéau wrote, "what will prevent the establishment of a corresponding order in the interior administration?"[60] Indeed, the principles of architectural order—proportion, symmetry, and regularity—were synonymous with the demands of administrative order.

> The forms of distribution adopted by the architect for the building should with rigor be physically and precisely representative of the order that it is possible to establish in the service.[61]

The circle thus created order; it distributed many functions equally with respect to service and accommodation; it was simple; and, finally, it provided what all devotees of the circle had claimed since the menagerie of Le Vau at Versailles: "the facility to see everything from a single point."[62]

This apparent prefiguration of the Panopticon should not be too quickly identified with Bentham's mechanics, however. What was to be viewed in the Poyet hospital was the chapel, center of religious observance for the sick and dying, not the observation cage of a director. It was the inhabitants of the ward who looked in; the doctors did not benefit in overall surveillance by this plan. There was an additional and perhaps overriding reason for Poyet's choice, one that referred more to the demand for architectural expression than to a disciplinary determinism. "The first advantage," wrote Coquéau, "presented by this imposing form is that of reminding us of one of the finest monuments of Rome, the Colosseum; being decorated in the same way, it does not demand the expenses of decoration that other forms need."[63] That is, the circle was in itself a monumental form and one that easily recalled antique precedent. The Colosseum, a grand public building, was a suitable reference by virtue of its simplified orders, which were abstracted even more in Poyet's version. Raised from the river level on a massive, rusticated base with cavernous, semicircular river-entries, it recalled the Piranesian fantasy of the Cloaca Maxima, or the Castel Sant' Angelo. Similarly, the chapel, raised on a rusticated podium, referred to the rotunda of Bramante or to the Temple of Sibyl.[64]

The Poyet plan seemed to many contemporaries to have solved the architectural question of the hospital once and for all, bringing together, in a single, easily repeatable form, a suitable characterization with an economical disposition of needs. Much later, in the *Annales de Musée,* the architect-historian Jacques-Guillaume Legrand concluded a long and eulogistic description of the project by recommending its application to other building types.

> The beauty of this plan and the commodity of its distribution could be applied with an equal success to a barracks, to a house of detention, to an immense manufacture, finally, to all large establishments where one wishes to bring together a large number of men without confusion and in the smallest space of land possible.[65]

To others, however, whether supportive of a number of single, large-scale hospitals (like the members of the Académie commission set up to evaluate its qualities) or against the centralization of health care (like Pierre Samuel Du Pont de Nemours), the Poyet project stood for the rest of the century as the emblem of institutional folly; its apparent expense, its restricting and inflexible plan, and its pretensions to a grand architectural statement drew strong criticism. It had the effect, as Coquéau noted in another defense of the plan against Du Pont's attacks, of "exciting a general fermentation," over which the government still debated years later.

SCIENTIFIC CALCULATIONS

The response to Poyet's dramatic scheme by the commission established by de Breteuil in 1784 under the aegis of the Académie des sciences was prompt and critical.[66] As de Breteuil had no doubt anticipated, the tangible presence of an architectural solution stimulated scientists to undertake a comprehensive enquiry into the state of the hospitals of Paris. As good experimentalists, the scientists asked for detailed statistics and measurements of the existing establishments, but they found little or no usable information. "We needed all the facts; we asked for them; and we obtained nothing," stated the commissioners.[67] Few of them were experts in the field: Lavoisier might provide information about the behavior and composition of the air; others, such as the astronomer Bailly, the mathematician Laplace, and the physicist Coulomb, might understand the use of statistics; but only Jacques Tenon, chief surgeon at the Salpetrière and sometime intern in the Hôtel-Dieu, combined actual experience of the conditions of "cure" with a long-standing passion for collecting information relevant to their reform. The commission's first report drew largely from Tenon's accumulated knowledge and reflected his opinions; it also propelled him to a new career, one modeled on that of John Howard in England, as an indefatigable enquirer into the state of hospitals and prisons and a polemicist of possible and necessary reforms.[68] From 1785, Tenon guided and to some extent controlled the reform movement, as he subjected administrative, medical, and architectural proposals to scientific scrutiny, visited the hospitals of England, carried out a wide correspondence with doctors and architects, and published his own schemes for new institutions (plate 60).

The commission's survey of existing conditions at the Hôtel-Dieu—assessing its size, management, and facilities with regard to the needs of Paris—preceded its scrutiny of Poyet's plans.[69] Eschewing sentimental and hyperbolic descriptions, the commissioners nevertheless felt repugnance at the sight of so many sick of all kinds in the same beds, the poor ventilation and waste disposal, and the administrative confusion in the old hospital, which mingled the sick, the dying, and the convalescent.[70] Lavoisier contributed precise calculations of the air; Poyet himself provided measurements of the wards; Tenon advised on the conduct of surgical operations and mortality rates; all reinforced the conclusions of the original report of 1773, that the Hôtel-Dieu was inadequate on every count, from site to organization.[71] But this did not move them to accept the centralized solution proposed by Poyet. Unanimously they found its density too high and its distribution faulty; three stories of wards were difficult to service; their layout and ventilation were calculated poorly. Further, the Ile des Cygnes, while healthy enough, was too far removed from the needy population residing in the faubourg Saint Antoine. The most serious criticism, however, was that of size.

> A hospital of 5,000 sick patients is a city, and a city more populous than three-quarters of the towns of France. It is already a great inconvenience to enclose so many inhabitants in a disproportionately small space; but a hospital, however well organized, is always a receptacle of ills and misery.[72]

The "frightening picture" of a single building housing so many sick, multiplying the problems of care and ventilation, suggested to the commissioners that Poyet was simply duplicating at a larger scale the execrable conditions of the Hôtel-Dieu:

> To think that one would thus continuously burden the same volume of air, not only with the emanations of 5,000 individuals, but with the miasmas and infection of ill bodies, from which the most airy and vigilantly cleaned place cannot be entirely rid. Ah! What a complication for he who gives rise to the movements of this huge machine! What a burden for the administration that should preside over it! What inconvenience of service! What abuse in the details! What inevitable neglect in the distribution of alms and remedies![73]

In place of Poyet's *grande machine,* the commission returned to Ledoux and Chalgrin's proposal of 1773, ruling in favor of four smaller hospitals sited on the edges of Paris, each housing up to 1,200 sick.[74] The commission further considered the circular forms of Petit and Poyet no better than the old square courtyard layout that allowed contagion to spread through adjoining, connected wards. Tenon and his colleagues suggested instead the distribution of pavilions advanced by Le Roy. Here each ward might comprise a small, isolated hospital of its own and, separated by green spaces for the convalescent, all wards might be aligned to the best orientation. Similarly, the chapel and ancillary services would find their best position. It was this type, promulgated by Tenon and later drawn by Poyet under Tenon's supervision (plate 61), that became the official hospital of the next century.[75] Durand published it in his *Recueil* (plate 62) and in his *Précis des leçons;* Bruyère elaborated it in standardized permutations; and when, in 1866, the old Hôtel-Dieu was finally rebuilt on the Ile de la Cité, the architect Gilbert adopted a variation of the same camplike distribution.

THE POLITICAL GEOGRAPHY OF HEALTH

The Académie rigorously criticized Poyet's project for its plan and function; but it was the attack of the physiocrats, begun by the abbé Baudeau and continued by Mallet du Pin, Du Pont de Nemours, and Condorcet, that most clearly revealed the political parameters of the debate over hospitals.[76] In the Académie's criticism, the question was one of programmatic concern, of rival geometries of architectural and administrative order; for the physiocrats, it was an urban and social question, touching the roots of Old Regime authority.

Du Pont de Nemours was a disciple of Turgot who, as intendant of the Limousin, had written to Daniel Trudaine, with characteristic antagonism toward unnecessary government regulation, of the uselessness of monuments in the face of the value of men and the cultivation of the soil. In 1786, Du Pont published his *Idées sur les secours à donner aux pauvres malades dans une grande ville* as a rebuttal to Poyet's plan, addressing himself to the Académie commission both as advocate of the poor and as economist of public funds.[77] Thus he supported self-help ("it is not found in nature to ask of others what one can do oneself without much effort"), family care ("society owes every individual, even in infirmity . . . only an addition to the aid that he can gain from his family"), and an extension of voluntary charity ("every natural sentiment can be turned toward good, and self-interest can make perfect mores if it is set on the right road by an intelligent charity").[78] All care, he argued, should originate in the parish, a unit small enough to be personal and economical at the same time. In this way, the major cost of care—the construction of buildings—would be removed together with the ever-present danger of decay, corruption, and abuse in a large state institution. Obviously, there would have to be institutions for the migrant poor and for those without families, but their scale would be as close to the familial as possible. In these domestic asylums a kind of "parental charity" would reign: "one should be able to say 'I am not in a hospital; I am supported by my friend.'" The physiocratic principle, that the state itself holds no property but simply acts to transform natural resources into real wealth for the society, was hereby transferred to the domain of the passions.

> The passions are the forces of the soul, and the wisdom of governments consists in turning the energy of all individual passions toward the public good, rendering them useful to society.[79]

Mallet du Pin, in his 1786 review of Coquéau's *mémoire* for the *Mercure de France,* was even more emphatic in combatting the very idea of a large hospital.

> The frightening assemblage of three or four thousand sick, attacked by a hundred different illnesses, beneath the same roof, would seem . . . to lead to the same excessive mortality.[80]

Illness was but one of Mallet's complaints. The monumentality of Poyet's building was equally an affront to decorum: "Why this *beautiful monument?* Why an imitation of the Colosseum?" The amphitheater of Vespasian seemed to have little in common with a house of charity—one could just as well build a prison according to the model of the Capitol, he observed ironically.

> Let us reserve to each building its appropriate character. Let catafalques, palaces, and theaters occupy the Arts and amuse public curiosity by the magnificence of their forms; only rarely is luxury allied with utility, and nothing would make the heart heavier than the sight of misery hidden behind Corinthian columns.[81]

Mallet countered Poyet's claim that fifty small hospices would cost more than a single big hospital. His model, like that of Du Pont, was drawn from English examples, as described by Howard, of small hospices distributed by quarter, each with no more than 200 patients, where all "idea of magnificence and agglomeration has been banished." Condorcet, a member of the commission of 1784 but not a signatory of its report, argued in a similar fashion for a network of parish hospices, the combined results of the cooperation of the rich inhabitants of the quarter and local architects, mathematicians, doctors, surgeons, physicians, lawyers, merchants, administrators, civil servants, and political scientists.

> Let each *curé* thus assemble the men of his parish from whom he would expect the most knowledge and help; let him ask them to choose among themselves a certain number to be charged with drawing up a plan for the most advantageous hospice for the parish; let this plan then be discussed and examined by the parishioners.[82]

According to Condorcet, this collective community work would not only use resources hitherto ignored by the centralized government, but would also stimulate the charitable instincts of the entire quarter.

Coquéau replied once more to these criticisms, admitting the value of Du Pont's sentiments but repeating his estimate of an almost equal cost for both centralized and decentralized schemes.[83] Decentralization would produce redundancies of service and inefficiencies in care. A single large hospital clearly would announce its purpose: over its door would be engraved, "enter and you will be healed." Thrown into these "vast tombs of the human species, towns," the poor ought to be able to find one place for help and cure. The general administration of such an establishment would act, so to speak, like the paternal eye of the king, "the paternal house for the unfortunate." Thirty separate hospices would be more like thirty strange and alienating lodging houses; within them, the plight of the poor would be hidden from the general view. Finally, in one hospital a single apparatus of surveillance would be required instead of thirty.

The political argument was clear: Coquéau promoted the idea that all public monuments were the direct expression of monarchical beneficence; Du Pont and Condorcet held a republican vision of private morals and charity. In Coquéau's ideal monarchical government, a centralized and presumably impartial gaze would correct the inequalities of private fortune and interest. In a republic, private and moral forces would work freely to support the public administration.

During the revolutionary period, the physiocratic vision of the natural distribution of assistance coincided, as Michel Foucault has noted, with the utopia of a "natural" medicine, returned to its natural origins in the family: prevention, in the form of dietary instruction and universal exercise, would finally render doctors and hospitals obsolete.[84] However chimerical this ideal, its social and environmental field was one of the bases on which an entire discipline of urban pathology would be developed after 1789, beginning with the *Essai sur la topographie-physique et médicale de Paris* by the doctor Audin-Rouvière, and ending with the urban "surgery" of Haussmann.[85] The premise of prevention also affected the designs of many postmedical urban utopias in the modern period, from Ledoux's Ideal City of Chaux, which refused the degradation of the hospice and the need for hospitals in a realm where nature, aided by architecture, would sustain a generalized health, to Le Corbusier's Ville Verte, an open city itself built on the principles of the pavilion hospital.

This search for an urban utopia was perhaps, for architecture, the most significant legacy of the hospital debate, for when the details of a "hospital-architecture" were worked out in a tacit treaty between the professional designers and the doctors, under the Convention and the Empire, it proved to be little more than an obvious embellishment of need. They simply added the reduced and dignified attributes of monumental neoclassicism to a diagram otherwise established by an economics of spatial distribution. The expert in this compromise was Nicolas Clavareau, student of Viel and architect of the new entrance to the Hôtel-Dieu.[86] In a long apologia for the architect's contribution to hospital building, Clavareau tried to assimilate the doctor's special wisdom to the architect's general knowledge, according to ancient Vitruvian doctrine; equally important to him was the "character of grandeur" necessary for expressing the monuments of public utility.

> But independent of the real utility of these establishments, the government wishes to impress them with the character of grandeur that belongs to all its works; it is here that the artist merges himself with the friend of humanity and forces himself to honor his country by the charm of his designs as much as by the importance of his conceptions. O incomparable strength of the arts! They aggrandize and embellish still more everything that is grand and beautiful in itself.[87]

Even as Rome and the republics of Greece had recognized public virtues in monumental buildings, so in modern France "should not the aim of architecture, always grand, become even more touching when it is concerned with the asylums of humanity?" In this way, calling on Laugier's scornful remark, "houses to house the poor should themselves exhibit something of the same poverty," Clavareau justified the stern Doric portico added to the Hôtel-Dieu, itself an echo of Boffrand's entrance to the nearby Enfants-Trouvés, a composition that had provoked the argument over suitable character in the first place.[88] In his design for the School of Clinical Medicine, built within the ruined shell of the church of La Charité in the rue des Saints-Pères, Clavareau developed an iconography for the entrance facade based on Pausanius's description of the Temple of Aesculapius at Epidorus—completing his return to "appropriate" architectural embellishment (plates 63–65).[89] Even in this building, however, it is clear that the only truly architectural gesture was that of the plan, forced now to take account of a formal order described not solely by academic conventions but by the spatial logic of use.

THE DESIGN OF PUNISHMENT

CONCEPTS OF THE PRISON BEFORE THE REVOLUTION

Let us open up the prisons; humanity groans at the sight of their revolting abuses! Let us describe them, if it is possible, if the very pen does not fall from our hands. A citizen, born free, is suddenly besieged by a crowd of parasites, attacked, bound, strangled, dragged off with a disgraceful clamor, with the most pointed insults, to the frightful abode that harbors the criminal.

J.-P. Brissot de Warville, *Théorie des lois criminelles*, 1781.[1]

THE DISCOURSE on imprisonment in eighteenth-century France was ambiguous: on the one hand, philosophes and journalists alike railed against the very idea of loss of liberty in a well-run state, dreaming of an order where prisons would be obsolete and crime extirpated by the removal of its causes; on the other hand, the conditions of imprisonment in the hospitals and *maisons de force* called for hygienic and administrative reform, with the same criteria as those advanced for the Hôtel-Dieu.[2] Thus literary and aristocratic former prisoners from Diderot to Mirabeau universally condemned the state of individual privation, dwelling on the frightening aspect of solitude and incarceration as survivals of medieval tyranny, evocative of all the literary and artistic figures connected with the terrifying sublime, while reformers and writers from Tenon to Brissot concentrated on the redefinition of the prison, its specialization by types of crime and modes of punishment, and its spatialization for the needs of health, administrative order, and surveillance. This division in part reflected the enormous difference between the prisons properly so-called—the fortresses of Vincennes, the Bastille, the Châtelet, La Force, the Fort l'Evêque—and the establishments of the Hospital-general—the Conciergerie, la Salpetrière, Saint-Lazare, Charenton, and Bicêtre. These institutions housed different kinds of "criminals": the former, the political prisoners of the state and those confined by *lettres de cachet* in the prisons, the latter, those awaiting the galleys or deportation to colonies and those whose only crime was to be out of work and poor in the hospitals and workhouses.[3] As Philippe Roger has noted, this heterogeneity meant that one might more easily speak of imprisonments in the eighteenth century than of a unitarily defined prison, either as institution or place.[4]

If the prison had a clear form, it was only in the vision of artists and architects who saw it as a direct illustration of the sublime, a place of terror and power, of the kind evoked by the jails of antiquity and the Dark Ages and signaled most dramatically by Piranesi's Carceri fantasies and by George Dance the Younger's designs for Newgate in London. Certainly, the existing prisons in Paris reinforced this aesthetic image.

THE STATE OF THE PRISONS

The first official assessment of the need for prison reform came from the same body that would launch enquiries into the hospitals five years later, a commission established under the initiative of the finance minister Necker, consisting of Tenon, Tillet, Lavoisier, Duhamel de Monceau, Trudaine de Montigny, and Le Roy.[5] Their *Rapport sur les prisons* was recorded in the registers of the Académie des sciences on March 14, 1780; its first and most immediate objective was to assess a set of plans submitted by Pierre-Louis Moreau-Desproux, architect of the city of Paris, for a new prison to be built on the site of the Convent of the Cordeliers, which would replace the old Grand and Petit Châtelet and Fort l'Evêque.[6] As Tenon described it, Moreau's plan conserved the original cloister and its surrounding buildings but divided them equally to form "on one side a civil prison, on the other a criminal prison." All the services, kitchens, and rooms for the administrators and guards, as well as the *cachots* or cells for solitary confinement, were on the ground floor; the upper floors housed the prisoners and contained courtyards for indoor and outdoor exercise; special prisons for women and debtors were distributed on the rest of the site.[7]

Led by Tenon, the commission had visited the Châtelet prisons and the Conciergerie in February, setting itself this question: If a tribunal of parliament has need of a prison, what should it adopt as a model? The commission enumerated the disadvantages of existing buildings, however renovated by subsequent architects, and noted the horror of the underground *cachots,* "that unhappy idea," wrote Tenon, "of placing men beneath the earth before they are dead." He concluded, "It would be better to build a new prison according to suitable principles, than to make do with buildings that had another purpose."[8] In his own *mémoire* to the Académie, Tenon firmly criticized the administration for asking the advice of professionals "not on the absolutely best construction of a prison, but on sites and buildings already constructed." As with the case of the hospitals, the doctor could not admit that any existing structure would fulfill the proper requirements of ventilation and order.

> A prison placed in the middle of a large town should be considered both in relation to the prisoners of all kinds that it confines and in relation to the numerous population that surrounds it, because if one should take care of the health of the prisoners, one should at the same time prevent epidemic and contagious illnesses born within its walls from expanding outside.[9]

To this extent, no existing prison was adequate. Tenon concluded, "My intention is not at all to favor these existing prisons. Justice demands that they should be destroyed, and I make remarks only with regard to the establishment of new ones." He thus detailed the "horrible spectacle" of these prisons, with their small, ill-ventilated courtyards, their ill-lit rooms, their primitive and unhealthy means of sanitation, disgusting drains, their wet and vermin-filled *cachots*. "Everything must be torn down, everything reconstructed," he pronounced.[10] Accordingly, the commission immediately rejected Moreau-Desproux's scheme for the Cordeliers site. It lacked all of Tenon's principles: "cleanliness, an abundant water supply for washing and drinking, the free circulation of air, and a general administrative regime that all individuals could be made to follow." Sufficient ventilation and water were unobtainable, and the rooms were too small to avoid piling up several prisoners in the same bed. The arguments were the same as those advanced for hospitals. At this stage, the definition of the prison was still bound up with that of the mixed Hospital-general, and, as Tenon noted, it was concerned simply with the hygienic and administrative needs of "a large number of men gathered in a very small space."[11]

Necker, concerned with immediate reforms, nevertheless pressed forward schemes for replacing the Châtelet. In March 1780, he appointed Boullée to take measurements of another possible site for a new prison, that of the old Hôtel de la Force; in August, Boullée's plans for reconstruction were approved by the Académie d'architecture, and at the end of the same month Louis XVI ordered construction to begin; the prison opened two years later.[12] Boullée's scheme, like that of Moreau, was simple enough: it consisted of adding to the existing buildings in order to form internal courtyards that would separate the different sections of the prison—for prisoners in transit, debtors, convicted criminals, women prisoners, and beggars. Unlike Moreau's plan, however, Boullée's provided enough courts for ventilation and divided the quarters into smaller rooms containing one to four beds; these, as well as the general dormitories, were heated, and each department of the prison was supplied with abundant running water. Covered galleries allowed for exercise in bad weather; a common kitchen and dining room, two chapels, and an infirmary, divided between men and women, completed the services. It was, in fact, generally regarded as a model prison, as John Howard reported on his visit in 1783. For Howard, and for many reformers, Boullée's greatest innovation had been the suppression of the *cachots*.[13]

A MODEL PRISON

It was in this climate of reform, following the examples of Howard and Bentham, that the young polemicist, Grub Street journalist, and would-be philosopher Brissot de Warville drew up a plan for an entirely new criminal code. He proposed to classify crimes "exactly," to understand their "natures," and to trace them to their original causes as a practical complement to the analytical "system of laws" of Montesquieu or to the enlightened criticism of Voltaire.[14] It was Brissot's aim to make the state a beneficent "machine" that would "bind force and violence by the ties of peace," directing all harmful passions subtly and inexorably toward the public good. Poverty would be extinguished through the goodwill of government, the amelioration of morals, the reform of public education, and the encouragement of science. In a Rousseauesque fashion, he laid out the means for increasing the happiness and security of the rural population, for protecting it from the parasitic and corrupting influence of the towns, and for establishing institutions, from rustic fêtes to schools of morality and politics, that would at once sustain morals and root them "naturally" to the soil.

> In effect, if you destroy begging, you will see few thieves and almost no assassins. Return morals to their original purity, restore power to public opinion and luster to the realm of letters, ameliorate the education of the people, and the vices that conceal the germ of most crimes will no longer appear so frequently.[15]

His solution to all such ills was a wise and calculated institutionalization that would replace the generalized confinement of the Hospitals-general.

> Multiply the public institutions, build hospitals and asylums, let, finally, the gaze of the administration be fixed on the neglected interest of the poor, and France will no longer be soiled with so many perpetually renewed crimes.[16]

In such an ideal world, the prison would be an institution of last resort; in the present state of France, it was "an unhappy necessity." Nevertheless, it could be operated with humanity and a measure of enlightened self-interest. If the sources of crime were social, then the social conditions of the *maison de force* created as much crime, if not more, than they cured. Taking his cue from John Howard, whose *State of the Prisons* had been published four years before, Brissot drew a lugubrious picture of life in the prison.

> I see this unhappy man [the newly arrested prisoner] in the infernal dwelling prepared for him: archers, jailers, executioners, vile beings who, even in defending society, are regarded with a kind of horror. . . . They lead him finally into an obscure labyrinth of corridors to his sad dwelling where triple irons and gloomy bolts remove his liberty. . . . He enters the iron heart of sadness in this sink of infection, where a thousand miserable beings share among themselves the slow poison of death, where the most dangerous miasmas are exhaled. . . . The assassin, the thief, the libertine, all become friends . . . desiring to exercise on the newcomer a kind of despotism even amidst their chains. . . . He must pay homage to this association of new hosts.[17]

Such *maisons de force,* he argued, needed to be transformed into *maisons de correction.* Necker's initiative, which Brissot had noted, and Bentham's observations on Howard and Eden's proposed Hard Labour Bill, which had been published five years before, allowed for a certain optimism.[18] Bentham's remarks in particular served as a guide for Brissot in drawing specific administrative and architectural plans for a model prison.

In this early work, recognizing the value of both Burke's aesthetics of the sublime and Howard's reformist functionalism, Bentham had articulated the twin role of the house of correction as that of instilling terror in the prisoners while ensuring a secure and healthy imprisonment. "The business is, then," he wrote, "to make the necessary provisions for the purposes of safe custody and terror without excluding the fresh air."[19] Safety, he concluded, might be obtained through the siting, plan, and administrative regimen of the institution; a judicious mixture of rewards and punishments would ensure the continuous and productive labor of the prisoners, while isolation from surrounding structures would hinder escapes. Each prisoner would be held in isolation in a cell no smaller than twelve by eight feet, furnished with a bedstead and heated from a central furnace by means of ducts, with proper provision for drainage and ventilation. The prisoners would exercise in fresh air—on the roof rather than in enclosed yards—or, in bad weather, beneath the building itself in ground-level arcades. Twenty years later, Bentham was to incorporate these suggestions into his panoptical schemes.

In concert with these hygienic and security measures, Bentham envisaged a repertoire of environmental techniques that would act on the mind of the criminal. Echoing Burke's prescriptions for an architecture of the sublime, Bentham proposed that an atmosphere of gloom envelop the prisoner's life; the absence of daylight would encourage fear and lead to reflection.

> In the imaginations of the bulk of men, the circumstances of descent towards the center of the earth are strongly connected with the idea of the scene of punishment in future life.[20]

Such gloom might be enhanced by silence, the cells for hardened criminals being constructed at a distance from the main block, as well as by an air of strangeness encouraged by the unfamiliarity of the architecture. Here he converted the precepts of sensationalism into instruments for the production of a state of mind. Aesthetics was in fact an instrument of utility; the issue of expense was secondary to that of mental pressure: no "inconvenient expense" should be spared "in screwing the sentiment of terror up to the highest pitch."

The functional and decorative architectural details of the prison should be calculated to this principle. The open gratings recommended by Howard in place of glass windows for the cells, while not conducive to the health or comfort of the prisoners, would certainly, Bentham agreed, contribute to giving "a gloomy or distressful appearance to the outside of the prison." He suggested placing such gratings on the cells of the worst criminals and toward the public side of the institution, another sign to the passerby of the rewards of crime. In addition, he proposed an apparatus of mottoes and emblems reminiscent of the iconologies of an earlier period. Suitable inscriptions would be placed over the entrance to good effect: "they would contribute to inculcate the justice, to augment the terror, and to spread the notoriety of this plan of punishment." Mottoes, such as "Had they been industrious when free, they need not have drudged here like slaves" and "Violence and knavery are the roads to slavery," might be supplemented by devices or emblems.

> Over the door there might otherwise be a bas-relief or a painting, exhibiting a wolf and a fox yoked together to a heavy cart and a driver whipping them.[21]

In the background of the picture would be a troop of wolves ravaging a flock of sheep or a fox watching a hen house. Such bas-reliefs, manufactured in artificial stone, could be cast in great numbers and distributed to all labor houses; emblems of monkeys surmounting inscriptions, such as "Mischief, rapine, knavery are the roads to slavery," would be fitting alternatives if there were not the danger that monkeys would incite "merriment by their drollery [rather] than displeasure by their mischievousness."[22] Bentham was critical of the various devices proposed by Howard for the walls of European houses of correction: with too strong an appeal to antiquity, there would be the risk of idealizing the role of the hard-labor house. He concluded this inventive catalogue of the emblematics of incarceration with a plea for its serious purpose.

> Let me be not accused of trifling: those who know mankind know to what degree the imagination of the multitude is liable to be influenced by circumstances as trivial as these.[23]

Brissot found many of these recommendations excellent and some of them "ridiculous," but he especially liked Bentham's proposal for the playing of music on Sundays (a way, thought Brissot, "of purifying a gangrenous soul"). He proceeded to draw up a rationalized version of the Englishman's scheme, a "sketch of the plan for a general prison." This was to be a type, a plan suitable for every large town, which might be duplicated as many as three times in each place, according to need. Following the choice of a site, well drained and ventilated and of a proper size, the prison was to be laid out with geometric precision: "the building will be four stories, divided into four parts. Each part will have its own, separate courtyard."[24] This division corresponded to that of the prisoners: women and children; debtors; libertines; murderers and those condemned to the galleys or the mines. In each of these four quarters, prisoners would have separate cells with high ceilings and barred windows and doors; four infirmaries, operated like small hospitals, would reinforce the separation of offenders; finally, four workshops (heated in winter, cooled in summer) would provide work for each prisoner. The work itself would be calculated precisely to the nature of the crime and the criminal.

> The works will be proportioned to the strength or the delicacy [of the prisoner], to the nature of the crimes, etc. Thus the vagabonds, the libertines, and the criminals will be occupied in cutting stones, polishing marble, grinding colors, and performing other chemical operations in which the life of honest citizens is ordinarily in danger.[25]

In this way, as Michel Foucault has pointed out, the punishment would not only fit the crime, it would in some way be destined to work on the morals of the recipient, polishing and honing an otherwise rough, irregular soul.[26] It would also increase, Brissot anticipated, the productive forces of the nation, "harmlessly" diverting noxious and dangerous tasks to the criminal class. The administrative regime would be equally as strict; every minute would be accounted for, regulated by a timetable similar to that of the *manufacture réunie*. At the center of the establishment, a chapel, indispensable arm of secular administration, would provide Mass each day and music on Sundays. Nor did Brissot ignore Bentham's admonition to provide a source of terror.

> Over the door of the prison, a terrible epigraph, crossed chains, walls painted in black, sentinels, surveillants.[27]

The terror would not be confined to the prisoners, for twice a year the doors of the prisons would be opened and the citizens given "the spectacle of the atonement for crime." The workshop of crime had been transformed into its own theater.

DISCIPLINARY RHETORIC

In his repertoire of building types and their appropriate characters, Blondel had listed the prison under *architecture terrible,* a strong style marked by deep recesses and strong projections, high, thick walls throwing long shadows, a style almost theatrical in its effects. Such an architecture of terror, when used in *maisons de force,* prisons, and *cachots,* would, he stated,

> in some way announce on the outside the disorder of the life of the men detained inside and, as a whole, the necessary ferocity toward those condemned to irons.[28]

Blondel distinguished varieties of this *genre terrible* for different kinds of prison: for debtors' prisons, a rustic decoration combined with the simplicity of regular forms; for prisons confining persons of ill-repute and libertines, a *corps caverneux,* an "irregular architecture" representing the unruly and disreputable state of those imprisoned; for criminal prisons, a barbarous style, decked with the attributes of justified torments, representations of human humiliation and punishment.

Such "images of chastisement" abounded in prison designs of the 1760s and 1770s. In 1768, Jean-Charles Delafosse explored the limits of the available iconography in a project where all the imaginable "hieroglyphic attributes" for imprisonment taken from baroque stage sets and Piranesian fantasies were displayed on a single facade[29] (plate 66). François Cuvilliés, Daubanton, and, later, Houssin presented variations on the theme, from classic severity to Gothic horror.[30] These, and their many imitations in project and theatrical decor, notably by Pierre-Adrien Pâris, Blondel would no doubt have censured as taking the *genre terrible* to a ridiculous extreme, an abuse. An expression closer to that imagined by Blondel was that designed in 1764 by one of his students, Jacques Gondouin, for the prison facing the entrance to the Ecoles de Chirurgie, with its blind facade of horizontal rustication relieved only by a niche for a public water fountain (plate 67).[31]

Among the projects advanced by architects in the 1780s, the only one to go beyond the traditional solution of a barracklike plan decked with the commonplace attributes of heavy rustication, chains, ankle-irons, and figures of justice was that of Ledoux, designed between 1782 and 1785 for Aix-en-Provence in tandem with a new Palais de Justice (plates 68–69).[32] In this scheme, only the foundations of which were built before the Revolution suspended work, Ledoux forged an architectural language expressive of a program that in every respect corresponded to Brissot's recommendations. His prison, like Brissot's, was four stories high, square in plan, and divided into four parts by galleries crossing at the center; each part was reserved for one of the categories of prisoner suggested by Brissot. At the intersection of the galleries, in the space formed by the crossing of their barrel-vaults, stood a chapel. Without compromising these reformist distributions, Ledoux designed the institution with an idea of its proper characterization. The walls were stripped of all rustication and emblems, allowing the geometric combinations of form to read severely, themselves emblematic of Burkean "privation." The heavy, tomblike roofs of the corner towers, the primitive curved "pediment" over the entrances seemingly cut out of a single block of stone, the narrowly spaced, baseless Doric columns of the porches, the small slits of windows, all contributed to the effect. Only a single motto carved over the door confirmed the purpose of the building: *Securitas publicae*. So powerful was the impact of doom in this monument, even in its engraved representations, that over eighty years later Charles Blanc illustrated it in his *Grammaire des arts du dessin* as an example of an architecture characterized by a dominance of surfaces over voids.[33]

Ledoux's attempt to weld characteristic genre to model plan contrasted with a project designed by Boullée during the same years for a Palais de Justice and its associated prisons.[34] Boullée, who had in fact supported Ledoux's design in the Académie when it was challenged by the archbishop of Aix, joined palace and prison in an associative allegory, favoring the "poetry of architecture" over any reform of distribution. Where Ledoux had separated the two functions, Boullée preferred to use the contrast of justice and crime to endow his design with symbolic content.

> I thought that in order to introduce the poetry of architecture into this project, it was good to place the entrance to the prisons beneath the palace. It seemed to me that in presenting this august palace raised on the shadowy lair of crime, I would not only be able to ennoble the architecture by means of the oppositions that resulted, but further present in a metaphorical way the imposing picture of vice crushed beneath the feet of justice.[35]

While he seemed to echo the sentiments of Ledoux, who also spoke of "the enlightened temple of justice" forming a "salutary opposition to the dark places given over to crime," Boullée subordinated plan to character, noting only of the prisons that, "as their distribution offers nothing of great interest," he did not bother to detail them. In this work, as in most of his idealizing designs after the mid-1780s, Boullée thus effaced emerging programmatic concerns in favor of the pictorial and theatrical expressions of sublimity.

During the Revolution, this kind of dematerialized architecture was conserved, appropriately enough, in the ephemeral stage sets of festivals and didactic tableaux for the Champ de Mars and, especially, in the series of drawings prepared by A. L. T. Brongniart for the fêtes of Thermidor in 1796. These depicted in sequence a dance on the ruins of the Bastille (symbolizing July 14, 1789); a dance and mock insurrection in front of a palace and its destruction (memorializing the establishment of the Convention on August 10, 1792); the overthrowing of an allegorical prison (to signify the 9 and 10 Thermidor and the end of the Terror); and, finally, a triumph of liberty on the promulgation of the constitution in Year III.[36] The third scene was described in these terms:

> Almost all the houses of a large street are transformed into a prison. On a temple of the Fates, three Furies are seated on a throne of iron. The Furies' assistants emerge from the Temple, dancing like cannibals to suitable music.[37]

In the drawings, the People are then shown being dragged inside the prisons by cannibals while Justice veils her face; but soon the populace cries out, the sky replies with a burst of thunder, the veil is lifted from Justice, and the Furies and their prisons are destroyed. Brongniart's design showed a huge rock temple and, beneath it, the entrances to the prisons in a low, rusticated, "buried architecture" in the manner of Ledoux, Desprez, and Pâris.

The grand, symbolic gesture of the storming and razing of the Bastille, which had the effect of releasing no more than eight prisoners and dispersing the personal effects of the Marquis de Sade (who would himself have been liberated had he not been transferred to Charenton ten days earlier), did not, save in myth, initiate reform of the prison system. The National Assembly, through its Comité de mendicité and under the Convention, launched successive enquiries; but the grim reality, marked by the terrible massacres of September 1792, was that criminal and political prisons were the inevitable by-products of revolutionary liberty, and their numbers were swollen by dozens of makeshift houses of detention in convents and *hôtels* as the Terror advanced. Certainly, the Constituent Assembly of 1791 established the framework, later consolidated by Napoleon, of a comprehensive judicial code, including a rational categorization of prisons from *maisons d'arrêt* (within which "good order and tranquility" was administered without punishment to protect the rights of the yet untried) to *prisons pénales* for condemned criminals. But, as the lawyer and doctor François Doublet pointed out in the first systematic report after 1789, little was actually done to administer such laudable aims.[38] Neither the translation of Howard's studies nor Bentham's summary of the panopticon principle for the Assembly met with an active response. What reports were prepared, including those of Doublet and even of the Marquis de Sade, echoed the wisdom of Tenon and his commissioners. Only the indefatigable and much disliked Pierre Giraud, following Desmaisons as architect of prisons in Paris, claimed to have improved the existing establishments, but this seemed to be no more than retrospective boasting.[39]

In this climate of simple pragmatism, the aesthetics of the sublime were reserved for the victims of imprisonment under the Terror; Hubert Robert painted the hopeless and barren corridors of Saint Lazare, and Ledoux, in La Force, "dreamed and spoke only of columns," according to a witness. When Durand, in 1801, outlined the principles of prison design for his students at the Ecole Polytechnique, it was with scorn for those "who sought to render such a place horrible by the ridiculous spectacle of columns, chained, piled up, or in some way incarcerated in the walls."[40] Reviewing Durand's own project for a prison, designed with Thibault in the mid-1790s, Detournelle commented:

> The disposition of the plan is new and very suitable; the elevations have a good character; there are small buttresses that rise up the entire height of the buildings, so that the whole composition, with art distributed over its smooth walls and in its openings, gives an example of the severe and straightforward style and not a ridiculous assemblage of fortifications. What could be more grotesque than the cornice of Sainte-Pélagie; pediments, stones cut in diamond forms, chains, are the

> images of sadness and ferociousness; they insult the innocent and even the guilty not yet condemned by law.[41]

Durand's prison was a perfect example of his repertoire of simple, gridded, institutional schemes (plate 70): a central service court divided the women's quarters from the men's, each composed of single rows of cells, while at each corner, a square, higher block housed the refectory and infirmary, the workshops, and the guard-house. And if Detournelle had been too premature in proclaiming the death of rhetoric, in the face of what, in any other kind of rendering but Durand's simple line drawing, would have looked equally as forbidding as a project by Boullée or Ledoux, Durand's restrained rhetoric became a model for the nineteenth century. Looking back on the 1780s from the vantage point of the Restoration, Louis-Pierre Baltard, sometime assistant to Ledoux for the *barrières* of Paris, wrote:

> Architects, carried away by these examples [of medieval prisons], thought that it was proper to give to prisons an aspect and character of terror, and they devoted themselves to composing the facades of prisons according to the same principles as those applicable to theatrical decoration, suitable to inspire terror and to serve as a backdrop to a scene from a melodrama.[42]

Correctly enough, Baltard had identified the connection between the inevitable exaggeration of a true *architecture parlante* and the origins of melodrama, itself rooted, as Peter Brooks has observed, in the expressive aesthetics of Diderot.[43] It is significant that the only "built" examples of this genre of prison architecture were the painted scenes of the theaters themselves; after the Revolution, any sublimity in the prison, whether panoptical or not, had to be found solely in the implacable silence of a mechanism wherein, as Baltard put it, "the buildings functioned like a machine submitted to the action of a single motor."[44]

THE ARCHITECTURE OF THE LODGES

RITUALS AND SYMBOLS OF FREEMASONRY[1]

The coterie of the Anti-Formalists was made up of twenty persons, absolute enemies of ceremonies and forms. The place where they met was of a peculiar shape. It was almost completely in the form of a ball and, as it did not take up a great deal of space and its foundations were not fixed and firm, it could be transported almost as easily as a tent; also it often changed its position, lending a grand variety and distraction to their meetings.

L. Bordelon, *The Coterie of the Anti-Formalists*, 1716.[2]

THE FLOURISHING ASSOCIATIONAL life of the clubs, circles, and Masonic societies of prerevolutionary France was confirmed by the architecture of its meeting rooms. The apartments, salons, and lodges that served as the active centers of bourgeois sociability in the closing years of the Old Regime were all planned, or at least decorated, to characterize and ratify the intimate life of the group, to affirm its nature as an institution.[3] Even as the earlier forms of brotherhood—the professional and trade confraternities—had identified themselves with particular chapels for their worship and meeting, and as the tavern societies and wine circles of the first quarter of the century had established themselves in cabarets and inns, often renting entire premises, so, too, their lay successors found the need to incorporate themselves, so to speak, by means of their *salles de réunion*.[4] Fashionable pleasure societies in the capital, like the quasi-Masonic Fendeurs ("Hewers"), took over forest estates and fabricated elaborate settings for their bacchic festivities; more serious philosophical and fraternal associations developed precise rules for the layout of their rooms and the décor of their rituals.[5]

The names adopted by these societies marked the extent to which space was seen as a mode of constitution; often the group would be named after its place of assembly. Thus the young artisans of Provence, meeting in emulation of bourgeois circles, called themselves "chambers."[6] The Freemasons, who met in lodges, named their social organizations and assemblies "lodges."[7] Without such proper homes, a society felt hardly formed. The astronomer-royal, Jérome de Lalande, opening the first permanent home of his Freemasonic order, the Grand Orient of France, told of their search for "a house that could provide for our needs."

> In effect dispersed until now and wandering in all directions, we had a place neither for our secretariat, nor for our archives, nor for our assembly; without a fixed asylum, we were forced to carry our workshops to the houses of our brothers. Without a Temple, we had neither security nor decency.[8]

In a climate of severe political and religious censorship, where any secret group was read as a potential threat to state order or a conspiracy against morals and dogma, the word "asylum" was particularly apt.[9] The "asylum of peace," the "asylum of virtue," the "asylum of letters," the "asylum of philosophy," and the "asylum of friendship" were terms by which these new institutions characterized their meeting places. Even by the 1780s, when the Masonic order had become generally accepted by the authorities, the lodges still felt the need for anonymity and privacy. The Lodge of Friendship at Arras was "a house like any other house" on the street; nothing designated its particular character.[10] Much earlier, in the late 1730s, when lodges were subject to police action, the need for security, for "an inviolable place of refuge," was even more acute. The isolation provided by a secure home would further strengthen the social and ideological ties of essentially fragile and heterogeneous associations: "the more we are isolated and separated from the great number," wrote de Lalande, "the more we hold to that which surrounds us."[11]

Such isolation allowed the social relations of those otherwise divided by class, economic, or religious barriers, and permitted the free discussion of topics forbidden in public: free will, comparative religion, ideal commonwealths with egalitarian constitutions, changing moralities, and the scientific exploration of potentially heretical subjects. For certain groups, it undoubtedly furthered sectarian, politically subversive, or even pornographic ends. The principal result of this self-enforced bond was the identification of mutual interests, the resolution and propagation of common beliefs, and the mediation of conflicts within and between classes. In this way, new, mobile capitalists formed alliances with the governing aristocracy, philosophes touched the fonts of power, and professionals encountered patronage.

The means by which this social isolation was organized differed widely with the nature of the society: the qualifications for membership might be intellectual, professional, ideological, or financial. The divisions might be drawn along class boundaries, common interests, or recreational pursuits. An academic society would sponsor prize competitions, accept the recommendations of its membership, and hold elections, while an eating or gaming club would respond more strongly to the advice and consent of its already accepted members. Almost every society, however, formalized the process of entry into the inner brotherhood with an induction ceremony, a rite of passage. Initiation, remarked Dupuis, a historian of comparative religion, was "one of the ways philosophy has endeavored to civilize societies and perfect mankind."[12] Many of the societies developed rigid hierarchies for their governance and controlled admission into these upper echelons; it was important that the inner life of the society represent a larger world, yet differentiate itself from its contemporary milieu.

While formal induction, together with the ceremonial activities that made up the daily life of the societies, constituted the primary social bond of the society, by far the most influential agent of their isolation and institutional existence was the architecture of their domain. At once the expressive and characteristic statement of their nature and the physical outline of their social life, the design of the space that enclosed, protected, and enhanced these *asiles du bonheur* was as much a part of their definition as were the rules of admission and conduct. The "space of brotherhood" would protect and inform; the influence of proper surroundings was held to be no less important for the development of sociability than the carefully constructed organizational codes that they ostensibly mirrored.

THE FORMATION OF THE LODGE

> There was not a town that did not have confraternities of artisans, of bourgeois, of women; the most extravagant ceremonies were set up around sacred mysteries, and it is from these that, escaped from time, the society of Freemasons comes, the society that has destroyed all the others.
>
> Voltaire, *Essai sur les Moeurs*.[13]

It is not entirely clear by what stages the original Masonic craft guilds ("operative Masons") were gradually superseded toward the end of the seventeenth century by the societies of bourgeois and aristocratic association. Certainly in mid-seventeenth-century England, operative Masons began to receive nonpracticing members ("speculative Masons") into their ranks, and a number of these societies, from London tavern societies to the gentlemen's discussion clubs of the provinces, began to constitute themselves as wholly "speculative" circles. Among the group of philosophers and scientists involved in the establishment of the Royal Society were some of the earliest recorded nonoperative Masons, including Elias Ashmole and Robert Morey. By the turn of the century the operative form was more or less extinct; in 1717, the Grand Lodge of London was established to regulate the constitutions of the various societies already in existence. The book of *Constitutions,* collated by James Anderson, was published in 1723 and marked this stage of unification by bringing together the heterogeneous rules, mythologies, and histories of Masonry, some dating from the middle of the fourteenth century, that had served the different lodges.[14]

Imported into France after 1725 as a wholly fashionable society, Freemasonry was at its inception in Paris (where the first known lodge of 1726 was located) connected to a group of aristocratic, Jacobite émigrés led by Charles Radclyffe, the future Lord Derwentwater. The order rapidly became popular with aristocrats, bourgeois, and intellectuals (Montesquieu was recorded as having been initiated in London in 1730) and attracted the attention of the Paris police from 1737. The Church of Rome issued its first Bull of Condemnation in 1738. The period between 1737 and 1755 was one of considerable growth under the loose regulation of the early Grand Masters, the Duc d'Antin and the Comte de Clermont. Police harassment continued until 1745; a second papal bull was issued in 1751. Nevertheless, the order flourished, first under the Grand Lodge (from 1743), then under the Grand Orient (from 1773); by 1778, there were at least eighty-two lodges active in Paris alone. Between its foundation and the Revolution, the Grand Orient counted some 8,500 members in the capital, and beyond these there were the schismatics of the Grand Lodge, a large number of military lodges for officers, women's lodges, called lodges of "adoption," together with hundreds of breakaway and autonomous sects.[15]

The development of a type form for the lodge building emerged slowly. The earliest groups of French Masons, suspected and ultimately banned by Rome and harassed continually by the local police, were unable to establish any really permanent home. The first known, regularly constituted lodges met in private houses or in the many eating rooms of the Left Bank quarter of Saint-Germain. Between 1726 and 1735, as the order gradually attracted a more substantial middle-class patronage, the cabarets and taverns of the rue des Boucherons, a noted gaming precinct, and two gambling houses on the right bank (the Hôtel de Soissons and the Hôtel de Gesvres) were known to be the haunts of the *fri-maçons*. In an effort to escape the surveillance of the police, they repaired to the inns and *guinguettes* of the *banlieue* after midnight. Police reports dating from 1737 mention "five bands that meet in cabarets in different quarters of Paris." The Hôtel de Chaulmes, the center of the renowned literary circle of the Duc de Chaulmes—"le Parnasse de Chaulmes"—attracted to its soirées many well-known Masons of the Lodge Louis d'Argent, while the Hôtel d'Aumont, owned by the director of royal entertainments or *les menus plaisirs*, was the scene of many quasi-Masonic banquets.[16]

Between 1740 and 1750, police and church spies frequently reported having surprised groups of Freemasons assembled for receptions, deliberations, and, most often, dinners; indeed, the royal procurator, Leclerc de Douay, writing from Orléans, hazarded that the "pleasure of the table makes up the principal object of the association."[17] These reports provide a detailed picture of the meeting rooms and their ceremonial equipment at mid-century. In 1744, in the house of M. Ozouf, for example, thirty men and six women were arrested while "seated at long tables, singing, drinking, and eating dessert," as the commissioner of the Châtelet district wrote.

> We observed that the said room, which was long and narrow, was hung with curtains, so that one could only see clearly by lamps, and that the entry to this room was also curtained off. We observed also that the entry to a small garden, whose trellis formed a square, was hung round from the top of the trellis to eye-level to prevent anyone seeing what was done in the said square of garden.[18]

The police raided a more elaborate lodge the next year in the rue des Martyrs; on the first floor, beyond a courtyard, they found the Masons holding an initiation ceremony in three consecutive rooms, all with blocked windows. In comparison, the apartments of the Hôtel de Soissons were lavish: on the second floor, beyond the grand staircase, the Masons had established themselves in six rooms. The police found fifteen or so individuals waiting in the first apartments and twenty-five more in the sixth. These latter were dressed alike and guarded by a brother holding a drawn sabre.

The precarious social position of the Masons, save perhaps in the most highly protected personal lodges—those of Chevalier Beauchaine in La Nouvelle-France or of the Duc de Clermont, for example—did not lend itself to a permanent architecture. The lodge was composed of its members, its rituals, and, above all, its ritualistic equipment—the costumes, emblematic tools, furniture, and tapestried décor.

THE ROUTE OF INITIATION

The police described the Masons of the rue des Martyrs as arranged in two rows around a "form of carpet marked on square tiles with white stone." This "carpet" represented, among other symbols, the sun, the moon, compasses, squares, levels, stars, and columns. In the Hôtel de Soissons, the Masons were reported grouped around an actual carpet of linen spread out on the floor, which, "at the end a portico of two columns with a sun and a crescent above, a star in the middle, represented two different levels of Masonry, and other things."[19]

Easily erased after a meeting, or rolled up and carried, these chalk "floor-drawings" and "floor-cloths" were the temporary, but typical, form by which the early Freemasons defined the space of their ritual and marked the emblems of their "craft." The earliest-known representation of these figures is British, from the so-called Carmick Manuscript of 1727; triangular in form, it represents the warden or master seated at the east point, with two steps at the west and the brethren in seats along the sides; it contains the compasses, rule, gavel, trowel, and two candle-holders found in later renderings. Above the drawing is written, "This figure represents the lodge."[20] Accounts of the English rituals from 1733 mention "foot cloths" and "drawing boards,"[21] but the first systematic depictions appeared in France in 1744 and 1745, among the groups of "exposures" of Masonic secrets that were published between 1737 and 1751; according to the journalist Louis Travenol, these designs were "properly called the lodge."[22]

The drawings were allegories of the first Temple of Solomon and its attributes and, evidently, were laid out to describe a route from the point of entry into the lodge to the point of reception—the route of initiation. The drawings were differentiated according to the ordered stages of the initiation process and the three grades of initiation of apprentice, companion, and master. From contemporary accounts, it is clear that the stages depicted in these drawings played an active part in the reception rites (plate 71). A sponsoring brother prepared the aspirant by stripping him down to his shirt, bandaging his eyes, and leaving him alone for a long time in an antechamber, sometimes called the chamber of reflections. Then the inductee was ritually cleansed and led to the door of the lodge itself, where the sword-bearing brothers staged a mock battle for entry; once inside, the "journey" commenced. Still blindfolded, the aspirant had to walk three times around the floor-drawing, a "kind of representation in crayon of the Temple of Solomon," the brethren all the while making a great noise, throwing gunpowder on the candles, and clashing their swords. Some candidates confessed to fright and exhaustion as they encountered obstacles at each step. "Those who have undergone the ceremony," confided the abbé Pérau, "declare that there is nothing more tiresome than this blindfold perambulation. One is as much fatigued as after a long journey." Finally, the blindfold was suddenly removed, the lights turned up, and the candidate delivered to questioning by the master.

> The lights, the brilliance of the swords, the singular ornaments that adorned the Grand Officers, the sight of all the brothers in white robes, form a spectacle bewildering enough for one who has been deprived of light for some two hours.[23]

The candidate, thus thrown into "bewilderment and perplexity," was ready to receive the knowledge of his attained grade.

In these rituals, which were elaborated rapidly as grade was added to grade, the floor-drawings—the primitive type, as it were, of the lodge—performed all the roles of architecture itself: signifying the stages of entry into the society by entry into the temple, they were icons of three-dimensional spaces; they were the textbooks of the emblems of the grades; they differentiated the sacred space of the brotherhood from the profane space of the temporary apartment. Some of the most detailed representations of floor-cloths for higher grades, those of the abbé Larudan, were even drawn as perspective projections of actual architectural spaces (plates 72–74).[24]

THE CIRCLE OF BROTHERHOOD

"The ceremony ended and the explanation given, the Candidate is called Brother, and they seat themselves at Table, where they drink to the health of the new Brother."[25] Invariably, the ceremonies of initiation—and most of the police reports support this—ended in a banquet, the center of the sociable life of the Masons. From early in its life, the order had been seen as a kind of eating society: author of the tract "The Order of the Freemasons Betrayed," the abbé Pérau spoke of the various associations, the *sociétés bacchiques,* of the first years of the century, from which he assumed the Freemasons derived.[26] Rumors of the licentious feasts of this secret society were rife by mid-century: Couret de Villeneuve defended the celebrations of his brothers, admitting that "we do, it is true, have a taste for fine and delicate voluptuousness, but it is not uniquely sensual; the Table is a pleasure of tolerance—in itself it is no crime."[27] Pérau similarly dismissed these slurs on Masonic reputation, citing the rule against political or religious discussion in the lodge as well as the punctilious nature of the toasts and dining ceremonies: "There is no military academy where the drill is performed with greater exactitude, precision, pomp, and majesty."[28] The abbé Laugier, whose relationship to Masonic circles remains unclear, wrote a poem defending the order against the strictures of the papacy.

> In sobriety our banquets are prepared;
> By an intimate union the bonds are drawn closer.[29]

For the Freemasons, this "intimate union," forged by initiation and cemented by continual festivity, defined their life of sociability. Gathered around a semicircular or horseshoe-shaped table, sharing a common repast, the brothers experienced the pleasures of friendship and mutual support.[30] "Let us join

37 Pierre Touffaire, Royal Foundry at Le Creusot, 1785.

38 Barthélémy Jeanson, Queen's Glass Works at Le Creusot, perspective view, 1785.

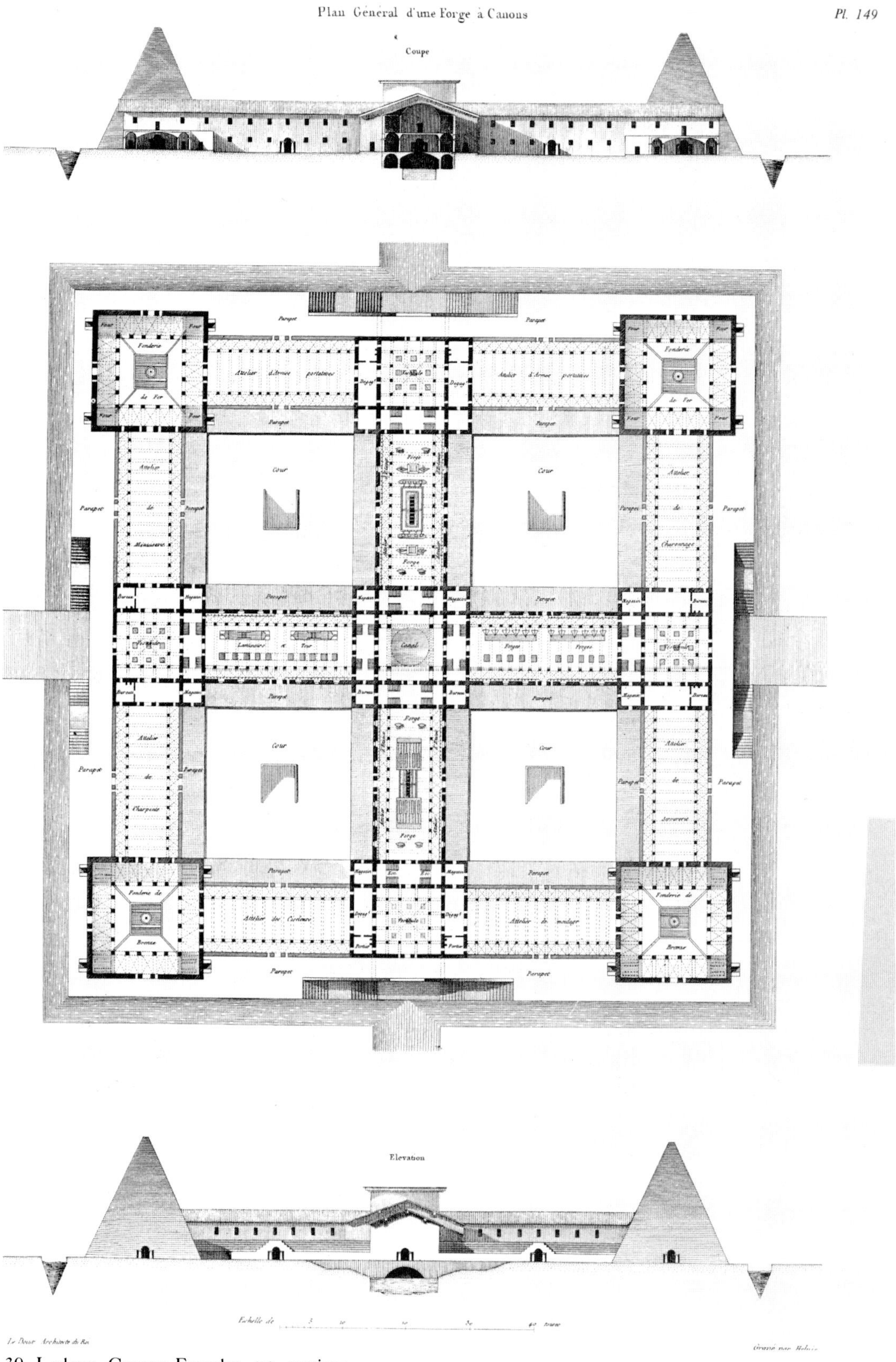

Plan Général d'une Forge à Canons
Pl. 149
Coupe
Elevation

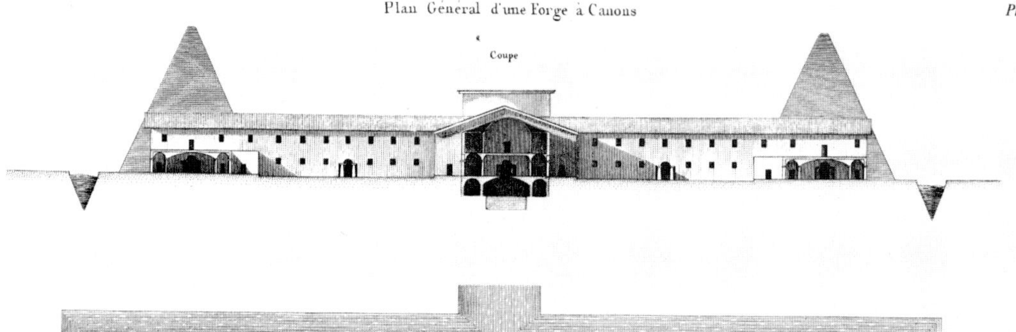

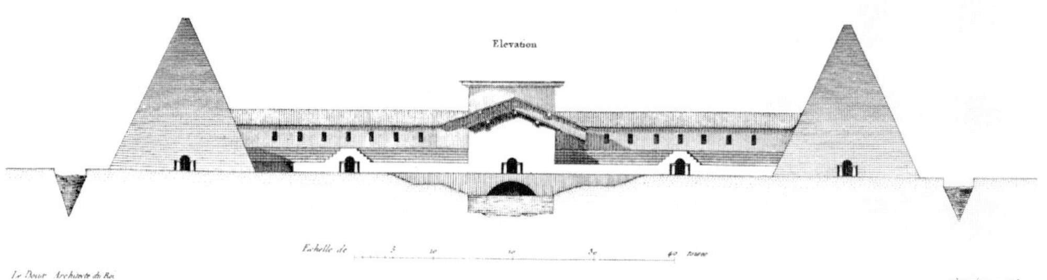

39 Ledoux, Cannon Foundry, *top*, section; *center*, plan; and *bottom*, elevation.

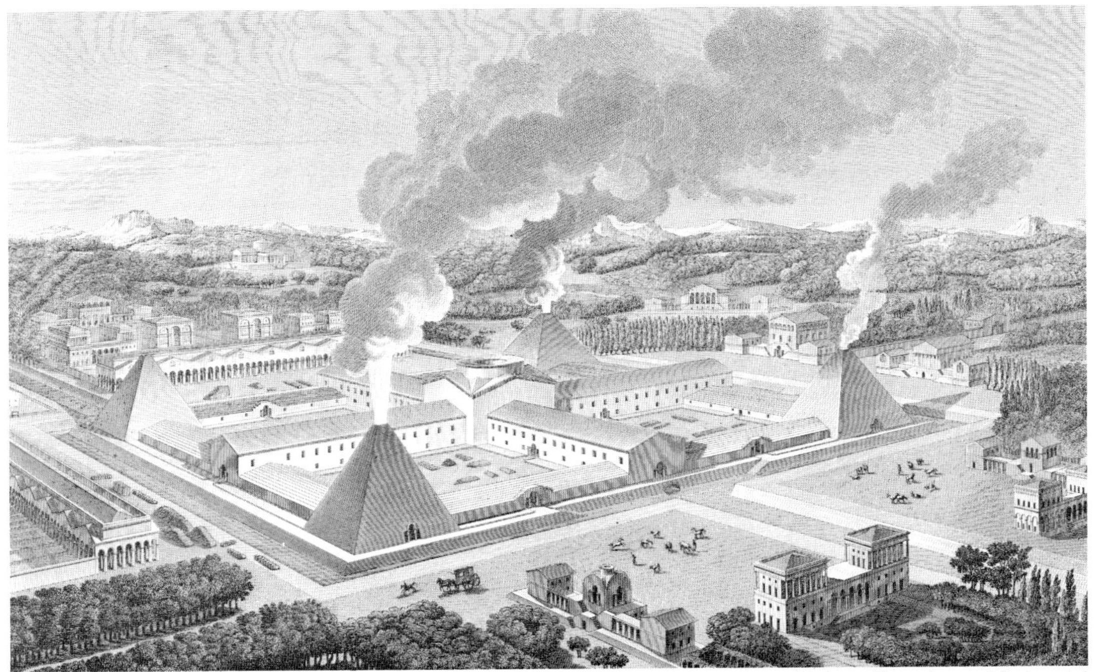

40 Ledoux, Cannon Foundry and Industrial City, perspective view.

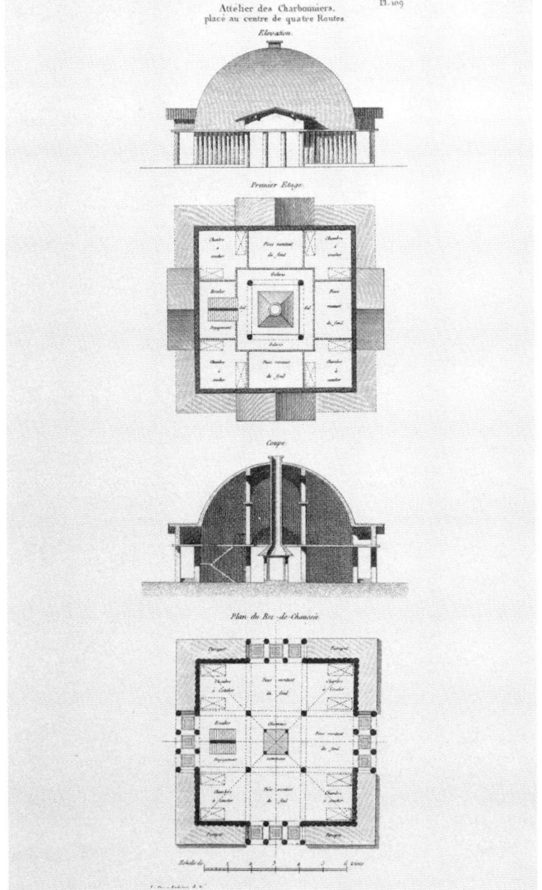

41 Ledoux, charcoal-burners' workshop "placed at the center of four routes," *top to bottom:* elevation, plan of second floor, section, and plan of first floor.

43 Ledoux, woodcutters' house, perspective view.

44 Ledoux, woodcutters' house, perspective view.

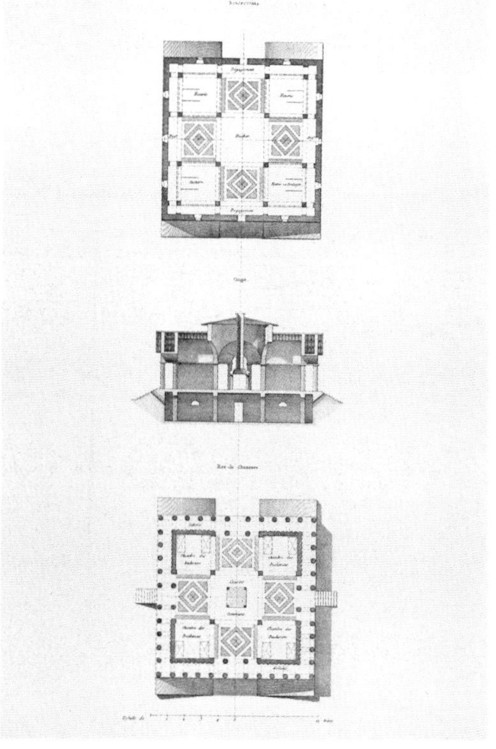

42 Ledoux, woodcutters' house, *top to bottom:* plan of basement, section, and plan of first floor.

45 Charcoal-burners at work. From the *Encyclopédie*.

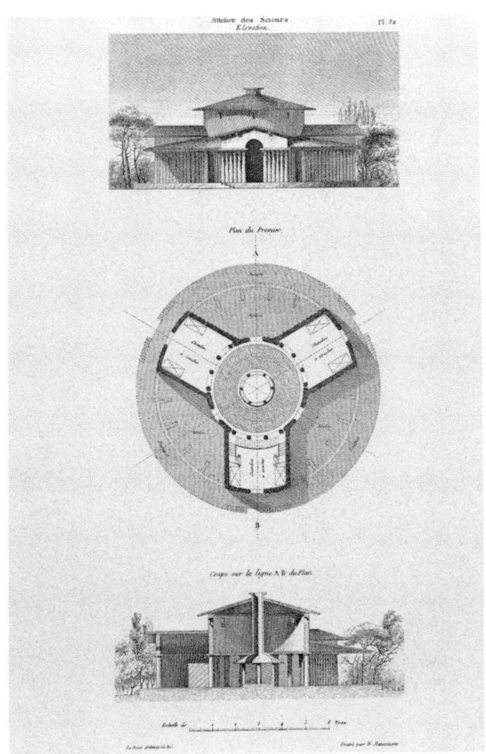

46 Ledoux, sawyers' workshop, *top to bottom:* elevation, plan of second floor, and section.

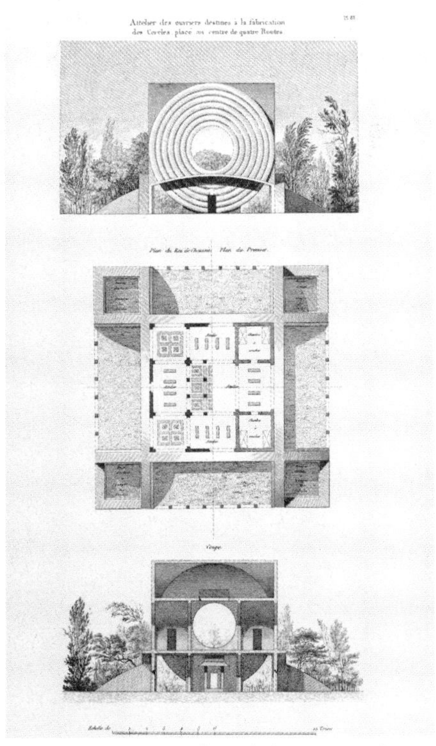

47 Ledoux, coopers' workshop, *top to bottom:* elevation, plan of first and second floors, and section.

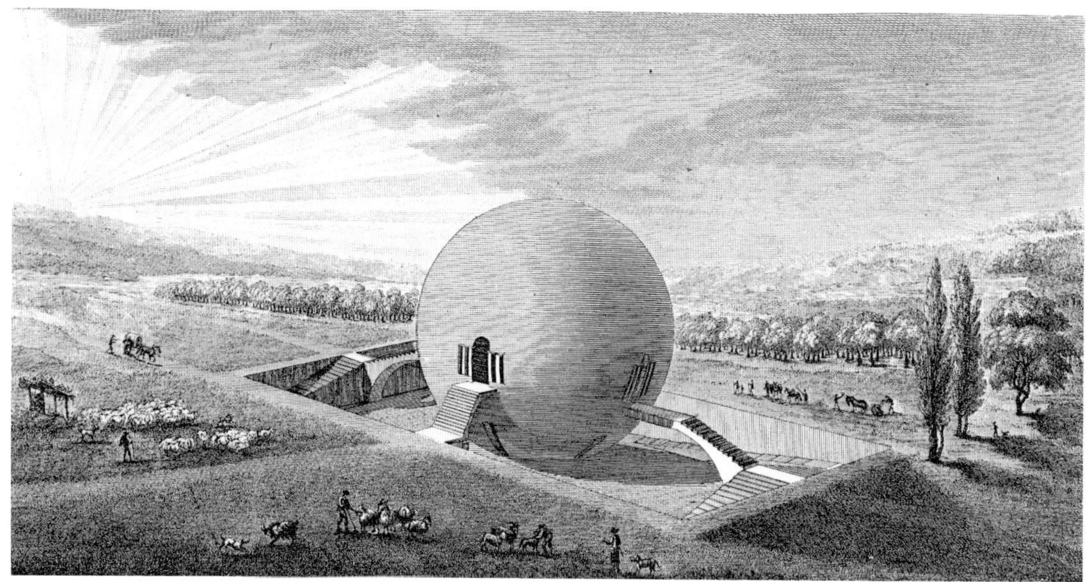

48 Ledoux, house of the agricultural guards at Maupertuis, perspective view.

49 Ledoux, house of the directors of the River Loüe, perspective view.

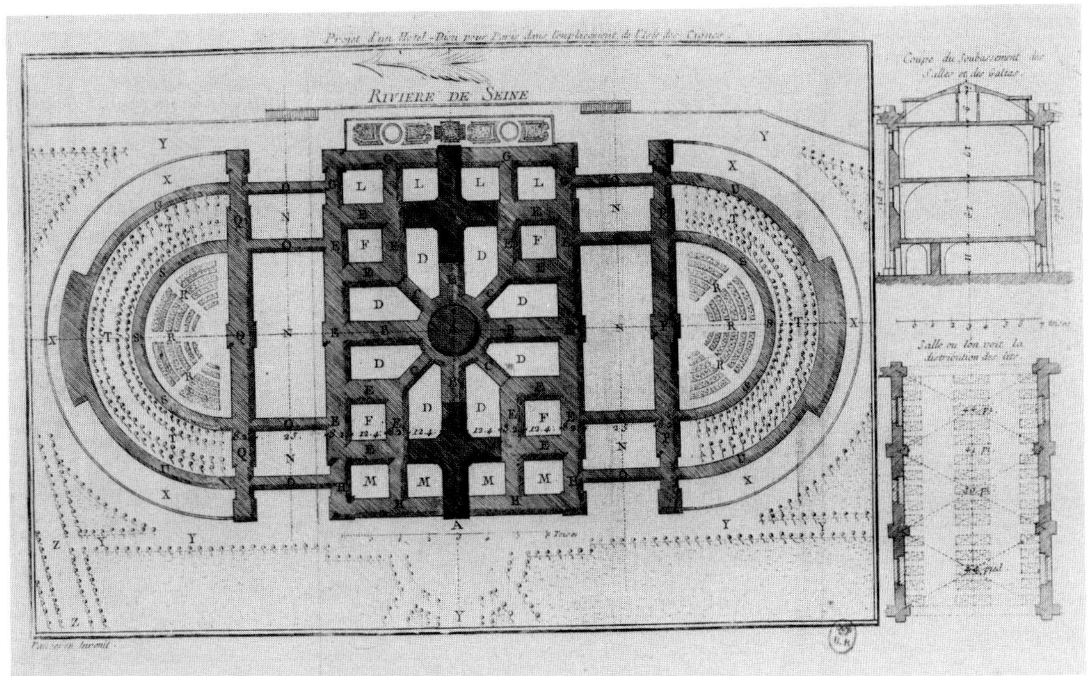

50 Pierre Panseron, Project for a Hôtel-Dieu for Paris, on the Ile des Cygnes, *clockwise from left:* general plan, section, and plan of a typical ward-block, 1773.

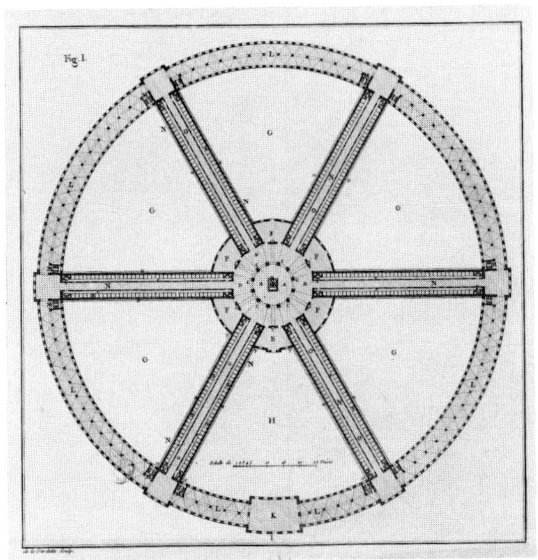

51 Antoine Petit, project for a new Hôtel-Dieu, plan, 1774.

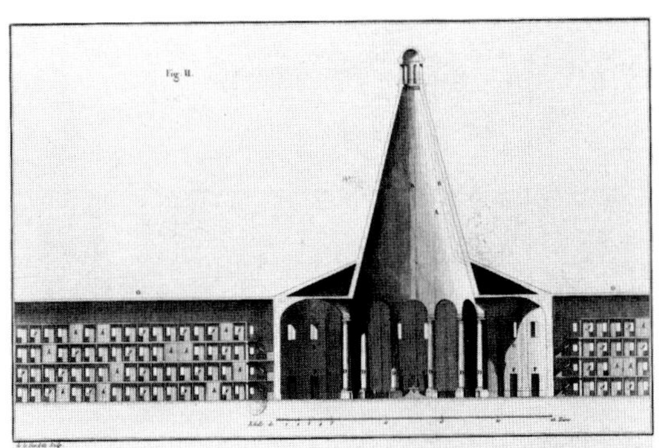

52 Petit, project for a new Hôtel-Dieu, section.

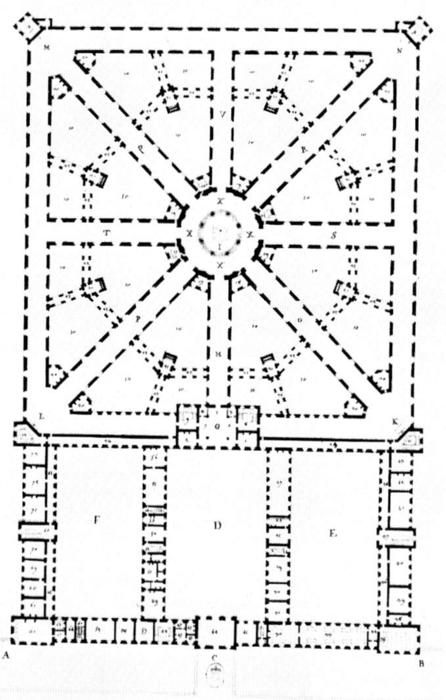

53 Antoine Desgodets, plan for a Hôtel-Dieu, 1727.

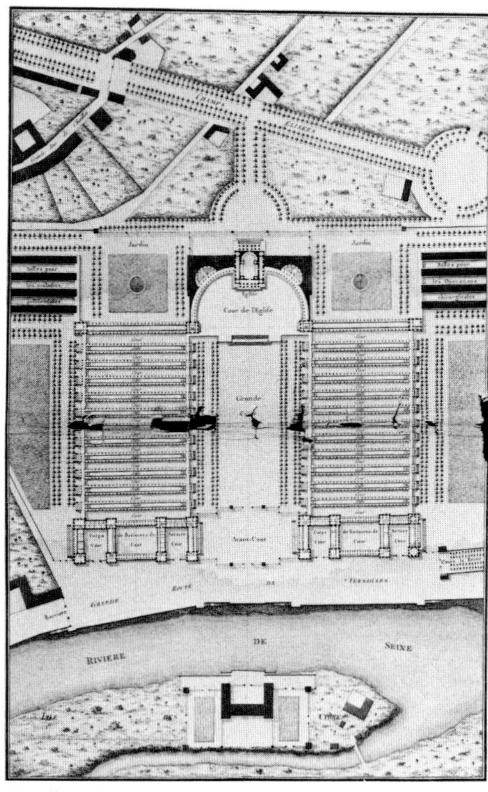

54 Jean-Baptiste Le Roy and Charles-François Viel, "General Plan of a Project for a Hôtel-Dieu," conceived in 1773, published in 1787.

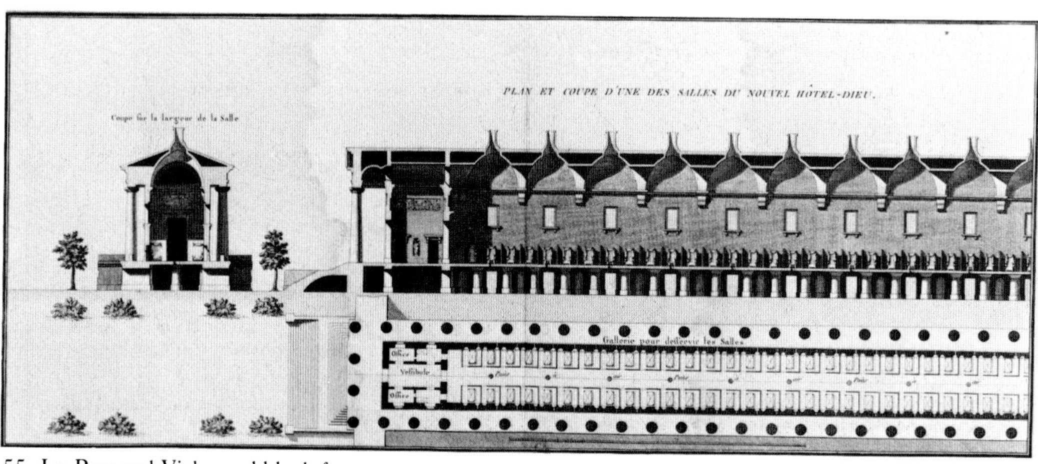

55 Le Roy and Viel, ward-block for a new Hôtel-Dieu, *clockwise from left:* cross section, long section, and plan.

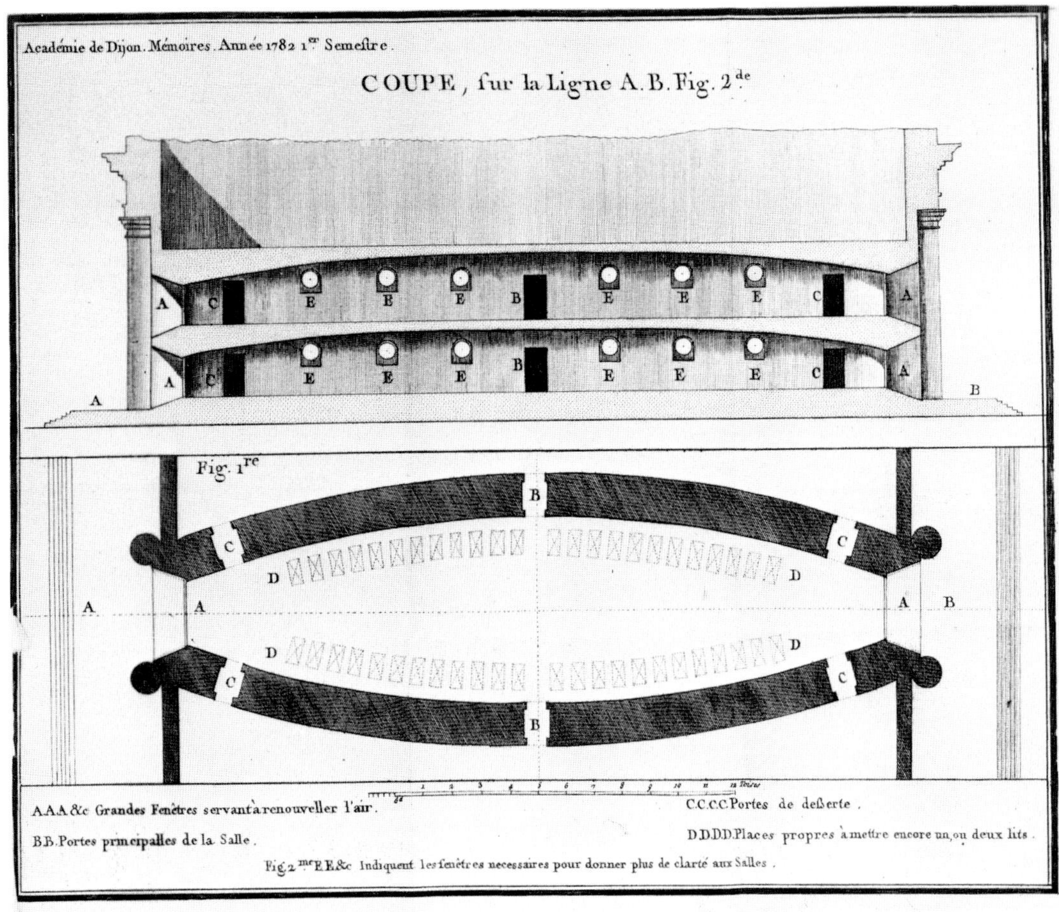

56 Jacques-Germain Soufflot and Hugues Maret, project for a hospital, a typical ward-block, *top*, section; *bottom*, plan, 1782.

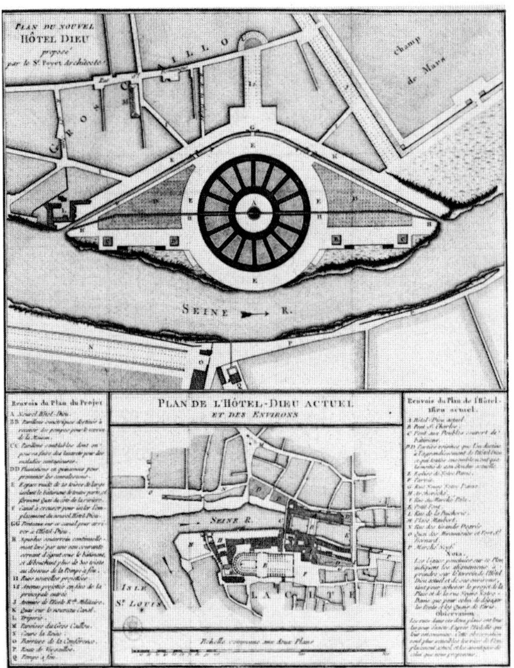

57 Bernard Poyet, *top*, plan of a new Hôtel-Dieu; *bottom*, plan of actual Hôtel-Dieu and its surroundings, 1785.

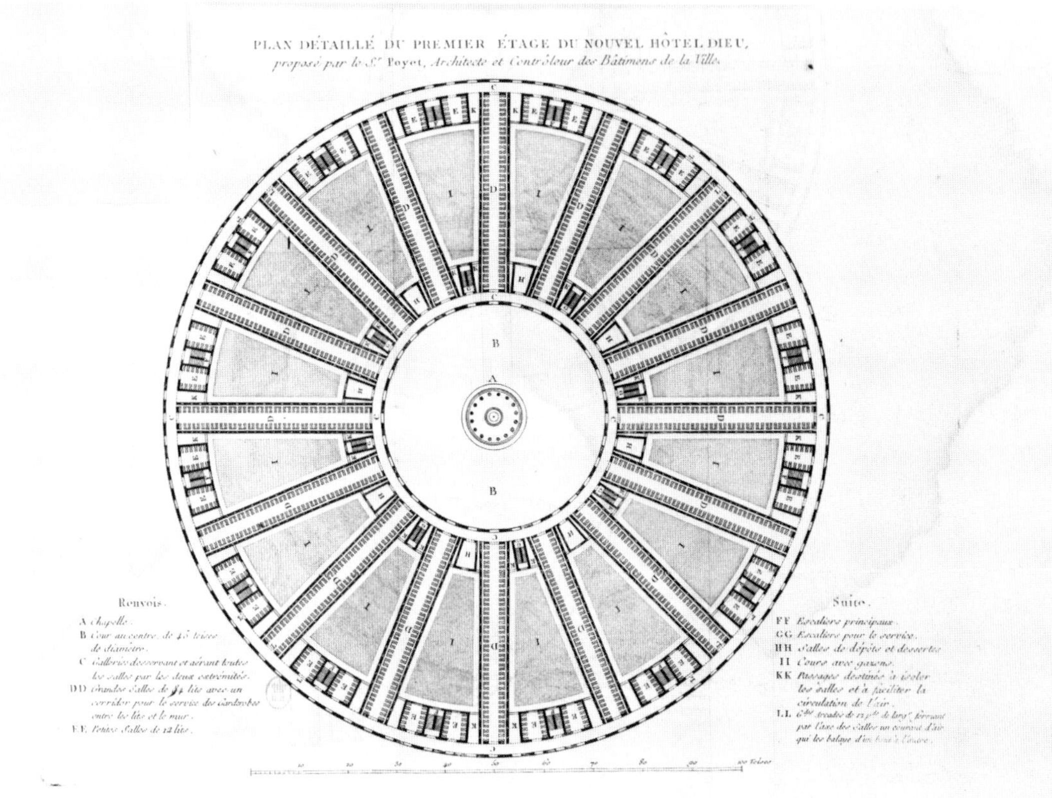

58 Poyet, "Detailed Plan of the Second Floor of a New Hôtel-Dieu."

59 Poyet, perspective view (*top*) and sectional perspective (*bottom*) through the courtyard of a new Hôtel-Dieu.

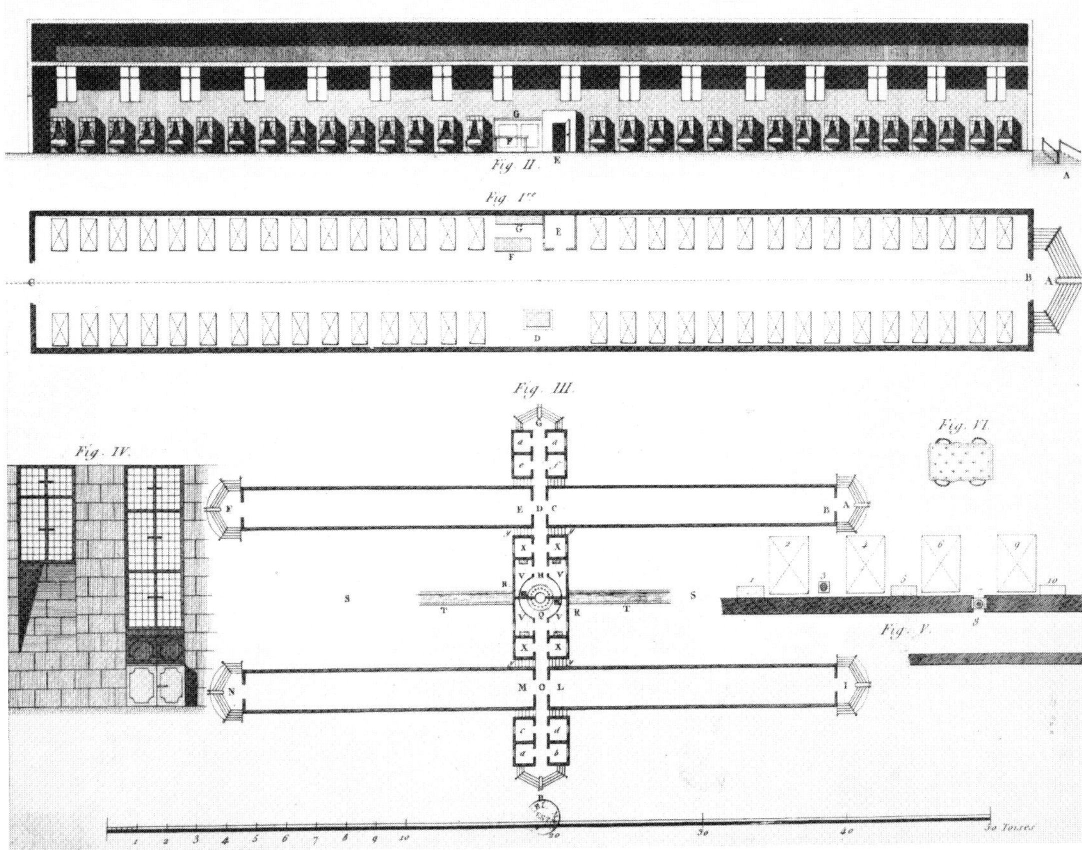

60 Jacques Tenon, project for a model hospital, 1787.

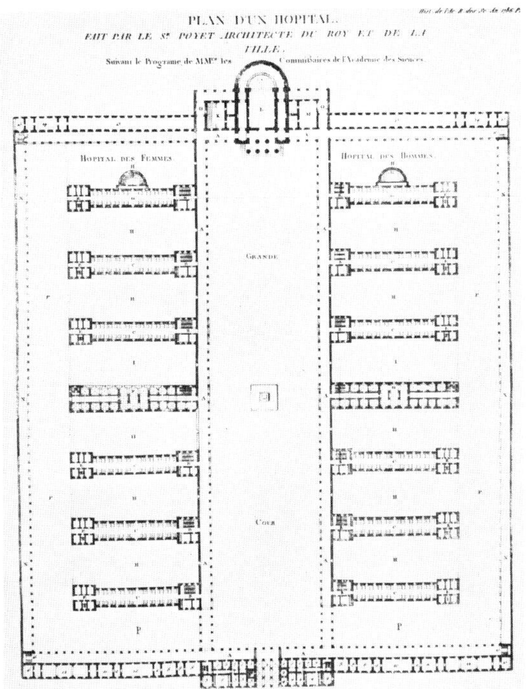

61 Poyet, "Plan of a Hospital, Following the Program of the Commissioners of the Académie des sciences," 1786.

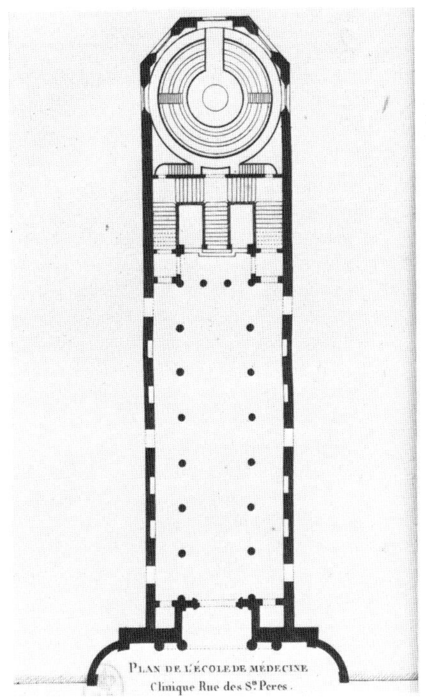

64 Clavareau, "Plan of the School of Clinical Medicine," constructed in the former chapel of the Hôpital de la Charité, 1795.

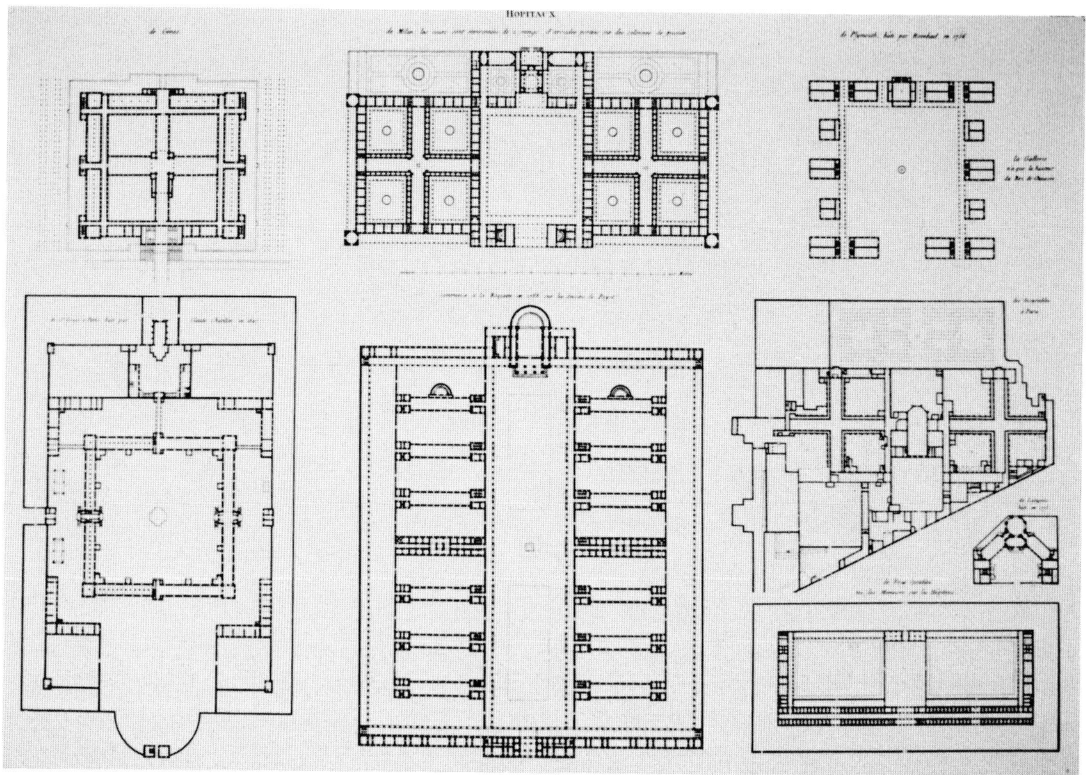

62 J. N. L. Durand, comparative plans of hospitals, 1799.

63 N. M. Clavareau, "Facade of the New Entrance to the Hôtel-Dieu de Paris," 1805.

65 Clavareau, facade of the School of Clinical Medicine.

66 Jean-Charles Delafosse, project for a prison, watercolor.

67 Jacques Gondouin, project for prisons opposite the Ecole de Chirurgie, 1780.

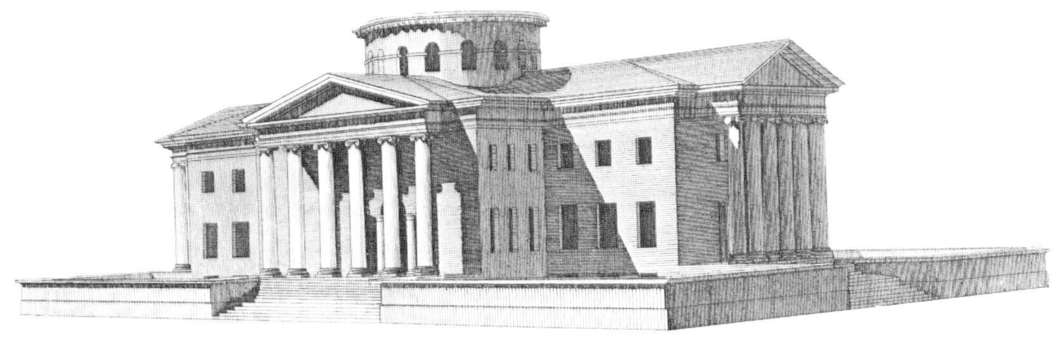

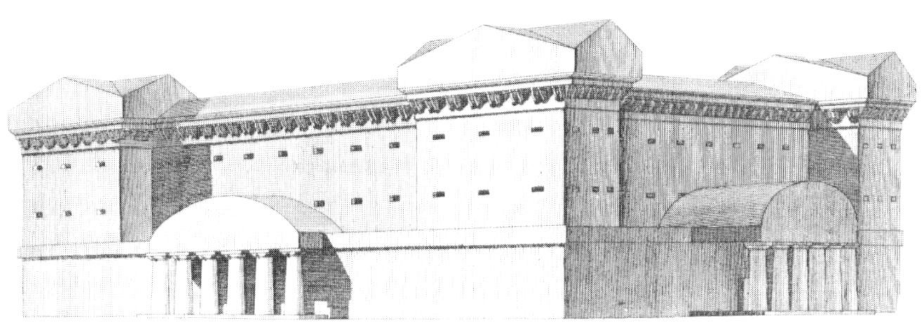

68 Ledoux, project for prisons at Aix-en-Provence, perspective view, 1783–1785.

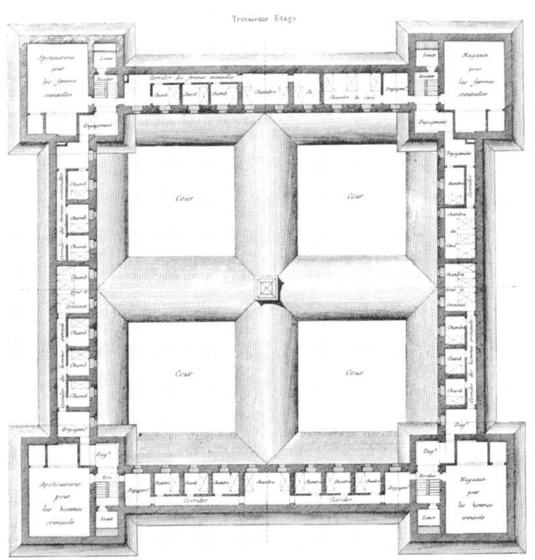

69 Ledoux, project for prisons at Aix-en-Provence, plan of second floor.

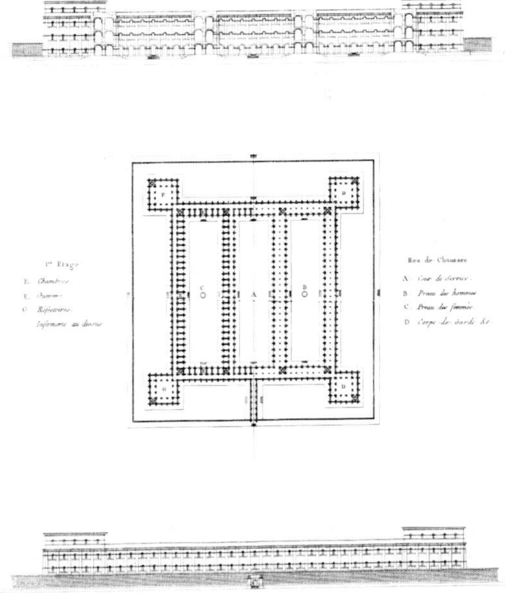

70 Durand, prison.

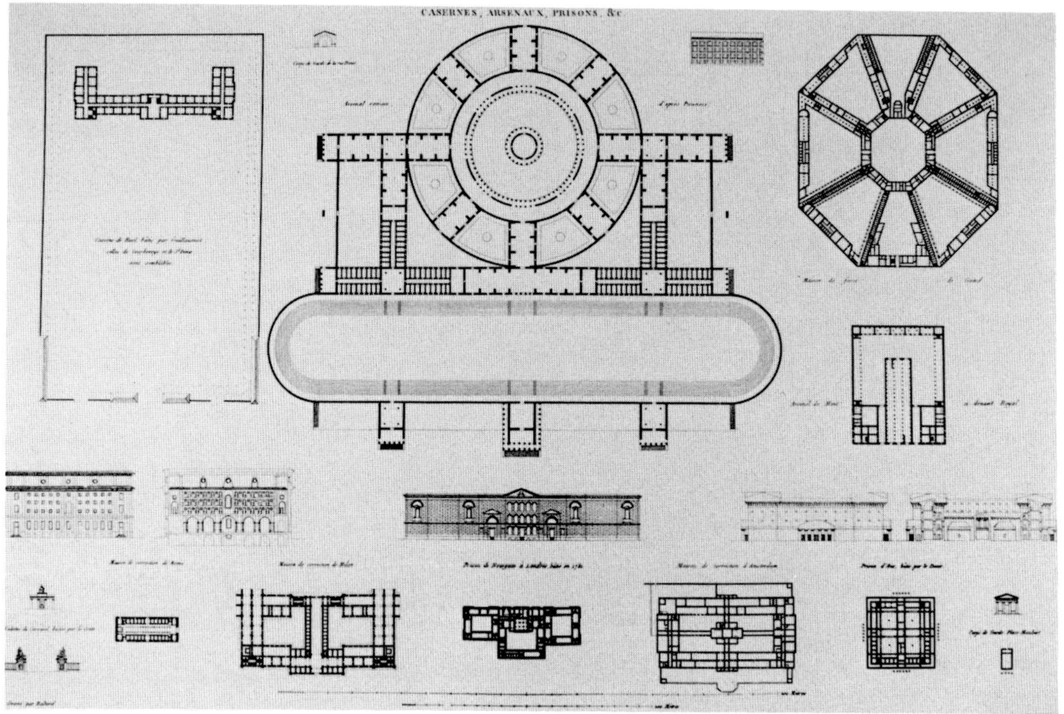

70a Durand, comparative prisons.

72 Abbé Larudan (Arnaud de Pomponne), floor-drawing for the reception of an Apprentice Mason, 1741.

71 Gabriel-Louis Pérau, reception of an Apprentice Mason, 1742.

hands, let us hold close together," they sang, and with every toast reminded themselves of the bonds that joined them closer than any family.[31] In the confines of their small band, they alone had perfected the true art of living.

> The law of equality, a soul tender and sociable, sweet mores, love for the fine arts, the decency and harmony that reigns in our festivals, this is the inextinguishable source of our happiness.[32]

In the celebration of the banquet, the Masons thus took part in the "search for origins," for the primitive roots of happiness, a search common, as we have seen, to many discourses in mid-century. Even as Rousseau had described the first festivals, where, gathered around a common hearth, natural men felt the first and sweetest sentiments of humanity, singing, and dancing,[33] so an anonymous Mason compared his brotherhood to "the first times, when men were always ready to care for their mutual needs."[34] Protected from the corruption of the world by the physical and social asylum of the lodge, continually renewed in moral and spiritual vigor by the endless catechisms, rituals, and social observances of their order, the Masons established a calm center, a place of repose and tranquillity that would in itself provoke "a good nature and a moral society."

These first festivals of the Freemasons were essentially reproductions, survivals, and revivals, in form at least, of earlier celebrations, religious and secular. In towns where Masonry assumed the role of professional confederations and guilds with little opposition from the authorities—in Arras, for example—the festivals replicated the patron-saint fêtes of the corporations and included the saying of vespers the night before, grand mass preceding a banquet in the town council meeting halls, followed by another vespers for the deceased of the fraternity. Similarly, the Masons of the Fidelité Lodge in the same town held a banquet on the day of Saint-Jean d'Eté, ostensibly to mark the inauguration of the new building. Initially confined to private dinners, by the end of the century the convivial life of the society had developed an almost public character: the pomp and strange iconography of the Freemasons' processions were satirized widely.[35]

THE TYPE OF THE LODGE

The descriptions of the police raids and the so-called "exposures" show clearly that, by the late 1760s, the plan of the typical lodge was fixed. The abbé Larudan drew a diagrammatic plan of what he called the Berlin Lodge; whether he had visited Berlin is not known, but in any event, the outline closely resembled the apartments of the Parisian Freemasons. Downstairs were the rooms used by the serving brothers, the concierge, cook, and confectioner; a grand staircase led to the second floor, where the apartments of the lodge were arranged *en série*. The first room, or "quarter," as Larudan called it, was "the place of darkness"; it had two small *cabinets* for the use of waiting candidates. In the second "quarter" were the purification facilities, bathrooms, and two other small *cabinets*, whose use was unspecified. In the chamber of initiation, the main room of the lodge, the floor-drawings took up an eight-by-four-foot rectangle in the center of the floor. Beyond this hall was a banquet room where, "during the ceremonies, the serving brothers prepare the meal or refreshments to follow, so that when the Mysteries are over, the Brethren can pass at once to this well-appointed room."[36]

In 1774–1775, the years of his first initiation into the lodge Des Coeurs Simples de l'Etoile Polaire, the architect Charles De Wailly made two drawings of a typical lodge viewed from the east and the west (plate 75). An entry space is framed by two prominent columns; the central room is flanked by stepped seating; and the Orient is raised up by three flights of stairs that lead to the Master's dais.[37]

This plan was in general use for the remainder of the century, with certain elaborations according to the cult. The Lodge of Friendship in Arras, for one, probably also designed by the architect Charles De Wailly and inaugurated in his presence in 1786, was an example of an entire building given over to a society. There was no indication on the outside that the lodge was in any way unlike the other houses on the street; inside, on the ground floor, a grand salon, measuring some thirty-three feet by twenty-one feet, was surrounded by a gallery that overlooked the benches and tables of the assembly. On the next floor was a "chamber of hospitality" for visiting and indigent brothers and a banquet hall furnished with a great, horseshoe-shaped table looking out onto the garden. In this room were held the balls and festivals of adoption—the reception of women into the affiliate lodge. At the foot of the grand stair were the waiting rooms for candidates and visiting Masons.[38] The only changes in the layout of the typical lodge called for by Louis de Béyerlé's unified code in 1784 were the provision of adequate archival storage and the addition of three separate lodge rooms for the three grades of initiation.[39] The dimensions of these lodges roughly conformed, although by no means consistently, to the proportions given as those of the inner sanctum of Solomon's Temple: the two columns of Jakin and Boaz surmounted by their globes invariably stood at the entrance; and the east, which represented the Orient, was treated as the most sacred space.[40]

THE HUT AND THE TEMPLE

The form of their lodge was of particular importance to the Freemasons, not only to endow the new society with institutional confirmation, but also for the immediate extension of their adopted terms of discourse and the representation of the forms of their ritual. Reviving the terminology of the old operative Masonic guilds, the aristocratic and middle-class fraternity of the mid-eighteenth century still talked of "building the Temple" and "constructing the social edifice." Anderson's *Constitutions,* translated into French in 1736, stressed this architectural analogy, repeating, this time for a non-guild audience, the miscellaneous myths of the origins of architecture and the various "histories" of architecture contained in Masonic charges since the thirteenth century. The *Constitutions* presented architectural history as an active metaphor for social development: the origins of architecture symbolized, and in some way participated in, the reestablished order of a natural society. The Mason had no need to construct an artificial philosophic system to unite paradigms in architecture with those in society; his mythology proposed that one was bound up with the other. The original art of geometry was an allegory of the original social structure; the rebuilding of Solomon's Temple was referential to that of a society and, at the same time, realizable in architectural terms as the first stage of regeneration.

Thus the engraved Frontispiece to the original publication of the *Constitutions* of 1723 depicted an architectural perspective: the colonnades that flank the central gallery recede to infinity. The Orders are ranged in their "historical" chronology, with Composite to the front, then Corinthian, Ionic, Tuscan, and Doric. The rear of the picture shows the path of columns disappearing into a primitive, pre-architectural landscape. This quasi-ritualistic and allegorical stage-set demonstrates the double character of the Masonic "return to origins," celebrating at once a rebirth founded on primary truths and the civilized "route of progress."

"Artisans of our own happiness," stated a mid-century Masonic writer, Couret de Villeneuve, "we work on Plans traced by Nature and compassed by Reason, to reconstruct a moral edifice, the model of which, executed in the first ages of the world, we have conserved by the universal idea of the [Masonic] order."[41] The task of the Freemason was to "reintegrate" the elements of this edifice, mutilated by time, to "reestablish" its original proportions in their "primitive purity," and to bring all the ornaments into accord with the whole. The model to which Couret referred was, of course, the Temple of Solomon, described at the high point of Anderson's narrative. When mention was made of the Temple in Masonic texts, it was generally this one, built, according to legend, by Hiram Abif, Solomon's architect.

The relation of the Temple to the idea of society was well understood by Freemasons and philosophers alike (plate 76). Jean-Baptiste Willermoz, the Masonic mystic of Lyons, wrote to the Duke of Brunswick:

> Fundamentally, Freemasonry has essentially no other aim than the knowledge of man and of nature; being founded on the Temple of Solomon, it cannot be a stranger to the science of man, since all the sages who have lived since its foundation have recognized that this famous Temple has existed for itself in the universe solely to be the universal type of man in general in his past, present, and future states, and the figurative emblematic picture of his own history.[42]

Elsewhere, the same writer spoke of the Temple of Jerusalem, the universal type of the science of man, as having been substituted, "because of its perfection, for all the types and symbols that preceded it." The proportions of the Temple provided specifications for the lodge building, and the apocryphal hierarchy established by Hiram Abif among master, companion, and apprentice became allegorical for Masonic degrees. The endeavors of scholars, from Jean Bautista Villalpanda and Perrault to Newton, to reconstruct the Temple graphically contributed to the establishment of this form as the type of Masonic building.[43] The most graphic of these Temple reconstructions is that by De Wailly (plate 77), recently discovered by Monique Mosser, in which the conventional plan developed by Villalpanda and Fischer von Erlach is reelaborated according to the stages of Masonic ritual in order to depict the route of initiation in a grand sequence of stairs and open courtyards leading toward the sanctum itself, a combination of Greek Temple and Roman Pantheon types later to be repeated in Vaudoyer's project for the completion of the Madeleine.[44]

But Villeneuve's terms seem to have implied an even more fundamental origin, whose design was first delineated by nature and only subsequently encompassed by the architect's rational geometry. His allusions were to an Edenist primitivism, not to the luxury of Solomon's developed type. The emerging importance of this primitivist model may be seen in comparison with Anderson's *Constitutions* of 1723. Here the prehistory of the Temple, from Adam to Solomon, is sketched roughly and quickly. Adam, "created after the image of the great Architect," is represented as having taught his sons geometry; his son Cain built a city with this knowledge. Then came Noah, the building of the Ark, and the construction of the Tower of Babel, the translation of architectural knowledge to Egypt after the Tower's fall, and the instruction of the tribes of Israel during the Captivity. There was no mention in Anderson's account of Adam being more than the simple transmitter of geometric wisdom.[45] Adam was not yet depicted as a builder, only as the receiver of original knowledge.

In Villeneuve's text of 1748, however, Adam was finally given a primary constructive role: despite his fall, he had not lost the knowledge received from the Grand Architect, and he "applied his science to the needs of human life." Leaving the *lieu de délices,* he set to work to guard himself against the injuries of the air.

> The retreat he built himself must naturally have had geometric proportions, this science making up part of his knowledge: it is thus that the first man was the first Mason.[46]

In the gradual fusion of the anthropological and religious models of origins, Adam became identified with natural primitive man as Rousseau would describe him two years later. Perhaps there was a more than coincidental relation between the civilized primitivism of these Enlightenment Masons, with their desire to return to the source always couched in the metaphorical language of architecture, and the paradigm of the "primitive hut," described by their brother or sympathizer, the abbé Laugier, to such effect in 1753.[47]

It is easy to see how such legends of Masonic origin became themselves of fundamental interest to an architectural theory preoccupied with the return to a basic, original order. Conversely, such a paradigm or type of original architecture was immediately connected, in a way that Laugier had only implied, to the paradigm of a new social order, and for the Masons, the *architect*-Freemason gained special importance, marked as the delegate of the Great Architect of the Universe. Indeed, the architect was held to be the paradigm of the Mason: in 1784, Béyerlé argued that the wide range of knowledge required of the architect and his special facility in interpreting the foundation myths constituted him as the very "type of the Freemason."[48]

FREEMASONIC ARCHITECTS

Between 1774 and 1789, over 120 architects belonged to lodges in Paris affiliated with the Grand Orient; of these, many were well known in the development of neoclassicism, as the authors of influential texts or important designs.[49] Among them, varying degrees of commitment to the ideals and the social life of Freemasonry may be distinguished. J. B. de Puisieux, chief architect of Sainte Geneviève under Soufflot, was a Mason from 1727 to 1773 and a high officer of his lodge; his treatise on geometry reflected his intense belief in guild Masonic doctrine.[50] Jean-Jacques Lequeu, on the other hand, alienated and probably half-mad, used the imagery and quasi-occultist concerns of lodges in Rouen and Paris in a highly eclectic and often satirical manner. In between was a large body of professionals who considered Masonry as either a simple extension of the social life of the salons—a ready-made patronage circle—or a theoretical doctrine, even if they did not use symbolic Masonic themes directly in their designs. This latter group included official architects like Moreau-Desproux, architect of the city of Paris, theoreticians and scholars like Quatremère de Quincy, as well as the important designers Nicolas Le Camus de Mézières, Bernard Poyet, A. L. T. Brongniart, Antoine Vaudoyer, Charles De Wailly, J. F. T. Chalgrin, Rondelet, Pierre Rousseau, and Jacques Cellérier.

Some of these professionals seem to have found specific lodges more attractive than others, either for reasons of friendship, intellectual affiliation, or patronage. The Neuf Soeurs Lodge was inevitably popular among intellectuals and the philosophic circle, including five architects in its membership, among them Charles Alexandre Guillaumot, architect of the Gobelins factory, and Bernard Poyet. Les Amis Réunis, the lodge of the linguist and antiquarian Court de Gébelin and the painter Hubert Robert, only attracted three architects (although two, Petit-Radel and Moreau-Desproux, were notable). Of all the lodges, the one with the highest proportion of architects was Les Coeurs Simple de l'Etoile Polaire, which had ten architects out of a total of ninety members between 1775 and 1777. Pierre Poncet, Chalgrin, Le Camus de Mézières, De Wailly, and Billiard de Belizard were among them. A clear example of patronage membership is that of Brongniart, who, as a member of the circle of Madame de Montesson, also belonged to the lodge of Saint-Jean Ecosse du Contrat Social with other friends of de Montesson and the Duc d'Orléans, such as Moreau jeune the painter, Sacchini the composer, and, more important for Brongniart, Anne-Pierre Marquis de Montesquiou, his patron at Maupertuis. A special case was that of Jean-Rodolphe Perronet, the engineer and professor of the Ecole des Ponts et Chaussées, who in 1787, with his entire faculty and student body, formed a lodge of civil and military engineers named Uranie.

Not all architects entered into an active relation with their brotherhood. Few established themselves so firmly as de Puisieux, dean of all the venerables of Paris, or Poncet, who designed the headquarters of the Grand Orient. Many architects were content to derive a convivial social life and a comfortable patronage from their membership in this bourgeois club par excellence. Some, however, and especially those concerned with the development of architectural history and theory, found in the analogical terms of the Masonic doctrines—the terms by which architectural metaphors referred to society—a particularly redolent and evocative discourse. Certainly Quatremère de Quincy, in his theoretical work before the Revolution, exhibited all the characteristics of one who was influenced by his Masonic affiliations: his emphasis on idealist typology and his academic interest in Egyptian architecture well before Napoleon's expedition to Egypt easily coincided with what may be regarded as legitimate Masonic concerns. Some architects, such as Boullée, Ledoux, and especially Lequeu, took seriously implications of the Masonic "analogous theory" of architecture as a means by which to join their work, in theory at least, to more utopian ends. In this attempt, Freemasons and non-Freemasons alike were supported by an unprecedented proliferation of Masonic imagery, symbolism, and publicly acknowledged festivity. Boullée, probably not himself a Mason, and Ledoux, certainly associated with an offshoot cult, drew their vocabulary of symbolic form not simply from classical tradition, but also from motifs already charged with this new set of social connotations. Lequeu, younger and unabashedly reveling in the signs of the lodges, displayed them in profusion in the ideal lodges he designed between 1786 and 1825.

MASONIC STAGECRAFT

The foundation of the Grand Orient of France in May 1773 and the installation of the Duc de Chartres as grand master, with the Duc de Montmorency-Luxembourg as his regular substitute, marked a new phase in the institutional development of the order, confirmed by its rising public popularity. The almost public nature of the festivals, the dramatic increase in membership, and the expansion of the order throughout the provinces under the regular surveillance of the Orient, openly confirmed what had emerged as a fact over the preceding ten years: that the Masonic order existed as the primary form of institutionalized sociability appealing to aristocrats, intellectuals, churchmen, professionals, and shopkeepers alike.

The celebration of the new grand mastership was an occasion of elaborate pomp and brilliant display; held in the duke's private quarters on the rue Folie-Titon, in the faubourg Saint-Antoine, the ceremonies were conducted in a vast salon "clothed in mystery."[51] The entire ritual was set amidst scarlet tapestries beneath azure vaults scattered with golden stars; the hall was lit with nearly 150 lights, which were arranged according to a mystical number theory.

Even more splendid, and certainly more significant for the order, was the inauguration of its new quarters in the fall of the next year.[52] Pierre Poncet, the architect for the Grand Orient, converted the building of the old Jesuit Novitiate in the faubourg Saint-Germain for the use of the lodge. Raised above street level, the lodge rooms were approached by a flight of twenty-four steps and a screen of columns. The three halls of the lodge were placed in sequence, much like the Berlin lodge: the first decorated in flowered cloth of different colors, the second in a watered blue and white and furnished with a double row of benches; both were lit by many lamps suspended from a crystal chandelier. The *salle des travaux* itself was seventy-eight feet long and twenty-one feet wide and was divided into two parts. The main room, fifty-one feet long and twenty-one feet high, with a blue ceiling, was again furnished with a double row of benches; to the west were the triangular tables of the Surveillants, next to which stood two columns "of the most pure metal, crowned with capitals, which carried a cluster of fifteen stars." The Orient, reached by steps from this hall, was twenty-seven feet long and thirty-five feet high; a three-tiered platform mounted to a grand throne, with the officers arranged in a semicircle on the first stage. Beyond this hall was a large banquet room, which was almost the same size as the lodge room, again decorated in blue and red with a blue ceiling and a raised dais for the grand master. "It is in this place," stated de Lalande, "that we build a temple to the Grand Architect and to virtue, which belongs to all the regular Masons of France; it is in this sacred asylum that the Orient will give itself up to its sublime works with the decency and dignity to which it is suited."[53]

The initiation of Voltaire was perhaps the most celebrated and certainly the most publicly discussed festival held in these quarters. One month before his death, in the spring of 1778, the ailing and by all accounts slightly bewildered philosophe was initiated into the lodge of the Neuf Soeurs with all the pomp the intellectual elite of Paris could muster.[54] The ceremony took place in the Grand Orient and was attended by some 250 prominent Masons; it lasted the entire afternoon and concluded with a sumptuous banquet. The antiquarian Court de Gébelin, together with the count Strogonof, privy councillor to Catherine of Russia, assisted the venerable of the lodge, de Lalande. Among the crowd were Sebastien Mercier, the playwright and chronicler; Savalette de Langes, fanatical mystic and ubiquitous Mason; the Marquis de Saisseval; and, of course, Benjamin Franklin. Voltaire was prepared by nine specially chosen members of the lodge and led into the main hall supported by de Gébelin and Franklin, passing between the two columns and submitting to a shortened version of the ceremony composed of various "philosophical questions," which he answered with "vigor and wit." The Masons presented him with the apron of Helvétius and gave short speeches; beautiful music played in the background, and men of letters recited pieces of verse composed for the occasion. Court de Gébelin then presented to the lodge a volume of *Le Monde Primitif* and read a passage from it concerning the Eleusinian mysteries; a royal painter sketched the eminent guest, who, tired and bemused by the whole event, reportedly was unable to face his food at the ensuing feast. "They made in his honor a formal reception," an anonymous witness wrote. "They read to him much bad verse; they then made him eat an even worse dinner."[55]

Even more remarkable was the *pompe funèbre* held in honor of Voltaire in November of the same year. The Temple was hung in black throughout, save for arches in gold and silver that held transparent banners with wise sayings of the master and, in the middle, a large cenotaph composed of a pyramid on four high steps; three broken columns holding urns filled with perfume as well as the works of Voltaire fronted this monument. At the end of long speeches, poetry readings, and musical pieces, the "sepulchral pyramid disappeared with a great noise like a clap of thunder," a bright light dawned, and to the strains of sweet music a picture of the "Apotheosis of Voltaire" appeared.

Contemporary observers were quick to note the emergence of Freemasonry into accepted social life. The confidence of the members, as they allowed themselves the liberty of "leaking" the circumstances of Voltaire's initiation to avid reporters, was matched by a jump in membership of the lodges, which nearly tripled in the following year. The so-called "mysteries" of Freemasonry were indeed hardly mysterious by the late seventies; the publicity surrounding the interdictions of the church, the gossip that inevitably accompanied every "indiscretion" of a brother, talk of conspiracy from right and left, together with the evident popularity of the brotherhood itself, had led to exposures, counterexposures, and a considerable production of Masonic "scholarship." Ostensibly with the right to issue charters to new lodges and to oversee the ideological and social life of all existing lodges affiliated with its central control, the Grand Orient was now in a strong position to maintain and propagate a unified form of association and, in the words of the Duc de Luxembourg, to "concentrate all Masonic operations under a single authority."

Yet a number of breaks appeared almost immediately: the schism that divided French Masons between the Grand Lodge and the Grand Orient led to the continuing defection of many lodges under the administration of the former, exacerbating the "ideological" split between those devoted to a "pure" English Masonry with three grades and those espousing the artificial, multigrade "Scottish Masonry" that had developed after 1740. These divisions were no doubt reinforced by the predominantly class lines along which their membership tended to align, accentuating the heterogeneous tendencies of an order that had always held the potential for ideological eclecticism. Indeed, within a few years after the foundation of the Grand Orient, what the historian Pierre Chevallier has called "an eruption of mysticism" developed inside and outside the lodges, led by individual mystics, ideologues, sectarian leaders, and charlatans who elaborated their personal visions of perfect Masonry, establishing breakaway sects and quasi-Masonic cults. A brotherhood united by the general idea of fraternal bonds seemed to disintegrate around individualistic and charismatic leaders; the names that appeared in the late seventies were no longer the sober bourgeois or aristocratic venerables, but the fanatical mystics, ascetics, eclectics, womanizers, and quacks of this "preromantic" era.[56] All the tendencies already embodied in the received doctrines of Masonry but hitherto buried under the philosophic Deism of the mid-century—alchemical lore, cabalistic language, hermetic philosophy—surfaced in this "flowering of the cults."

The social bases of this efflorescence were diverse. The early affiliation of the lower bourgeoisie and artisan classes to the complicated grades of Scottish Masonry was only the first stage of an increasingly sharp division between the "purism" of the aristocratic administrators of the Grand Orient and the eclecticism of the schismatic Grand Lodge.[57] The accomplishment of high and obscure grades seemed to offer a kind of ennoblement to the ever-aspiring *petite bourgeoisie,* but even in the philosophic lodges, the historical explorations of Masonic intellectuals such as Court de Gébelin had contributed to the increasing elaboration of initiation rituals by borrowing from the rites of past civilizations. In purely intellectual circles, and rapidly in the "nature" cults of the leisure classes, the idea of self-knowledge and individual revelation gained a strong following after the death of Rousseau. Writers and painters took increased pleasure in the delights of aesthetic contrast, of the sublime, of the bizarre and the grotesque, experimenting with the world of sensation.

Thus, the séances of Mesmer in 1784 were not only enormously popular, but also studied by serious scientists; Cagliostro, introducing his "Egyptian rite" to Paris two years earlier, had received a warm welcome from eminent Freemasons' wives eager to gain adoption into his lodge. The presence of the legendary figure of the Comte de Saint-Germain was often rumored but never proven as the reportedly 130-year-old mystic slipped in and out of the capital. Frightening stories of vast and politically seditious conspiracies were spread; one such story claimed that the Illuminés of Bavaria were in Paris, holding secret meetings to undermine the fabric of Masonry itself. The mystic Mason Savalette de Langes organized an international conference of Masonic sectarians in 1785, the Conference of Wilhelmsbad, in a vain attempt to resolve these differences.[58]

The lodges of these heterogeneous sects generally followed Masonic precedent, with many well-advertised variations. That of Mesmer, held in the Hôtel de Coigny, was called the Lodge of Harmony; its arrangement was parallel to that of Masonic lodges, the floor drawing replaced by a giant tub filled with mesmeric fluid. For Mesmer, initiation was a pseudoscientific ritual in the form of lectures and communal séances around this central basin; the ritual was supposed to induce transported states of mind among the participants.[59] The lodges of Cagliostro were often purpose-built; the Egyptian rite, emulating the descent of Orpheus into the underworld, his trials, and his eventual initiation by the Egyptian priests, required a sophisticated *mise en scène*. In the lodges of adoption supervised by Cagliostro from 1782 to 1788, aspirants were blindfolded and ritually submitted to the trials of fire, water, and air, with much noise, smoke, and an acceptable level of boisterous indelicacy.[60]

These sectarian developments had a strong influence on the formation of a specifically Masonic architecture. They were marked by two parallel and mutually supporting themes: the theatrical elaboration of the forms of initiation and their final confirmation, not in emblematic floor-drawing or in the ephemeral *mise en scène* of decorative hangings, but in the spatial sequences of the lodge itself.

EGYPTIAN MYSTERIES

On the occasion of Voltaire's initiation into the Neuf Soeurs Lodge, the historian Court de Gébelin had read a detailed account of the Eleusinian mysteries, an extract from his *Monde Primitif.* A contemporary Masonic rite was thus supported by historical precedent: the primitive type of initiatory ritual itself, the rites of Demeter and her daughter Persephone. For de Gébelin, these rituals, together with those of Orpheus in the underworld and those described in Vergil's *Aeneid,* were typical of the first initiation conducted in Egypt, the home of hermetic magic, by the Egyptian priests for the benefit of Hermes Trismegistus, first magus. De Gébelin quoted from classical authors concerning the horror of the mysteries and the enlightenment of the initiate:

> The horror of it is augmented by everything frightful that human industry could imagine. Thunder rolls from all sides; thunderbolts fall with a great tumult; the air is full of monstrous figures; the sanctuary trembles; the earth itself bellows. Finally, calm succeeds the tempest; the scene is opened and extends into the far distance; the end of the sanc-

tuary opens; and the initiates see a pleasant pasture to which they repair to dance and rejoice.[61]

In this way, the basic structure of initiation (a reenactment of descent into the underworld and the following trials or proofs of the candidate's worth) was supported historically and placed in the domain of the theater.

The literature of Freemasonry had already proposed this essentially artificial quality of initiation in several quasi-historical novels that treated Egyptian rites and their elaborate settings. That of the abbé Terrasson, published first in 1733, was perhaps the most celebrated. His novel *Séthos* described in detail the trials of his hero following the steps of Orpheus in the underworld (plate 78). Séthos was subjected to three trials, by fire, water, and air, before being admitted into the temple precinct. The ritual was administered by priests in realms that stretched beneath the Great Pyramid, from the horror-filled caverns of Hades to the brilliant and perfumed Elysian fields.[62]

If the prototypes of the ritual of initiation were Egyptian, so the ruins of the great temples themselves seemed to be the remains of ritual structures. The new Masonic iconographers studied the forms of this architecture for any signs, patterns, and dispositions that might inform the development of ritual procedures and higher Masonic grades; even as legend held that the architecture of the Egyptian priests had been deliberately constructed to affect the states of mind of the aspirant by providing, as it were, the stage set for his initiation, might not lodges be planned in turn for their restored rites? Willermoz noted the implications to be drawn from Egyptian practice:

> [The Egyptians] employed all their Emblems and allegories to exercise the intelligence of the Aspirants and prepare them for the development of the mysteries that were their object. Thus the Triangular form of the pyramids, which in Egypt cover the underground vaults destined for initiations, the form and number of the Routes that lead there, all the ceremonies that were there observed, offered to the aspirants a sense of mystery, relating to the principal object of initiation.[63]

The rediscovery of Egypt and, specifically, the reconstructed plans of the temples, thus lent a particularly formal vocabulary and, more important, an architectural plan for the representation of the initiatory route. Thus Quatremère de Quincy, who wrote the earliest scholarly dissertation on Egyptian architecture before Napoleon's expedition stimulated accurate excavation, described the temples of Thebes and Karnak according to his understanding of the mysteries they housed (plate 79):

> It was in the shadows of these underground vaults that the initiations were born, whose secret was the first law. The secret was deified under the name of Harpocrates. . . . Numerous doors, closed by curtains, which added to respect, followed one after the other and led to vestibule after vestibule, allowing sight of the true temple or sanctuary only from afar.[64]

Door after door, the succession of vestibules along an extended axis, these were the formal elements of Pococke's reconstructions; they also emphasized the route as the primary space of ritual.

Lequeu provided the most graphic example of this fashion in a drawing of a lodge, designed after his reading of the three-stage initiation described by Terrasson (plates 80, 81, 82, 83, 84). Exposed in a detailed section, elaborately annotated with quotations from *Séthos* and instructions to the builder, this fantasy lodge shows, from left to right, the deep well-shaft, the three-headed dog (looking for all the world like a Parisian puppy), a great furnace hung with instruments of torture and, adopting the section of the English glass kilns sketched by Bélanger, a deep river and a huge windmill-like wheel, which, after the initiation by fire and water, deposited the aspirant, as if by air, in the Temple of Isis, beneath the statue of the goddess herself. On the far right of the drawing, Lequeu depicted the cups of forgetfulness and of memory described by Terrasson.[65]

THE TEMPLE IN THE GARDEN

In the various occultist and mystical lodges designed or built in the period of Masonic "disintegration" between 1780 and the Revolution, the spatial order of the early lodges was gradually transformed by an increasing emphasis on the initiatory route. These routes, like those traversed by the legendary initiates, were no longer confined to the space of the lodge building itself, but extended out into the landscape. For a second and equally powerful vision of initiatory space had asserted itself in the late seventies as the corollary to the Egyptian temple: that of the *jardin-anglais,* the allegorical representation of the landscape of the Elysian fields.[66] Rousseau had proposed the natural landscape as the site of mankind's regeneration; now the increasingly popular forms of the English landscape garden were adopted as the environmental agents of the initiatory state of mind. What in England had been the poetic conceits of Pope at Twickenham or Henry Hoare at Stourhead, now became invested with emblematic meaning by the Mason-proprietors of the new and fashionable *Elysées.*[67] The emergence of the individual patron and of the individual mystic supported this development; the patron, the resident magician, the secluded estate, all combined to establish the particular forms of the new cultist lodges. The temple built in the garden was an individual asylum, a retreat of the privileged.

The small pavilion built in 1781 by Cagliostro for the banker Sarasin, his patron, on Sarasin's estate near Basel epitomized this trend (plate 85). Constructed in the most remote part of the grounds, the two-story building was specifically conceived as a lodge of "Regeneration" according to the formulae of Cagliostro's so-called Egyptian rites, invented some five years before.[68] Here an aspirant would be confined for forty days, undergoing trials and performing ceremonies that recalled those of the occultist *élus-cohens.*[69] On the first floor were the main rooms—the entry, the reception room, and the lodge room; a spiral staircase led to the salon or so-called billiard room and to two small chambers for the aspirant and his hierophant on the second level.

In this way, the lodge was invested with the quality of garden *fabrique,* and as such it readily entered the general vocabulary of landscape gardening in such gardens as the Désert de Retz and the Parc Monceau, and certainly in the garden built for the Comte de Bouville, the wealthy Mason who was perhaps the only significant patron of Jean-Jacques Lequeu before the Revolution.[70]

Lequeu's Temple of Silence, built around 1786 on the count's estate near Portenort, was the private lodge par excellence (plate 86; for two other Lequeu Temples, see plates 87 and 88). Both dwelling and quasi-Masonic lodge, it demonstrated the extent to which the celebration of Masonic rites had been individualized. The iconography was clear: a figure of Harpocrates, god of silence, in the pediment, an owl of night over the doorway, and occultist turtles in the metopes. Within this personal lodge a complex sequence of spaces led from the entrance through to the final gallery, serviced at points by trapdoors and underground passages.[71] At Retz, the eccentric Racine de Monville engaged the architect François Barbier to build a ruined column, perhaps referring to the "incomplete" Temple, as a house at the center of a garden elaborately furnished with emblematic *fabriques.*

Similarly, the *fabriques* designed by Brongniart for the gardens of the Marquis de Montesquiou at Maupertuis may well have marked stages along a kind of ritualistic route through the *jardin-anglais,* called by Montesquiou "Elysée." The garden itself was approached through a subterranean grotto beneath a huge stone pyramid (a "descent into the underworld") (plate 89), while in the park, among other "follies," sat a rustic temple beside a small spring dedicated to "the Eternal" and a round tower dedicated to the arts (plate 90). The quasi-Masonic nature of these pavilions is confirmed by others that were planned by Ledoux but never executed for the same client—notably, the spherical house of the agricultural guards and the ideal village of Maupertuis, with its curious half-Doric, half-pyramidal temple in the center.[72]

William Beckford, the English mystic, gives us further evidence of Ledoux's Masonic affiliations in his description of another esoteric lodge of the 1780s (plate 91).[73] This lodge, which Beckford claimed to have visited in 1784, in Ledoux's company, resembled those depicted in contemporary accounts of the sect called the Eveillés; according to Beckford, it was situated some distance from Paris in the midst of a deserted garden, surrounded by endless alleyways of woodpiles.[74] The entrance to the structure was in the largest of these pyramids; one passed through a sequence of chambers, each markedly different from the other. These seem to have depicted a kind of "history of civilization" in architecture, from the initial "primitive hut" to a "barnish hall," medieval and gloomy, then to a small, rustic, eighteenth-century cottage overlooking a sunlit garden, then to a cubical anteroom, and, finally, to the great salon itself, with a coved ceiling richly painted in mythological subjects. In the center stood a giant laver, filled with liquid; in front of the fireplace sat an ancient and "grim-visaged" man. The visions presented to him in the surface of the evidently "mesmeric" fluid filled Beckford with horror; he was even more disturbed by the sight of the final chapel, lit by a single ray of light, in which a clearly unorthodox service was being held.

As Beckford described it, the route from the primitive forms of the charcoal burners' piles to the final chapel of revelation was the predominant spatial form. The celebration of brotherhood had returned to its religious patrimony, readopting the forms of ascetic mysticism. Ledoux, who claimed to Beckford that he had designed at least the main salon and stairs of this lodge, was evidently an adept in the mysteries of the sect.

Beckford's tale seems to have taken its place within a fully developed romanticism in which the edges of fantasy and reality were blurred. The spaces of the lodge were calculated to influence the state of mind of the neophyte. Beckford's story might indeed form an indistinguishable part of his own novel *Vathek,* an Oriental, mystical romance first published in French two years after Beckford's visit.[75] Beckford himself was willing to believe that Ledoux, in his role as guide, was indeed master of some occult magic. Even had the entire tale been fabricated, a product of Beckford's wayward and fantastic imagination, the discourse that joined the author to the architect, object of his speculation, would have been the same; for it was in the very nature of the cults themselves to merge the facts of everyday life with their mystical extensions into feeling and sensibility. The idea of an aesthetic of sensation was first and foremost tied to the creation of a trompe l'oeil for the feelings. Few members believed wholeheartedly in the mysteries, yet few were prepared to deny the possibility of witnessing the unseeable; here the boundaries between stage effects and their apparent reality, between the artifice that stimulated and the sense that recognized, remained unclear. The essence of the eighteenth-century associational experience lay in this moment when everyday life and a utopian vision were confused in a form of lived utopia enacted in the festival and the banquet.[76] That the forms of this existence were translated into the domains of literary and, especially, of architectural utopias during the 1780s was simply a logical extension of the conditions of sociability.

Between 1780 and 1802, Ledoux was to develop a galaxy of such utopian associational forms; his Ideal City of Chaux, projected as an extension of the real saltworks of Chaux, may be read in this context as an entire city of lodges.[77] Groups of families, groups of charcoal-burners, groups of woodcutters, philosophers, and barrelmakers, lived around their common hearths, common tables, and common meeting spaces. There were lodges of trades, of relations, of crafts, of social functions of all kinds; there were ritualistic temples where youths were inducted into the mysteries of sensuality, with elaborate processionals developed along phallic-shaped routes. There were, finally, symbolic public lodges of virtue, peace, memory, and union. "Union," he stated, introducing the most purely Masonic of all the ideal lodges, "is the source of happiness; believe me, do not disdain this honorable institution." In his prospectus to the unfinished work, Ledoux spoke of buildings for "gatherings of brothers" and "gatherings of friends":[78] "also you will see," he noted slyly, "that my city contains houses for Brotherhoods."[79]

In this way, the forms developed for the associational lives of bourgeois brotherhoods were raised as ideals, to be dispensed by the beneficence of the architect—the "delegate of the Creator," as Ledoux called him—to cure the ills of all mankind.[80] The Masonic *institutions of happiness,* called by the Masons *asyles du bonheur,* gradually were transformed from voluntary societies into the architectural bonds of instrumental reform. By the time of the Revolution, men of goodwill were speaking of hospitals and prisons as *asyles forcés.*[81]

Ledoux had completed the construction of his wall of toll booths for the "benefit" of the population of Paris, and the period of articulated confinement had begun. When the idea of an architecture of sociability was again pressed into service to make a utopia, in Fourier's model of "associational architecture," social utopianism had been turned inside out to become utopian socialism. It was symptomatic of the powerful image of sociability projected by the Freemasons of the eighteenth century that Fourier's prototypical form of social habitat, the Phalanstère, developed on behalf of the working classes of the nineteenth century by a concerned bourgeois, finally adopted the order as its model. The Freemasonic order, wrote Fourier in 1808, "is a diamond that we disdain without knowing its value." As one of a number of autonomous and isolated corporations developed before the Revolution, it was a small paradigm of association that could be generalized; it was even a means toward social reform.[82]

ASYLUMS OF LIBERTINAGE

DE SADE, FOURIER, LEQUEU

Libertinage . . . is the practice of yielding to the instinct that carries us to the pleasures of the senses; it does not respect mores, but it does not pretend to defy them: it is without delicacy and justifies its choices only by its inconstancy; it holds the middle line between voluptuousness and debauchery.

D. Diderot, "Libertinage," *Encyclopédie.* [1]

THE RATIONAL WORLD of institutional reform imagined by the philosophes and technocrats of the Enlightenment was, during the last years of the eighteenth century, subjected to radical criticism by a number of writers and artists who objected not so much to the general idea of a new social order brought about by architecture, but to the specific nature of that proposed by the Encyclopedists and their followers. Imprisoned by the State, as was the Marquis de Sade; confined by poverty and psychological alienation, as was Fourier; or passed over for promotion and opportunity by a revolution that had seemed to offer hope, as was Lequeu, they all in some way emerged as the self-proclaimed victims of rationalism, of the implacable bourgeois philosophy of confinement and cure, sociability and happiness. Deprived of institutional means of expression, their protest was itself confined to private texts, often unpublished or, if published, suppressed. Their schemes for social liberation and their programs for architectural language were without issue, at least in their proposed forms; their elaborate blueprints for alternative societies and means of expression remained symptoms rather than sources of change.

Conceived and realized on the level of the text, however, the apparent content of the critical utopianism of de Sade, Fourier, and Lequeu—its pornography, social programming, and iconography—was less determining than its linguistic form, which in each case took the methods of reason and enlightenment to their logical and ultimately "mad" conclusions. In the writings of de Sade and Fourier, objects, activities, and functions were listed and classified as exhaustively as in a program for a hospital; in the annotated drawings of Lequeu, attributes, orders, motifs, and styles were catalogued and represented as in a botanical encyclopedia. In this exercise, of course, all three were entirely dependent on existing language for their material; their method lay in its transformation by calculated procedures of cutting, recombining, and neologism. As Roland Barthes suggested, in the case of de Sade and Fourier the result was a literary enterprise perversely divorced from its avowed social aims; an attempted social mimesis was defeated by the form of the text itself.[2] Thus de Sade's "eroticism" emerged as "boredom," flattened by endless lists and the repetition of words and phrases, while his fantasies of dismemberment bore equally on writing as on the body. Fourier's passionate dreams of social harmony were disguised beneath a fanatical care for the coupling of words and the invention of new ones. Lequeu's meticulous drawings represented less buildings to be built than an internal exploration of a purely graphic discourse. In searching for oppositions, these radical hermits often simply achieved reversals. The new "building types" of de Sade and Fourier were in this way assembled out of the fragments of existing forms—the monastery, castle, palace, theater, Masonic lodge, hospital, prison, and passage. The "language" of Lequeu was a bricolage of ready-made signs.

THE INVENTION OF LIBERTY

> I know enough about architecture and I have sufficiently studied all the beauties of this art in Italy, where I spent all my time with people of this profession, to decide if an idea is beautiful or not.
>
> Marquis de Sade, 1782.[3]

De Sade took a decidedly professional interest in the architecture of prisons, hospitals, and asylums.[4] He was, after all, an expert witness: first imprisoned for less than a month at the age of twenty-three in the royal keep of Vincennes, he subsequently spent more than twenty-five years in the prisons and hospitals of the Old Regime, the Revolution, and the Empire. He thus had an intimate knowledge of the administrative and environmental conditions in Vincennes, in the Bastille, and, later, in the hospital of Charenton, as well as in numerous temporary prisons during the Terror. It was, therefore, entirely appropriate that he was employed, in the brief period of his liberty between 1789 and 1794, as a member of the commission established by the Convention to oversee the hospices and hospitals of Paris. In this position he assiduously gathered information, visited institutions, and proposed reforms; his *mémoires* were entered into the reports of the commission and many of his recommendations were accepted. His public statements were reformist; castigating the procedures and buildings of the monarchy, he nevertheless argued for reconstruction rather than destruction, offering the works of Chamousset as containing excellent views on the administration of hospices.[5]

De Sade did not undertake this work as revolutionary commissioner entirely in bad faith; his dedication to the nature of imprisonment coincided precisely with his primary interests in the theory and practice of libertinage. Indeed, as the site of his writing after 1777, the space of the prison not only served to convert practice into theory; it also offered itself as the paradigm for the space of libertinage. Absolute liberty, free from interference, demanded the security afforded to all prisoners held in complete isolation; the libertine, to act as if beyond all constraints of law and morality, required an impenetrable and total solitude, the thick walls of a *cachot*.

De Sade first reflected on this coincidence between imprisonment and liberty while traveling in Italy. On a visit to the Roman catacombs in 1775 he noted, "These impenetrable underground caverns would be very secure retreats for crime if the monks in the house built above them had some interest in committing it."[6] The theme of the monastic retreat as the privileged locus of the libertine society, with the underground cell as its center, was to be repeated in numerous literary permutations, from *Les cent vingt jours de Sodome* to *Justine*. De Sade described each of his fictional seraglios with care. Its plan, sequence of spaces, furnishings, special equipment, and, above all, its defenses against the outer world, were developed in such detail as to suggest, correctly, that the reader was being presented less with a realistic background to the action than with a specification for building. De Sade supplied precise measurements where any ambiguities in section or layout might occur, or where specific lines of sight were necessary to the mechanics of pleasure or retreat.

In *Justine,* the design of the infamous convent of Sainte-Marie-des-Bois, which the abbot and his fellow monks had transformed into a haven for every cruel, licentious desire, rivaled the meticulous contrivance of Bentham's Panopticon in its architecture of surveillance (plate 92).[7] As described by the unfortunate Justine, it was approachable only by a single, underground route, which was entered through a disguised door in the sacristy of an otherwise normal chapel; this tunnel wound through the earth, dipped beneath the outer moat of the establishment, and ended in the cellars of the house of pleasure. This house, a prison for the victims, an asylum of liberty for the monks, stood at the center of an elaborate system of hedges, six impenetrable ramparts of thorn bushes three feet thick and sixty feet high, separated by *allées* six feet wide; an equally thick wall and the outer moat completed the ramparts. The seraglio itself was invisible from outside these walls, only fifty feet high and covered with a flat lead roof overgrown with grass, trees, and shrubs—the Sadian *toit-jardin.* Inside, the cellars contained a grand salon surrounded by twelve smaller rooms, six for wine storage and six *cachots* for punishing unwilling victims; above, a dining room was at the center of twelve more rooms, six highly decorated and luxurious rooms furnished with instruments of torture for the monks' pleasures, two for food storage, one kitchen, one office, and two mysterious rooms that no one but the monks might enter; above these, in the mezzanine, were rooms for the monks, their servants, and the jailers; in the top story were two dormitories for the male and female victims, barred and guarded.

The entire building, set within concentric circles of *allées,* might have been designed by Ledoux—we recognize the quasi-Palladian plan of the central pavilion and the emphasis on circles within circles—but it was also a self-conscious transformation of the post-Platonic utopia—the city of Atlantis surrounded by its labyrinth—and the Renaissance ideal city. The old world here contrasted with the new to reinforce the power of the transgressive oppositions, as the church and convent acted as convenient disguises for the modern *machine à plaisir* built under cover nearby.

De Sade was equally specific about the arrangement of the Château de Silling, retreat of the four libertine brothers-in-crime in *Les cent vingt jours.*[8] Following de Sade's program of morality, this asylum was even more inaccessible than the convent of Saint-Marie.

> A retreat, lost and solitary, as if silence, distance, and tranquillity were the powerful vehicles of libertinage and as if everything that, by virtue of these qualities, impresses a religious terror on the senses must evidently lend a greater degree of attraction to lechery.[9]

De Sade evoked the principles of the natural sublime, never far from his aesthetics, to heighten the terror of the victims and, thereby, the pleasure of their torturers. Indeed, the journey to the château reads like a late-eighteenth-century travel account in which the danger and inhospitality of the terrain adds to the beauty of savage nature (plate 93). Thus the band of companions and its chosen subjects travel first to Basel, cross the Rhine, and plunge deep into the Black Forest; the road narrows to the point where they are forced to leave their carriages and follow a difficult track, impassable without a guide. At the boundaries of the property, they encounter an "evil hamlet of charcoal-burners and foresters," almost all of whom are thieves and smugglers instructed to let no others pass. A five-hour climb up a mountain almost as high as Saint Bernard is followed by the dangerous crossing of a narrow wooden bridge over a precipice a thousand feet deep. The summit of the mountain conceals a flat plain surrounded by rocks whose peaks touch the clouds; at the center of this stands the château, surrounded by a thirty-foot-high wall, a moat filled with water, a second defensive wall, and an archers' gallery. Inside, the libertines have remodeled the rooms of the old castle to their specifications, forming what de Sade called a veritable school of morals, the culmination of which is reached beneath a stone in the steps of the chapel altar, down a spiral stair of three hundred steps to the mountain's bowels: a kind of "vaulted *cachot,* closed by three iron doors, in which is found everything that the cruelest arts and most refined barbarity can invent." In such a cell, the libertine might finally feel at ease:

> He was at home; he was outside France, in a secure country, at the heart of an inhospitable forest, in a retreat in this forest that, by means of the measures taken, only the birds of the sky might breach; he was at the very heart of the entrails of the earth.[10]

Nostalgia for his own isolated asylum in the family seat of La Coste was here mingled with the replication of the moats, walls, posterns, triple doors, locks, and bars that enclosed de Sade in Vincennes and the Bastille, now with their roles reversed to bar the "criminals" and "monsters" who condemned him to jail from the realm of liberty.

THE DISTRIBUTION OF PLEASURES

> On one page of your notebook of characters, draw the plan of the château, apartment by apartment, and in the blank space that you leave beside it, put down the kinds of things you would have done in such and such a room.
>
> De Sade, Note to himself while writing *Les cent vingt jours,* 1788.[11]

Central to the activities of any brotherhood was the careful distribution of spaces by function; not only were the ritual relations among different tasks and pastimes cemented by such a sequence, but the distinction and specificity of the institution would be confirmed by the type-form that resulted. Thus de Sade made it clear that the libertines of *Les cent vingt jours* were not simply occupying an old castle, acting out some Gothic romance within medieval walls. The Château de Silling was "not as it once was, but in the still more perfect state of embellishment and solitude accomplished by the care of the four friends," a château, that is, completely rebuilt for its new purposes.

Indeed, de Sade's description revealed a plan and section entirely rationalist and nonmedieval in character; some alterations of detail would transform it into Fourier's Phalanstère, which it anticipated by some twenty years. As in the Phalanstère, the dwellings were arranged around a great courtyard and connected by a vast gallery that stretched from one to the other of the two major wings at first-floor level. In one wing, in sequence, were the "public" functions of the establishment: the dining room, salon, assembly room, and bedrooms for the use of the libertines; in the opposite wing were the apartments of the libertines, their servants, and victims of both sexes. Again leading to comparisons with Fourier's later model, these main rooms were raised above service, storage, and kitchen facilities, with vertical hoists between kitchen and dining rooms. Each space was carefully proportioned to its needs; larger rooms led to smaller ones, horizontally and vertically; their intricate interconnection mimicked the equally complicated division of activities among the actors during the day. Analogies of festivals, religious ceremonies, battlefield tactics, and theatrical performances served, as in Fourier's narratives, to give shape to otherwise incomprehensible actions and to reinforce their transgressive character. Thus the entire community mocked the Freemasonic brotherhoods with which de Sade was familiar (he was later to invent the "Society of Friends of Crime" with statutes and secret lodge as an elaborate anti-Masonic jest).[12] He turned the chapel, "that small Christian temple," into a wardrobe to store costumes specially designed for the stimulation and exercise of lechery. The assembly room, the active nucleus of the whole building, transformed the notion of theatricality from public performance to private emulation. This "theater of lubricity" was fittingly the most complex of de Sade's inventions; a combination of Masonic lodge, theater, and bedroom, it was constructed, as Barthes observes, as a space in which language and its correlates reigned supreme.

The overall form of the assembly room was, like an antique amphitheater, semicircular (plates 94–95); but in place of ramped seating for the audience, de Sade arranged four niches, one for each of the libertines, mirrored and furnished with large couches.[13] Behind each of these niches a door led into a private wardrobe or secret *cabinet*. The reclining libertines looked out from their niches toward a throne set against the rear wall of the space and raised on four steps. This was for the "historian" or narrator, whose daily accounts of past experiences in a long life of prostitution were the object of close attention by the libertines, who were then fired to emulate them with the help of their victims, ranged in front of the throne on the steps. On either side of the throne stood two freestanding columns, like those at the entrance to the Masonic lodge, but here hung with every conceivable instrument of torture in the eventuality that, as was often the case, some victim required stern correction. De Sade was explicit in drawing on the theatrical analogy; placed on the throne, he noted, the historian "finds herself situated as an actor in a theater, and the listeners, seated in the niches, are as in an amphitheater." The reciprocal relations between storyteller and audience, the mimesis of the narratives enacted by the libertines, turning audience into actors, has been characterized by Barthes as constituting a machine for the production of texts, the one leading to the other across the space of the theater.[14]

Architecturally, however, de Sade had designed a complex reversal of the political connotations of theatricality in the late eighteenth century. Whereas, for example, in the Saline de Chaux, Ledoux had placed the subject-audience in direct geometrical relationship to the supreme power at center stage, the theater of Silling regained for the elite brotherhood the privileged loges of courtly theaters; it was their stories that were told on stage and their subjects that were displayed at the front of the scene. Power, absolute in isolation and freedom, indulged in self-reciprocity and fed on its own image. De Sade, the last of the classical libertines, was not preoccupied with the surveillance of large numbers of potentially recalcitrant members of society; the problems of prison guards, factory owners, and hospital administrators were not his. He was concerned solely with the potentials of unfettered freedom wielded by men without scruples who recognized no law. The codes they obeyed, and equally brutally transgressed, were erected by choice to maintain "order" and thereby prolong pleasure. The architecture that framed these codes was solipsistic and without rhetoric; unlike the ruined prisons of Piranesi, the prisons of de Sade literally "said nothing." They had, after all, nothing to do but listen.

This absence of rhetoric, perhaps the most pervasive characteristic of the functional architecture of de Sade, is exemplified by comparison with the projects conceived by Ledoux for similarly licentious programs. The Maison de plaisir, designed by Ledoux for Paris around 1787, and his later scheme for an Oikéma, or brothel, for the Ideal City of Chaux, took the ritualistic architecture of the late eighteenth century, quasi-Masonic in origin, to a logical conclusion, spatially and figuratively.[15] Overtly, both institutions resembled classical temples, with colonnaded porticoes and apsidal sanctuaries; both were organized along a "route of pleasure" that had obvious initiatory connotations. The Maison de plaisir for Paris was planned to stand on the summit of the hill of Montmartre; its circular precinct, in fact, encompassed the entire hill, which was reshaped accordingly as a giant cylinder (plates 96–97). Those to whom the temple was dedicated were to traverse a route from the foot of the mount, up winding stairs to the doors of a public lodge and from there, like neophytes to Masonry, through anterooms and grand salons to the final destination, the oval sanctuary at the center of the composition.

Ledoux predicated a similar route in the Oikéma, an institution envisaged to protect the ideal society from the impetuous desires of its youth (plate 98). According to the quasi-Ovidian description provided by Ledoux, it was to offer every means of satiating such disturbing sensations, returning its initiates to the world outside spent and remoralized, ready to enter into marriage. The central spine of the temple was in fact organized like a long gallery of delights, with bedrooms lining it on either side and a second-story balcony for display and coquetry; the conclusion of this route was again a circular room. All these practical distributions were accomplished within a simple geometrical schema; no baroque attributes on the outside revealed the libertine nature of the institution. In both cases, however, Ledoux retained an overriding figurative dimension that was secret—known only to the architect because hidden in the plan—but that nevertheless spoke of its function. Both plans were witty plays on an obviously phallic theme.

On the other hand, when de Sade drew up his plan for what Gilbert Lély has called "an establishment of lechery," an institution conceived, during his detention at Charenton after the Revolution, as part of a scheme to provide thirty-seven licensed houses of prostitution for Paris, all such rhetoric disappeared (plates 99–100).[16] The plan, sketched and annotated by de Sade himself, might have been that of any prison by Baltard or hospital by Gilbert. He divided a vast, square compound, surrounded by double walls and an *allée*, into three equal precincts, one for offices and entrance, one for the women's dwellings and a central prison pavilion, and one with six radially organized blocks for specific activities ranging from sodomy and flagellation to murder. On the other side of the wall, a cemetery would receive the bodies of the victims. Nothing in the plan indicated that this institution was to be any different from those being built to police the modern city in the first quarter of the nineteenth century. Emptied of its imaginary "content," de Sade's establishment might well have served as an efficient hospital. A "pure" functionalism, stripped of aspirations toward communication, had developed a series of interchangeable parts that would, as Hugo noted in 1832, assume a kind of rhetorical status of their own as "institutional," but which had no need to be differentiated for a specific visual character from building type to building type.

HARMONIOUS ARCHITECTURE

> You ask me if I have found Paris to my liking? Without doubt; it is magnificent, and I who am not easily astonished have been amazed to see the Palais-Royal. The first time you see it, you think you are entering a fairy palace. There you find everything you could desire: spectacles, magnificent buildings, promenades, fashions. . . . And the boulevards, where you see grottoes of rocks, small houses, all very pretty. . . . You could say that this is the most agreeable landscape there is.
>
> C. Fourier to his mother, January 1790.[17]

Fourier's interest in architecture was aroused early in his life and confirmed by his visits to Paris in 1790; it remained to the end of his life a dominant force in the designing of his society of harmony. Born in Besançon, not only the site of Ledoux's new theater but also close to the Saline de Chaux, Fourier found in Ledoux—and especially in the individual *hôtels* of the 1780s—his paradigmatic architect. A long footnote in his *Traité de l'association* of 1822 mourned the demolition of the Hôtel Thélusson; a similar note described his initial inspiration for a theory of social architecture, which occurred in front of two small *hôtels particuliers* (plate 101):

> It was thirty-three years ago when, walking for the first time in the boulevards of Paris, their aspect suggested to me the idea of a unitary architecture whose rules I immediately determined. I owe this invention principally to the Boulevard des Invalides, and especially to two small hotels set between the streets of Acacias and N. Plumet.[18]

He was in the habit of recording the plans of these dwellings on small postcards, delineating their plans and elevations, carefully marking their dimensions as if to determine the proportional rules of their composition.[19] In elaborate equations he laboriously investigated the mathematics of architectural harmony. It was said of Fourier that, like Le Corbusier a century later, he carried a marked cane to measure a particularly pleasing facade on his walks; he recorded his findings on his postcards, yellowed and polished from the inside of his pockets, as evidence of the slow steps civilization was taking toward harmony (plate 102).

In 1796, Fourier took the developing pattern of the western quarters of Paris, with their freestanding neo-Palladian hotels set in miniature *jardins anglais,* as the prototype of a garden city, which he suggested to the city of Bordeaux as a replacement for the demolished Château Trompette.[20] He felt it was a necessary stage in the transition from the disaggregated architecture of the present to the unitary architecture of what he called "association" or the final, sociable stage of man's progress. On the one hand, the "code of architecture" he outlined, which was expanded and published by his followers as the utopian socialist solution for *cités ouvrières,* was purely numerical, concerned with the areas of plot and building, height and spacing of constructions, width of roads and proportion of green spaces—all of which became the commonplaces of the garden city movement; on the other hand, he attacked the increasing monotony of modern cities from Mannheim to Philadelphia, arguing for variety and embellishment to be written into building regulations. Fourier called for the modeling of facades, bas-reliefs, and exterior frescoes; filled with flowers, variegated shrubs, and gentle cats, like his own apartment, his utopia was above all to be pretty.

But for Fourier, architecture was more than a means of beautifying an existing state; if, as he wrote to an anxious follower in 1819, there could be no testing of his schemes without buildings, it was because buildings themselves generated social order.

> You tell me that your society would like to see simple Association tested in Franche-Comté. That cannot be, because its foundation requires buildings. There is no way of using the buildings of Civilization.[21]

Each epoch not only crystallized its social forms in specific building types; those types sustained and developed society as well. Architectural surroundings, like the natural environment, acted on individuals and groups through sensations of sight, smell, touch, and hearing; these sensations were the very springs of social activity. Thus a building calculated to the desired social order would automatically help bring that order into existence. "I am going to prove," Fourier wrote in one of his notebooks, "that a man of taste could, on his own, perfect a general architecture to metamorphose civilization."[22]

Some time between 1803 and 1805, Fourier completed his first scheme of what such a transformational architecture might look like, part of a series of unpublished *mémoires* designed to prepare the world for the imminent coming of harmony and to list its universal benefits. In 1808, he published a longer version of the prospectus to these papers, omitting the details of the new architecture (no doubt as a precaution against the theft of his original ideas), under the title *Théorie des quatre mouvements;* it was this work that established Fourier's reputation as harmlessly mad, relegating him to oblivion for nearly twenty years.[23]

His manuscript plan for what he first called a Tourbillon and, later, a Phalanstère is, however, evidence that the outlines of the well-known prototype for utopian socialist communities were established much earlier than is generally recognized, more a product of the late Enlightenment and its institutional utopias than of the positivist socialisms of the July Monarchy.[24] Indeed, its forms, as depicted in Fourier's own drawings, the most complete of which certainly dates from before 1815, tie the Tourbillon, which in its final, simplified version looks no more interesting than a three-courtyard palace with a recessed center block, to an older tradition of hermetic memory systems and ideal cities. Generated in the quasi-Masonic and mystical circles of Lyons, in whose journal, edited by the romantic visionary Ballanche, Fourier published his first articles, the Tourbillon emerges as a composite of revived number magic and rationalist distribution. Its overall plan is determined not by the classical palace type but by the traditional circle of many ideal cities; its subdivisions are calculated according to a gridded "map" of the universe (plates 103–105). Its internal arrangements, however, are as functional as any by de Sade.

In Fourier's "historical" account of the necessary advance of society, the building of this Tourbillon was to be preceded by another type, an intermediary between the garden city and the final, all-consuming collective. This "halfway house" to harmony was briefly described in the *Théorie des quatre mouvements,* where it is called the Tribustère or home of the associated tribe: "To establish this tribe," Fourier wrote, "one must plan a building suitable to house a hundred people, unequal in fortune."[25] Apartments of different rents, meeting rooms for public activities, and a complex of dining facilities characterize this communitarian dwelling, the genetic antecedent of universal association. It was still a primarily urban type; Fourier envisaged the redevelopment of the city, block by block, on this model. Its most important architectural innovation, however, with regard to the future form of the Tourbillon, was the system of covered galleries that allowed passage between blocks.

> The palaces or manors of the neighboring tribes should communicate between themselves by means of covered galleries, sheltered from the injuries of the air, in such a way that the relations of pleasure or business are guaranteed against the inclemency of the seasons, from which one suffers at every step in Civilization.[26]

These arcades, modeled on those of the Palais-Royal, which in 1790 Fourier had described as a "fairy palace," would be heated and ventilated to encourage social intercourse of every kind, day and night, in Fourier's festive city.

The Tourbillon was a far more complex structure than the Tribustère (plate 106). It was designed to house over twelve hundred persons of every sex (Fourier envisaged at least three), talent, wealth, age, and proclivity. For such a group, the buildings had to be prepared well in advance; two years of work would precede the assembly of the communitarians, who then, enclosed by spaces calculated for their every need, pleasure, and whim, would quite naturally attain a state of social harmony. As opposed to his followers, who loved to turn fantasy into strict doctrine, Fourier intended that each commune assume different characteristics, both from the nature of the different sites and from necessary rivalry among groups. His descriptions, therefore, are typical and exemplary, advising only as to the most essential, structural, and functional conditions.

The Tourbillon was to be a vast building, with some five to six thousand windows, many wings, peristyles, porticoes, domes, and apartments; at first it could be built out of wood and brick, but it was to be rebuilt in stone as soon as possible; the apartments, carefully graduated in size and position according to the wealth of their inmates, would be arranged around a large number of halls for council meetings, balls, and dining. Educational facilities would include a museum, a theater, and an observatory with a beacon and a telegraph for communicating with neighboring Tourbillons. Outhouses, stables, storehouses, and workshops would be distributed around the main building. At the corners of its spreading territory would be four kiosks, or cafes, for the recreation of its agricultural workers.

Two architectural elements stand out as central to the incessant activity of the house: the gallery and the Exchange. Fourier gave the gallery, retained from the Tribustère, a primary constructive role, for the society as for the building; running above the ground-floor service arcades, continuously around every courtyard and along every wing, the gallery would unite, in plan and section, all the functions of the commune. Taking up the full three stories to the roof, it would literally combine all the apartments that looked down into it, as well as become a huge, enclosed glass winter-garden for promenades and dances. By its means, every conceivable social relationship would be possible, and many illnesses—colds, inflammations, fevers—prevented.

> In the height of winter, one can go to the ball, to the theater, to the workshops, in colored shoes, in light clothes, without feeling the cold or the humidity, however distant the place one wishes to visit, because the enclosed communication extends outside the palace, by glazed corridors, by tunnels, by galleries crossing at the height of the first story; all these passages lead to the workshops, the stables, the caravanserai, the opera, etc.[27]

If, as Roland Barthes has observed, the foremost concern of this immense institution was communication, then the gallery was its literal agent and principal symbol. It of course facilitated more than the simple coming and going of busy Phalanstèriens; the warmth and security, exoticism, and almost stifling excitement of this giant greenhouse would also stimulate its inhabitants to experiment endlessly in the forms of sensual pleasure, thus bringing about the Nouveau monde amoureux, which, delineated by Fourier with a mathematical systematics that would have amazed even de Sade, was the true mark of harmony.[28]

At the heart of this organism, regulating its work and play, was the Exchange; if the gallery was, as in Fourier's dialectics, the harmonious counterpart of those civilized centers of commercial and sexual barter later to be described by Balzac in *Les Illusions perdues,* the Exchange was to be the precise opposite of the new Bourse of Paris. Here not money but pleasure was marketed. The exchange was the central point of all the intricate and balanced arrangements between individuals and groups, the hall in which each bargained for its next day's tasks, affirmed the menus and entertainments for banquets, and confirmed the amorous relations among the sexes.

> Each day, around midday, all the groups scattered in the countryside and in the workshops return to the palace to assist in the Exchange and then to dine. . . . The interval between 12:00 and 1:00 is employed in negotiations, and as every individual, rich and poor, man, woman, and child, likes to vote on the meeting of the groups of which he is a member, each goes as often as possible to the Exchange, which is very entertaining for its many intrigues.[29]

With the volume of negotiations approaching 1,000 each day, the Exchange would rival those of Paris and London; certainly a new method of negotiation would be needed to accomplish all this trading in an hour or so. Fourier carefully described the manipulations of the various officers—the brokers of harmony—and their different responsibilities. From their activities a plan is derived.

The great hall of the Exchange is surrounded by a score of offices for the officiating negotiators, each of whom organizes the affairs of fifty groups. In front of each is an enclosure formed of balustrades, behind which sit the officers of each group or sect engaged in the negotiations. From there, in the main body of the hall, they confer with the public, who walk around, passing each office in turn. At times the officers dispatch their acolytes to run messages to other offices. At the center of the hall is the office of the Director of the Exchange. The officers bargain in complete silence by means of an elaborate code of signals; the banners of each group are carried to the office where the negotiation is taking place, while acolytes standing on a gallery above each office exchange signals over the banner to convey the variations of trading to the public. A new language of signaling is created, similar to marine signals and the telegraph.[30]

Fourier's method is clear: he transforms the evil practices of civilization into their opposites, solely by means of language. He uses the tricks of neologism and dialectics to redefine the old codes. The magic wand of linguistic play, disguised by an apparently exhaustive systematization, turns every bad into a good. As in writing, so in architecture: the gallery and the Exchange are only two of the well-known spatial elements to which he gives beneficent connotations—the theater, the opera, the factory sheds (with their elegant "rustic orders" as perfect as the council chambers decorated in Corinthian)—are all turned inside out and upside down. Fourier fondly dreamed that eventually everything would become its opposite: the lion would change into a giant pussycat and the seas overflow with lemonade. His was, of course, a fundamentally *petit bourgeois* utopia dreamed in a single, cramped, rented room, crowded with flowerpots and cats, by a *célibataire* who suffered from incessant indigestion and ailments, real and imaginary, who returned to his room at noon each day to await the coming of a prince who would finally build his scheme and appoint him head of Harmony.[31]

When, at the end of his life, a few of his followers actually raised the financing for an initial experiment, he rejected them with bitterness, jealous and scornful of the architect they hired who could not begin to imagine the delights of a truly harmonious architecture, preoccupied as he was with closet doors.[32] It is paradoxical that the most concrete legacy of Fourier's fantasy was the gallery-street, a leitmotiv of every communitarian building from the Familistère of Godin to the Immeubles-villas of Le Corbusier, and one of the bleakest attributes of modern social housing.

In trying to translate textual utopia into architectural schema, de Sade and Fourier not only shared the positive predilections of nineteenth-century institution builders, but prefigured them in intention and method to an uncanny degree. Fourier, like de Sade, attempted to achieve an absolute transparency between an activity and a space; he accomplished, naturally enough, only a transparency between the account of an activity and the (narrated) assumed properties of a space; which is to say that no real "translation" actually occurred, merely the transformation of both society and architecture into a text. This "fiction of functionalism" paralleled that other fiction emerging so strongly within the profession of architecture during the same period: the fiction of the program, a text based on the assumption that a systematic listing of functions and requirements would ensure an appropriate social response, thereby denying architecture either an autonomous life of forms or a cultural history of signification.

THE ARCHITECTURAL UNDERGROUND

> As for Lequeu-Architect, having lost the goods of his ancestors by the Revolutionary laws and by other misfortunes that resulted from them, he is consoled by his wisdom in the paddock of the old Grand Cerf. There he cultivates the arts and the sciences he loves: wearied with the world (deceiver) and its extravagances, he searches in the solitary paths of the Fields for the secrets of nature, the course of the stars and the heavens (whose God-given inventions are great); but above all, he applies himself to cultivate his soul in virtue (pure), that gift of God. Jean-Jacques Lequeu is the son of Jean-Jacques François Lequeu, Draftsman and contractor of joinery, but issue of the noble family of Gaillon: having the same right of burial in the Tomb of his Ancestors.
>
> J.-J. Lequeu, 1815.[33]

If Jean-Jacques Lequeu had been a writer, he doubtlessly would be considered a member of the literary underground characterized so evocatively by the historian Robert Darnton, the crowd of Grub Street journalists, hacks, and would-be philosophes who fed the commercial presses of the late Old Regime and the Revolution with translations, political broadsheets, gossip, popular treatises, and pornography.[34] Among the architects of the late eighteenth century, Lequeu had no recognized place: the son of a provincial carpenter, without formal training in architecture or prior education, he had no access to salons or patrons; nor was he considered fit company by architects either of his generation or older.[35] He belonged definitively and throughout his life to what might be called the low life of architecture. But, like his literary compeers, he had a skill that earned him a modest living until retirement, in his case draftsmanship. Of all the draftsmen of his generation whose work survives, Lequeu was indeed among the very best. His drawing teacher in Rouen, the academic painter Jean-Baptiste Descamps, attested to Lequeu's merit while Lequeu was still a student: "he has won the best prizes in our establishment; he draws well and has genius and conducts himself well."[36] It was as a draftsman that he found his first job in Paris, and successive bureaucratic administrations after 1800 used his talent to their advantage. The evidence of the hundreds of drawings he deposited in the Bibliothèque Royale in 1825, just before his death, shows his technical excellence in drawing and rendering to be little short of perfect.[37]

Like many inhabitants of Grub Street, Lequeu felt that his "genius" deserved more than it received in the way of patronage, encouragement, and public recognition. From the beginning to the end he thought of himself as an architect, worthy to stand beside the best and most celebrated architects of the age. His failure to persuade others of this had two results: the exaggerated paranoia and sense of persecution that ran through his writings and designs, many of which seem to have been conceived in revenge against more successful peers; and the suite of architectural fantasies that, to spite the same peers and to record his genius for posterity, he drew in his spare time between 1789 and 1825—drawings that leave the interpreter both silent in front of their meticulous accuracy, with all the beauty of anatomical and natural historical representations, and disturbed by their obsessive qualities.

Undoubtedly, Lequeu was something of a neurotic. He deserves and has received psychoanalytical interpretation, of the order Ernst Kris has afforded another late-eighteenth-century physiognomist, the sculptor Messerschmidt.[38] Certainly, as Jacques Guillerme has pointed out in his incisive essays on Lequeu, "the plastic expression of the obsessions of a neuropath is a feast for the aesthetician and the psychiatrist."[39] In Lequeu's case it was not only his pervasive narcissism and physiognomical fixations that qualify him as neurotic, psychotic, or schizophrenic, but also his preoccupation with names and smells (both perfumed and putrified), and with purification by air, water, and fire (as well as by soap), and his self-attested professional paranoia and resentment.[40] His symptoms indeed uncannily match those of Messerschmidt, who similarly spent much of his later life sculpting images of his face in every conceivable distortion, whose resentment of the "academic gang" that persecuted him professionally was well known, whose study of physiognomy included self-portraits as a lecher, as afflicted with constipation, as responding to strong smells, as beaked like a bird, or as Priapus, and whose castration anxiety (Kris affirmed) was such as to lead him to embody the feminine in each of his portraits.[41] On the evidence of his writings and drawings, Jean-Jacques Lequeu suffered from a similar ailment, which the psychoanalyst summed up tersely as "a psychosis with predominating paranoid trends, which fits the general picture of schizophrenia."[42] It would seem that such a personality, whether driven mad by circumstances or not, might well have provoked many of the insults he imagined.

Certainly, he was neither literate nor *mondain;* his letters and drafts of letters as well as the fragments of text that cover his drawings are written with the autodidact's sense of spelling and reference, while his numerous self-portraits simply confirm the mediocre appearance verified by his official description as five feet tall with blue eyes, a large mouth, a prominent, straight nose, and chestnut hair.[43] His life reveals no event outside his own thoughts that would have supported his ideas of grandeur; from Descamps' free drawing school in Rouen, he entered the office of Soufflot in Paris, where he worked under the older architect's nephew, François Soufflot, who had just returned from Rome.[44] Here Lequeu drew up details for the orders and dome of Sainte Geneviève and, later, for the younger Soufflot's Hôtel de Montholon.[45] The few private commissions he mentions before the Revolution may well be fictitious, for imaginary clients, or developed with more hope than substance. None of them was built, with perhaps the exception of the Maison de Plaisance of the Comte de Bouville, which Krafft later recorded as having reached first-floor level before 1789.[46]

Lequeu submitted a project for the Hôtel de Ville of Rouen in 1786, which led to his reception as *adjoint associé* of the Rouen Académie in the same year, and he drew up a hospital design for Bordeaux in 1788.[47] During the Revolution he acted as head of one of the public workshops in the faubourg Saint Antoine, until their suppression in 1791; he tried to attract attention by a number of "revolutionary" designs—a triumphal gate, "Gate of Paris" or "People's Arch" (1793); a "monument to the glory of a number of illustrious men"; a "monument for the exercise of the people's sovereignty" (1793). And in 1793, he ended by taking employment in the Bureau du cadastre as draftsman, first class. His salary of 2,000 francs a year was reduced to 1,800 francs; in 1797, he was working for the Commission of Public Works; in 1802, he moved back to the cartography department of the Office of the Interior as a geographical draftsman, working on a new plan of Paris; he then worked in the bureau of statistics as a *premier dessinateur géographe;* his task was studying and delineating, cartographically, "the limits of vine cultivation, the limits of countries where French is spoken, their customs, commerce, etc., all the surfaces of the earth that act as pastures for all the different beasts, and also the smallest and largest farms"; finally, he moved, still in the Interior Department, to the drawing office of the Bâtiments civils, again registering the plans and lot lines of Paris buildings.[48] On August 12, 1815, he received a letter from the secretary of the Minister of the Interior, the historian de Barante, informing him that, "forced by the need for strict economy in the expenses of the minister," he was to be retired, but with a pension, a result of the new government's desire "to proceed with justice."[49]

From 1786, Lequeu had lived in the same apartment, in the cul-de-sac called the Passage du Grand-Cerf, off the rue St. Denis, quarreling incessantly with the landlord through letters complaining of the noisy tenants on the fifth floor, who night and day dropped bottles on the floor, making his ceiling tremble and his windows shake: "you remember that my room is a study where I work, that people in my house should not hear an uproar . . . since I myself have nothing in common with that sort of worker."[50] In this retreat, "the *enclos* of the old Grand Cerf," Lequeu prepared the final drawings for his *Architecture civile,* never to be published, and advertised vainly for customers who would buy his work, publicizing in little paragraphs, as if talking to his only audience, his illnesses and his final change of address to 8, rue des Deux-Portes St. Sauver, "the first stair to the left." He warns the public that he is "little known in the confines of this courtyard."[51] A year later, he took all his drawings, the manuscript copies of pamphlets on subjects ranging from "A Natural Method Applied to the Elementary Principles of Drawing Leading to the Graphic Perfecting of the Outline of the Head" to a "Letter on Washing, Which One Could Call the Soaping of Paris, Addressed to Mothers of a Family," and deposited them in the Bibliothèque royale. Nothing more was heard of him.[52]

On one level, such a career is noteworthy only for its typicality. If he had been more of a writer, Lequeu would have been known for the kind of scurrilous and libelous tracts common in politics and pornography, which thrived on rumor and innuendo. Indeed, outlines for several *libelles* of the kind common before the Revolution are to be found in his papers. During the Revolution, he copied, no doubt for future reference, a placard posted on the Louvre attacking the reputations of the academic and royalist "party" headed by "the septuagenarian Boullée, a kind of madman in architecture," and comprising the "fawning Ledoux," "the phlegmatic charlatan Le Roy," and others accused of rigging the jury appointed by the Convention to benefit their students.[53] Lequeu's explanatory note, written in the same tone, implied, indeed, that he might well have been the author, who had signed himself "le juste." Similarly, on the back of his letter of retirement, Lequeu drafted a long and bitter exposé of architects and employees of the ministry whose "crimes" had gone unreported and unpunished; he called the exposé, "Long note on the Shady Dealings *(tripotages)* in the *Bâtiments civils.*" It gave details of payoffs to architects and experts, from Rondelet ("arrogant") and Bruyère to Gisors ("stonecutter"). Other notes, couched in the form of dramatic dialogues, indict Brongniart (for stealing the decorations of Ledoux's Hôtel de Montmorency during the period of Revolutionary vandalism), Bélanger (for his prerevolutionary mistresses, present debauches, and financial dealings), Chalgrin ("jealous and dishonest"), Cellérier ("passionate for the beautiful singers of the Opera, who prostituted himself"), and others.[54]

But his chief mode of attack, lacking literary skills, was through design, by means of which he succeeded in satirizing and throwing into question all the sacred conventions of the academy and fashion alike. At the same time, he revealed his peculiar graphic version of an unending warfare against authority in every form, from other architects and writers of books to political factions and ministerial employers; but by the same token, these antagonistic drawings were also the instruments by which he might appeal to the very patronage of those he attacked. The project for the "Porte de Parisis," exhibited in the Salle de Liberté in 1792 and then later inscribed with irony, "Drawn in order to save me from the guillotine," was only the most celebrated example of a continuous practice in which Lequeu would apparently affirm a position only to deny or neutralize it by a superscription either ironic or resentful. He subjected classicism, traditional iconography, institutional programs, religions, exotic styles, Freemasonic practices, and individuals to this relentless play, which took the form of a kind of architectural dismemberment, a physiognomy *en abime*, which mocked all the verities of the theory of character even as it established, however unwittingly, the subversive codes of a libertine architecture.

THE LIBERTINE GAZE

> Lechery is in the eyes, in the countenance, in the gesture, and in the discourse.
>
> D. Diderot, "Lubrique, Lubricité," *Encyclopédie*.[55]

It has often been pointed out that Lequeu was as interested in his own face as he was in the spelling of his name. Philippe Duboy has listed nineteen variants of his signature; some simple differences in abbreviation or appellation, others obvious puns on "*la queue*" (tail) or "*le queux*" (cook).[56] There are as many self-portraits, some drawn as such, others hidden, others more subtly implied or transformed. The earliest, dated 1786, is of "Jn. Jacques Le Queu, twenty-nine years old," presented in profile with curled wig, hair drawn back by a ribbon, silk cravat, and top-coat (plate 107); it is the portrait of an upwardly mobile professional, confident at the beginning of a promising career, surmounting an imaginary coat of arms that played on Lequeu's Masonic connections and included a rebus of his name. It appears that it was drawn to celebrate Lequeu's election as an associate member of the Académie de Rouen.[57] The second portrait (plate 108), dated 1792, is of "Jean Jacque Le Queu Jur. Architect."[58] He looks out from an architectural niche, as from the private box of a theater, his head resting on his right arm, elbow propped on a pile of folios bearing the titles of Lequeu's graphic works since 1789. He is dressed in his draftsman's jacket; his hair is short, parted in the middle, and slightly curled at the ends. His face is in studied repose, neither haughty nor submissive, his gaze direct but serious. It is the portrait of a grave man, "one who never laughs," as Diderot might have defined it, certainly the opposite of frivolous; he is resting his reputation on his works, others of which are hidden in the recess below his window, but he has the air of having submitted with difficulty to his fate.[59] The third portrait (plates 109–110), which logically enough carries no date, is that of "J. J. De Queux"; it is represented carved in bas-relief on his tomb, surmounted by two variants of an appropriate iconographic monument, one with all the emblems of Freemasonry that symbolized his *métier* as draftsman, "ornaments of instruments suitable to worldly men and that replace the cross of Christ," the other hidden beneath, on a flap of paper, with a cross marking the resting place of "the author, brother of Jesus; he has carried the cross all his life."[60] The face is again in profile, facing left, and shows Lequeu as if on a classical coin, dignified like a Caesar. It is the portrait of an emperor buried with full honors, his tomb bearing the tears of mourning, a truncated column carrying the motifs of his triumph.

It is clear from these three representations alone that Lequeu had a taste for staging his identities, not only by respelling his name and by substituting the aristocratic "de" for "le," but also by dramatic changes in convention. These conventions are not, however, as straightforward or as readable as they seem at first glance. Each portrait seems to hide as much as it reveals: that of 1786 has no gaze, showing only the projecting profile, as if drawn by Silhouette or Lavater; its apparent confidence is belied by the coat of arms, which hides behind a bar, on which is displayed the rebus "LE" followed by a quail's tail, which represents, of course, "Le-queue"; to this is added a Masonic column and, behind that, a plumb line. The second portrait, which presents a full gaze, not only hides the titles of the folios, but also hides all emotions, in an enigmatic and entirely veiled expression. The third portrait is classical but wavers between monumentalizing a Christian and a Freemason.

The ambiguity of these self-portraits becomes more pronounced in the physiognomical self-portraits, where Lequeu used himself as a model for registering the transformations of the face by different moods and passions. Here Lequeu gave a twist to this common pursuit in self-portraiture, begun by Lavater in the 1770s.[61] Ostensibly, the series of five drawings falls readily into the Lavaterian convention, one also explored, as we have noted, by the sculptor Messerschmidt and by the many artists who contributed to Lavater's own illustrations, including Henry Fuseli.[62] According to his own nomenclature, Lequeu shows himself pouting *(la moue)*, pursing his lower lip *(l'homme à la lippe)*, sticking out his tongue *(Je tire la langue)*, winking *(le borgne grimacier)*, and yawning *(le grand bâilleur)* (plates 111,112,113,114,115, respectively).[63] Each attitude seems to imply a personality, an impression reinforced by the other attributes of the portraits—the hair, headgear, and dress. The pouter has a bandage on his head, rolls his protuberant eyes, and tenses the sinews of his neck; his torso is bare, as in a medical or anatomical view. The pursed-lip face has half-closed eyes, and the hair is covered by a cap institutional in character, tattered and identified by the number "12"; Lequeu is wearing a simple jerkin, open at the neck. The winking face has a closed left eye while the right side of the mouth is drawn in a grimace; its title, "The One-eyed (or shady, suspicious, disreputable) Grimacer," endows this portrait with underworld undertones, while the pointed cap and the scarf wrapped round the neck seem to evoke the garb of a *sans-culotte*. The tongue-sticker is full face, with eyes half closed and closely cropped hair. The yawner, eyes tightly closed, mouth fully open displaying both rows of teeth, hides his bandages under a bowler hat and wears a top coat. A superficial interpretation would find the pouter slightly mad and place him in an asylum; the lip-purser about to break down in childlike tears from disappointment; the tongue-sticker in an attitude of brazen defiance of the world; the winker as a sly but sad revolutionary *gamin;* and the yawner as near breaking point, perhaps with bureaucratic ennui. But these emotional states, measured on the face by line and posture, are what Lavater would have called the mobile and transitory effects of changing moods, as he distinguished between physiognomy proper ("the art of interpreting mental powers") and pathognomy ("the art of interpreting the passions").[64]

Lavater held that each pathognomical state might add to knowledge of a total physiognomy but independently could provide very little of general interest. In these terms, Lequeu's pathognomical portraits would be a measure of his physiognomical nature only if they added up to a coherent characterology.

Again we are in the presence of a staging, a posturing. Consistent in his attempt to trick the viewer, Lequeu turned himself into a model of those varied types that Lavater urged the artist and psychologist to study in hospitals, prisons, and asylums. What Géricault accomplished by visits to institutions, Lequeu simulated in his bedroom. Indeed, he was suspicious of physiognomical wisdom, noting the difficulty of "determining the true combination of passions" on the face because of their infinite number; one should, he concluded, "always examine all appearances with great care so as not to betray or disparage virtue."[65] Here he might have been paraphrasing the article "Physionomie" in the *Encyclopédie,* which warned:

> One must not judge from physiognomy. There are so many traits mingled in the face and bearing of men that it can often confuse, not to mention the accidents that disfigure natural features and prevent the soul from manifesting itself, like smallpox, thinness, etc. One might do better to speculate on the character of men by the pleasure they attach to certain figures that respond to their passions, but one would still be tricked.[66]

The double play of Lequeu's knowing trickery was, on the one hand, to "explore" in an apparently scientific way all the appearances of madness, rage, despair, and pique, as if to ward off the attribution of these emotions to himself, on the other, to reveal his "true" feelings without dissembling them, thus following the path of the confessional. Such a stance allowed Lequeu, in his particular morality, a certain license, which was echoed by the inconsistency of his tomb. Here the deliberate confusion of truth and lie was reinforced by the question raised in the graphic method by which the two designs for the tomb are presented, the crucifix hidden beneath mundanity: is virtue hidden beneath falsity, or is the falsity, as appearance, the real truth? Would Lequeu prefer to have been a man of the world, worthy of his attributes, or a patient and virtuous cross-bearer?

The hidden self-portraits scattered through his drawings better reveal the nature of Lequeu's self-dispensed latitude, what he might, according to his self-imposed morality, permit himself. His unmistakable face peers out from the top of columns, as in the invented "Symbolic Order" (plate 116), and from the heads of statues. He is discovered in amorous engagement in a "Hammock of Love." More significantly, he emerges as Lequeu-*femme,* first in Arethusa's grotto, then in the bed of the wife of "the Beglierbejs de Rumelie," and then again directly in a self-portrait leaning back, dressed in a corsage, unlaced to reveal his full breasts.[67] Here Lequeu's private transvestism, carried to anatomical extremes, is covered once more by a supposed scientific interest, one that caused him to draw detailed studies of his own body as well as those of women, no doubt inhabitants of the same lodging-house, to explore the physiognomies of sexuality before, after, and even during the reproductive act (plate 117). A series of biologically accurate, textbook details of the male and female organs is accompanied by a textual gloss that turns them into pseudo-

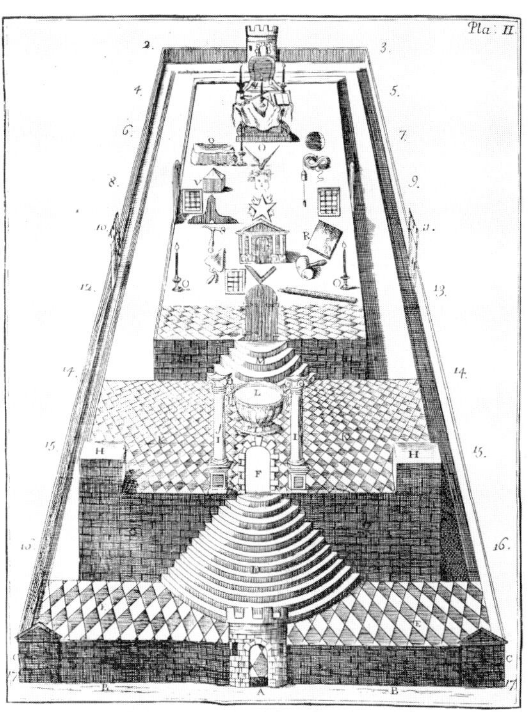

73 Larudan, floor-drawing for the reception of a Companion Mason.

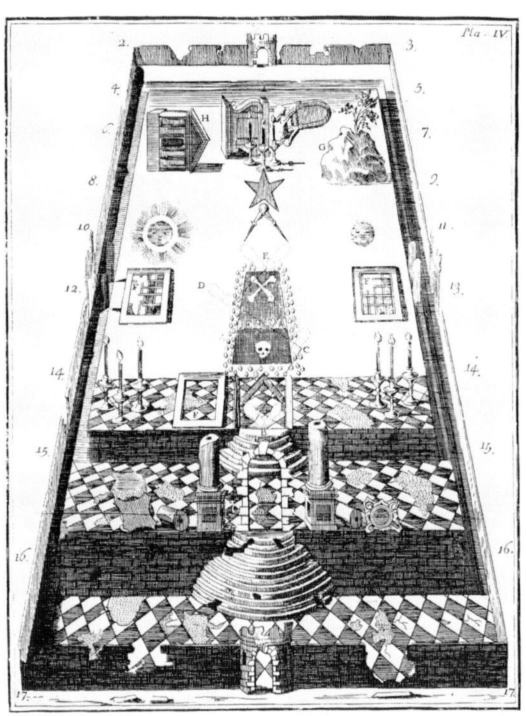

74 Larudan, floor-drawing for the reception of a Master Mason.

76 Anonymous (late 18th-century German), Symbolic Masonic Temple.

75 Charles De Wailly, project for a Masonic lodge, view toward the Orient, 1774.

77 De Wailly, restoration of the Temple of Jerusalem, engraving.

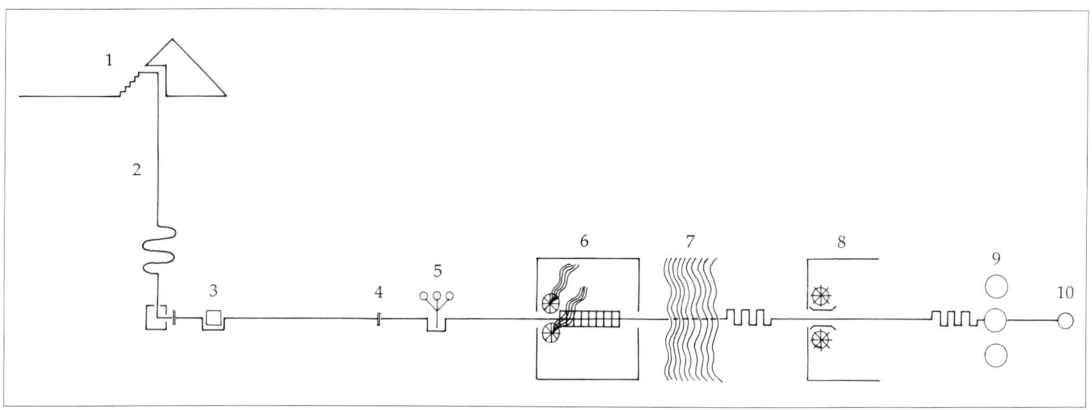

78 Diagram of the journey of Séthos into the Underworld, according to abbé Terrasson, 1731.

1 Great Pyramid; *2* shaft; *3* warning inscription; *4* bronze doors; *5* Cerberus, the three-headed dog; *6* initiation by fire; *7* initiation by water; *8* initiation by air (drawbridge and wheels); *9* statue of Isis; *10* cups of Lethe and of Mnemosyne.

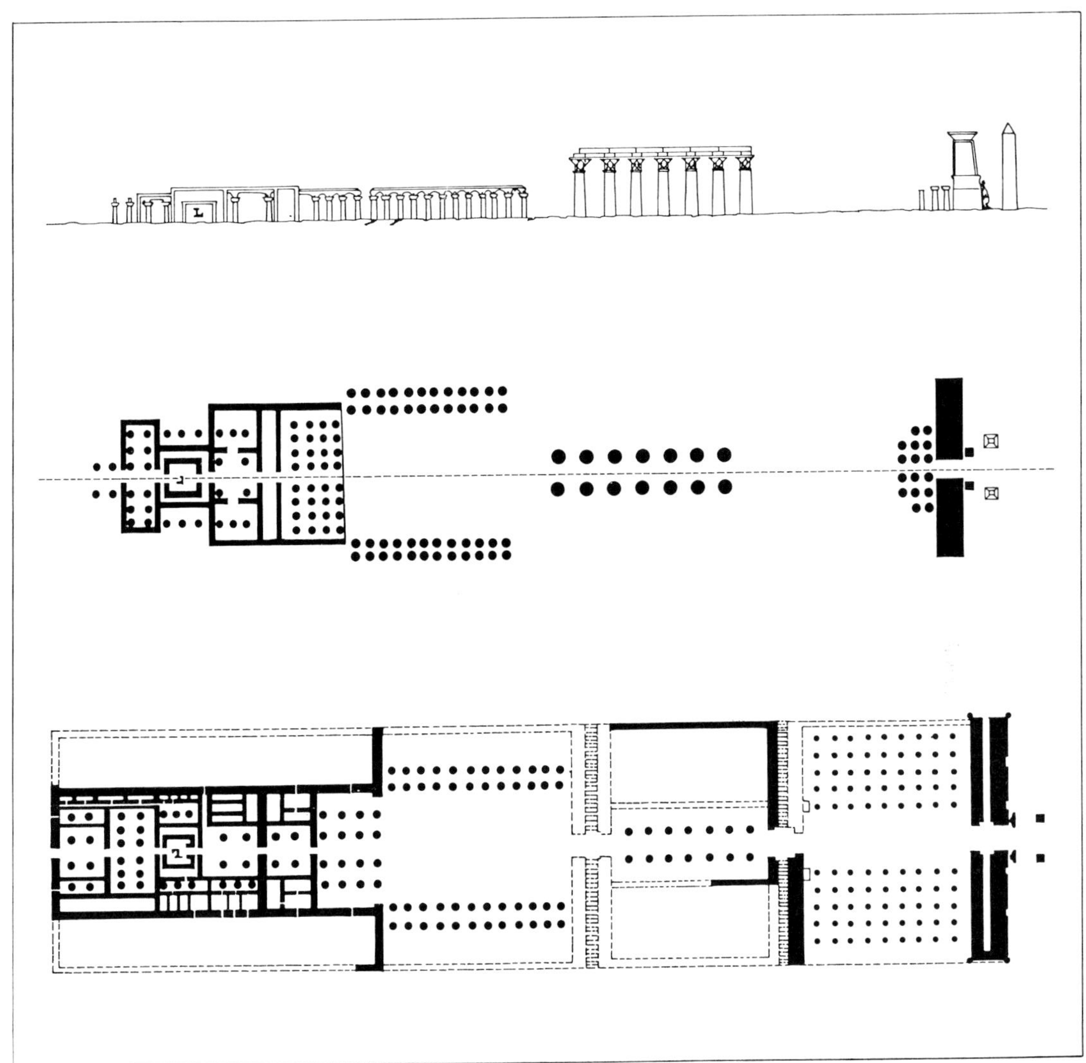

79 Antoine-Chrysostome Quatremère de Quincy, plans of Egyptian temples, after Pococke, 1803.

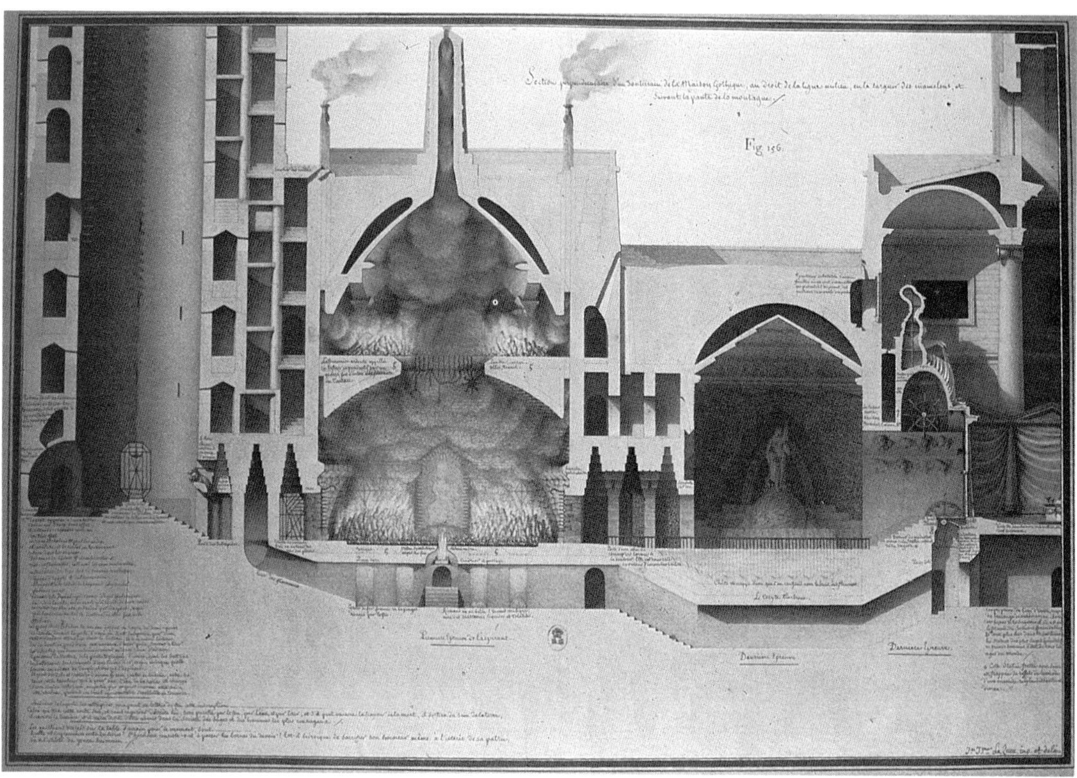

80 Jean-Jacques Lequeu, "The Gothic House," section through the cellars.

81 Lequeu, detail from "The Gothic House," the first stage of initiation, Cerberus.

82 Lequeu, detail from "The Gothic House," the second stage of initiation, by fire.

84 Lequeu, detail from "The Gothic House," the final stage of initiation, by air, and entrance to the Temple of Isis.

83 Lequeu, detail from "The Gothic House," the third stage of initiation, by water.

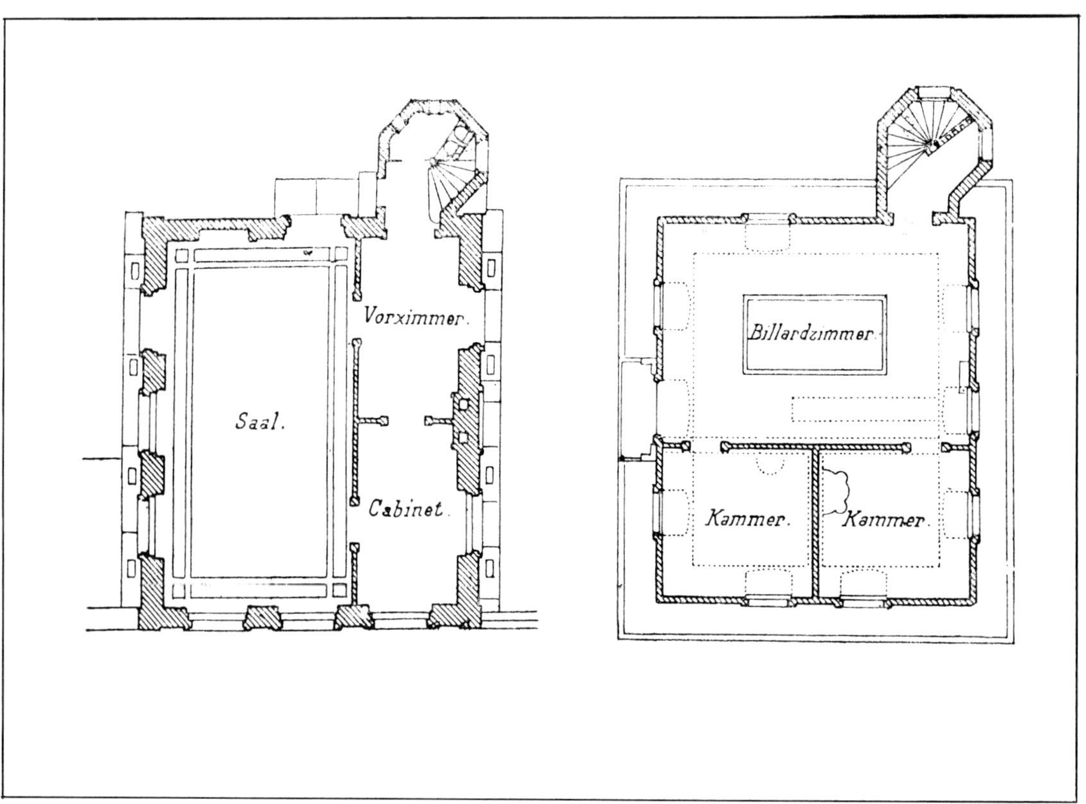

85 Pavilion of Regeneration, built for Cagliostro on the Sarasin estate at Riehen, plan, 1781.

86 Lequeu, Temple of Silence, near Portenort, 1786.

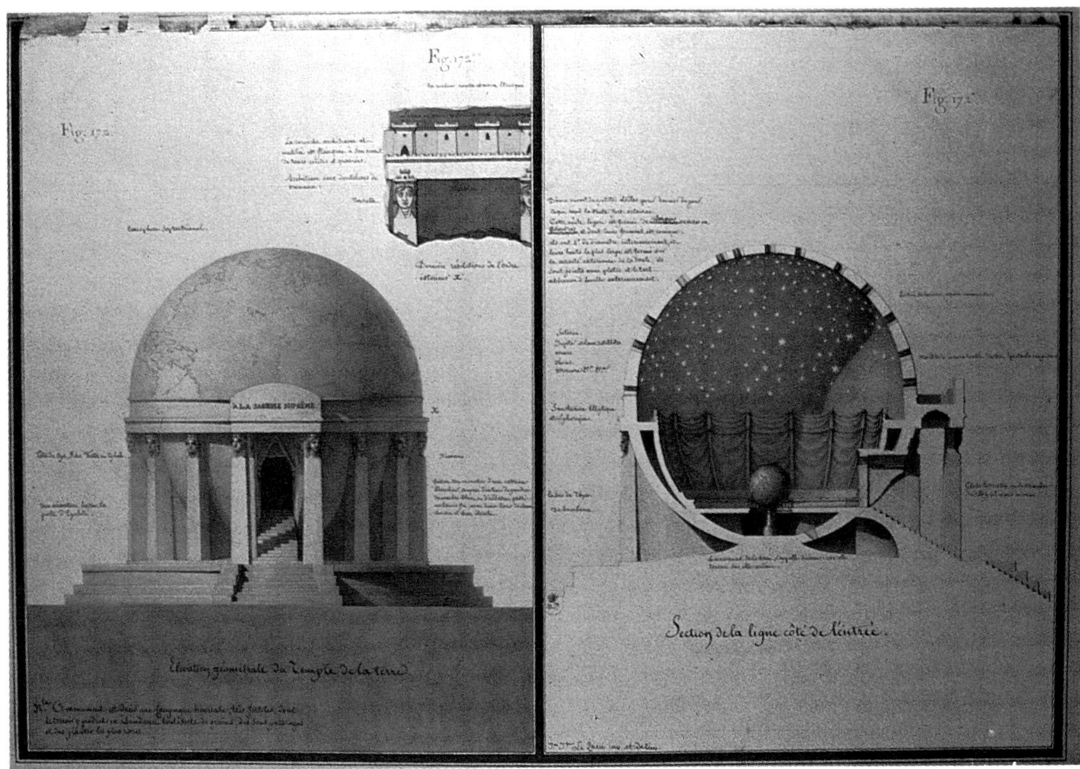

87 Lequeu, Temple of the Earth.

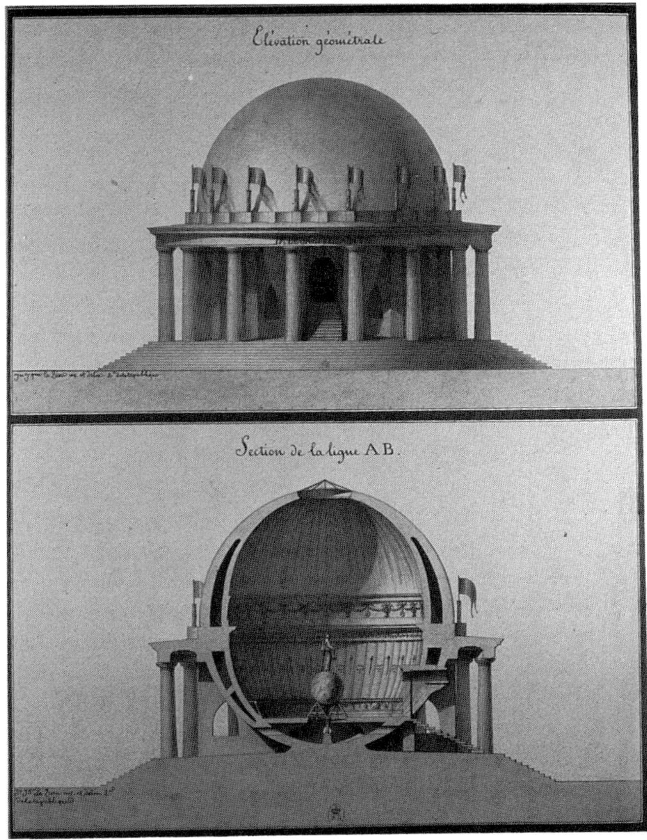

88 Lequeu, Temple to Sacred Equality, 1793.

89 A. L. T. Brongniart, pyramid at Maupertuis, c. 1783.

90 Brongniart, rustic temple in the gardens of Maupertuis.

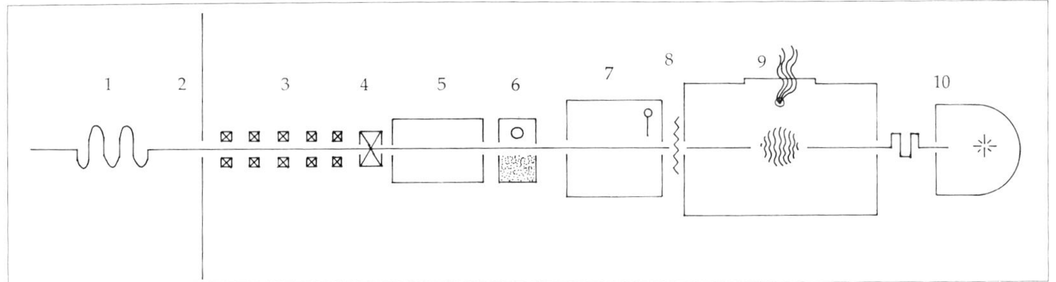

91 Diagram of Ledoux's "Lodge," as described by William Beckford, c. 1784. *1* route from Paris; *2* wall of the estate; *3* wood-piles; *4* pyramidal entrance; *5* "barnish hall"; *6* cottage and garden; *7* antechamber and cockatoo; *8* curtain; *9* main salon, with laver and fire; *10* chapel and tribune.

91a Masonic landscape with temple and pyramid, Frontispiece to Anonymous, *Athenée des Francs-maçons* (Paris, 1808).

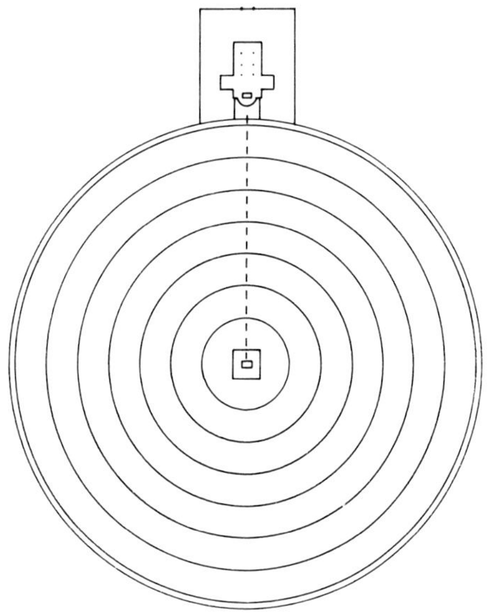

92 Diagram of the plan of Sainte-Marie-des-Bois, as described by the Marquis de Sade in *Justine*.

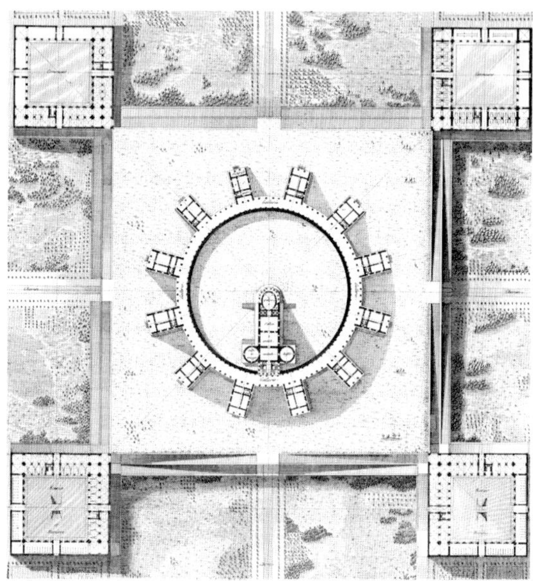

96 Ledoux, Maison de Plaisir, for Montmartre, Paris, plan, c. 1787.

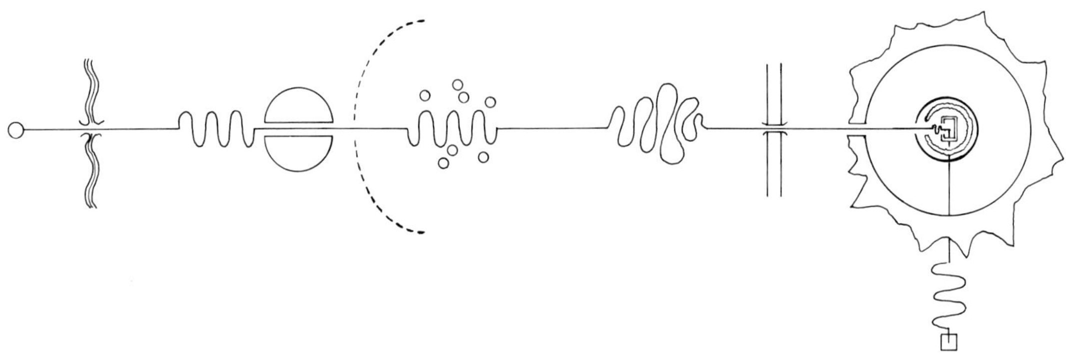

93 Diagram of the route to the Château de Silling, as described by de Sade in *The 120 Days of Sodom*.

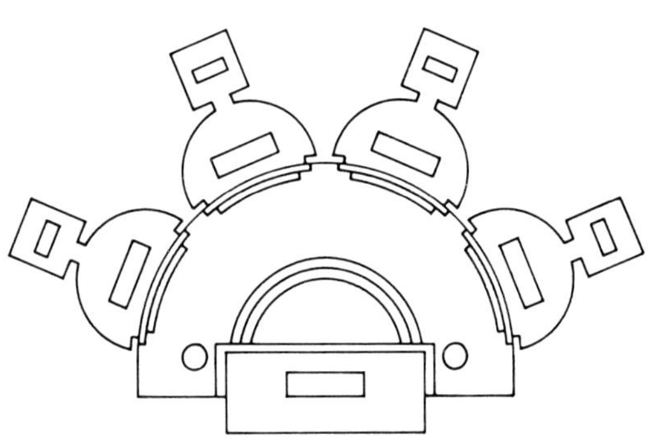

94 Diagram of the plan of the *salon d'assemblée* in the Château de Silling.

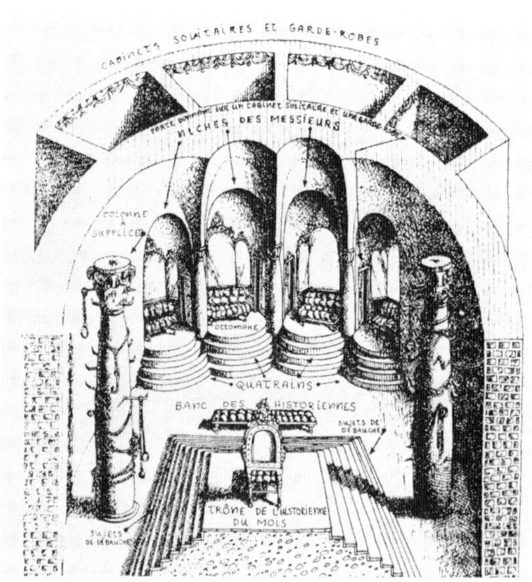

95 Ramon Alejandro, imaginary view of the *salon d'assemblée* in the Château de Silling.

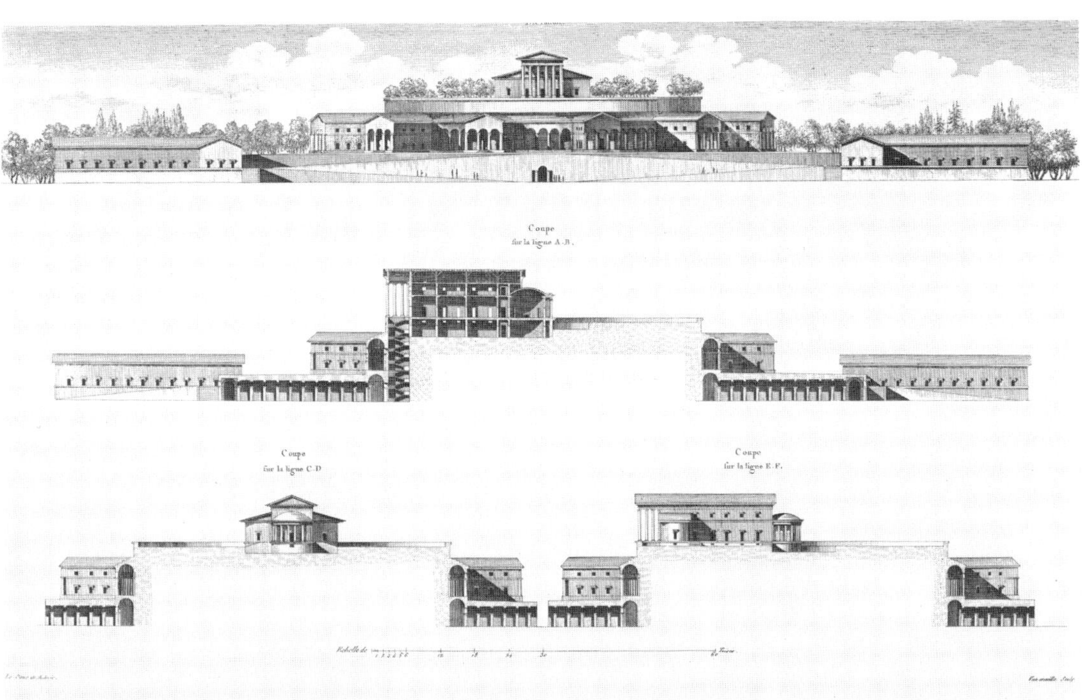

97 Ledoux, Maison de Plaisir, section.

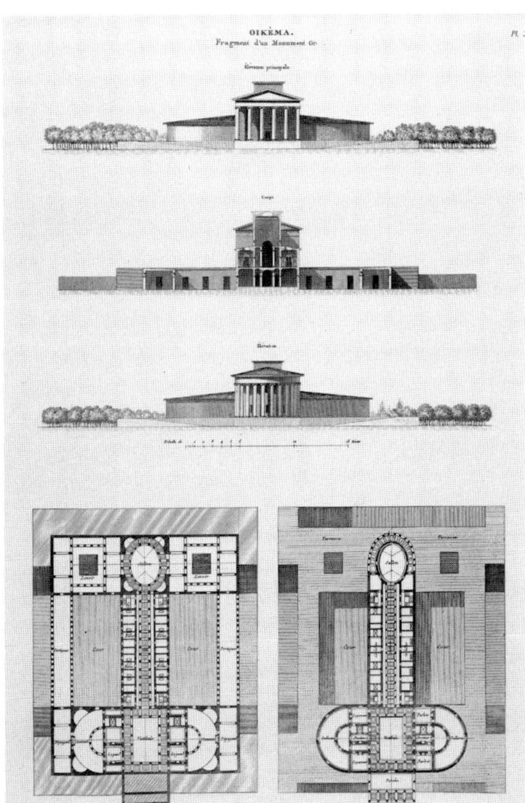

98 Ledoux, Oikéma, project for the Ideal City of Chaux, *from top to bottom:* principal elevation, section, elevation, and plans of first and second floors, c. 1790.

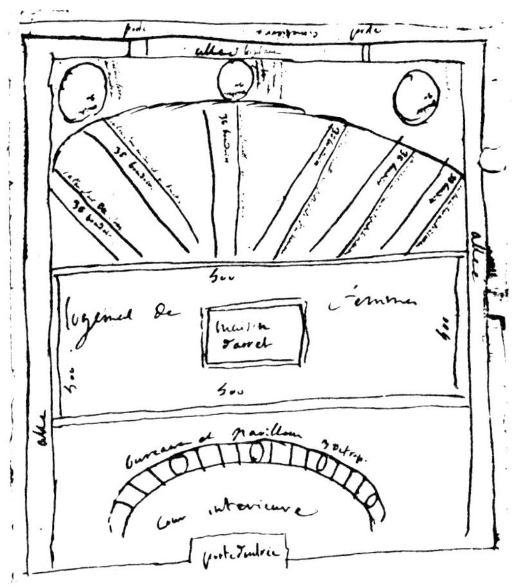

99 De Sade, Institution of Debauchery, for Paris, c. 1805.

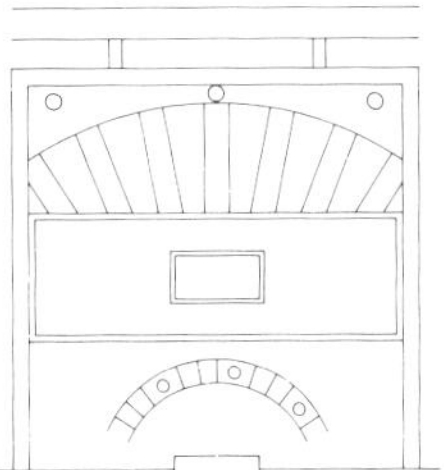

100 Diagrammatic plan of the Institution of Debauchery, from drawing shown in plate 99.

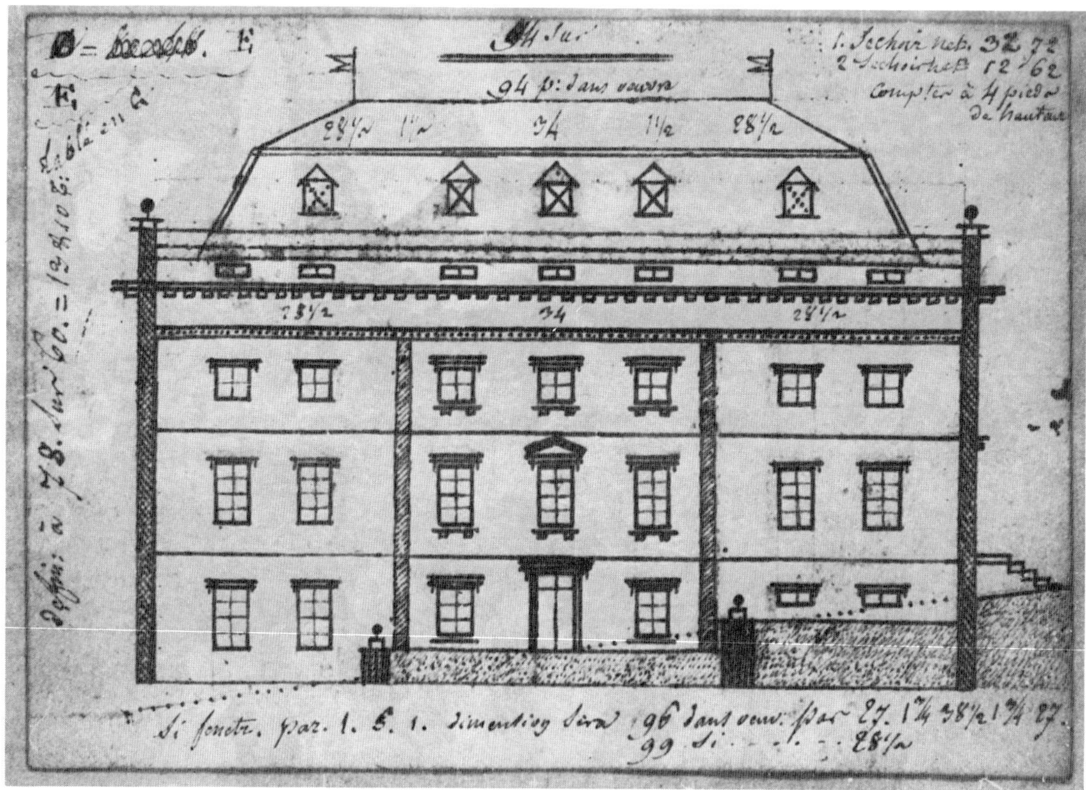

101 Charles Fourier, drawing of a *hôtel particulier*, c. 1800.

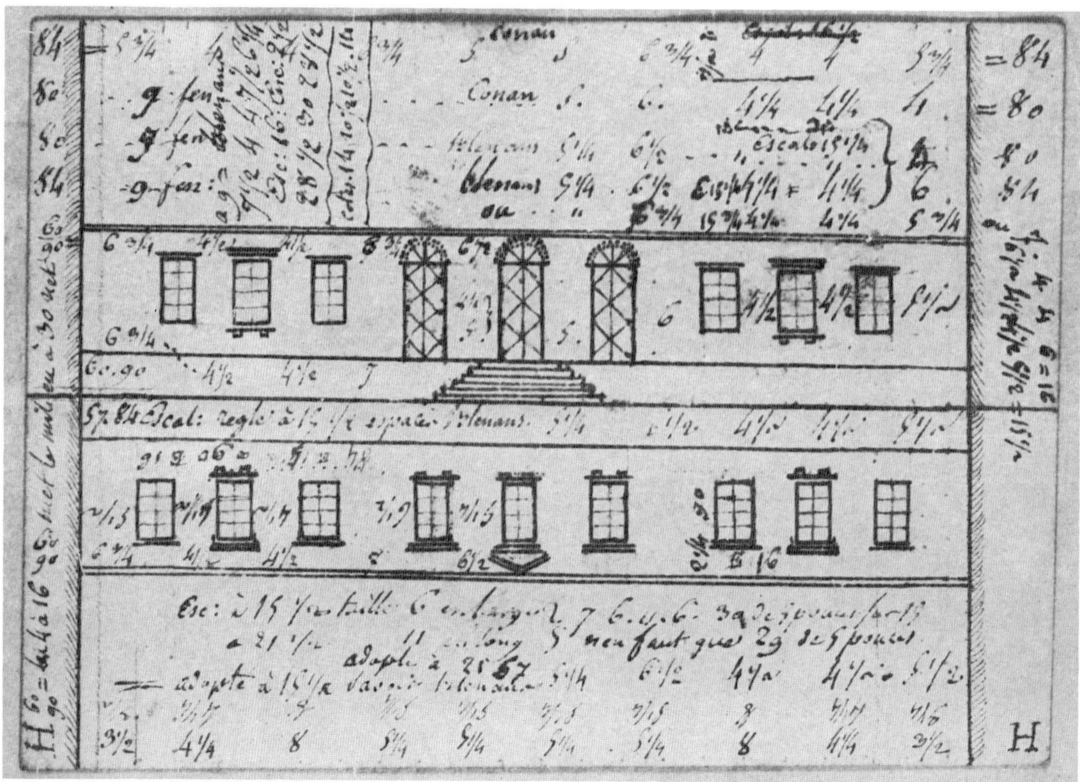

102 Fourier, drawing of a facade, with proportional measurements, c. 1800.

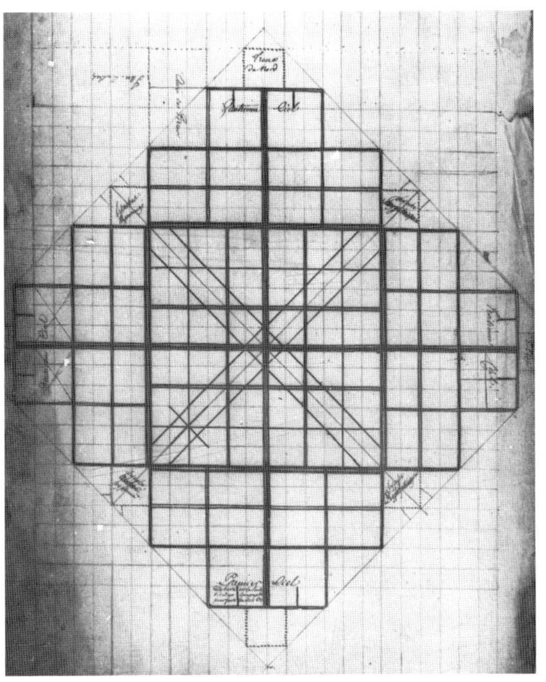

103 Fourier, cosmological grid, before 1808.

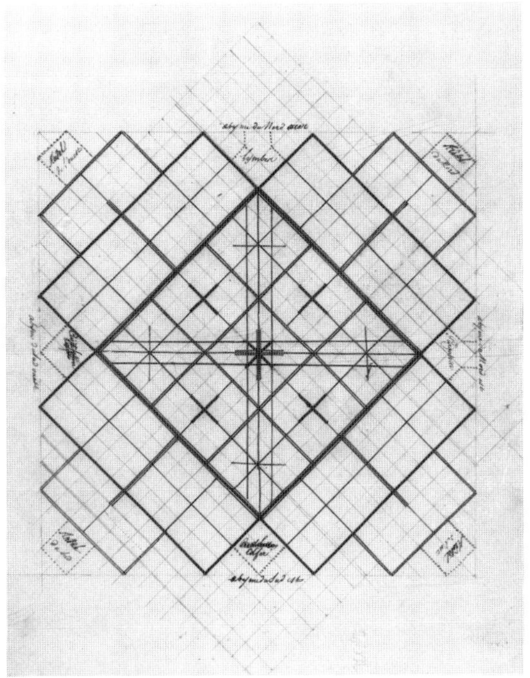

104 Fourier, cosmological grid.

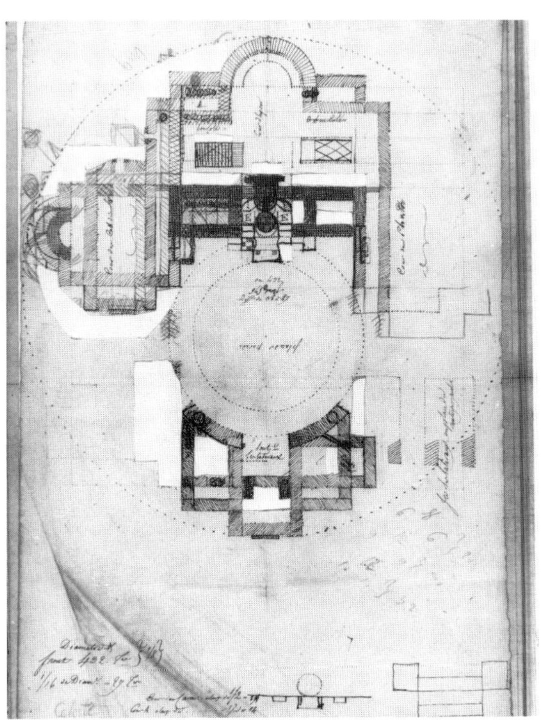

105 Fourier, plan of the Tourbillon or Phalanstery, before 1814.

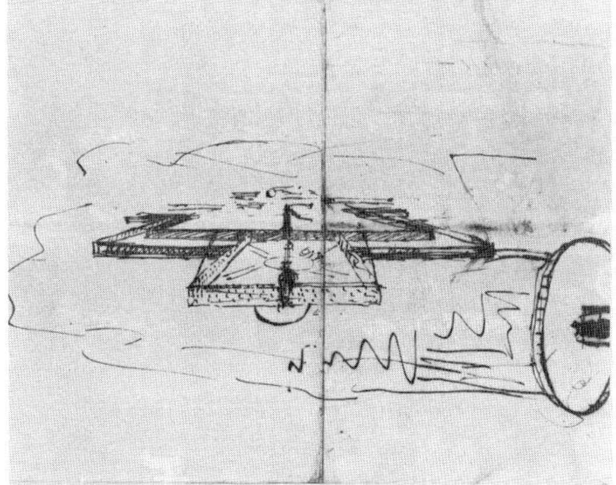

106 Fourier, aerial perspective of the Phalanstery, c. 1814.

107 Lequeu, self-portrait, 1786.

108 Lequeu, self-portrait, Frontispiece to his *Architecture civile*.

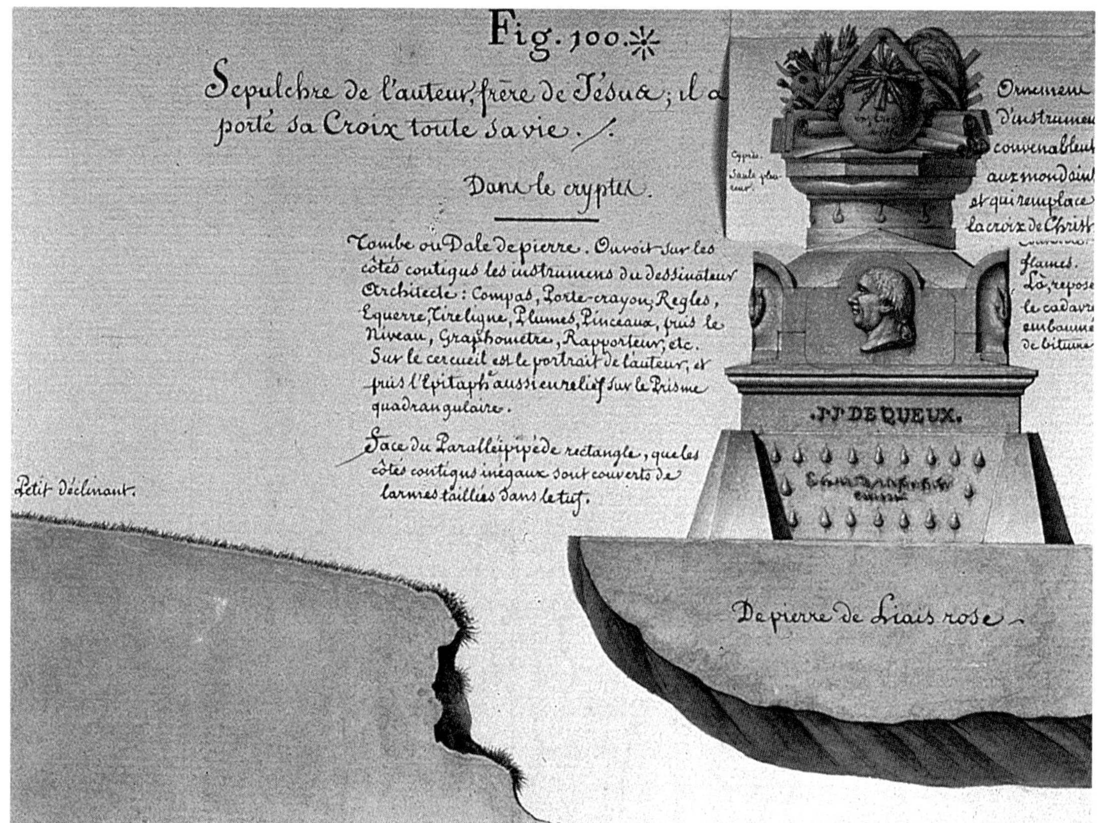

109 Lequeu, self-portrait for tomb, with architectural attributes.

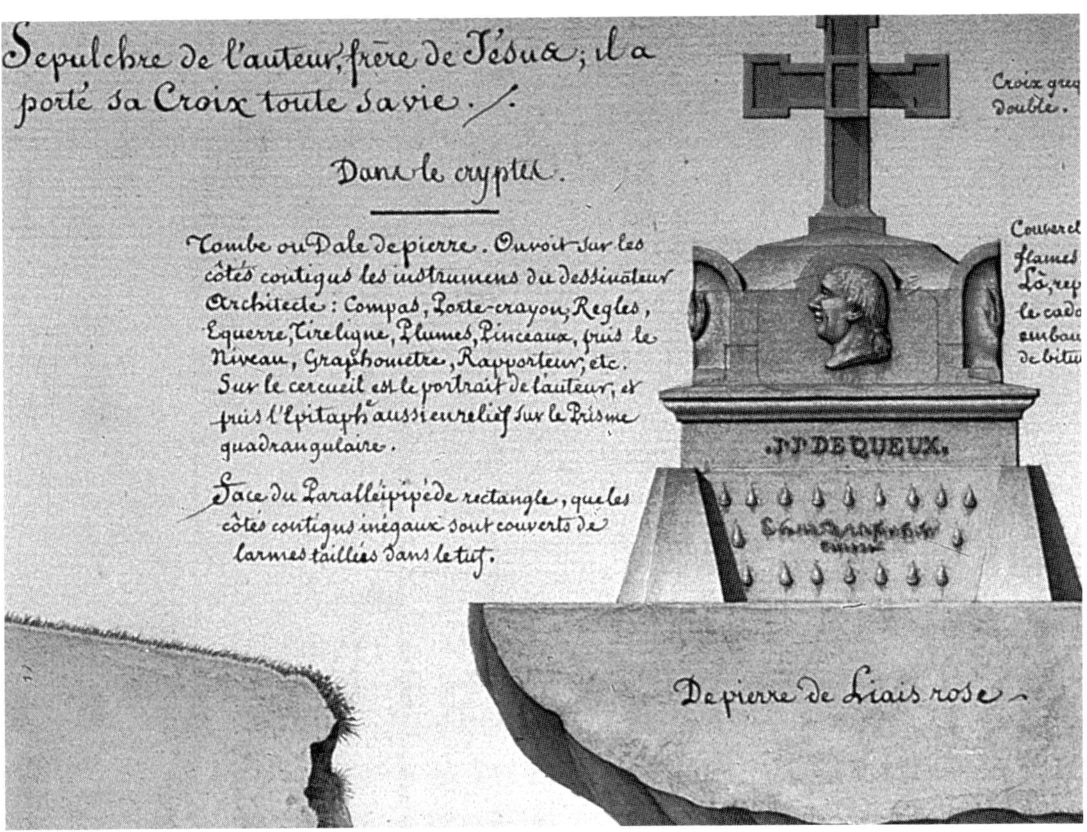

110 Lequeu, self-portrait for tomb, with cross.

111 Lequeu, physiognomical self-portrait "The Pouter."

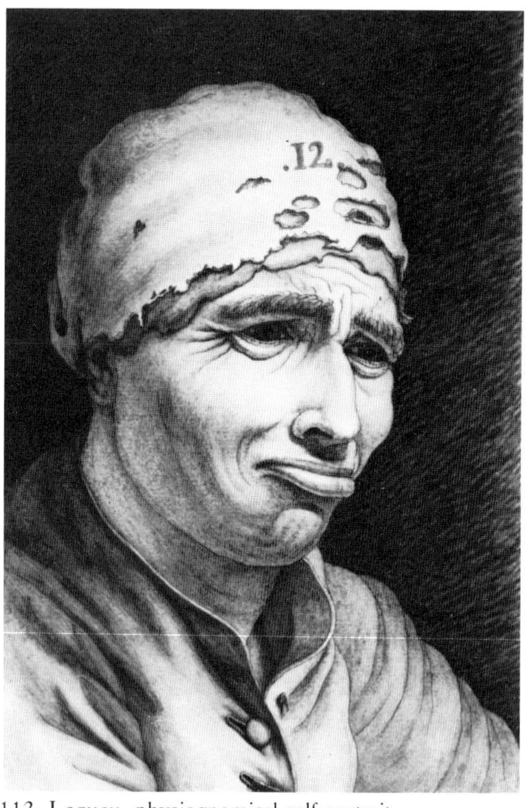

112 Lequeu, physiognomical self-portrait
"The Lip-Purser."

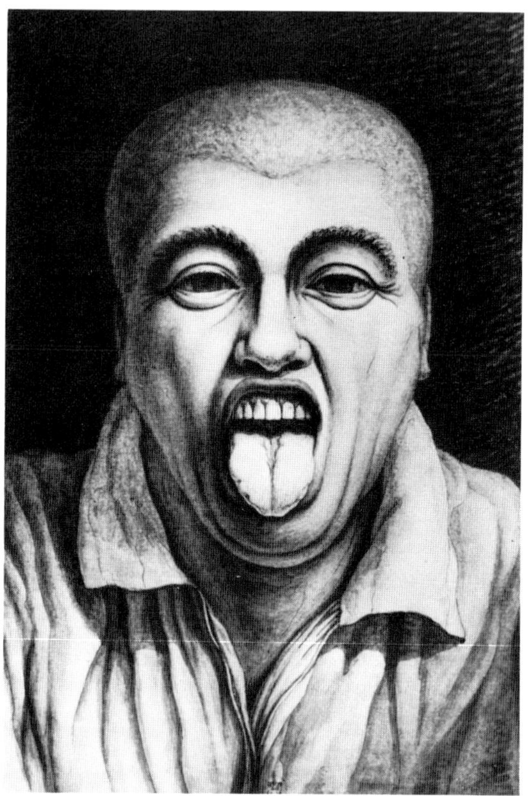

113 Lequeu, physiognomical self-portrait
"The Man with His Tongue Stuck Out."

114 Lequeu, physiognomical self-portrait
"The Winker."

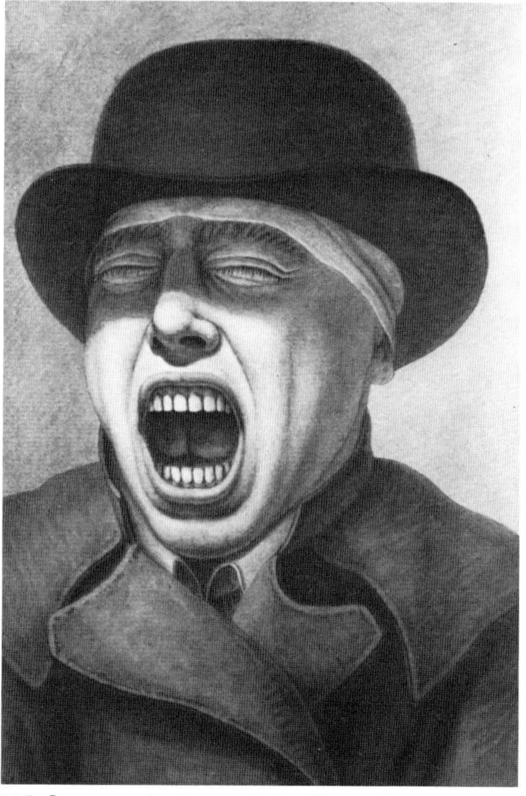

115 Lequeu, physiognomical self-portrait
"The Yawner."

pornographic displays—"pseudo" because the texts hide their message in apparently moralizing epigraphs. There is a drawing, obviously a self-portrait, of a male member "soft, and hanging without movement," which is labeled contradictorily, "Lewd Posture of Bacchus," and another, completing the classical pantheon, of the female organs viewed from between raised legs, entitled, "The Infamous Venus Lying Down, Lewd Posture *D'après Nature.*"[68]

Lequeu-narcissist, was, then, also Lequeu-*voyeur;* he showed himself as such in a drawing that places him in a garden, in a "lecherous posture," slyly listening in on the conversation of two young lovers (plate 118). Other portraits, evidently of prostitutes, some dressed in religious habit, some asleep in bed, others signaling from windows and niches, all drawn from life, reveal an artist without studio or models, whose desire of the eye at least was satisfied by his fellow tenants in the brothel of the Passage du Grand Cerf.[69]

Such physiognomic excursions would be of little interest, best consigned to the history of sexuality before Krafft-Ebing, if it were not for the fact that Lequeu was consistent in at least one level of representation, that of the lubricious gaze, applying it not only to the more obvious subjects but also, with significant effect, to architecture. For these naturalistic studies of self and others were simply the preface to his more "serious" designs for buildings, a kind of prearchitectural research into what Lequeu clearly regarded as the science of architectural physiognomy.

The application of the idea of physiognomy to architecture was not new: the comparison of facades and faces was entrenched in the classical anthropomorphic tradition. But it had gained in currency from the mid-eighteenth century with the attempt to develop a coherent theory of character for different building types. Blondel had even superimposed human profiles on architectural profiles, comparing in this way the Tuscan Order, as drawn by Scamozzi, with the head of a young warrior à la Leonardo, and the same order by Andrea Palladio with the head of a bearded sage.[70] The concept of physiognomy was similarly adopted by Ledoux and Quatremère de Quincy, and especially by Le Camus de Mézières, to refer to the way in which lines and shapes might evoke certain sensations, as they did in nature, thereby refining the architect's knowledge of characterization.[71] Ledoux's prison at Aix was designed expressly to bear the countenance of crime.[72] As such, the analogy between buildings and faces was useful enough and persisted in theory and criticism well into the nineteenth century. Lequeu, author of a treatise on facial representation, took the idea to its extreme and most disruptive conclusion: that with all its potential for emotional description and personal expression, every building has a face, not simply as analogy, but in fact. It is significant that in more than two hundred drawings, almost without exception, Lequeu presented his designs in elevation or section; his buildings always have an orthographic personality, but rarely a plan.

His most obvious physiognomic studies for buildings are well known and often cited as examples of *architecture parlante.* There is the huge replica of a cow that stands as a cowshed waiting to receive the cows through an entrance between its forelegs (plate 119). There are the various temples—the Temple of Divination, with its literally "oracular" facade, entered through a giant keyhole (plate 120); the half-eyed, almost blind mausoleum to Voltaire and his family (commemoration of his genius or celebration of his death?) (plate 121); and the almost carnivorous entrance to the grotto of Mary Magdelene. Rural *fabriques*—the henhouse and the dairy (plate 122)—are invested with the characteristics of their inhabitants. Giant doors open like mouths, in warehouses for gunpowder storage (plate 123) or as entrances into Chinese temples of light. Not surprisingly, these faces have the same enigmatic qualities as Lequeu's self-portraits—they might be characterized as having moods as they wink, frown, orate, defy, hide, or protect their inner recesses from the viewer.

Each of these drawings reveals a somewhat different procedure, drawn, as Emil Kaufmann has noted, from the repertory of characterization established by late-eighteenth-century architects, from the simple application of attributes or carved symbols that designate the building's purpose, to the genre or expressive effect of the facade as a whole, whether elegant or terrifying.[73] But Lequeu's method differed fundamentally from these general attempts to make architecture "speak to the eyes," precisely because, while Boullée and Ledoux worked with all the apparatus of classicism and the abstract forms that comprised its logical, rational foundation, Lequeu, for the first time in so extensive a manner, constituted his "buildings" with nonarchitectural elements. He fabricated them, that is, using natural, inorganic, or manufactured objects that directly related to the subject of the composition, but which were not in themselves drawn from a known architectural lexicon. The difference might be measured by a comparison between, for example, Ledoux's House for the Coopers and Lequeu's Cowshed. Ledoux used abstract geometry to construct a house with simulated "hoops" on the facade, and in three dimensions the house formed an intersecting barrel-vault, simulating the object of fabrication; the whole was conceived within an analogical framework whereby a recognized architectural or geometric form stood for something else. In Lequeu's Cowshed, on the other hand, mimesis was taken far beyond any such architectural figuration, and a giant sacred cow, natural and asymmetrical in stance, became a direct picture of its inhabitants. Similarly, Lequeu's "attributes"—the milk jugs that serve as waterspouts, the rooster that crowns the henhouse, the animal heads that ornament the gateway to the hunting park—were neither conventional architectural motifs nor conventionalized in any way that would make them "architectural." They were simply replicas of their originals, if not the originals themselves.

In an analysis of the portraits of Arcimboldo, built up out of vegetables, flowers, shells, and kitchen utensils, Roland Barthes has pointed out the particular techniques involved in such picture-language: in assembling his "composite heads" so that they are first broken into forms that resemble those of food prepared for the kitchen and then recomposed so that these kitchen forms themselves signify not themselves but the parts of a face, Arcimboldo, claims Barthes, "made a true language out of painting."[74] This language is based on metaphor; the "canvas," concludes Barthes, "becomes a true laboratory of tropes": a shell stands for an ear, metaphorically; a school of fish stands for water, metonymically; fire becomes, allegorically, a flaming head; spring fruit stands allusively for spring; fish that one time stand in for mouths, other for noses, create antanaclases. All these substitutions make up an encyclopedia of things representing other things.[75] In this sense, Barthes observes that the painting of Arcimboldo is less painted than *written;* it becomes a dictionary not of words but of images: "the 'things' are presented didactically as in a book for children."[76]

In much the same way, Lequeu's buildings are made up not of columns, pediments, waterspouts, and windows, but of the objects of life, if not of the kitchen. His design for a tavern uses wine bottles as waterspouts and wine casks piled on top of each other as rusticated columns, while soup bowls, salad plates, and wine glasses form the surroundings of windows; the dome of the henhouse is composed of an egg. Lequeu-*cuisinier* similarly treats architectural elements as nonarchitectural: the transposition of a keyhole to the entry of the Temple of Divination, the combinations of exotic and historical elements without regard for stylistic homogeneity or antiquarian accuracy, and the mechanical assemblage of fragments of observatories for the Rendez-vous de Bellevue (plate 124) show that architecture itself has become subjected to the same operations as Arcimboldo's kitchen objects, a disassembled lexicon of already formed images to be reassembled into something else that is not architecture. Here Lequeu has moved one step beyond Arcimboldo, as if, having decomposed a face into its principal shapes, he then remade the face with facial elements that stood for other facial elements—the mouth for the eyes and so on. Such a process cannot, properly, be called *architecture parlante.* It is instead a transformation of architecture into writing, an *écriture architecturale;* rather than forcing architecture to speak of its own character, it makes writing out of architecture. Lequeu's draftsman's revenge on architects is to absorb their *métier* into his, thereby completely undermining all of its codes.

Thus Lequeu's libertine gaze did not stop at the specifically erotic, pornographic, and obscene. Certainly, instances of phallocentrism are multiplied throughout his architectural drawings: overtly, as in the garden statue of Priapus (plate 125), with his face represented in the traditional manner as a composite of a cock's head, male member as nose ("an extraordinary member," noted Lequeu), and human neck; or covertly, as in the phallic symbolism of the chapel dedicated to the Revolutionary cult of Theophilanthropy, its credo partly hidden behind a tall, round-topped column reminiscent of Pococke's and Norden's depictions of Eastern standing stones.

Lubricity, as Diderot noted, "betokens a violent temperament," and Lequeu's drawings, without exception, dramatically assaulted the received images of architecture.[77] De Sade, also libertine, in practice as well as in imagination, used architecture as the setting and confirmation of his fictitious rites, institutionalizing a kind of topsy-turvy carnival of oppositional mores; Fourier, more gentle, but still resentful, found solace in a world designed, so to speak, from its foundations. Both de Sade and Fourier in a sense left architecture where they found it, de Sade with the conventional spaces of eighteenth-century theatricality and institutional form, Fourier in the simple extension of the programmatic, protofunctionalist discourse that purported to render plans transparent to use. Neither of them seriously undermined architectural codes or explored questions of representation. Manfredo Tafuri has pointed out that a truly Sadian architecture is not to be found in de Sade; nor, similarly, is a truly utopian architecture to be found in Fourier. Lequeu, however, directly implicated in representational problems, discovered the way to undermine architecture at the very point that late-eighteenth-century theory had proposed to situate its authenticity: the proper expression of truly rooted character.

THE AESTHETICS OF HISTORY

WINCKELMANN AND THE GREEK IDEAL

When I began to engrave this collection, I first had in mind the man of letters who seeks in monuments only their relations with the testimony of the ancients. I seized on these relations when they presented themselves naturally and when they seemed clear and evident to me; but being neither a scholar nor patient enough always to use this method, I often preferred another way that will perhaps be of interest to those who love the arts. It consists in studying faithfully the mind and hand of the artist, penetrating his views, following him in their execution, and, in a word, looking at monuments as the proof and expression of the taste that reigns in a century and in a country.

Comte de Caylus, *Recueil d'Antiquités égyptiennes*, 1752.[1]

THE CHOICE BETWEEN a history of antiquities that relies on textual evidence and one based on aesthetic judgment, between, that is, a consideration of objects or non-literary sources as illustrations of an otherwise literary history or as artistic artifacts in their own right, was in the second half of the eighteenth century perhaps the most important among the many choices that confronted the historian of art. To an amateur, connoisseur, and collector such as the Comte de Caylus, his decision against pure scholarship in favor of erudite taste seemed perfectly natural and even without serious methodological problems. He was, after all, following a long tradition of art appreciation established in the Renaissance. But in his tentative gestures towards a more systematic correlation of textual and aesthetic evidence with a definite chronology and geography and in his assumption that, out of such a rudimentary method, some general classification of art objects in time and place would emerge, that "monuments presented under this point of view distribute themselves in a few general classes relative to the country in which they were produced, and that in each class they range themselves in an order relative to the time in which they were born," he was going somewhat further than his antiquarian predecessors.[6] He was, almost ingenuously, adumbrating a problem that would become the central methodological issue for art history in the late eighteenth and nineteenth centuries: the problem of reconciling an external, context-related history of art objects to an internal, formal, and aesthetic treatment.

As assayed by historians in the late eighteenth century, it was a question that crystallized around the implicit oppositions between a typology of objects classified according to ahistorical criteria, whether functional or aesthetic, and a narrative treatment of the same objects in relation to the chronological history of their appearance. One proposed a normative, systematic arrangement, parallel to that of the natural and physical sciences; the other subordinated considerations of judgment to those of relative significance and social change.

These questions, not fully apparent until a more overtly relativist historicism had been defined in the following century, were, in the 1750s, easily buried by a growing enthusiasm for an "aesthetic history" that articulated an overt criterion of judgment—generally an idealism of the "high period" of Greek achievement—within a kind of chronological typology of epochs and their monuments. According to aesthetic convenience, history was divided into periods, each defined by and manifested in a specific style of art; the succession of such periods, symbolized by their products, formed a normative trajectory of artistic accomplishment that measured the rise and fall of taste across the centuries. This model was no doubt taken from Vasari's history of Renaissance art; in its ideas of progress and subsequent decadence, it originated in classical histories themselves. But its reworking in the eighteenth century incorporated a number of new themes: the systematic comparison of building types in their development over time—the "*parallèle*" as utilized by Julien-David Le Roy, Durand, and Séroux d'Agincourt; the application of Greek aesthetics to the judgment of antique art, as practiced by J. J. Winckelmann and Quatremère de Quincy; the imaginary "restitution" or "restoration" of statues or buildings, according to a mixture of visual and literary evidence; and the synthetic incorporation of history and archaeology into a narrative that treated of cultures as a whole, politically, socially, and artistically, as sketched by Winckelmann and elaborated by Edward Gibbon.

THE ORIGINS OF ART HISTORY

> The object of a reasoned history of art is to return it to its origins by following its progress and variations to their perfection and by marking its decadence and fall to the point of its extinction. A history of art conceived according to these principles should make known the different styles and the diverse characters of peoples, times, and artists; it should establish the facts, as far as possible, through study of those monuments of Antiquity that remain to us.
>
> There have appeared some works under the title "History of Art," but art has had little place in them. The authors of these works, not having studied their material sufficiently, have been able only to provide us with commonplaces. There are few writers who have known how to make us understand the very essence of art.
>
> J. J. Winckelmann, *History of Ancient Art,* 1764.[3]

Introducing his *History of Ancient Art* in 1764, J. J. Winckelmann consciously developed the themes outlined by de Caylus into a manifesto for art history.

As such, his book has been traditionally represented as a foundation moment in the development of the discipline, a preparation for the developed historicism of the nineteenth century. From Herder in the 1770s to Friedrich Meinecke in the 1930s, this interpretation of Winckelmann's contribution has been more or less unshakable.[4] Certainly, measured by the influence of his stated intentions and aesthetic judgments, this assessment has to be partially correct; but a closer reading of the *History,* perhaps more interesting for the identification of methodological problems in the eighteenth century, reveals several barely hidden contradictions that, despite the unifying attempt of his rhetoric, mirror the divisions among the philosophical, philological, antiquarian, and historiographical traditions of the seventeenth and eighteenth centuries.

In the first place, Winckelmann posited an apparently ahistorical basis for his undertaking: the return of art to its origins, a familiar refrain in the 1750s. Second, once found, these origins would be treated as the starting point for an already plotted narrative—following art in "its progress and variations to their perfection . . . marking its decadence and fall to the point of its extinction"—hardly the relativistic standpoint championed by the nineteenth-century historicist. Third, complicating the foundations of the discipline still further, Winckelmann compared his own attempt to "make known the different styles and the diverse characters of peoples, times, and artists" with previous self-named historians of art, claiming that what had been lacking hitherto was a sense of the nature of art as it takes its place in history: "there have been very few who have known how to make us understand the very essence of art." This essence, of course, was aesthetic and, though Winckelmann proposed to return it to its origins in different peoples, times, and places, it was in his eyes a normative aesthetics, based on the idealizing Neoplatonism of the seventeenth-century classicists; from this superior standpoint, it would be relatively easy to trace the rise, fall, and decay of art in any period. In these terms alone, without reference to the often dubious historical evidence used for his sweeping conclusions, it would be possible, as many of his contemporaries and successors attempted, to unravel Winckelmann's text in order to return his thesis to its own origins in the methodologically heterogeneous climate of mid-eighteenth-century historical connoisseurship.[5]

In the process of developing his historical aesthetics, Winckelmann brought together two apparently contradictory kinds of evidence and, thereby, juxtaposed two traditions of scholarship. The first was the body of rules governing taste, form, composition, propriety, and genre, generally understood as the "theory of art." The second was the account of the remains of the past commonly understood as "history," sometimes chronological, sometimes heterotopical, sometimes arranged by juxtaposition, similarity, or resemblance. The theory of art was the domain of the critic, the theoretician, and the artist himself; history was the realm of the philologist, antiquarian, and collector. The abbé du Bos, for example, was a celebrated authority on taste, while Bernard de Montfaucon and Francesco Bianchini were noted for their archaeological interests.[6] For Winckelmann, neither of these traditions, deployed separately, offered plausible explanations of art in history. Connoisseurship, eulogies, travelers' tales, and bric-a-brac, descriptions of works that in many cases were never seen by the writer, these had no claim to historical value. Similarly, the anachronisms of collectors' catalogues had to be avoided. Even the great Montfaucon passed judgment on the evidence of drawings rather than on experience; "at a distance from the treasures of ancient art," he "saw with the eyes of others."[7]

While this was a gross simplification, if not a slighting, of the work of the Benedictines of Saint Maur, Winckelmann's burden was clear: what he termed "history" had to be understood in the "widest sense of the word," combining a narrative chronology with "a sketch of the system of art," of the "very essence of art itself." This is what he meant by the idea of "returning the work of art to its origin," by which he referred neither to the materialist origins common to the philosophes, to the structures of Condillac or Laugier, nor to the biblical origins still evoked by many theorists of language or metaphysics, but rather to a complicated notion of aesthetic origin, specific to and comprehensible in the work of art itself.

Hence the celebrated method of Winckelmann, based on a combination of personal vision and a meticulous reading of the objects, in his case the statues first of the Dresden Museum, then of Rome. His rule was first to distinguish carefully between the modern and the antique (the general criterion was that the projecting parts of statues, above all the arms and hands, were probably restorations) and second to develop a certain empathy with the work observed. "I have always looked at works of art with a certain enthusiasm," noted Winckelmann. From this appreciative state, he hoped to derive an appropriate style of description: "The description of the Apollo demands the most sublime style." Not only is the statue "motivated" by its relation to its epoch, an almost natural sign of its culture, but the historian's description would itself be motivated by the object described.[8]

These first principles were applied at the most detailed scale of close observation: the depth of navels, the flare of nostrils, the projection of nipples, the size of knees, all contributed to stylistic knowledge.[9] Thus in the *Reflections,* a long dissertation on the representation of the skin in sculpture prefaced the conclusion that Greek bodies formed better objects of imitation than modern bodies. As Walter Pater summarized it, Winckelmann caught "the thread of a whole sequence of laws in some hollowing of the hand or dividing of the hair."[10]

The history of art became, in this sense, no longer a catalogue of remains and objects to be reconstructed by means of *a priori* rules, but a history of forms, whose material surfaces, masses, and contours were clues to higher ideas, inner forces, and spiritual concepts. The task of the historian-critic was, as it would be throughout the nineteenth century, to derive from the work its own ideas, to become a connoisseur of lines and planes as the inscriptions of those ideas, in a way to become an aesthetician of the invisible by means of abstraction from the visible.[11]

But the objectives of a history of art, Winckelmann cautioned, could not stop at the appreciation of a single work: each form was part of a life of forms that was itself symptomatic of the life of societies and cultures. Here he incorporated that classical legend of the sequence of the ages, given new power by

Turgot and the philosophes of progress, which posited an organic development for culture, society, and art. Like Turgot, who compared the development of societies and nations to the infancy, adulthood, and dotage of a human being, Winckelmann stated that "the fine arts have, like the human species, their period of infancy," and drew conclusions about the crudity of primitive styles. He spoke of the "march of human nature," which crept by degrees from the first crude, vehement, and impetuous movements of man to a calmness and regularity emblematic of an achieved maturity.[12]

In this story of rise and fall, Winckelmann claimed to follow Aristotle:

> For as every action or event has five parts and, as it were, stages—namely, beginning, progress, state of rest, decline, and end—in which lie the ground of the five scenes or acts in dramatic pieces, so it is with the succession of time in art. . . .[13]

Avoiding the later Hegelian conclusion of the death of art, Winckelmann dismissed the "end of art" as logically beyond the consideration of art itself, thus reducing the epochs of artistic development to four. As applied to Greek art in particular, this meant the recognition of four periods, to which he assigned characteristics or styles: the most ancient period, which lasted until the time of Phidias, was characterized by a "severe and hard style," powerful and vigorous, which emerged at the moment when art became recognizable, when it had "attained a form and been reduced to a system"; the second period, which lasted from the death of Phidias to the time of Praxiteles, was characterized by its "grand and lofty" manner of expression, in other words, by the sublime as defined by Longinus; the third period, from Praxiteles to Apelles, was that of the "beautiful" style; while the fourth and last period was that of decline, when imitators held the field and "art gradually bowed itself to its fall."[14]

In accordance with the organic analogy, there was in this sequence an inner principle that forced one epoch into the next, endowing its successor with some of its own traits, in an almost Hegelian manner. Thus in the second stage, the "grand and lofty" style preserved some of the "severe and hard" characteristics of the ancient manner, strengthening its loftiness by severity of expression. In the accurate drawing of the grand style, Winckelmann saw the traces of an ancient art of hard outline. Such a principle of inheritance might well, he noted, be a general rule; modern artists should have "been instructed by the sharp outlines and strong development of all the parts" of Michelangelo's art, using clear, outline drawing to achieve truth of form, a lesson that was not lost on neoclassical artists in the 1790s.[15]

In this double scheme of aesthetic judgment and chronological pattern, Winckelmann summarized the contradictory genre of art history for generations. He also brilliantly obscured the hardening dividing line between philosophes and *savants,* simply by positing that proper observation of a nonliterary source would provide essential historical knowledge, without which a history of art as opposed to one of politics, law, institutions, or wars could not be written. By at once insisting on the verification and close reading of sources, and at the same time incorporating his observations in a grand scheme of progress, he satisfied antiquarians and philosophers alike. By asserting that the development of art was bound to principles of social and cultural origin, he claimed the attention of Encyclopedists such as Diderot and left the way clear for a modern art, while in claiming the time of Praxiteles as the apogee of all artistic achievement, he confirmed the prejudices of partisans of the ancients such as the Comte de Caylus, Diderot's *bête noire.*[16] Finally, the sweep of his narrative and the power of his images—he had taken the lessons of Longinus to heart—furnished a convincing model of a history that need neglect neither art nor fact, neither effect nor cause.

The structure of the book itself reinforced his methodical message. Book I treated the origins of art and its development from Egypt, Tuscany, and Greece; Books II and III sketched the nature of early art among the Egyptians, Phoenicians, Persians, and Etruscans, that is, before the emergence of art as a fully developed system; Books IV and V dealt with the essential aesthetic nature of Greek art, its idea of beauty and its application in different kinds of sculpture, moving from general principles to detailed examination of the parts of the body; Book VI concluded this discussion with an analysis of drapery; Book VII studied the mechanical and technical aspects of sculpture in different materials; and Books VIII to XII traced the history of art in relation to what Winckelmann called external causes—politics, institutions, and mores—from early Greece to late Rome. The work thus deployed its argument in a continuous movement from the aesthetic nature of art to its historical context, with a pivotal section on material fabrication as a key to the relationship between intention and form. However limited Winckelmann's archaeological knowledge, mistaken his judgments, faulty his history, or misguided his understanding of technique, no eighteenth-century art historian could ignore the dramatic intent of the book and its implications for a "unified method."

THE HISTORY OF ARCHITECTURE

Winckelmann fully developed the application of his method in his study of Greek sculpture; the other arts, including painting, received much less attention. But in two essays published before the *History of Ancient Art,* "Observations on the Architecture of the Ancient Temple of Agrigentum in Sicily" (1759) and "Observations on the Architecture of the Ancients" (1760–1762), and in a surprising number of passages of the *History* itself, he presented at least the outline of an architectural history or, rather, provided the aesthetic and historical criteria for one.[17] In the earlier essay, he made explicit his historical intentions.

> Those who until now have wished to write the history of Greek architecture have been obliged suddenly to pass, with Vitruvius, from the time when the need to guard against bad weather taught men the art of building huts and houses to the time when architecture found its highest degree of perfection.[18]

The contemporary discovery of early Doric architecture in Sicily would allow the historian to understand the "ancient style of this order." Even though Winckelmann had not visited the site, the observations of his friend Robert Mylne, the Scottish architect, were sufficient for him to "undertake the task of filling the lapse in time that transpires between these two periods of art."[19] In his view, he was describing one of the oldest Greek buildings in the world and thus, according to principle, he was returning the art of architecture to its origins. Further, a study of the moment when the first rough system of art was formed from early experiments in building would afford insight into the essential, aesthetic qualities of Doric architecture. Here the first discrepancy with received wisdom was the difference between Vitruvius's ideal proportion for the Doric (seven diameters high) and that of Agrigentum (five diameters). In an attack on the Vitruvian canon, which was rejoined in the *History of Ancient Art,* Winckelmann was scornful:

> This author, Vitruvius, wanted to determine his dimensions of architecture, like those of the human body, in part according to the mystery of certain numbers and in part according to harmony; he has been able to give no other reason for these seven diameters than his mysterious number seven, an idea that places him on a level with the dreams of those moderns concerning the seventh in music.[20]

Rather than trying to find a universal justification for the temple's proportions, Winckelmann argued for reasons to be found in the plan, which provided a simple ratio for the height of the columns in its relation between length and breadth. Proportions, he concluded, were not derived from any external rule, "something foreign to the building," but from the nature of the building itself. Indeed, the "conical form" of the columns was not a result of proportional theory, but a direct response to the function of the column as support, calculated according to the weight of the entablature. Finally, the entire aesthetic of the building differed markedly from the Doric described by Vitruvius; its ornaments were simple and massive: "the ancients searched for the grandiose, in which consisted magnificence; this is why the parts of this temple are strongly projecting, more than in the time of Vitruvius."[21]

In this short essay, Winckelmann outlined principles that he would apply to architectural history as a whole, remarking, in conclusion:

> Everything depends on the way one looks at things. Spon and the most learned travelers have limited themselves to searching for inscriptions and old books. Cluvier and Holstein have occupied themselves with ancient geography, but until now no one has thought of art. There are still many things to be said about the works of ancient architecture, both in Rome and its surroundings. Desgodets has only measured; it remains for another to provide observations and general rules for this art.[22]

Winckelmann's second essay on architecture, "Observations on the Architecture of the Ancients," was written in 1760 and published in Dresden two years later. Carlo Fea, Winckelmann's editor, considered it to be one of his best works, a kind of third part to the *History,* completing its coverage of the three visual arts.[23] In the preface, Winckelmann resumed previous attempts to write architectural history, especially the history of the earliest remains of Greek art on Roman soil, the temples at Paestum and Agrigentum, and that of Greek architecture itself. He summarized the contributions of Cluvier, the results of ten years of Englishmen's visits to Paestum, the work of Paoli and Galiani; he recorded his eager reading of Le Roy and Stuart and Revett as they depicted for the first time the monuments of Athens and the mainland (plate 126). He based his own claim to architectural expertise on the approach "of a *savant* studying antiquity," acknowledging the invaluable help of Cardinal Albani, his patron; Clérisseau, his friend; Wille, the Parisian engraver; and Füssli, the father of the emigré painter Henry Fuseli, translator, into English, of *Reflections on Imitation*. Winckelmann had read all the available antique authorities—Vitruvius, Strabo, Pausanius—and most of the moderns—Alberti, Perrault, Le Roy and Piranesi.[24]

For Winckelmann, architecture consisted essentially of two elements: its material construction and its ornamentation; these corresponded, in sculpture, to the nude figure and its drapery.[25] His essay was similarly divided, moving from a consideration of materials, the art of construction, foundations, walls, the form of buildings, their elements—columns and the orders—and parts—roofs, doors, windows, stairs—to a detailed study of the art of exterior and interior ornament. His exhaustive investigation of ancient techniques of building is conducted with similar enthusiasm and parallels his investigation of sculpture in the *History*. In the first instance, architecture must, he implied, be defined by its material nature and limitations, its aesthetic to be derived from practical experience. The qualities of brick, its composition and fabrication; the nature of stone, its regional variations and use; iron and its corrosion by the weather, all endowed a building with its character. As the procedures of sculpture—from modeling to the extraction of a figure from a single block of marble—in some way emulate the movement of the artistic idea from the outside to the interior and back, so the building of a wall, an eminently practical activity, leads inevitably to its worked, expressive quality. Thus, describing the construction of antique stone walls, Winckelmann derived the principle of symmetry—treated as an exterior principle of composition by Vitruvian academic theory—as a natural result of stonecutting.

> In the most distant times, they used for construction the largest blocks of stone they could find, which has given rise to the saying that these were the works of Cyclops. For the same reason, the people of the locality still call the ruins of the Temple of Jupiter at Agrigentum in Sicily, the Palace of the Giants. The stones are in general so accurately squared and finely cut that the joints resemble a fine thread; some writers have called this *armonia* (αρμονια).[26]

A word that, as Winckelmann noted, was translated from Pausanius by most commentators as "symmetry," was thereby returned to its true material origin in the laying of stones.

Winckelmann was, in fact, obsessed by the techniques of joining materials. He described city walls joined without cement; surfaces paved in white; polished stones cut into different forms, such as pentagons, hexagons, and heptagons, fitted together *al'antica inserta;* the surfaces of Roman roads, walls, aqueducts, and triumphal arches.[27] Like Piranesi, he celebrated the precision of workmanship, studying every variety of the technique known as *spina pesce,* or herringbone pattern, correcting Perrault for not realizing that the name was derived from the ancient *opus spicatum,* or wheat grain patterning. In every case, the material technique of building was translated into its aesthetic principle, its outer form presenting its inner construction.[28]

In much the same way, ornament, Winckelmann's second element of architecture, possessed its own "nature," as essential to building as to construction, its embellishment and the source of its pleasure.

> A building without ornaments can be compared to a healthy body in a state of poverty that by itself cannot complete the happiness of man, as Aristotle remarks.[29]

Ornament provided variety, and the precepts of rhetoric held for building as for writing.

> Monotony can become as vicious in architecture as in the style of a book and in all other productions of art. It is variety that is the source of pleasure; in discourse, as in architecture, it serves to flatter the mind and the eyes. When elegance is joined to simplicity, beauty results.[30]

To provoke such an effect, architectural ornament should be at once suited to the general purpose of the building and proportioned to its specific use; thus, as an organic supplement to propriety, it should remain and express itself as an accessory or addition; subordinate to the nature of the specific building, it should not in any way alter or disturb that to which it is added. In this sense, ornament was like a dress, covering the "nudity" of a structure; "the grander a building is in its plan, the less it demands ornament, like a precious stone that should be chased, so to speak, only in a gold thread, the better to conserve its brilliance."[31] The principle of decoration was clear: structure and ornament should complement each other but in no way be confused; ornament should clearly stand as ornament, changing the nature neither of its own position nor of the building's function. Ornaments were like the drapery of the vestal virgins, which "never obscured the beautiful contour of the nude body, visible to our eyes without restraint."[32]

Ornament thus had its principle, but it also had its history. Winckelmann traced the origin, development, perfection, and decline of ornament from "the first times of art" to the late Renaissance. Ornament was rare at first (the earliest buildings were bare of moldings or projections of any kind); it emerged with the taste for variety, movement, and diversity; it initially took the form of accessories to architectural members. But the desire for variety and elegance was fatal, leading to the inevitable decline of ornament and, therefore, to the decline of architecture. Winckelmann paraphrased Vitruvius in what, by the eighteenth century, had become a commonplace of critical rhetoric:

> When good taste began to be lost and appearance became more important than reality, ornaments were no longer regarded as simple accessories; places that had hitherto remained bare were covered. This is what produced *le goût mesquin* in architecture, because when each part is small the whole should be small as well, as Aristotle says. It is the same in architecture as with ancient languages, which became richer as they lost their energy and beauty, as is easily proved for Greek and Latin; as architects saw they could neither surpass nor even equal their predecessors in beauty, they tried to supply it by richness and profusion.[33]

Thus was born the "useless ornament," an invention of the corrupt reign of Nero, "a taste . . . that was adopted more and more under the emperors who followed him."[34] This stricture also held when applied to modern art, as it had for Bellori a century earlier.

> One could make a comparison between the art of decoration among the ancients and among the moderns and, to make the point better, use engravings. With ancient ornament, simplicity always ruled, whereas with the moderns, who do not seek to imitate the ancients, the opposite is true. The ornaments of the ancients all present among themselves a certain accord and harmony, like branches belonging to the same trunk; but the moderns present disparate forms where often, as one says, one finds neither rhyme nor reason.[35]

Even Michelangelo, "whose fertile genius could not be contained within the economy of the ancients," abandoned himself to novelties, and Borromini surpassed him in bad taste, creating a fashion that continued to the mid-eighteenth century.

As a whole, and in its parts, architecture thus participated with the other arts in the great historical narrative of birth, rise, perfection, decay, and death; despite the randomness of reference to buildings in the *History,* Winckelmann indicated at each stage how architecture might be incorporated into a universal history of art. First, architecture had to be distinguished from the other arts with regard to the nature of its imitation. It is this fact that slowed its gestation.

> Among the Greeks, the arts of sculpture and painting attained a certain excellence earlier than architecture, because the latter has in it *more of the ideal* than the two former; it cannot be an imitation of anything actual and must therefore of necessity be based on the general principles and rules of proportion. The two former arts, which originated in mere imitation, found all the requisite rules determined in man, whereas architecture was obliged to discover its own rules by repeated trials and to establish them by general approval.[36]

From this, Winckelmann derived his refutation of Vitruvian proportional theory and the need to develop formal criteria that depended not on rules but on aesthetic experience for judging architectural beauty. If a column could not be judged according to a fixed principle, such as the relation of height to diameter, its form had to be subjected to an analysis similar to that of sculpture; its beauty had to be analogous to, not derived from, the human figure.

Winckelmann drew the comparison in an especially suggestive passage:

> The forms of beautiful youths resemble the unity of the surface of the sea, which at some distance appears smooth and still like a mirror, although constantly in movement with its heaving swell. . . . So it is with the beautiful youthful outline, which appears simple and yet at the same time has infinitely different variations, with that soft tapering, difficult to achieve in a column and still more so in the diverse forms of a youthful body. Among the innumerable kinds of columns in Rome, some appear preeminently elegant on account of this very tapering; of

these I have particularly noted two of granite, which I am always studying anew.[37]

The complicated curves of columns and bodies were thus subjected to the same aesthetic criteria; the building and the body were seen to hold similar tensions and compressions in their subtle outlines.

However, despite his reading of Le Roy and Stuart, Winckelmann said almost nothing about Greek architecture, presumably following his own principle (more often than not honored in the breach) of commenting only on works he had seen. Thus by far the most references to architecture in the *History* occur in the final two books, where he treated of Greek architecture under the Romans, the remains of which he had studied in Italy.[38] Here he saw the decline of art as an inevitable consequence of the decline of Greek values in Rome and of the decline of the Roman Empire itself, until the extinction of both art and Rome under Constantine; the monuments erected by the Emperors illustrated and confirmed this decay. In a way that proved redolent for future historians of this period, Winckelmann described, among others, the temple of Fortuna at Praeneste, built by Sylla, the first despot; the Forum and public buildings of Caesar; the monuments of Augustus, including the tomb of the Plautias at Tivoli; the temple at Melasso in Caria; the works of Vespasian, noting especially the temples of Virtue, Honour, and Peace; the arch of Trajan at Ancona; Hadrian's Castel Sant'Angelo, and his villa at Tivoli; the baths of Caracalla and of Diocletian; Diocletian's palace at Spalato; the so-called temple of Bacchus in Rome, later a Christian church; and, finally, the Arch of Constantine. For the most part, these buildings were characterized in order to add to the picture of continuous decline. Thus, both Sylla and Caesar deployed private wealth, "erecting sumptuous edifices" at their own expense. An increasing love of display showed itself in the transition from single-story, simple courtyard houses to the multistory dwellings of Rome and the *campagna;* the temple of Melasso, built in honor of Augustus, exhibited "an unusual license" in its mingling of the Roman Order (the porch) and the Ionic Order (the sides) and in the decoration of column bases with carved leaves. He found similar departures from Greek taste at Castello, in the Nymphaea, where Ionic was mixed with Doric, and at a tomb near Agrigentum, where Ionic pilasters were surmounted by Doric triglyphs. Vitruvius himself had accused the Augustan age of a decline in literature and decorative art. A momentary respite was afforded by the "parsimonious" and economical Vespasian; but he was succeeded by Trajan, whose taste for monumentality was balanced only by his reputation as the last of the cultivated emperors and by his careful restoration of antique works. Not even the antiquarian eclecticism of Hadrian at Tivoli, where a sense of theatrical historicism modeled the "representation of the most celebrated regions and edifices in Greece," including the Elysian Fields, could save art from its descent; the spirit of imitation was impoverished beyond recall.

> The spirit of liberty had departed from the world, and the source that had given birth to lofty thoughts and glorious deeds had disappeared. . . . The assistance Hadrian rendered to art may be likened to

> the food prescribed by physicians to their patients, preventing them from dying, but yielding them no nourishment.[39]

From there it was a short step to the final "downfall of . . . architecture": the reign of Constantine, in which buildings were constructed from the remnants of antique structures.

Only the reign of Diocletian was partially exempt from this picture of universal distress, for, although Winckelmann criticized his baths ("the entablature of the columns is suffocated by the heaps of carved work, as were the spectators by the deluge of flowers that was showered upon them at the plays he had performed"), he was pleasantly struck by Adam's drawings of Spalato.[40] Winckelmann's explanation for architecture's late bloom (as compared to painting and sculpture) was "that architecture occupies itself principally with rule and measure, that everything is determined according to them, and that it is governed by more direct precepts than drawing and, therefore, could not so easily deviate or fall."[41] Nevertheless, the fatal flaw was still present; by the time of Constantine, architecture was dead, along with all the other arts. How else could one explain the "restoration" of the so-called Temple of Concordia in such a way that two columns of the porch were reset upside down? This image of an upside-down column, its function and supporting form negated, its tapering end pointing toward the earth, closed Winckelmann's historical account of architecture: "after the time of Constantine, we do not find much further mention made of art."[42]

Thus Winckelmann ended what had become for him in the last books a somewhat distasteful task.

> I have already overstepped the boundaries of the history of art and, in meditating upon its downfall, I have felt almost like the historian who, in narrating the history of his native land, is compelled to allude to its destruction, of which he was a witness.[43]

Only his mission as historian, coupled with a nostalgia for beauty, had impelled the "completion" of the story; perhaps the lessons learned from the picture of decline would serve artists in the present. In a sense, however, as Winckelmann's readers were quick to note, the entire book had been written in the shadow of this awful conclusion, which made the beauty of the high period of art seem the more fragile and exquisite. This is the tenor that appealed to the early romantics: irreparable loss coupled with succeeding horror; the beautiful beside the corrupt and the grotesque. Speaking of the restoration of works of art in antiquity, Winckelmann himself, in a negation that was to pervade the writing of the next generations of historians, from Gibbon to Séroux d'Agincourt, betrayed a fascination with the forbidden period of decline and fall.

> It was my intention to speak in this place only of those works that were damaged and then restored in ancient times to their original condition, not of those that have been dug up broken into fragments, such as those destroyed when the Northern tribes overran and devastated not only Rome but also Latium and other parts of Italy, to say nothing of Greece. It makes me sad when I reflect upon the consequences of

this fury; however, we are speaking here not of destruction but of completion.[44]

And yet the very incompletion of Winckelmann's own history opened the way for his boundaries to be overstepped. Later historians would admit the self-evident truth of his thesis, but, despite their aesthetic preferences, they would be drawn to the long agony of art's death out of sheer historical and intellectual curiosity. The period between Commodius and the Medici, after all, coincided with the rise of Christianity—a comfort to skeptics and philosophes, but something that at least called for explanation; for the architectural historian, it contained not only the traditional roster of canonical Roman buildings, but also those that evoked antiquarian and aesthetic interest—Spalato and Palmyra, the exotic East, not to mention the gamut of Christian architecture from the churches of Ravenna to Saint Peter's. It was a period that demanded assessment historically, if not aesthetically, according to the emerging taste for reappreciating the Gothic, following Soufflot in France and Walpole in England.

SYMBOLIC ARCHITECTURE

VIEL DE SAINT-MAUX AND THE DECIPHERMENT OF ANTIQUITY

The symbolic and allegorical genius of the ancients is the true key to antiquity—it presided over its fables, poetry, religion, festivals, calendar, and its entire agriculture.

A. Court de Gébelin, *Monde primitif,* 1784.[1]

AMONG THE PHILOSOPHES who concerned themselves with the origins of language, there was a general consensus that, as Rousseau pointed out, the first signs were figurative: "As the first motives that made man speak were the passions, his first expressions were tropes. Figurative language was the first to be born."[2] There was also agreement as to the power—didactic, moral, and political—of this original language, which relied for its effect on gesture: "one speaks much better to the eyes than to the ears," wrote Rousseau; "one even sees that the most eloquent discourses are those with the most images inserted."[3] The evidence for such a rhetoric of images lay in the history of writing, itself figurative from its beginnings. As Condillac had demonstrated, the origins of language included not only the grammatical and syntactical orders of thoughts and words, but also written signs—pictographic characters and hieroglyphs—and languages, that is, signs that "spoke to the eyes" and not simply to the mind. Condillac had included in his *Essai* a long exposition on the origins and development of writing, taken from the French translation of Bishop Warburton's study of hieroglyphs, and he had posited that the first "language of action," that "mixed discourse of words and actions," as Warburton had it, was accompanied by and made permanent with the invention of written characters.[4] Warburton had argued that the history of writing had developed in parallel to that of speech, moving quite naturally from a pictorial representation of the object signified (a picture writing, like that of the Mexicans) to a hieroglyphic stage, which used images for the analogy or the symbolic relation they held to the object represented (the Egyptian hieroglyphs), then to Chinese characters, which are more philosophical and arbitrary with respect to what they signify, and, finally, to the signs of the alphabet, which are entirely arbitrary and stand for sounds. By such a "gradual and easy descent," the general history of writing fell from picture to letter, from signs representing things to standing for sounds, themselves arbitrary signs of ideas.

What seemed especially important to Condillac in Warburton's analysis was the method by which he professed to decipher the hieroglyphs, which he regarded as rhetorical signs, or visual tropes. Warburton's "origins of tropes" distinguished three principal stages in the development of symbolic characters. The initial hieroglyphs were simple and rude; they merely made the "principal circumstance" in the subject stand for the whole. A battle would be represented in this way by two hands, one holding a shield, the other a bow, or by a siege by scaling ladder. Warburton called this first form "curiological"; in rhetorical terms, it is called *synecdoche*. With the application of more art and invention, the next form was invented, which he called "tropical," a form that "put the instrument of the thing, whether real or metaphorical, for the thing itself" *(metonymy)*. Thus an eye would represent God's omniscience. The final stage was a "symbolic" writing, which was more mysterious than the first and more conducive to the secrecy of the priesthood that made one thing represent another by "any quaint resemblance or analogy" *(catachresis)*. In this manner, the sunrise might be indicated by the two upstanding eyes of the crocodile.[5] Warburton thus laid the way for all picture-writing and, indeed, all ancient visual artifacts, to be interpreted according to the rules of rhetoric, as allegorical and symbolic. Condillac extended the theory to include all the arts of action and gesture, including not only writing but dance, song, pantomime, harmony, and music, which in his terms took their origins from the same root and formed the primitive figurative language of a more natural and spontaneous community.

For Rousseau, this origin was also invested with moral significance.[6] The language of natural man signified his natural state transparently. It was direct and forceful, unembellished by tricks and sophistries, equally visual as aural: "more objects strike our eyes than our ears, and figures have more variety than sounds; they are also more expressive, and they say more in less time."[7] Economical, but also speaking more immediately through the eyes to the soul, these first figures were clear: "The most energetic language is that where the sign has said all before one speaks." He gave the example of Darius I, king of ancient Persia, who while on attack received from his adversary, the king of Scythia, a message composed of "a frog, a bird, a mouse, and five arrows." Darius, no doubt aware of the meaning of "this terrible harangue," turned back.[8] Similarly Marc Antony, speaking silently through the presentation of the body of Caesar himself, was more eloquent than any professional orator.[9] This was, said Rousseau, the natural rhetoric of a time "when exterior appearances were always a reflection of the heart's disposition," when "differences in conduct announced at first glance those of character." Simple rustic clothes displayed a strength and vigor lost behind the masks of civilized finery. In this first world, the arbitrariness of the sign was reduced to a minimum; all signs, so to speak, acted on the level of onomatopoeia.[10]

The extension of this philosophical idea of energetic language to the interpretation of historical remains was logical enough: "All is emblem and figure in antiquity," stated Voltaire, resting his case on centuries of antiquarian investigation.[11] And while the philosophes themselves did not agree on the specific virtue to be attributed to hieroglyphic and emblematic expressions, their interpretative schemas were drawn of necessity from the increasing number of historical studies not only of writing and alphabets, but also of the whole range of nonliterary evidence hitherto the domain of the collector and antiquarian, but becoming essential for the construction of an ancient history that was more than a political or military chronicle. Gradually, from the last years of the seventeenth century, the criteria were worked out for interpreting charters, inscriptions, coins, vases, bas-reliefs, gems, statues, and other fragmentary remains, in a general attempt to construct what the historian Arnaldo Momigliano has called a "scientific iconography," to answer the fundamental questions, "Given a monument with images on it, how can we understand what the artist meant? How can we distinguish between what is only monumental and what is meant to express a religious or philosophical belief?"[12]

The list of such works in the early eighteenth century was long, and the philosophes were perhaps only too correct in their general disdain for so many tedious and often fantastic explanations. But where these antiquarian discourses did not simply repeat previous mythologies, they added considerably to the recorded repertoire of remains, assembling a kind of pictorial museum of scattered artifacts and, more or less systematically, they laid the foundations for a nonchronological history of society, customs, and institutions. The publications of Jacob Spon and, especially, of the Maurist scholar Bernard de Montfaucon, advanced this enquiry with a reasoned skepticism, contributing to the belief that all visual evidence should be understood as symbolic.[13] The abbé Pluche, Nicolas Fréret, the abbé Barthélémy, and, above all, the Comte de Caylus wrote *mémoires* on religious practices, inscriptions, and antiquities that were summarized and criticized in the *Recueil d'antiquités égyptiennes, étrusques, grecques et romaines* from 1752 on.[14]

On a more popularizing level, and with less erudition than determination, the protestant pastor Antoine Court de Gébelin joined to the philosophical obsession with origins the antiquarian conviction that symbolism and allegory were the keys to historical interpretation. In his eight-volume *Monde primitif*, published between 1773 and his death in 1784, de Gébelin traced to their origins the history of allegory, universal grammar, the calendar, etymology, heraldry, blazonry, numismatics, games, religious rites, and customs. He found the underlying principle for these domains in allegory:

> I see allegory shining on all sides, giving the tone to the whole of antiquity, creating its fables, presiding over its symbols, animating its mythology, mingling with history, incorporating itself in the most august truths, becoming the vehicle for human knowledge, furnishing it an indispensable support.[15]

The remains of the ancient world were thus so many poetic forms invented "to instruct men in their best interests, to touch them." The origins of all such allegories lay in the customs of agricultural peoples, beginning with the first tentative written characters.

> As for the causes of all these allegories, we have seen that in the earliest times men were deprived of a means by which to communicate

their ideas quickly by writing; they drew with broad outlines, on the walls of temples, figures of distinguished persons, each characterized by an appropriate symbol, representing each season, month, and its labor, each festival of the seasons.[16]

These first symbols were rooted in nature, provider of all primitive languages. It was a short step from this symbolic interpretation of the writing *on* the walls to the understanding that entire buildings and parts of buildings might hold iconographic significance, the symbolic reading of the writing *of* the walls.

In seven "letters" on architecture, published between 1779 and 1787, the antiquarian-architect Jean Viel de Saint-Maux described a symbolic history of architecture along the lines suggested by Montfaucon and Court de Gébelin.[17] Viel, a fellow member of Court de Gébelin's lodge, Les Neuf Soeurs, was both erudite in the history of architectural theory and relentless in his scorn for philosophic conceits.[18] Widely read in the scholarly literature, from Montfaucon, Richard Pococke, and Engelbert Kaempfer, to the Comte de Caylus, Viel assaulted the reduced models of architectural origins with wit and historical evidence, much of a dubious nature. In the eyes of this *érudit,* Vitruvius was full of contradictions, falling into error as he tried to cast all the orders from the same mold, a waste of his interpreters' time as they tried to decipher his "unintelligible books," which, Viel concluded, "could only be of use on Robinson's island."[19] He was equally scornful of successive attempts to explain architectural forms, too preoccupied with materials and construction and inattentive to their religious and spiritual meanings. Thus tree trunks were not the originals of columns, nor were ropes, iron bands, and weeds the originals of bases, capitals, and ornaments, any more (he added sarcastically) than the forms of pedestals were derived from women's slippers or rows of dentils from the imitation of false teeth. Rather, the origin of architecture was more profound, touching the origins of religion and social life.

> Its sublime origin, to the great astonishment of those who pretend to be the most clever on the subject, is agriculture itself and the form of worship that was its outcome; it is the *speaking poem* of agriculture; in its totality the ancients instructed themselves as from a book, not only in primitive theogony, but also in the combinations of their cosmogony; in a word, it is in honor of agriculture that all knowledge was brought together and depicted by ingenious allegories and unmistakable emblems.[20]

But it was not only in the sculptural and painted additions to architecture that such a "book" resided: "sometimes a rough stone produced the same effect; the aspect of a building, its totality and its height equally presented ideas transmitted to posterity in its construction."[21]

Thus the temples of the ancients exhibited not the traces of some primitive hut, but "symbols and mysterious types" dedicated to the fertility of the earth and the order of the heavens. Geographic maps of the known world, signs of the zodiac, calendars of the sun, moon, and seasons, allegories of science, were displayed on the walls and ceilings and in the symbolic forms of the buildings themselves, didactic and dramatic messages for an "enlightened and hard-working people."[22] Viel began his analysis with the most primitive architectural element, the column, which owed its origin, he argued, not to the material imitation of the tree, but to its symbolic nature in "the simulacra or types of agriculture." The first sacred places were marked by freestanding stones.

> Single stones, raised at some distance from each other, whose number equaled that of the planets, the months of the year, or, finally, the days of the month, established this sacred spot, which was the gathering place for families and neighboring societies.[23]

Such symbolic oratories, whether used as simple votive altars or, later, carrying the first hieroglyphs—"representational signs to which we owe the origin of painting and of language"—or, later still, "carved into mysterious columns," finally served as the supports for a roof and suggested the idea of the temple. A pyramidal stone would symbolize the divine flame; a round or pyramidal stone represented Jupiter Cassius; a column stood for Memnon or Minerva; cylindrical stones were the simulacra of Diana, the Sybils, the Vestals, even the sun; all formed in Viel's eyes a "rustic Pantheon" only gradually personified in sculpture by the addition of hands and feet or embodied in columnar architecture. With the invention of the vault, a new symbolism arose to substitute for the open sky: the signs of the zodiac were carved on the architrave, and domes were decorated with stars; the frieze, or "zophorus," was named for its zodiacal significance, and the triglyph was a representation of the sacred tripod. Circular temples were dedicated to the sun; the number of steps were calculated by the number of planets; the columns measured the days and months. Certain columns continued, in their form, to refer to fertility, covered with breasts and garnished with signs of agriculture and cosmology.[24]

Viel drew much of his evidence for this thesis not from the standard repertory of classical architecture in Greece or Rome, but from an increasingly fertile source of knowledge and conjecture: the illustrated travel accounts of the English, German, and French in the Middle and Far East. Grelot's *Relation d'un voyage de Constantinople* (1680) had been followed by a spate of similar and more lavishly published volumes, many of which were financed through subscriptions raised either on the author's return or, sometimes, before his departure. The most popular of these, which became standard references to this unknown territory for much of the century, were Richard Pococke's *A Description of the East* (1743–1745); Alexander Drummond's *Travels through Different Cities of . . . Greece* (1754), translated as *Voyage au Levant;* Chardin's much reprinted *Voyage au Perse* (1686–1735); Robert Wood's *Ruins of Palmyra* (1753) and his *Ruins of Balbec* (1757). The accounts of Frederick Norden in Egypt and of Kaempfer in Japan supplemented the travel journals of Cornelius de Bruin from the late seventeenth century.[25] Viel relied mainly on Pococke, Norden, Kaempfer, and de Bruin.

Viel was nevertheless critical of these writers, castigating them for limited interpretations or fanciful visions that did not contribute to his own: "in fact, error is so free in the better part of their accounts that they sustain a principle opposed to that which is demonstrated to us by the ancient monuments and customs of the peoples they have visited." Thus for Viel, de Bruin was no more than a mediocre draftsman filled with biblical mythology and unappreciative of the architecture: beside the drawing of a capital, useful enough, he depicted a duck that he had just eaten; he described birds he had killed, flies he had collected, and storks' nests on the columns of Persepolis. Norden, in Egypt, was still preoccupied with the Flood, thought the pyramids were built before the invention of hieroglyphs, and was totally ignorant of agricultural stones. Pococke, also in Egypt, wanted to align the measurements of columns with contemporary practice, not understanding the different genius of the ancients. Kaempfer, in Japan, was still "more ridiculous"; speaking of stars falling from the sky and of gems that are reduced in size when shut in boxes, providing a multitude of personal anecdotes, his work was more fantasy than fact. Nevertheless, Viel drew from Kaempfer all he knew of Japanese and Chinese architecture, and from Pococke, Norden, and de Bruin most of his Middle Eastern examples. His quarrel was not so much over description as it was over interpretation.[26]

Out of this heterogeneous mingling of antiquarianism and travelers' tales, Viel forged a theory that, at least for the architects of the late eighteenth century, seemed both plausible and desirable. Quite systematically, and with much repetition from letter to letter, he built an image of ancient architecture and its symbolic meanings that was directed unambiguously toward the reformation of architecture in the present.

First, he reconstructed the origins of the classical elements, literally from the ground up, as they might be understood from a nonmaterialist viewpoint. Bases and pedestals, seated on the foundation of agriculture—the soil itself—seemed to grow like plants and were even decorated with stalks and leaves, as in Egypt and Herculaneum. Capitals, "expressing the causes of nature and the genius of each people," were the very book of the ancients and, like the head from which they were named, were decorated with all the wisdom of religion and science. Entablatures depicted the myths of the people, embellished as they were with astrological signs, with emblems of music and mortality, with bas-reliefs and friezes, forming an image of the firmament as they connected the tops of symbolic columns. Both cornices and friezes, as Balbec's example showed, were decorated with globes born on the wings of eternity, bull heads, Medusas, and agricultural garlands. Pediments derived their triangular form not from the practical shape of a pitched roof but from the miraculous properties of the triangle and, when joined to the circle or sphere, constructed a universal symbolism used widely from Rome to India.[27]

Secondly, Viel joined this symbolic code to a parallel and supporting code of customs, rites, and festivals in Greece and Egypt, as well as in China and Japan, India and Persia, sketching a cultural history of architecture that was only implicit in the studies of antiquarians such as Montfaucon and de Gébelin. Viel's vision was close to that of a comparative anthropologist.

> In Africa, in Arabia, in Persia, and in the Indies, one sees peoples and even Empires, still agrarian, who live just as the first inhabitants of the earth: the same genius, laws, allegories in the objects of worship, the

same types and symbols in the monuments of architecture. Among them no mountain, no terrain can rest without culture, without lacking, as they say, providence and public order. Their dietary regime is almost solely composed of vegetables, in order to maintain their faculties of memory as well as the strength of their religious and political constitutions; they guard against innovations; they possess knowledge of the first world.[28]

Gardens, fêtes, and ceremonies, especially in Japan, were cited to attest to this living culture of symbolic design, out of which, like Lafitau some fifty years earlier, Viel proposed a comparative method of interpretation.[29]

With symbolic *fabriques* scattered through fertile countrysides as the centers of worship and education for diligent and moral populations, this image of a universal rurality was later echoed in the monumental schemes of Boullée and, even more closely, in the rustic landscapes and symbolic monuments of Ledoux's ideal designs for Chaux. In 1801, another historian, J.-G. Legrand, adduced a passage from Viel's second letter to explain the references to the zodiac and the spherical form of a *jeu d'esprit* that the young Antoine Vaudoyer had sketched while a *pensionnaire* in Rome: a playful design for a house imagined for a wealthy patron, the "Maison d'un cosmopolite."[30] As the reviewer of Viel's first edition of 1784 wrote in the *Mercure de France,* Viel's ideas were "too peculiar to be generally adopted . . . too remarkable to be passed over in silence."[31] Clearly, Viel summarized antiquarian scholarship in a way that supported a culturally expressive architecture against those contemporary architects, from Boffrand to Patte, who persisted in their support of a Vitruvian academicism; in his final letter, he even characterized Blondel as "the Charlatan of architecture" for his inaccurate and anti-symbolic "history."[32]

Viel's most trenchant criticism was, however, reserved for Ledoux, whose monumental entrance to the Hôtel d'Uzés had, Viel claimed, plagiarized a design of Legeay, and whose office building for the Ferme générale seemed to ignore all the traditional codes of signification. Anticipating Hugo's celebrated attack on Brongniart's Bourse, Viel pretended to be puzzled by the appearance of Ledoux's building, unsure whether it was a church, a hospital, a theater, a college, a *bourse,* or even a tobacconist's shop.[33] Such criticism of Ledoux, which became commonplace among critics in the late 1780s, reflected not so much Viel's antagonism to the breakdown of classicism, as would be the case for Quatremère de Quincy, but rather Viel's historical sense of propriety, based on a belief in the absolute value and meaning of symbols and on the possibility, demonstrated by his study of other cultures, of an architecture that would be immediately legible on the one hand and tied to the highest aspirations and customs of a society on the other.

It is significant that the only contemporary architect Viel mentioned with some respect was Jean-Laurent Legeay, who, upon his return to Paris from Prussia, found no occupation and, despite the many who had passed through his *atelier*, no patron and no student who would even visit him; Viel, it seems, found an affinity with the symbolic imagination of this alienated and poverty-stricken talent, who had been rejected by the profession and copied by his students without acknowledgment.[34]

It was this edge of fantasy in Viel's "history" that led Quatremère de Quincy, one year after the final edition of the *Lettres,* to rebuke those who would try to read into architectural form meanings that were not in fact intended. Implicitly directing his criticism to Viel, he warned against writers who

> no longer see in a pediment the representation of a roof, but because of the fortuitous relation of a form of necessity to a geometric figure, the roof is only in their eyes a mysterious triangle, emblem of the divinity. Columns are no longer supports created for the need to sustain roofs and architraves; they owe their origin to votive stones, to Hermes, or to other symbols or first types of the statues of gods. The pedestals of columns are transformed into altars. Friezes, entablatures, dentils, cornices, capitals, decorated with allegorical accessories, become, themselves, allegories.[35]

Perhaps we may see in this impassioned refutation the sensibility of a historian seeking greater accuracy of interpretation; it was also that of the neoclassicist who was working to establish a different and more aesthetically normative use of the word "type."

FROM THE HUT TO THE TEMPLE

QUATREMERE DE QUINCY AND THE IDEA OF TYPE

Type, from the Greek τυπoσ, a word that by general acceptance (and thus applicable to many nuances or varieties of the same idea) expresses what is meant by model, matrix, imprint, mold, figure in relief, or bas-relief.

Quatremère de Quincy, "Type," *Encyclopédie méthodique: Architecture*, 1825.[1]

THE IDEA OF TYPE in architectural theory, with its omnibus meaning of concept, essential form, and building type, was formalized as a part of academic doctrine for the first time in the late eighteenth century. It derived from a more or less logical combination of the idea of origins, as enunciated by Laugier and epitomized in the primitive hut as a paradigm of structure, and the notion of characteristic form, as both embedded in the classical tradition and newly adopted in the terminology of the natural sciences. In the early 1780s, this combination was expressed by the word "type," a term whose peculiar etymology and history of use lent itself especially well to an idea that was vague and precise at the same time: vague in its general reference to a world of ideal forms and metaphysical beauties, precise in its application to the expressive qualities of different building types.

For many philosophes, the word retained overtones of archaism and of religious mysticism, inherited from its original biblical usage. In Boyer's dictionary of 1727, for example, type is defined as "figure," "shadow," and "representation"; it was applied most commonly to the symbolic acts and emblems of Christian theology—the "types and shadows" that represented the divinity in the Old and New Testaments.[2] Type held the connotations of received law (the signs disclosed to Moses and Solomon); prophecy (as in the ark of Noah, type of the deluge); of hermeneutics (the symbol of mysteries and miracles). It was in this sense that Voltaire spoke of *miracles typiques*, and the *Encyclopédie* described types as moral models, figurative exemplars, even as, earlier, Newton had interpreted the prophetic books of the Bible, the vision of the heavenly city, and the Temple of Solomon as so many "types and phrases" constituting a mystical language of analogy that joined the "world natural and the world politic."[3] In this sense, antiquarians, historians, and biblical scholars routinely used the word to describe religious symbolism. Viel de Saint-Maux wrote of the temples of the ancients in which "everything presents symbols and mysterious types . . . the grand attributes of the Divinity."[4]

To such hermeneutical concepts, of course, was added a precise philosophical meaning, embedded in Platonic and Neoplatonic thought. "According to the Platonists," noted the dictionary of the Académie Française, "the ideas of God are the types of all created things."[5] Here the word was almost synonymous with its cognate "archetype," as when Voltaire spoke somewhat scathingly of Plato's *idées archétypes,* which "always resided in the depths of the brain."[6]

Neoplatonism also contributed the word type to aesthetic theory as, with the revived interest in antiquity, Greek authors and their academic commentators became the touchstones for the proper judgment of ancient and modern art. Here the stimulus came from Winckelmann, whose *Reflections on the Imitation of the Greeks in Painting and Sculpture* (1755) rewrote traditional imitation theory taken from Bellori and the seventeenth-century academics by referring it to its original in Neoplatonic thought and then to the practice of Greek artists themselves. Summarizing Winckelmann's views, with which he took some exception, Diderot noted in the *Encyclopédie:*

> Monsieur Winckelmann observes that . . . the Greeks have attained ideal beauty in all genres . . . habitually seeing beautiful people in the gymnasia, in the amphitheatres, in the baths . . . these Greeks, like the bee that makes its honey from the nectar of flowers, join the most admirable eyes to the most perfect mouth, etc., and compose by this means a *type* of beauty in the female genre.[7] (emphasis added)

Here Diderot applied the idea of type to the canonical ideal of Greek beauty, the result of the procedures of perfect imitation. Familiar with Winckelmann through translation and through Gessner, a friend of Frédéric-Melchior Grimm, Diderot was critical of Winckelmann's absolute belief in the Greek imitation of nature, espousing a more experiential view of antique perfection, which was less idealist than the traditional concept of *la belle nature* and less mechanical than the idea of a choice assemblage of ideal beauties, that is, one that arrived at what he called "a true ideal model of beauty" by means of a long process of refinement, trial, and error.[8] Nevertheless, by the 1770s, the idea of type, absolute or relative, was ubiquitous in the terminology of painting and sculpture, generally with reference to the Greek ideal. Quatremère de Quincy, as a student of sculpture in the 1780s, would have been familiar with this usage.

Most important to architectural theory, the word type was current in antiquarian circles, which, since Montfaucon, had preoccupied themselves with the interpretation of what Viel de Saint-Maux called "the symbols and mysterious types of antiquity." Originally restricted to emblematic or written characters such as hieroglyphs or symbolic motifs, this use of the word type to embrace architectural elements and entire buildings, was already a commonplace by the time Viel popularized the idea in the 1780s; it was also sustained by the theory of symbolic forms prevalent in Freemasonry, which considered Solomon's Temple the type of true architecture.[9]

It was thus at once as symbolic figure and aesthetic ideal that the idea of type entered into architectural theory in Ribart de Chamoust's idiosyncratic formulation of *L'Ordre français trouvé dans la Nature* (plate 127). Published in 1783, but purportedly written eight years earlier, the work attempted finally to resolve the long-standing debate over the form of a French order, a subject previously addressed by François Blondel, Claude Perrault, and Antoine Desgodets, among others.[10] Setting out to develop an Order with "all the proportions, graces, and richness found in Greek columns," with "that character of originality that should be suitable to it, an Order of architecture, elegant and rich, that would characterize the Nation,"[11] Ribart concluded that the solution rested in the method of design rather than in superficially new forms, a method that lay in following the original principles of development of the ancient Orders themselves. One must, he stated, not simply follow the Greeks step by step, but "return to the primitive theory, that is to say, to Nature herself." Only by, so to speak, growing an Order naturally from the soil of France in the same way that Greece had grown its own, might a true national version be evolved.

Ribart had evidently taken Laugier's metaphorical frontispiece entirely literally.

> The first two Orders of Greek architecture grew up, so to speak, by themselves from Nature or, rather, from the type that the Greeks selected in preference to Nature. The Doric and the Ionic owed almost nothing to creative imagination.[12]

Here Ribart followed the conventional theory of imitation: the selection of a type as a composite of nature's ideal beauties, a standard of perfection rather than a particular example, a typical tree as opposed to a specific one, and the imitation of this *la belle nature* to ensure the perfection of art. Nature provides the type; man turns it into art. Ribart maintained that even beneath the subtleties of the Corinthian Order, "the type, deprived of its simplicity, adorned with elegance, is still to be found."[13] Ribart's type was not, then, natural in itself, but rather a crucial step away from nature[14] (plates 128–29).

Except for the interjection of the word type, this explanation might have been derived from Laugier or Batteux. But Ribart went further. Behind every man-made type, which was the essential form of the Order, rests an archetype, in this case the tree (plate 130):

> One must go back to the source, to the principles, and to the type. I mean by this word *type,* the first attempts of man to subdue nature, to make it suitable to his needs and customs and favorable to his pleasures. The sensible objects that the artist selects with correctness and reasoning from nature in order to kindle and fix at the same time the fires of his imagination, I call *archetypes.*[15]

The development of a French Order according to these principles, he recounted, was surprisingly easy; the archetypes in fact were growing at the bottom of his garden. Some young trees, "placed in groups of threes, regularly enough, even though planted by chance," were clustered in such a way as to form a "kind of natural room, hexagonal and out of the ordinary." All that was needed was the intervention of the creative gardener; Ribart trimmed the tops of the trees to an equal height, superimposed lintels, and built a roof of beams over his outdoor room, thus "rediscovering the true Greek type, but in a new guise and with marked differences." Returning the next spring, he found that nature had completed his work, growing "capitals" out of young shoots, bases out of the roots.[16] Decked with flowers and garlands for a private fête, this *temple champêtre* seemed to epitomize the very essence of French architecture, ready to be dedicated to the god of love.

Ribart's Order was not only natural, it was also symbolic: the Masonic overtones of the triadic clusters of columns defining a hexagonal plan were unmistakable; similar geometric plays on the triangle existed in the Masonic garden temples designed by Charles De Wailly for Marigny at Menars and in the plans for a Freemasonic lodge published by Neufforge.[17] Ribart had, so to speak, joined Laugier's model of natural origins to the symbolic idea of type to establish a principle of representation in nature.

It was, significantly enough, another antiquarian and Freemason, Quatremère de Quincy, who, two years after the publication of Ribart's treatise, systematically extended the concept of type as the basis for his theory and history of architecture. In his prize-winning essay on Egyptian architecture for the Académie des Inscriptions, prepared in 1785 but not published in its entirety until 1803, Quatremère, whose training in sculpture and friendship with Canova had introduced him to Winckelmann's version of neoclassical idealism, readily applied the word type where Laugier and other more materialist writers had simply referred to "models."[18] Throughout this essay, type was used almost synonymously with model; architecture, Quatremère stated, "imitated" the "types or models presented by nature to art."[19] Likewise, it followed the rules established by the "first models of original dwellings in each country," among which the hut had become "the type of Greek architecture."[20] Returning to classical idealism, Quatremère concluded that the transformation of the type "hut" had been effected by the higher imitation of the "perceptible types" of harmony, proportion, and truth found in nature and applied to the art of building.[21] In these senses, the word type was being used to join the principle of origins to the aesthetics of classical imitation theory, two concepts essentially opposed to each other, which Quatremère would later distinguish again under the rubrics of "model" and "type."

The historical-theoretical sketch of the essay on Egyptian architecture, which contained almost all the ideas of Quatremère's mature theory, was extended and systematically reelaborated in a series of articles written between 1787 and 1788 for the first volume of the *Encyclopédie méthodique: Architecture.*[22] Here the notion of type reappeared as fundamental both for the history and for the aesthetics of architecture. Articles on "Architecture," "Cabane," and "Caractère" affirmed that the first *cabane de bois* was "indisputably the type of the Greeks, among whom. . . art found a model at the same time solid and varied." Type was again similar to model, a kind of "skeleton" of architectural form; the *cabane* was, like Laugier's hut, the description of which Quatremère quoted at length, a "principle, which to architecture would be what an axiom is to morality." At once origin—formed under the aegis of natural *besoin* and according to principles parallel to nature's own—and promise of future development, the type was both first law and fruitful seed.

> It is always, and in every age, that one should turn one's eyes to the type of the hut in order to learn the reason for everything that may be permitted in architecture, to learn the use, intention, verisimilitude, suitability, and utility of each thing. This type, which should never be lost from view, will be the inflexible rule that redresses all depraved customs, all vicious errors that are the inevitable result of blind routine and of the successive imitation of works of art. In the hands of the artist, it will always have the powerful virtue of regenerating architecture and of provoking those sudden changes and revolutions of taste to which art is always open. This precious type is in some way an enchanted mirror, in which a corrupted and perverted art cannot bear to look and which, by recalling it to its origin, can always restore it to its original virtue.[23]

Unlike Laugier, however, Quatremère, with his historical and antiquarian outlook, did not posit the *cabane* as the only original type of architecture; it was indeed the only principled type, but others existed and had to be accounted for. Thus the hut was assayed alongside two other founding models for architecture, the *cave* and the *tent*.[24] Each of these three types originated as the particular shelter of a kind of people in a particular place; that is, they were all bound by the law of necessity, whether of use, climate, or country. Thus the cave had formed the natural shelter of the hunter and the fisherman; the tent had been the response to the need of the herdsman for *maisons ambulantes;* the hut, finally, was the natural habitat of the more settled farmer and cultivator. Moreover, each of these types was in some way a genetic model for a particular kind of architecture built on and developing from its principles. The heavy, dark interiors of the cave had marked the religious architecture of the Egyptians; the light and mobile structure of the tent had left its trace in the thin wooden structures of the Chinese; the four-square hut, with its post and lintel construction, had been, when transposed into stone, the model for Greek architecture. The idea of type is here joined on the one hand to history—the plural origins of architecture crystallized in paradigmatic forms of shelter—and, on the other hand, to society—each type reflecting a way of life: "the three principal ways of life offered by nature to men . . . necessarily modified the first experiments in the art of building in very different ways." Only the hut, the type of classical architecture, however, was susceptible to the kind of development that allowed for its generalization as the origin of all civilized architecture, from the Greeks to the present. In this sense, type acted to explain regional and cultural difference while at the same time asserting a fixed and preferential standard, a kind of frozen classification of an otherwise endlessly relativized history.

TYPE AND MODEL

When, in 1825, Quatremère finally published his article on type for the third volume of the *Encyclopédie méthodique*, the role of type as an aesthetic control was reinforced, and with strongly Neoplatonic overtones.[25] Type became almost synonymous with the "Idea" celebrated by Bellori and Winckelmann, a metaphysical concept to which all physical manifestations might be related, but only imperfectly.[26] Thus, in a way that was by no means consistent before, type was distinguished from model; the latter, implying "literal copy" in common usage, had too many connotations of the empirical, the physical, the mimetic, to be properly used in a philosophical manner; it also recalled the endless primitive huts built according to Laugier's model in the landscape gardens of France, England, and Germany after the 1770s, the *chaumières* that hid beneath their fake rusticity a richness of materials and taste. Quatremère was no doubt attracted to the distinction between type and model following his preference for Greek over Latin etymologies, for "intellectual" rather than "common" usage: type from the Greek, meaning the "imprint of a blow, mark, character of writing," and model from the Latin, meaning the "measure, manner, method, rule," transposed to the arts by way of the Italian *modello,* the object of imitation.[27]

> The word *type* presents less the image of a thing to copy or imitate completely than the idea of an element, which ought in itself to serve as a rule for the model. Thus, one should not say . . . that a statue, or the composition of a finished and rendered picture, has served as the type for the copy that one has made. But when a fragment, a sketch, the thought of a master, a more or less vague description, has given birth to a work of art in the imagination of the artist, one will say that the type has been furnished for him by such and such an idea, motive, or intention. The model, as understood in the practice of an art, is an object that should be repeated as it is; the type, on the contrary, is an object with respect to which each artist can conceive works of art that may have no resemblance to each other. All is precise and given in the model; all is more or less vague in the type.[28]

When applied to architecture, this distinction by implication attacked those who too rigidly held to primitivist models, who insisted that "columns have to continue to look like trees, and capitals like the branches of a tree," who suppressed the tympanum, who admitted to no convention intervening between the wooden hut and its stone descendants, who thus refused typical status to the hut by their "servile copying." The difference between type and model also stood as a criticism against those who tended to reject all rules in architecture that depended on the idea of imitation, denying the existence of metaphorical ideas in architectural contents, in favor of a materialism that in the end led to "the most complete anarchy in the totality and details of every composition."

As an object, then, the hut that Quatremère imagined to be the origin of Greek stone architecture had neither precise form nor dimensions; no longer even a principled hypothesis of elements and their combination, nor an aesthetic canon (which, by definition, the primitive nature of the hut as "built need" refused), it was simply an idea of antecedence, a preexisting source, or, as Quatremère qualified, "an elementary principle, which is like a kind of nucleus about which are collected, and to which have been coordinated over time, the developments and variations of forms to which it is susceptible."[29]

Before being translated into stone, the hut itself had to undergo innumerable transformations until, gradually, "that kind of combination to which the use of wood is susceptible, once adopted in each country, becomes a type, which, perpetuated by custom, perfected by taste, and accredited by immemorial usage, must inevitably pass into undertakings in stone."[30]

Nor would this stone construction itself yet be exemplary of the principles of architecture; no building principally subordinated to necessity could be considered art. Only with the development of the idea and practice of ideal imitation, based on the idealized proportions of the human body, first in sculpture, then, more abstractly, in architecture, would the full aesthetic system of classicism be revealed.

> Only a people familiarized by its climate, its mores, and its institutions with the sight of the human body, could give birth to a system of imitation in which the limited idea of *a* man is transformed into the general idea of *man*, in which art can derive from its observations a universal type, which, unable to belong to any individual, becomes the presumed model that nature desires effectively to produce according to its general laws, one it would have surely produced if it only had in view the pleasure of the eyes in the generation of beings. This type was the *ideal* of human nature.[31]

Quatremère echoed Winckelmann in his identification of the ideal climate of Greece, its society, its formation of beautiful bodies, its imitation of the most beautiful aspects to produce a type of beauty crucial for the transformation of building into architecture.

> Beneath the most beautiful skies, amid the political and civil institutions most favorable to genius, sculpture, marching with slow but sure steps, followed a route unknown till then. Raising itself by degrees from the indication of the most unformed signs to the distinguishing of the principal dimensions . . . it finally arrived at the reasoned knowledge of the body of man and its proportions. This reasoned imitation of the human body opened for architecture, if not a new model, at least a new analogy for a model.[32]

Which is to say, a type.

But the embodiment of the ideal type of beauty in the type of architecture, producing the fully developed temple, itself a type for classicism, constituted only the most general level of the type, that which resided in the essential qualities of a place or a people. Quatremère also allowed the use of the word to refer to what, more specifically, might be understood as the type behind particular building types; he would have called this a relative as opposed to a general type. Here Quatremère insisted neither on the primacy of the program, as it was to be developed by Durand and Bruyère, nor on the simple application of antique precedents; indeed his analogy was surprisingly functionalist in the sense of a typical form responding to typical use, and it was drawn from the example of "certain mechanical arts."

> No one ignores the fact that a great number of pieces of furniture, utensils, seats, and clothes have their necessary type in the uses one makes of them and the natural customs for which one intends them.

> Each of these things has, truly, not its model but its type in needs and in nature. In spite of what the bizarre industrial mind tries to change in these objects, contrary to the simplest instinct, who does not prefer in a vase the circular form to the polygonal? Who does not believe that the form of a man's back ought to be the type of the back of a chair? That the rounded form should not be the sole reasonable type of a style of hair?[33]

The comparison between the form of a human back to the form of a chair recalled the earlier functionalist argument of Lodoli, who compared the form of a gondola's prow to the form of a chair, an analogy that gained wide circulation in the 1780s; reported to Quatremère's friend the painter Jacques-Louis David, this analogy had become the inspiration for a series of experiments in chair form, built to David's design by Jacob. Perhaps the most startling of these designs took pride of place as the centerpiece of David's *Brutus,* standing between two other chairs of evidently Etruscan origin that served only to indicate the modernity and typicality of the empty chair in the middle, the curve of its back strikingly similar to the prow of a ship and, more particularly, to that of the Argonauts as illustrated on the title page of Winckelmann's *Monumenti Antichi Inediti* of 1767.[34]

Applying this "mechanical" analogy to buildings, Quatremère spoke of the characteristic form of a building type, based on a primitive type that had given birth to the original. He gave the examples of pyramids, formed according to the type of the eternal flame, and the tumulus, based on the type of the primitive mound covering the coffin. Finally, he referred the architect to his own article on character, "where we have extensively demonstrated that each of the principal kinds of building should find in the fundamental purpose, in the uses to which it is given over, a type that is suitable for it."[35] Such a type should be recognizable in the building's outer appearance. Here the concept of type was revealed to be bound to another idea fundamental to the eighteenth-century architect: the idea of *character* or, as Blondel put it in his *Cours d'architecture,* the demand that "all the different kinds of productions that belong to architecture should carry the imprint of the particular purpose of each building; each should possess a character that determines its general form and declares the building for what it is."[36]

TYPE AND CHARACTER

As Quatremère well realized, the etymologies of type and character embody the relationship between the two. Type, in its more technical meaning as the physical instrument of printing, derives from the original Greek, which, besides referring to "model, matrix, mold," also and more directly meant "imprint" or "impression," the Greek *typos* having the sense of "to beat" or "to impress." The etymology of the word character was similarly linked to the act of marking.

> This word comes from the Greek χαρακτηρ (impressed mark, distinctive form), which is formed from the verb χαραδδειν (to engrave, to imprint). Thus *character* signifies a mark or figure traced on stone,

> metal, paper, or other material, with a chisel, a burin, a brush, a pen, or other instrument, so as to be the distinctive sign of something. In figurative language it means, that which constitutes the nature of beings in a manner that is distinctive and proper to each.[37]

The double notion of a physical impression or stamp and a written, figurative character, coincided nicely with the idea of an architecture that, in its relation to typicality, on the general and the specific levels, would be, quite naturally, a sign of its own nature. A true type would possess its own character, which would be unambiguously marked in its form.

Natural scientists such as Buffon and Adanson had already made this connection between typicality and characterization, on the one hand identifying what Buffon called "a general prototype for each species," and on the other identifying what Adanson called "general and particular characters," the visible signs of the type and its variations. For the botanist Carolus Linnaeus, the question of character had become central to taxonomical procedure, for the purpose of identifying fixed, formal properties of the species in question that might characterize its type—such as the stamens or pistils of a plant.[38]

In one of the longest essays of the *Encyclopédie méthodique*, Quatremère developed the theory of character along these lines, moving logically from a consideration of the general definition of the word character, its specific definition, and its signification when observed in nature, to the characteristics of peoples, places, and climates, their architecture and their types. For Quatremère, the passage from natural character to artistic character was seamless, moving down a chain of inheritance that was both organic and inevitable. The very use of the word in a figurative as opposed to a literal sense—the notion of a characteristic being or object as derived from that of a mark or written sign—was itself entirely natural: "as in the origin of societies, the material signs of objects were the first elements of writing and the characters from which it was composed."[39] Thus from the beginning, writing and its characters were transposed to nature and its characteristics; by systematic enquiry, an enlightened natural science had only reinforced the connection.

From such natural origins, the descent of characters in the world moved from the general and essential characters of nature—"the type by which nature makes its works recognizable"—to the distinctive or "accidental" character of the varieties in each species, caused by different agents in place and climate, and finally to the relative character proper to particular species or individuals. The first was recognizable by its overall power, its "strength" or "force" of character; the second was synonymous with physiognomy; the third identified in tangible ways the individual of the species. Quatremère thus followed Buffon in accounting for the numerous varieties and exceptions to any overall "prototypical" character that might be ascribed to a species by means of climate, race, place, and accident. And what held true for natural species also held true for nature in a more fundamental sense, precisely in those original causes of characteristic difference: the characters of climate, from hot to cold, and of landscape, from flat to mountainous, acted in predictable ways on the beings they nurtured. In Burkean terms, Quatremère called for definite character in landscape—vast plains with their horizons lost to infinity like the ocean, high mountains, varied and unexpected scenes—as opposed to flat and uniform conditions that offer little stimulation to the mind or to the senses. Similarly with climate: hot and cold climates produced distinctive physiognomies and mentalities, neutral ones only characterless inhabitants. The same influences determined the character of individuals, institutions, and peoples; from the physical character of the place stemmed the moral character of each nation and its society.[40]

In this way, language, poetry, and all the arts of imitation were impressed with their own character, which could only faithfully record the physical and moral qualities of nature, peoples, and individuals. The language of the passions, stated Quatremère, was everywhere shaped by that of nature, cold climates producing reason, hot climates excess, even monsters. He cited Winckelmann to support the view that only in Greece was the temperate balance achieved, where "nature, having passed through all the degrees of hot and cold, was fixed as in a central point," allowing for the equal mixing of reason and imagination. As in nature, artistic character also took on three modes: nature provided essential character, while political and moral causes formed distinctive and relative character.

As one of the arts of imitation, architecture necessarily followed these general rules. But by imitating nature less directly than the other arts, more by analogy than by appearance, its characters were conceived more abstractly. Quatremère argued that there was "an intellectual link of ideal forms and the moral character of architecture" with natural forms and the proprieties of a state. Here, too, the three kinds of character pertained.

> Is it not certain, when you say of a building that it has *a* character, that you mean a kind of originality, a special physiognomy, a manner of being belonging to it in particular. But when you say it has *character*, do you not mean those imposing qualities that strike the spectator, especially the height, the sturdiness, and the solidity of everything that approaches ideas of grandeur and power. And when, on seeing a building, you say that it has its *own* character, do you not mean to designate by this the idea of suitability and propriety, as if you were to say: the building announces, by its exterior and apparent qualities, its purpose, why it was built?[41]

The general and essential character of an architecture was the result of place and climate—hence the origins of the three types of architecture.

> The character of the architecture of different peoples consists in a way of being, in a conformation necessitated by physical needs and moral customs, and in the depiction of the climates, the ideas, the tastes, the mores, the pleasures, and the very *character* of each people.[42]

Despite the fact that, as in natural species, habitat and circumstances tended to, in Quatremère's words, "denature" and "decompose" first needs, the qualities of national and regional architectures might be traced to their roots. Quatremère detailed with great care the relationships between institutions and architecture. Thus the hot climates of Asia, with their violent political and social institutions, were represented by arabesques, by caprices, and by fantastic, unregulated, and licentious architecture. These tormented, exuberant, and irrational products were the natural result of *le génie de l'hyperbole*, the taste for the gigantic and for everything that breaks the bounds of the possible.[43] In Egypt, however, nature and society were constrained by "a sort of visible mechanism" where all was subjected to reason, leaving no space for the imagination (plates 131–133).

> Egypt has been prepared by this to become a sort of observatory, a kind of school for the sciences. Its pure sky without clouds provided the first elements of astronomy. Geometry was born of the need to recognize the properties lost in the element that fertilized them. The sciences of calculation joined themselves naturally to the needs of life, linking themselves to the memory of the past like a vision of the future. Everything must lead the spirit of this people to the calculations of necessity more than to the caprices of pleasure. Thus you see the blocks of marble from the quarries, cut with the greatest simplicity, placed one on the other according to the direction of the cardinal points to form the pyramids.[44]

Between the "license" of Asia and the "servitude" of Egypt lay the fair architecture of Greece, an architecture of order and harmony. The soil, the climate, and the temperature, the equilibrium that formed the national character, was transferred into architecture as balance, nuance, and delicacy. This formed the perfection of Greek architecture and gave it its general applicability.

> Leaving aside everything that the pleasure of a beautiful climate, the rich spectacle of an enchanted nature, the variety, magnificence, and delight of its soil should inspire in the sensations of its inhabitants, I cannot prevent myself from regarding the arts as fruits susceptible to being transplanted, saying that their perfection depends upon climate; and when I see that, in the midst of all architectures, there may be found one equally distant from all excess born in a climate equally distant from all extremes, I cannot misunderstand the direct action of nature on the essential and primitive *characters* of architecture.[45]

As Blondel had noted earlier, the problem with such a determinism of place and climate rested precisely with this question of transplantation, the particular appropriateness of the architecture of Greece and Rome for Northern Europe. The Gothic style, which would be identified later as northern par excellence, was in Quatremère's eyes no more native to Europe than the Greek. Following a number of writers such as Fontenelle and Christopher Wren, Quatremère believed that the Gothic derived its motifs from the Arabic.[46] Colder climates had nevertheless quite correctly adopted the Greek manner, gradually and insensibly adapting it to the specific needs of the north; but this process, in which "certain forms were altered and denatured to the point of losing the true characteristics," resulted in a loss of the essential nature of Greek architecture. Therefore, Quatremère concluded, there was an urgent need for rules and precepts to correct and bring back architecture to its original strength; thus the particular importance of the idea of type to didactic theory.

> In regions deprived of one of these causes or even of all, precepts and teaching become indispensable, because they can themselves enter into the order of moral things that influences the arts; even if they are

insufficient in their action on art in general, they will not be on some works in particular.[47]

To return all architectural principles to the type, however, only solved the question of character in general, that is, the character of the art as a whole; there remained the determination of what Quatremère termed "accidental," "distinctive," or "original" character, and, finally, "relative" character. Distinctive character, tied closely to general character, still belonged to the different architectures of peoples; it was the mark of Chinese, Arabic, Egyptian, and Greek architectures, in the sense that they might be said to have a character of their own. Quatremère called this the "physiognomical" character.

> It is to architecture what physiognomy is to the face, which while fixed and given does not prevent all the passions, all the sensations, all the movements of the soul being depicted in a most varied fashion; but as there are certain physiognomies where the play of passions is deployed more easily, there are also certain architectures whose distinctive character is so pronounced that the other kinds of character will hardly be manifested.[48]

Thus the lightness of Chinese architecture, the heaviness of Egyptian, the grace and harmony of Greek, the luxury of Roman, were all physiognomies that marked the work no matter what its particular function, more or less susceptible to variety and nuance.

Finally, there was relative character, the "synonym of propriety and suitability," by which Quatremère referred to the individual character belonging to different kinds or types of building. Quatremère analyzed every architectural level that might contribute to the unambiguous expression of a building's contents.

> The art of characterizing, that is to say, of rendering sensible, by means of material forms, the intellectual qualities and moral ideas that can be expressed in buildings; the art of making understood, by means of the accord and suitability of all the constituent parts of a building, its nature, its propriety, its use, and its purpose; this art, I say, is perhaps, of all the secrets of architecture, the finest and most difficult both to develop and to comprehend. This happy talent of feeling and making felt the physiognomy proper to each monument; this sure and delicate discernment that makes perceptible the different nuances of buildings that at first sight seem unsusceptible to any characteristic distinctions; this wise and discreet use of the different manners, which are like the musical tones of architecture; the adroit mixture of signs that can be employed by art to speak to the eyes and the mind; this precise and fine touch . . . can only be imperfectly outlined in theory.[49]

Such a ramified art naturally encompassed all the expressive means of architecture, together with their rules of application; Quatremère divided his consideration into two parts, the one concerned with what he called "ideal" characterization—the high poetics of the art—the other with "imitative" character—the character of specific building types. He took this division from the classical theory of painting and sculpture that distinguished between ideal and imitative beauty.

Ideal character consisted in the communication of ideas ("intellectual relationships") by means of architectonic forms; it was "to architecture what poetry is to language, the poetic language of the art." Invented by the ancients, it enabled them to convey the power, strength, grandeur, and majesty of temples dedicated to Jupiter; the seriousness, nobility, and gravity of temples dedicated to Hercules, Mars, and Minerva; the pleasure, delicacy, gaiety, and gentleness of those dedicated to Venus, Flora, Proserpina, and the nymphs of the springs.

Imitative character, on the other hand, conveyed specific messages connected to the nature of the building by means of a precisely calculated language of forms and attributes.

> This expression may be rendered either by the gradation of richness and of size in proportion to the nature of the building, as required by social decorum;
> or by the indication of the moral qualities inherent in each building, the feeling of which . . . seems to lie outside the bounds of rules;
> or by the general and particular forms of architecture;
> or by the kind of construction that may be employed in it;
> or by the resources of decoration;
> or, finally, by the choice of attributes. . . .[50]

In this way, each kind of building might be rendered according to its place in a hierarchy that ranged from the cottage to the palace; the qualities of each building might be marked by the richness or the poverty of decoration, from the opulence of the temple to the "nudity" of a hospice; the traditional forms of antique building types might be used, in whole or in part, to convey meanings long established by use and opinion, from the temple to the pyramid; materials and structure might be more or less appropriate; finally, decorative motifs and attributes might add a specificity to all these means, precisely labeling the type.

In the context of late-eighteenth-century practice and the increasing number of experiments in institutional form, Quatremère's discussion of relative character takes on added significance on two levels: one, as he set out the categories by which character would be understood and applied in the Ecole des Beaux Arts after 1795; the other, as his strict sense of neoclassical propriety measured the extent to which the traditional genres had already been exploded, in his terms "denatured," beyond recognition. Thus Quatremère insisted even more strongly than Blondel on the rigorous application of the hierarchies of luxury, "the gradation among the different buildings of the city," as a political and moral imperative that the general forms of architecture be returned to their original use—that the rectangular and circular temple replace the false, modern Greek cross; that the use of columns and peristyles be proscribed for all the functions of public security or utility from the arsenal to the barracks; that the character of the hospice and the hospital be carefully distinguished from the scientific academy and the public granary, that of the museum from the theater, the odeon, and the concert hall. Each building type in the city was listed and characterized to regain the sense of dignified and virtuous variety infusing the "restorations" of the Greek and Roman agora and fora, an architectural equivalent to the idealized descriptions of classical cities in the abbé Barthélémy's *Voyage du jeune Anacharsis.*[51]

Quatremère's rules for building forms, their elements and attributes, were all couched in terms that clearly demonstrated his conception of architecture as a language. The definition of the word character itself derived from an etymology of origins that recalled the linguistic theories of Turgot; the recognition of the figurative transposition of the idea of written marks to the metaphysics of characterization; the generic use of the figure in identifying the characters of nature; the fundamental definition of character as a sign; the understanding of language as the first of all the arts of imitation, model for all the other arts, with its deployment of figures and its example of enthusiasm in the "language of the passions," wherein lay the origins of poetry; the theory of language as influenced by climates, drawn from Rousseau; the idea of physiognomy as a language, these premises alone testify to the ubiquity of the linguistic model.

But Quatremère, like many of the Encyclopedists and ideologues of his generation—de Beauzée, Destutt de Tracy, and de Gérando—understood the arts of representation literally to be languages, and his prerevolutionary writings, less influenced by German idealism than those of the 1800s, adumbrated a comprehensive theory of what later became known as *architecture parlante.* Architecture was a language because, in the most general sense, it could be considered "a way of expressing or depicting something . . . rendering perceptible intellectual ideas . . . or particular uses"; its signs worked to this end on each level that Quatremère had distinguished for character, from the natural to the conventional. Of these signs the most important were, first, the "forms of architecture"—the partis of antiquity—which might be applied only according to strict criteria of traditional meaning, and, second, the decorative attributes, which more or less figuratively described a building's use and idea. Quatremère spoke of the general forms of architecture much in the same way as the scientist Lavoisier, speaking of the need for a nomenclature in chemistry, defined "a well-made language" composed of geometric signs; the geometric conformations of architecture could, as Quatremère claimed, "with these simple and varied means . . . at little cost and within the circle of a small number of elements, change the physiognomy of all objects." Thus he called for the use of an architectural geometry that would immediately signify interior character on the exterior, notably in the case of the theater, where the semicircle of the auditorium should be visible as the outer form of the monument—a maxim put into effect by Boullée.[52]

Properly speaking, however, it was decoration, comprising interior and exterior painting and sculpture, that constituted the language of architecture. Quatremère thought of decoration as "a kind of writing . . . a language whose signs and expressions should be endowed with a precise signification capable of conveying ideas." Perhaps the greatest resources of decoration beyond the simple art of embellishment were attributes: the figurative devices, emblems, and motifs, either taken from antiquity or invented by the artist, that were so many "signs of the different proprieties and qualities of buildings."[53] In Quatremère's view, they were far more potent than inscriptions for characterizing monuments, because they deployed all the potential associations of symbol and allegory. In fact, attributes might be understood primarily as a genre of allegory.

> The use of attributes offers to the architect the most vast and unlimited field by which to characterize monuments, because the invention of attributes has no more limits than the art of allegory. One can change them, modify them, renew them in every different guise; genius, the sole master in this realm, has nothing to fear but their being rendered obscure by the power of new combinations.[54]

The idea of allegory had been much elaborated in eighteenth-century aesthetic theory; it was an integral part of the doctrine of *ut pictura poesis*. It had also been much attacked by philosophes who were critical of the ambiguities of meaning and the academic attenuation of effect typical of the drawn-out and artificially forced allegories of the rococo. The abbé Pluche, in his *Histoire du ciel* (1748), had argued strongly against "these enigmatic figures" as a burden to art, unwanted by the public and untenable as devices for communication.[55] Other philosophes were more charitable, out of an interest in the early forms of writing, pictographic and hieroglyphic; they were content to characterize the different uses of allegory, in emblems, devices, and symbols, as a way to decipher what were thought to be metaphoric scripts.

De Beauzée summarized critical opinion in the *Encyclopédie méthodique*, using the work of Court de Gébelin on the origins of allegory in language and in writing, and setting out the principles both of proper allegorical interpretation in antiquity and of the good use of allegory in contemporary works. He agreed with Fréret on the potentially didactic use of the genre: "allegory is thus a means, in use for a long time, that often serves successfully to carry instruction."[56] Quatremère adopted this view, as well as de Beauzée's definition: allegory was the presentation "of a thought under the image of another thought in such a way as to render it more perceptible and striking than if it had been presented directly without any kind of veil."[57] As such, it might, he admitted, seem more a stranger to architecture than to the pictorial arts of painting and sculpture; but "true" allegories were possible in architecture, notably in the conscious relationships made between buildings. Thus the two temples built by Marcellus in Rome, dedicated to Virtue and to Honor, "enclosed a mysterious and sublime lesson" in their adjacency—it was only by way of virtue that honor is attained. Similarly, the circular temple of the sun in Thrace, the Temple of Vesta in Rome surrounding the sacred fire, and the portico of the temple at Olympus dedicated to the seven liberal arts, all expressed meaning in form allegorically. Hidden meaning might also be detected in the Egyptian temples, lost together with the key to the hieroglyphs.[58] Used in this way, allegory was a "figurative discourse" that "makes architecture an ocular language, a sort of hieroglyphic writing."

> The resources that decoration finds in allegory are such that the architect can treat all kinds of subjects. It is not simply by indirect relationships, by more or less abstract combinations, by a choice of analogical relationships, that architecture can arouse in our soul ideas that correspond to the qualities it displays. By means of allegory, the art of architecture is made *historian and narrator:* it explains to us the general

> and particular subject of which it treats, and it informs us of the moral aim as well as of the physical use of the building. Allegorical decoration takes the place of inscriptions; it says more, it speaks better, than all those legends that weigh down pediments and walls.[59] (emphasis added)

Such a primacy of the visual, emblematic sign over the alphabetic sign not only places Quatremère in the tradition of Condillac and Rousseau, but, theoretically at least, relates him to a number of architects to whom he was temperamentally and critically opposed, including, of course, Ledoux, whose celebrated axiom, "example is the most powerful of lessons," became a premise of the overtly emblematic architecture of the imaginary town of Chaux, and, closer to his own antiquarian interests, Viel de Saint-Maux, whose elaboration of Court de Gébelin's principle of allegory in the primitive world became the model for the young Antoine Vaudoyer. Quatremère held that allegory, in the hands of these symbolic architects, was taken far beyond its legitimate bounds. Under the heading "Abuse," he warned against any excess: "as with languages, there are many ways in architecture to speak against the rules of grammar." Viel de Saint Maux, with his proclamation of a universal symbolism, was a particular target of Quatremère's criticism, but in article after article Quatremère also castigated the work of Ledoux, especially as evinced in the *barrières;* here it was significant that not only was Ledoux taken to task for an architecture "denatured" and "decomposed" in its combinations of heterogeneous architectural elements and distortions of scale, but also for the indiscriminate mingling of antique types, none of which seemed to answer the requirements of monumental gateways. Ironically, Quatremère surmised that Ledoux had fallen into error by taking for his model the existing tollgates of Paris, the mean and broken-down huts of wooden boards. A correct "type" for imitation, that of the triumphal arch, he implied, would have led to a more suitable architecture for entrances to the city.[60]

The argument thus returned to its origin. Type controlled the language of character, even as propriety controlled decoration, in a chain of command from the hut to the temple and on to all its contemporary variants. History, and historical styles, were likewise strictly controlled.

Despite Quatremère's pretensions to antiquarian scholarship and historical connoisseurship, his idea of typicality, tied as it was to that of character, was inflected with only the slightest of historicized contents; indeed, its role seemed more calculated to master a history that might otherwise escape the bounds of classical taste than to account for historical difference and change. His pseudohistorical typology of origins was essentially static, establishing a plural root for architecture only to reestablish a preferred, single root. In this sense, Quatremère's theory opposed the increasingly relativized idealism of his German contemporaries from Herder to Schelling; it was, in fact, entirely at home in its methodological, Encyclopedist format. The very insistence of his arguments, together with their neat simplicity, appealed to a generation that looked in uncertain times to the comfort of a preestablished classical canon, a set of readily identifiable objects by which to recognize cultural excellence.

FROM RESTITUTION TO RESTORATION

While traveling as a student in Italy, Quatremère had dreamed of a project, the idea of which "he was more than once astonished had not yet arrived in Rome." Among the ruins of Catania, at the foot of Mount Etna in Sicily, he had visited the museum of the Prince of Biscari, "where all the genres of antiquity are found set out and selected with care and knowledge." This led him to imagine a program for "a museum of architecture, where one would bring together, with order, the scattered debris that is trampled underfoot and lost to artists and, in the end, lost to the arts."[61] Such a literal collection of fragments later became distasteful to his classicist idealism, but the idea of an exemplary collection of the best architectural and sculptural models continued to preoccupy him for the rest of his life .

On one level, ideal perfection might be found only in the imagination. Thus Quatremère saw the ruins of the Acropolis as a kind of silent witness to excellence, an active agent of criticism: preferably, all students of architecture should undertake the pilgrimage to Athens, but those who could not should "profit from the lessons of these eloquent ruins."

> One wishes that the architect who undertakes a building or project would place it, in his imagination, within the walls of Athens and that, surrounding it with the masterpieces that remain or those whose memory has been conserved by history, he would examine them, drawing from them analogies applicable to his own designs. Their silent and ideal witness would still be one of the most authentic kinds of advice he might receive.[62]

In the face of this "imaginary tribunal," architecture might regain its lost virtue.

On another level, the desire to secure a paradigm was exemplified in Quatremère's attitude toward restoration of statuary and architectural monuments. In his monograph on the Olympian Jupiter, he sought to establish scientific bases for the restoration of statues, later to be applied in his projected restoration of the Venus de Milo[63] (plate 134). In architecture he traced a seamless path from the act of "restitution" or imaginary evocation of a destroyed monument from contemporary descriptions or remaining fragments according to "the general theory of imitation," to the wholesale restoration of ruined structures.[64] He castigated those whose "frivolous tastes" caused them to perpetuate the ruined state of existing antiquities or, even more dangerously, to "provoke or accelerate their destruction in order to find in them models of ruins" for artistic imitation; he censored those "simulacra of antique ruins . . . broken columns, scattered stones" set in irregular gardens as a picturesque tableau; and he called for the conservation of ruins, clearing away debris and foliage, cleaning their stones, and replacing their materials.

> Should some kinds of imitation lose something of the picturesque from this, it is much more important, both for history and for the arts in general, to prolong the existence of architectural monuments, to arrest their deterioration and to complete them when there is still time by reestablishing what is lacking on the model of the parts that still survive.[65]

This was a simpler task for architecture than for sculpture because buildings were "ordinarily composed of similar parts that could, by means of measures, be identically reproduced or copied." In this vein, Leo von Klenze and Schinkel were to propose entirely serious restorations of the Acropolis, while Quatremère himself forged a short-lived alliance with the young Victor Hugo in the latter's "war against the demolishers" after 1825.

Here the ideal of type and the practice of restoration came together in their antimuseological stance; for, in Quatremère's view, a living culture required both types, or imaginary forms of perfection, and models, or exemplars of the type, chosen from the best examples. Museums, presenting only fragments detached from their original context or, worse, setting them against each other in a never-ending series of comparisons and differences, represented a historical understanding that could not, out of its own integrity, stop at the classical and ignore history as a whole; museums by definition were relativist and catholic in their inclusiveness. They were also in some sense "cemeteries of art" that, by removing works of art from "that totality of relations from which they receive, in some way, their life," caused them to lose their power over the observer's emotions. The choice, as Quatremère's supporters and adversaries recognized, lay between a normative aesthetics justified by history and a history of objects representing different aesthetic values.

ARCHITECTURE IN THE MUSEUM

DIDACTIC NARRATIVES FROM BOULLEE TO LENOIR

The Museum: one understands by this word the bringing together of everything nature and art have produced that is most rare and perfect. A Museum is the Temple of Nature and Genius. This definition indicates at once the idea and the proportions of a monument suitable to carry the title of Muséum français.

A.-G. Kersaint, *Discours sur les monuments publics*, 1792.[1]

THE MUSEUM, as an idea, was not, in the period immediately preceding the Revolution, tied as strictly as it was to be in the nineteenth century to an institution dedicated to exhibiting historical artifacts. Its literal meaning, home of the Muses, embraced a range of concepts, some real, some imaginary, from the quasi-academic gathering common in the 1780s to grand schemes for bringing together all the sciences and the arts in a single Temple of Knowledge.[2] The Grand prix program of 1779 had outlined such a monument "to contain the products of the sciences, the liberal arts, and natural history." Four years later, Boullée designed a project for a "Museum at the center of which is a Temple of Fame."[3] With its blind walls, a square plan divided into four courtyards and a huge central "Pantheon," Boullée's museum-temple anticipated a type that was later systematized by Durand and Schinkel. Boullée's grand design, however, had more to do with his experiments in the Burkean sublime than with any clear conception of classification or display.[4]

The word "museum" was nevertheless didactic by implication: it was often used to refer to a collection of examples of a particular art, especially in painting and sculpture. Winckelmann had demonstrated the value to the sculptor of a collection of plaster casts; similar arguments were used to support the salons and the permanent display of the royal art collection in the Palais du Luxembourg or the Louvre.[5] In the domain of architecture, Blondel and his successors were agreed on the need for an exposition of *chefs-d'oeuvre*. This might take the form of a collection of scale models arranged chronologically or systematically; or it might, as Boullée suggested, be composed of designs, taken either from the past or from the best current practice, that would serve the student as well as the patron in deciding through comparison the best solution to a particular program.[6]

> Supposing that the government gave to architects the same encouragement it gives to painters and sculptors, the result would be that we would have *examples,* which are as rare in architecture as they are numerous in the other arts. By means of the comparison of works, artists would be placed at the level their talent has acquired for them. With time, one would have a *museum of architecture* that would include everything one could hope from the art by means of the efforts of those who cultivate it. These numerous examples would serve as guides when circumstances required.[7] (emphasis added)

The advantage of such a museum was that it needed no permanent place of exhibition and could be owned by every interested amateur or professional in the form of a published *recueil* and accompanying catalogue. It was in this spirit that Boullée collected his exemplary designs and, before his death, wrote his commentary on them. Ledoux, similarly assembling his engraved works for publication, considered the result an "Encyclopedia or Architectural museum" in his 1800 description. Durand published in his remarkably successful *Recueil et Parallèle des édifices en tous genres* a "complete and inexpensive table of architecture," which artists and the students of the Ecole polytechnique "could look through quickly, examine without difficulty, and study fruitfully."[8] As we have seen, Lequeu adopted this course in his isolation, preparing, in conjunction with lessons in rendering shadows, a collection of "a number of buildings of different peoples disseminated throughout the world."

These architectural "museums," visual counterparts of the Encyclopedic discourse, were for the most part conceived systematically rather than historically. Stressing classification and comparison, their implied method was that of the natural scientist, not the antiquarian. Boullée stressed the need for comparison; Ledoux spoke of "abbreviating the annals of time"; Durand insisted on "classifying the buildings and monuments according to type" and drawing them to the same scale. Examples might be drawn from history, but, once selected, they merged into a timeless canon, supported by the fiction of a morphological perfection attributed to each "species" of building. Thus the historian Legrand, contributing an introduction to Durand's *Recueil,* stressed the importance of natural history, wherein the architect would find "general principles embedded in its immutable laws and diverse products."

> The formation of shells, the development of plants, the growth of minerals, the work of insects, are so many workshops open for his instruction, which should furnish him the means of putting his own in good order.[9]

The principles of observation outlined by Buffon—formal discrimination, selection of types, and ordering of species—also applied to architecture.

> In order to disentangle the true principles, to demonstrate them incontestably, one should make them stand out by bringing together all the monuments that deserve to be known; these monuments should be placed in a simple and clear order that makes their comparison easy, indicates their origin, their genre, their perfection, and their decadence.[10]

Legrand's belief in the typical, in the systematic method of study and judgment, coincided exactly with that of Durand.

> One sees without difficulty the advantages of this table of monuments of all centuries and of the works of nature distributed in different climates and having a relationship to architecture or serving as the type for some of its parts . . . above all, those of providing the surest and easiest means of establishing all the systems, of wrestling with them and judging them by experience.[11]

The idea of type, as derived from the natural sciences, here joined the classical notion of the aesthetic canon in such a way as to represent history, in concrete examples, as an undifferentiated field of ideal forms, a table of architectural species. Here typicality directly opposed temporality and its inevitable result: relativism.

It was in this spirit that the artist-traveler Louis-François Cassas conceived his museum of architecture. A collection of scale models of the best examples taken from every period, "restored" to their original state, it was in every way a three-dimensional realization of Durand's *Recueil.*[12]

In his catalogue notes to the display, first opened to the public in 1806, Legrand underlined its educational role:

> The collection of masterpieces of architecture, executed in models following their true proportions and related in suitable scales, alone offers a powerful means of instruction of its kind.[13]

The "reasonable selection" exercised by Cassas allowed a student immediate experience of only the most perfect models: out of some seventy-two exhibits, over half were Greek, Etruscan, or Roman. Among Cassas' models, supplemented by engravings that picturesquely showed the restored monuments in their present state of ruination, the student would have no sense of history in its changes over time. Instead, time was collapsed so that "one would see at the same instant, by traversing the interval of many thousands of years, what each building once was and what it is now."[14]

THE MONUMENTAL HISTORY OF FRANCE

> A museum should be instituted according to two points of view, one political, the other concerned with public instruction; from the political point of view, it should be established with enough splendor and magnificence to speak to every eye . . . ; from the instructional point of view, it should include everything the arts and the sciences could together offer to public education.
>
> A. Lenoir, *Musée des monuments français,* 1800.[15]

Partially forced by Revolutionary events, partially supported by an understanding of historical specificity and change derived from Winckelmann, there emerged in the 1790s a concept of the museum that in many ways was opposed to the universalizing idealism of the Académie: one open to the study of historical periods other than the classical, bound to the revalorization of a French heritage that included the Middle Ages, and immediately engaged in the struggle to counter the destructive acts symbolic of the death of the Old Regime. In this concept, a sense of chronology and of the relative importance of each epoch of French history countered a still strong allegiance to classical aesthetics and systematic comparison.

It was a paradox noted by many observers of the Revolution that the cultural vandalism of its early years, supported tacitly or openly by succesive governments, was accompanied by an emerging sensibility towards a national patrimony embodied in historical and artistic monuments.[16] The word "vandalism" was indeed first used in this context by one of its most outspoken opponents, the abbé Grégoire, who in a series of reports to the Convention listed the following reasons for preserving the records and monuments of the past: *nationalism,* recognizing French Gothic as "one of the most daring conceptions of the human spirit," an aid toward "happiness in being French"; *didacticism,* viewing the objects of the past as so many *chefs-d'oeuvre* for instruction in the crafts, art, and design; and *moral improvement,* to be derived from the exemplary nature of historical works.[17]

But, at least in the first three years of the Revolution, the patriotic nature of historical monuments was by no means universally accepted. For a combination of ideological and politically expedient reasons, what was called "vandalism" by Grégoire and his supporters was often openly advocated by administrators and legislators. A typical memorandum of a Parisian police official noted "complaints on all sides that the eyes of patriots were offended by the different monuments built by despotism in the time of slavery, monuments that should certainly not exist under the reign of liberty and equality."[18] The destruction of particular monuments even became public policy in the face of internal and external threats; thus in August 1793, in the face of renewed revolt in the Vendée and the success of the Allied armies, the Convention ordered the destruction of the tombs of the kings of France located at Saint-Denis.[19] From 1790, the contents of disestablished churches, monasteries, and ransacked châteaux were regarded more as lawful booty than as historical records—in fact, their very history rendered them culpable. A Commission des Monuments had been formed simply to catalog the new *biens nationaux* that were being transported en masse and unsystematically to provisional depositories in Paris and the Departments.[20] Roughly classified by type—machines, scientific instruments, books, manuscripts, paintings, and statuary—they were then sold as needed. Metal objects were melted down for cannons; statues and tombs were ground into powder for mortar; the abbey of Cluny and the château of Anet were treated as stone quarries, the cloisters of Saint-Nicholas at Rheims as horse stalls.[21]

Only in late 1793, with the establishment of a new Commission des arts as an arm of the Comité d'instruction publique, was there a perceptible slackening in the pace of defacement. From early in 1794, Grégoire's speeches in the Convention and his reports to the Comité d'instruction publique provided a rallying point for antiquarians, historians, artists, and architects concerned with the indiscriminate destruction.[22] In deliberate overstatements, designed to

117 Lequeu, cave in Gardens of Isis.

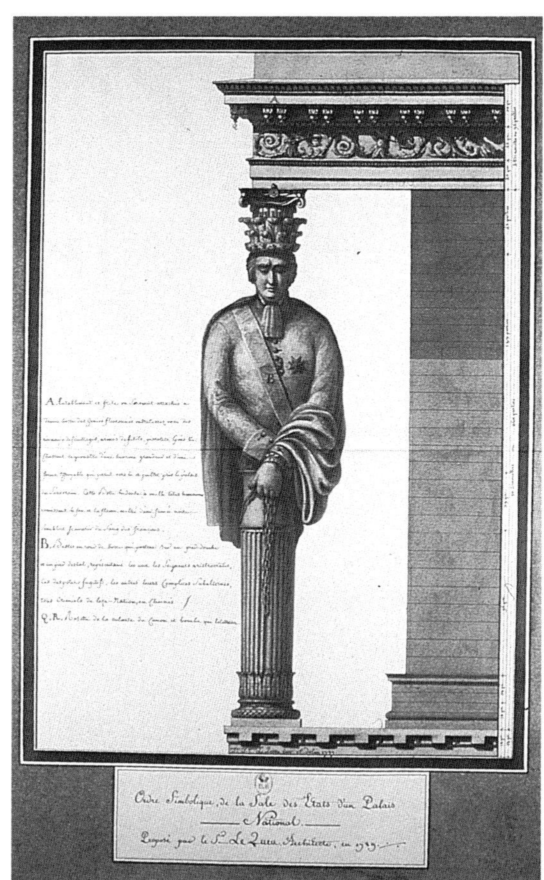

116 Lequeu, self-portrait as symbolic order.

118 Lequeu, self-portrait as voyeur.

119 Lequeu, cowshed.

120 Lequeu, Temple of Divination.

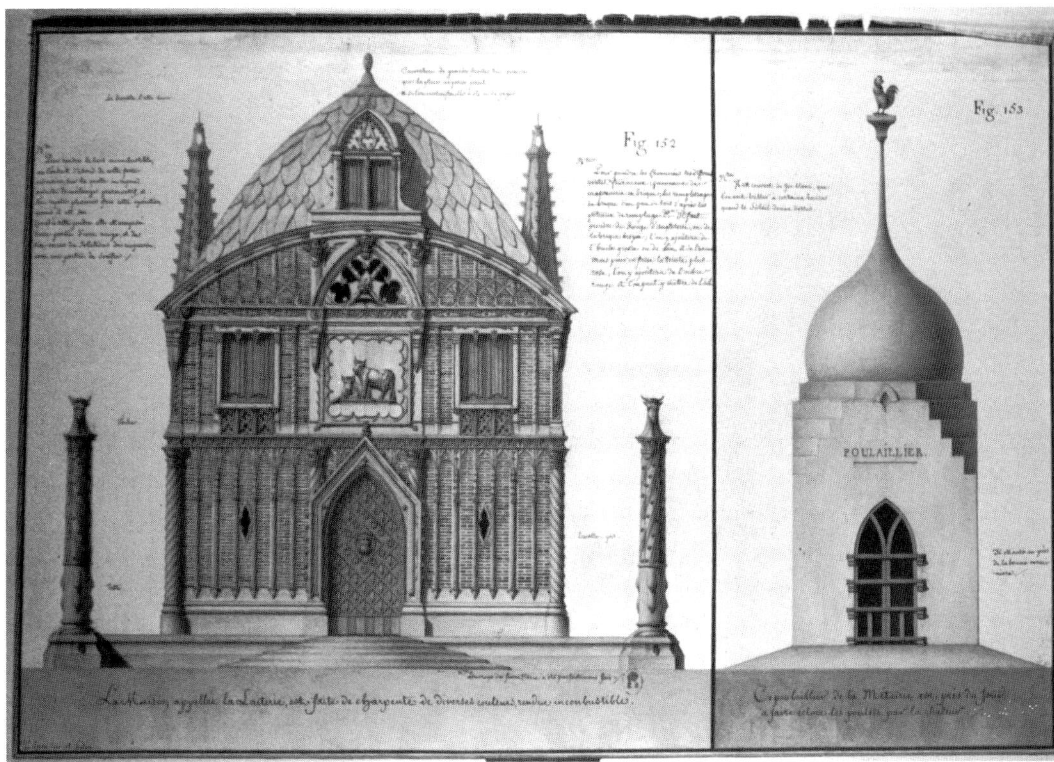

122 Lequeu, *left,* dairy; *right,* henhouse.

121 Lequeu, mausoleum for Voltaire and family.

123 Lequeu, *top,* Temple of Virtue; *bottom,* powder-magazine.

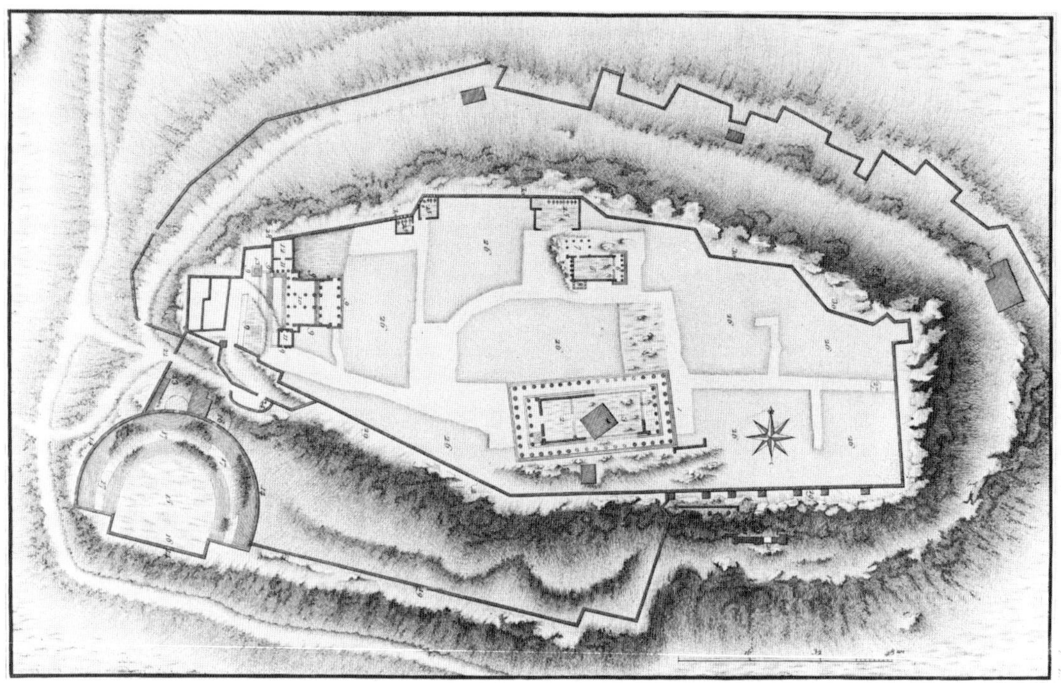

126 J.-D. Le Roy, "Plan of the Citadel of Athens," 1758.

124 Lequeu, *top*, primitive huts; *bottom*, Rendez-vous de Bellevue.

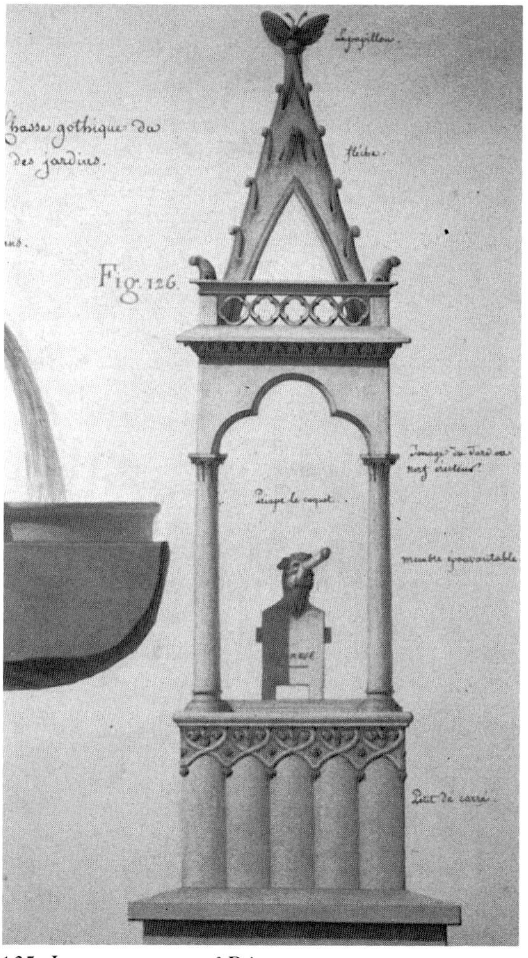

125 Lequeu, statue of Priapus.

127 Ribart de Chamoust, "The French Order As Found in Nature," 1776.

128 Ribart, "Type of the French Order."

129 Ribart, "The French Order Developed."

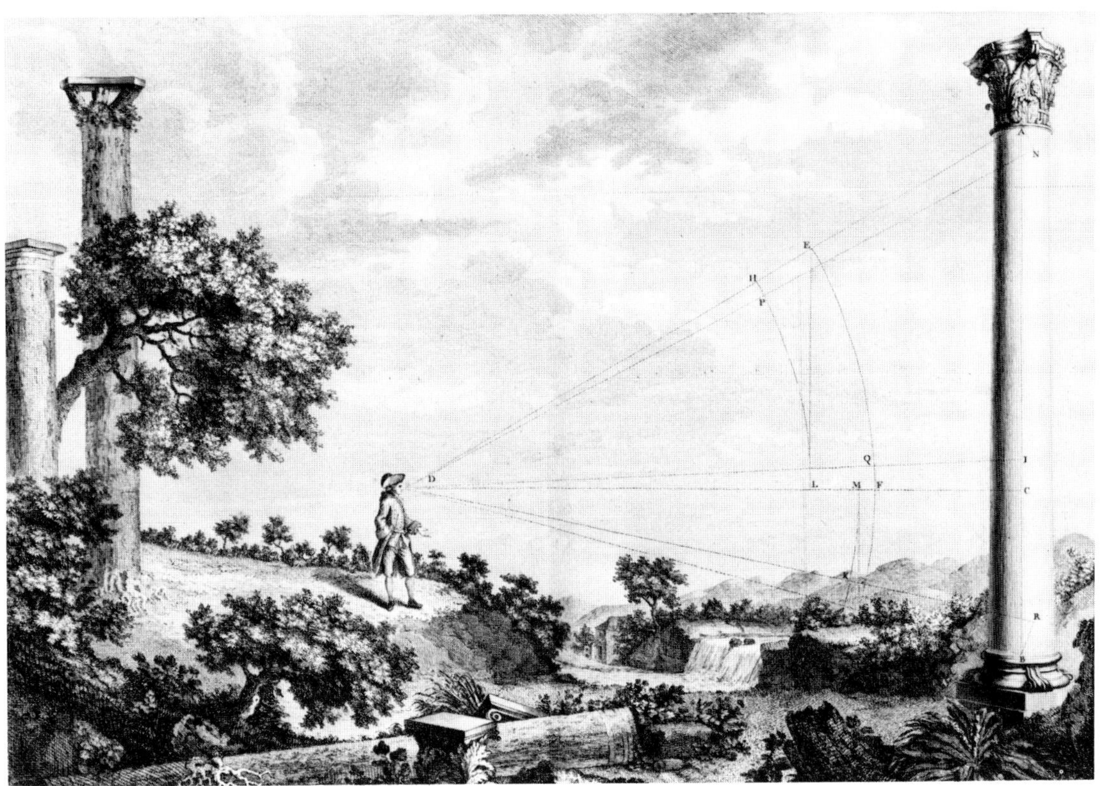

130 Ribart, "Origin of the Four Architectural Orders."

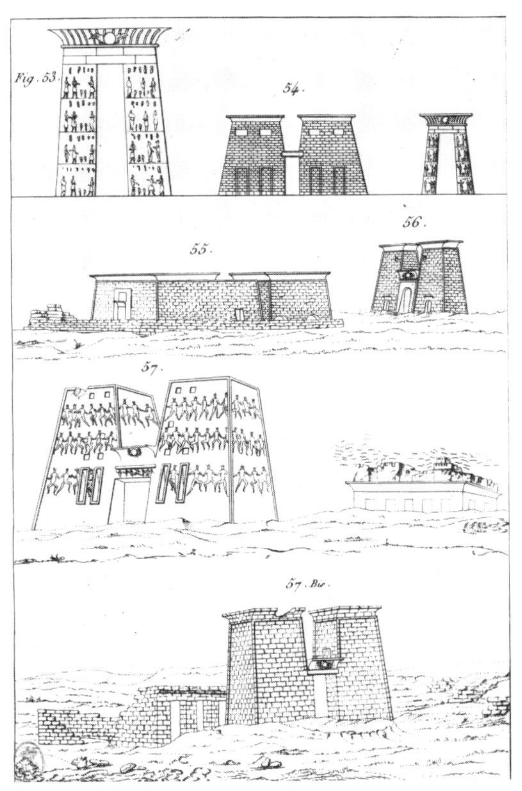

131 Quatremère de Quincy, "Entrances, Facades, or Propylaea," 1803.

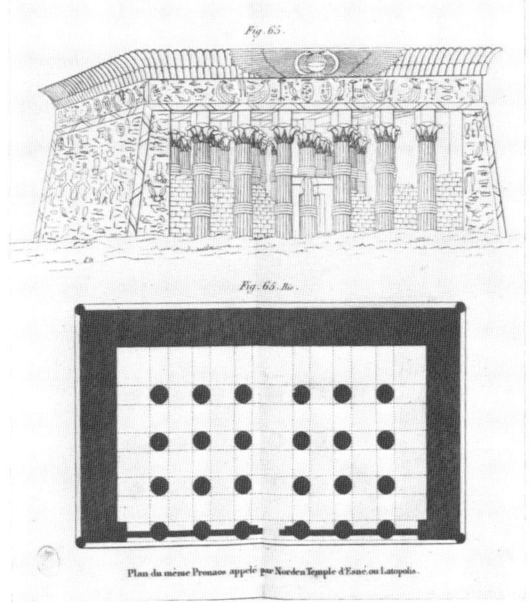

133 Quatremère de Quincy, an Egyptian Pronaos, called by Norden the Temple of Esne or Latopolis, *top*, perspective view; *bottom*, plan.

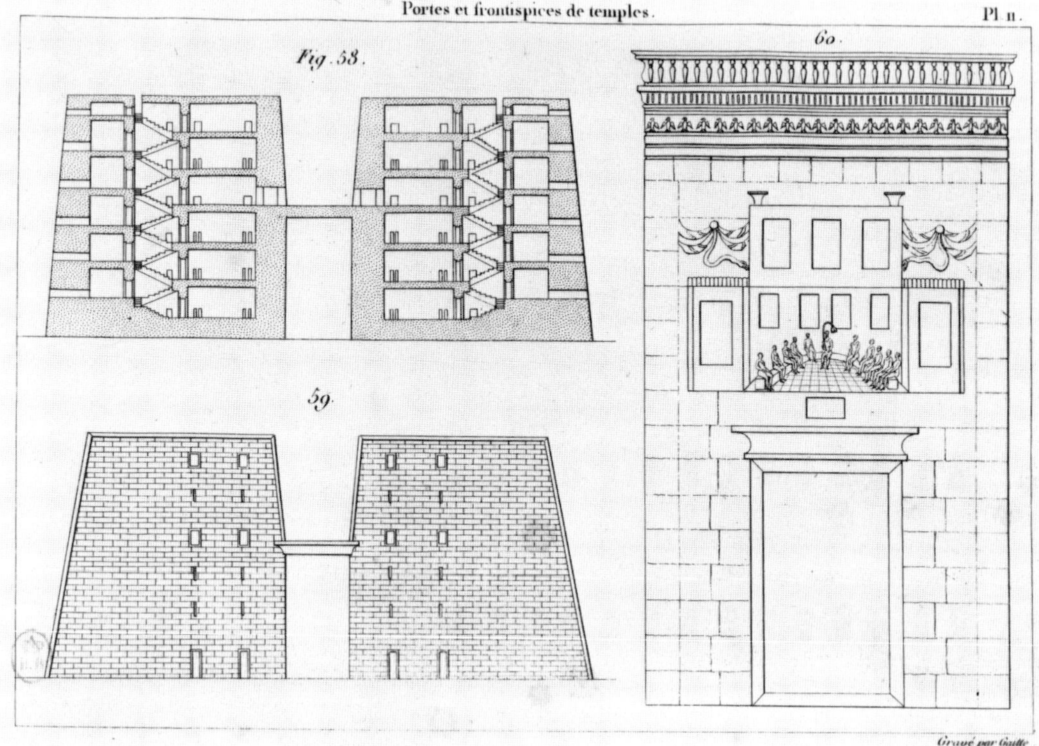

132 Quatremère de Quincy, "Entrances and Facades of Temples."

134 Quatremère de Quincy, "The Olympian Jupiter, seen on his throne inside his temple," 1814.

135 J. E. Biet, Frontispiece to his *Souvenirs de Musée des monuments français,* engraved by Normand fils, 1821.

137 Musée des monuments français, view of introductory gallery, drawn by Nauzelle, engraved by Lavallée, 1816.

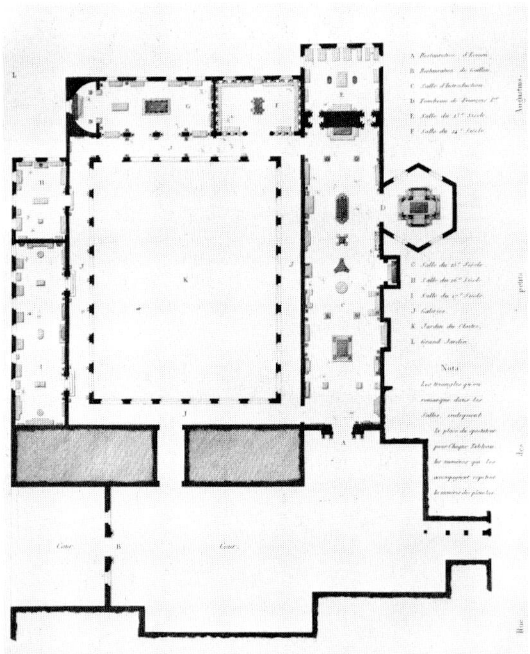

136 Alexandre Lenoir, plan of his Musée des monuments français, drawn by Biet and engraved by Normand fils, 1815.

139 Musée des monuments français, view of fourteenth-century gallery, drawn by Biet, engraved by C. Normand, 1816.

138 Musée des monuments français, view of thirteenth-century gallery, engraved by Lavallée and Réville, 1816.

140 Musée des monuments français, view of gallery leading to the sixteenth and seventeenth-century galleries, drawn by Biet, engraved by Normand fils, 1821.

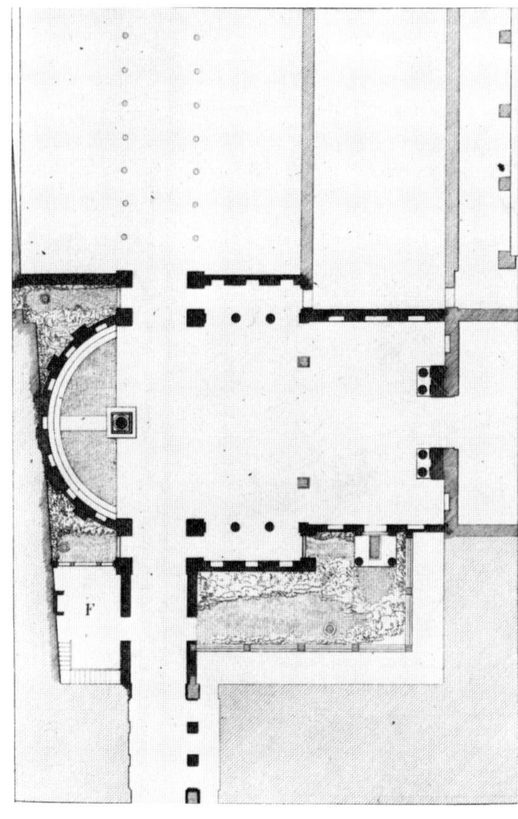

141 Musée des monuments français, plan of entrance courtyard, drawn and engraved by Percier, 1802.

144 Musée des monuments français, restoration of the Château d'Anet, in the first courtyard, elevation, drawn and engraved by Percier.

142 Musée des monuments français, entrance courtyard, perspective view from the rue des Petits-Augustins, drawn and engraved by Percier, 1802.

E. Vue perspective de la cour d'entrée, prise du Portique existant.

143 Musée des monuments français, entrance courtyard, perspective view from the front doorway, drawn and engraved by Percier, 1802.

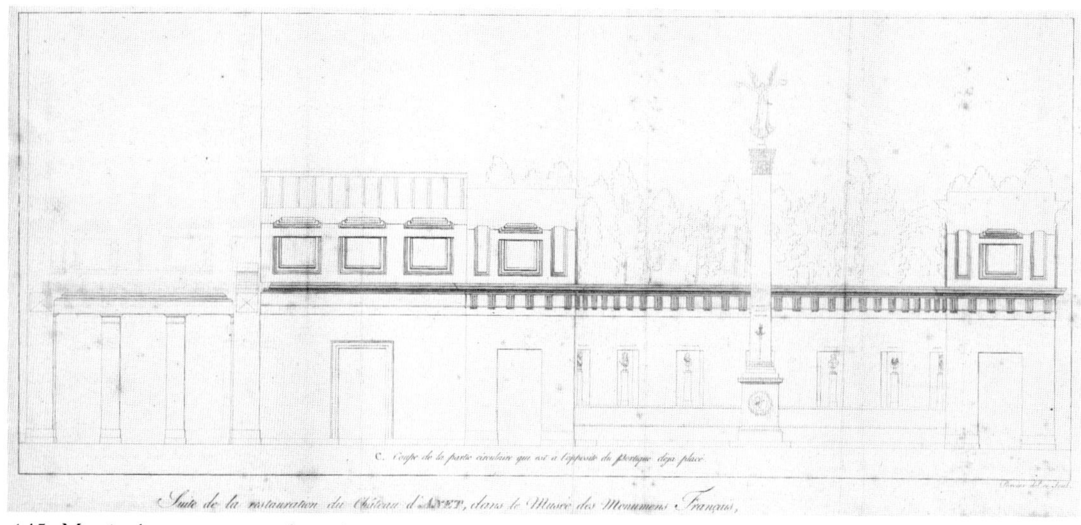

145 Musée des monuments français, restoration of the Château d'Anet, section, drawn and engraved by Percier.

146 Musée des monuments français, front facade of the Château de Gaillon, in the second courtyard, drawn and engraved by Percier.

147 Musée des monuments français, rear facade of the Château de Gaillon, drawn and engraved by Percier.

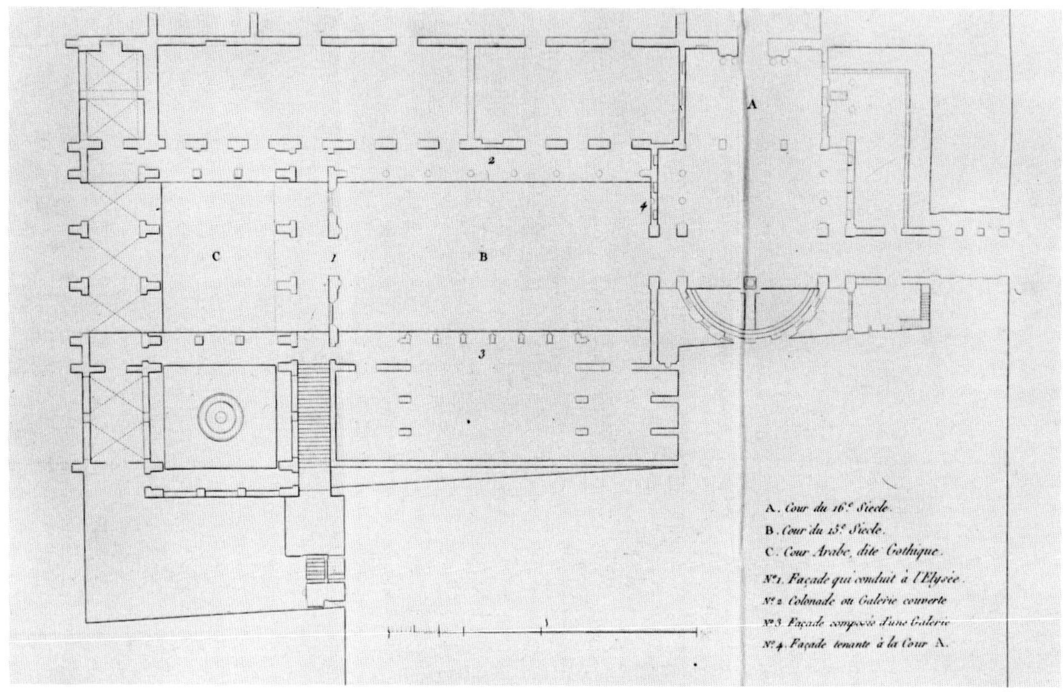

148 Musée des monuments français, projected plan for three courtyards, drawn and engraved by Percier.

149 Musée des monuments français, view of the garden called Elysée, tomb of Abelard and Héloïse, drawn by Biet, engraved by Normand fils.

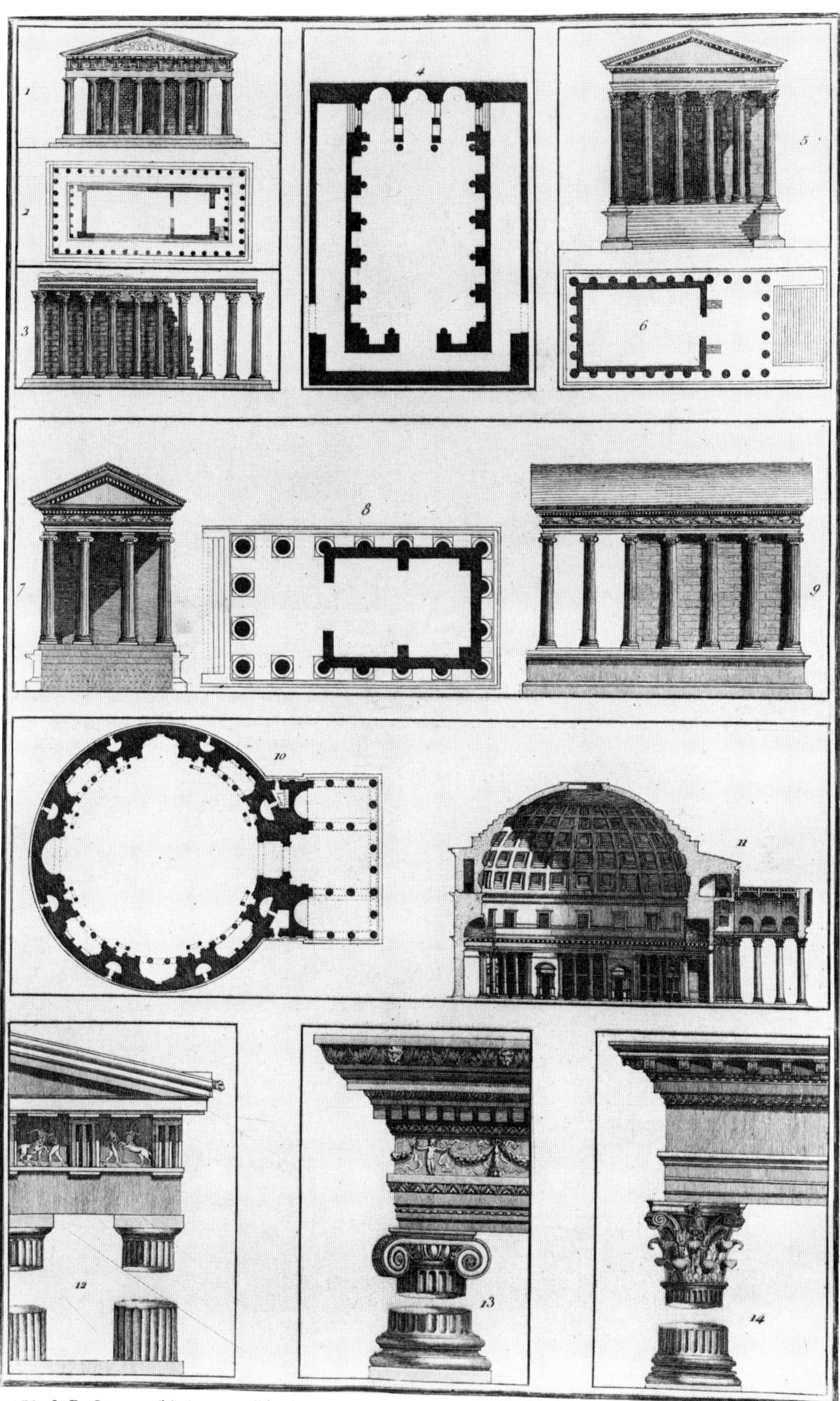

150 J.-B. Séroux d'Agincourt, "Antique Architecture in Its State of Perfection among the Greeks and the Romans," 1823.

151 Séroux d'Agincourt, "Conjectures on the Origin, the Various Forms, and the Use of the Gothic Arch in Well-Known Countries."

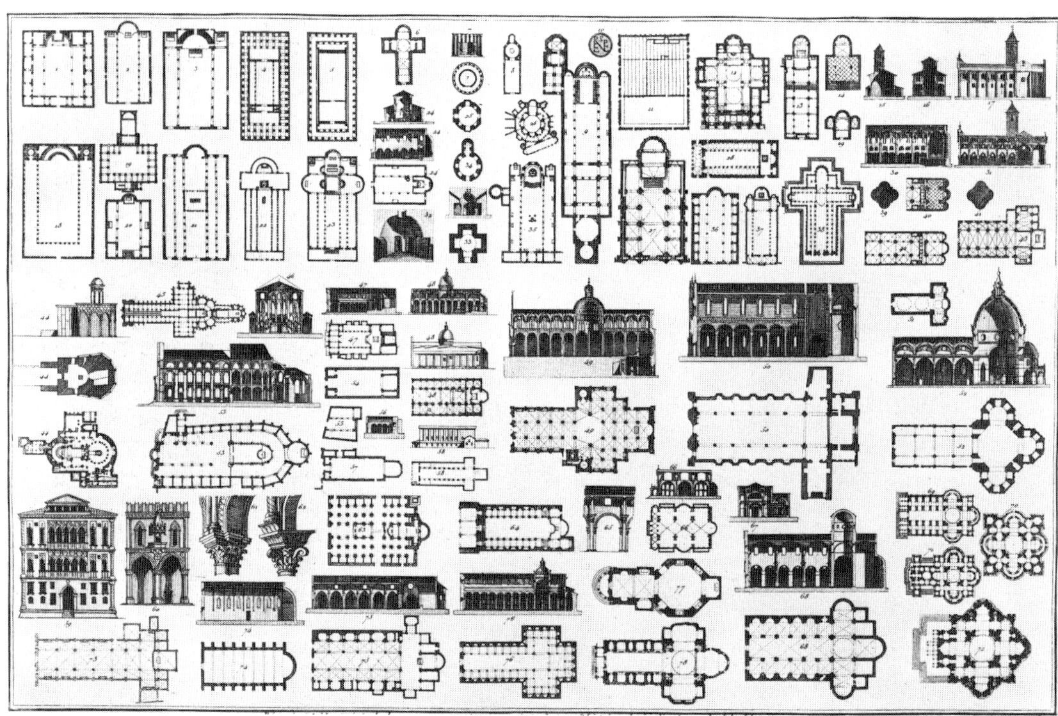

155 Séroux d'Agincourt, "Summary and General Catalogue of the Buildings That Constitute the History of the Decadence of Architecture."

152 Séroux d'Agincourt, "Historical and Chronological Catalogue of the Facades of Temples before and during the Decadence of Art."

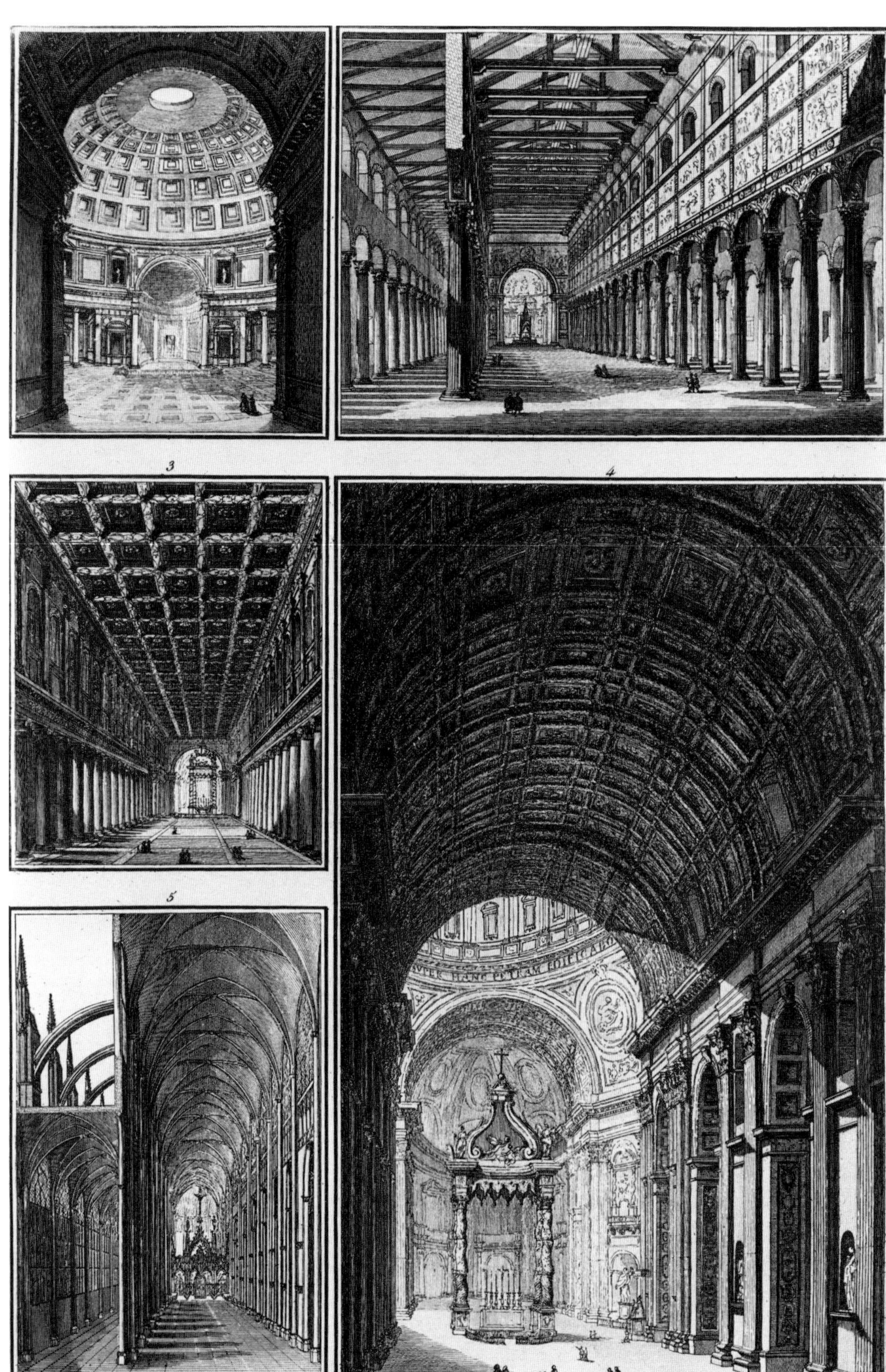

153 Séroux d'Agincourt, "Principal Forms of Vaults and Ceilings Used in Sacred Buildings during the Period of Decadence."

154 Séroux d'Agincourt, "Construction Techniques in Use before and during the Decadence of Art."

156 Séroux d'Agincourt, "Principal Monuments of the Architecture Known as Gothic Built in Various European Countries during the Fourteenth and Fifteenth Centuries, the Style's Most Brilliant Epoch."

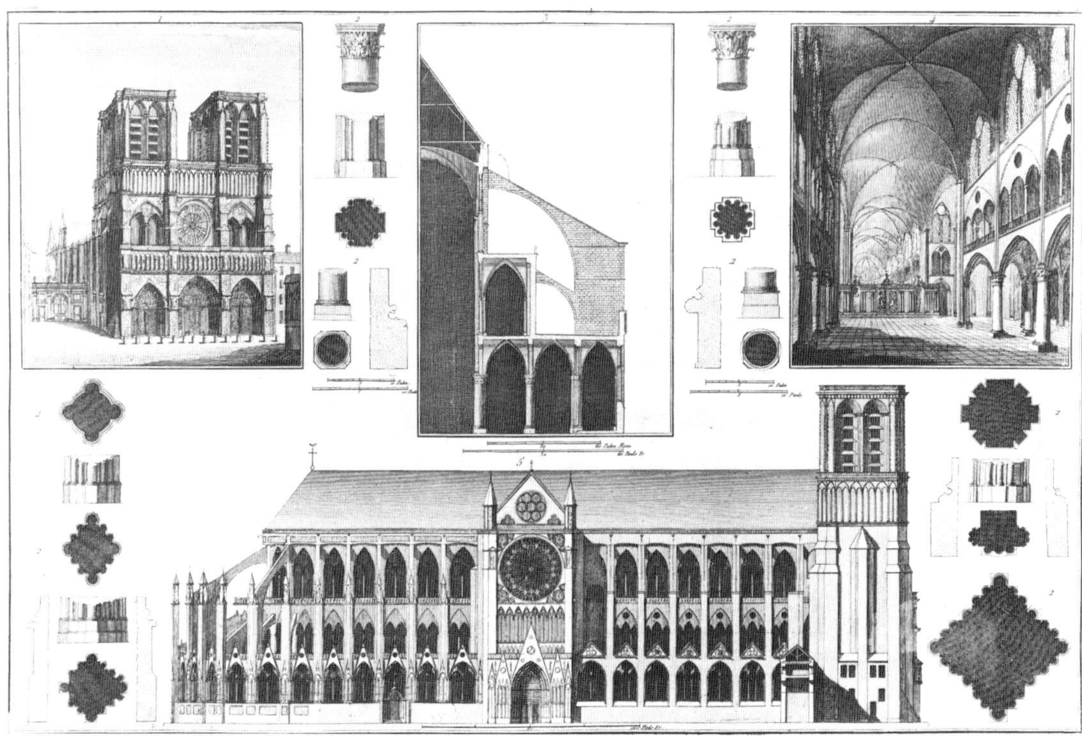

159 Séroux d'Agincourt, Notre-Dame, Paris, *clockwise from top left:* entrance, side elevation, interior view, and decorations.

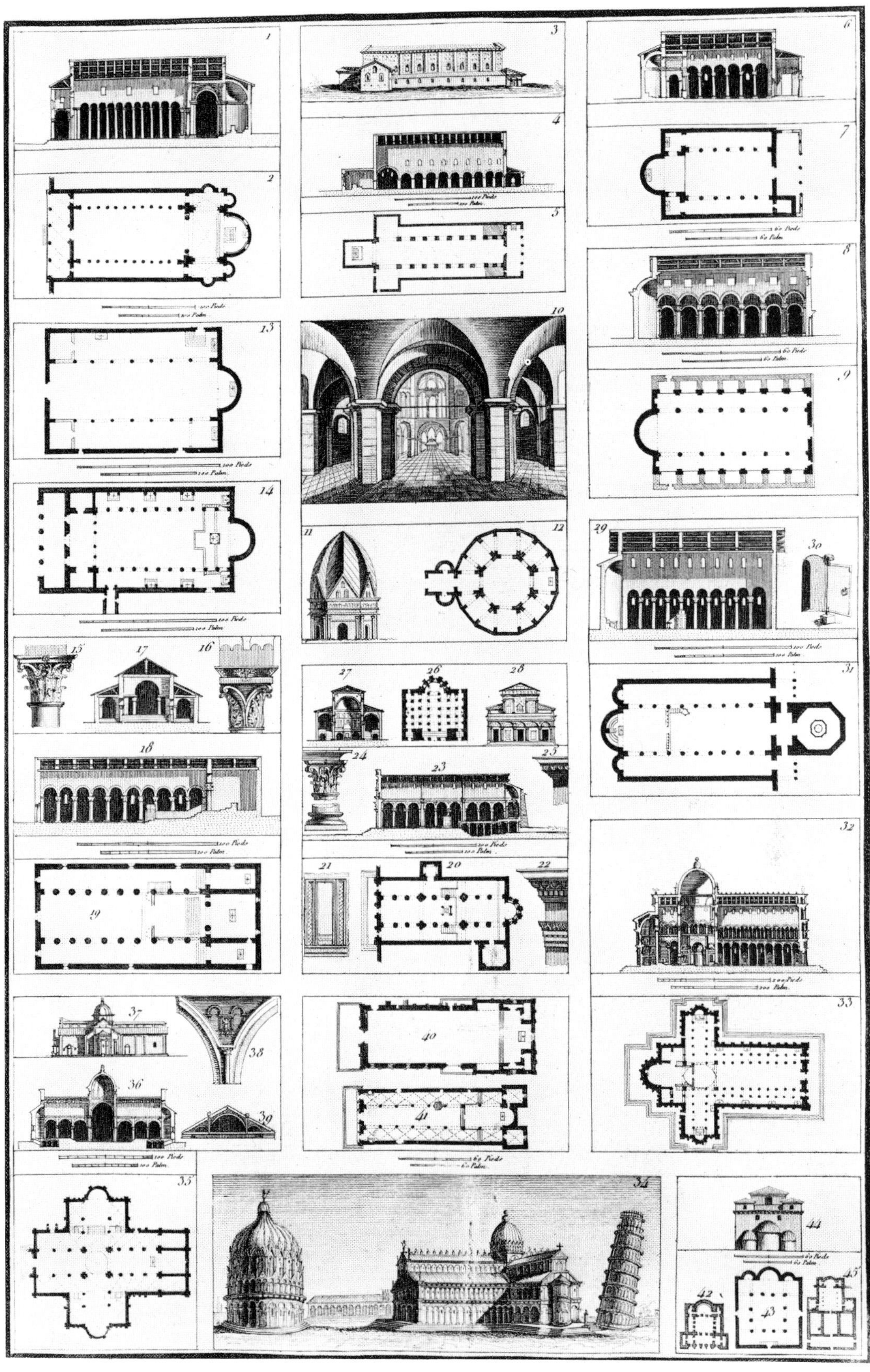

157 Séroux d'Agincourt, "Architecture As It Was Developed in Italy in the Age of Charlemagne, in the Ninth Century, and by the Pisans in the Tenth and Eleventh Centuries."

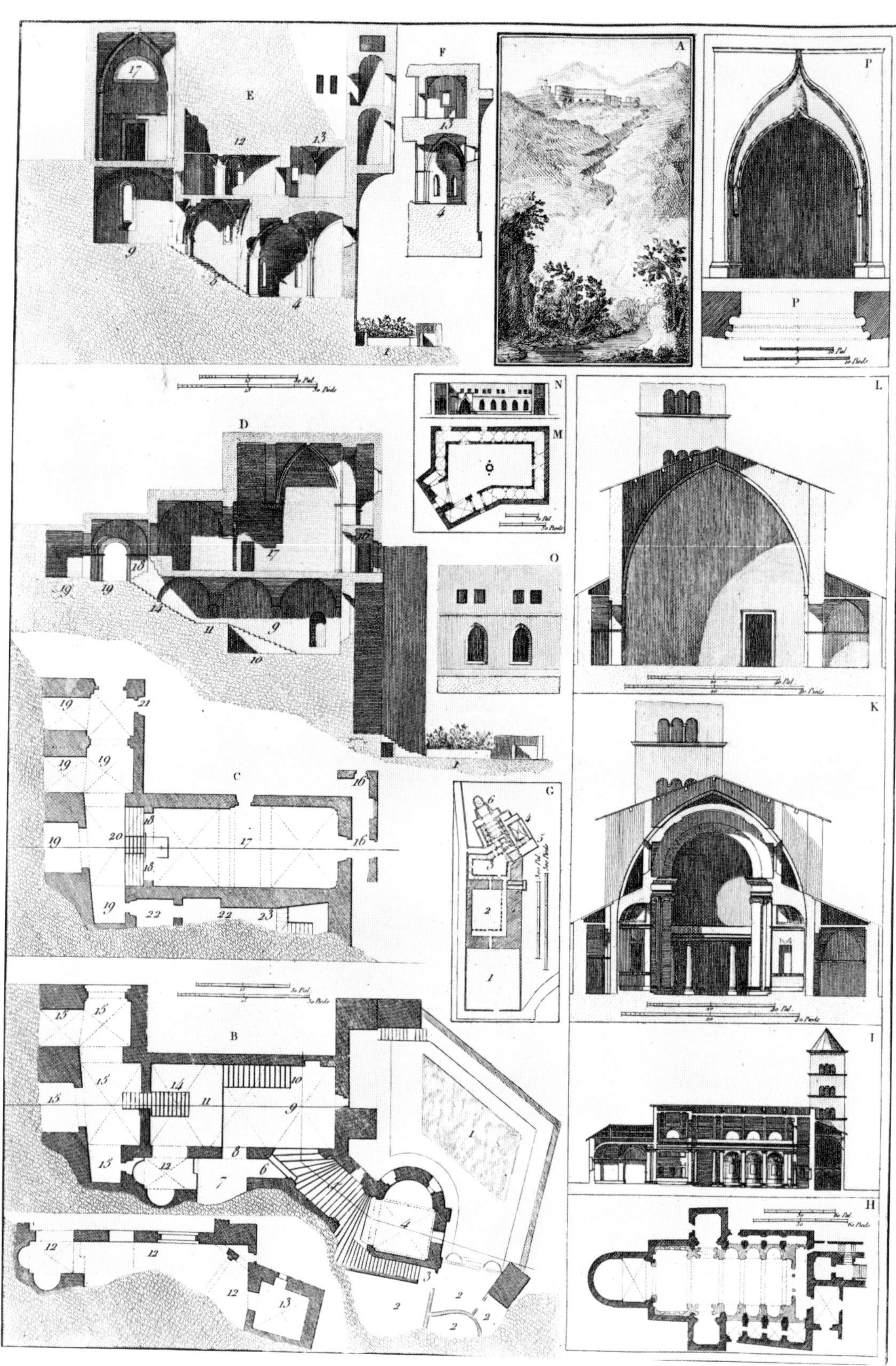

158 Séroux d'Agincourt, "First Traces of the Architecture Known as Gothic, in Italy, at the Abbey of Subiaco, near Rome, in the Ninth, Tenth, Eleventh, and Twelfth Centuries."

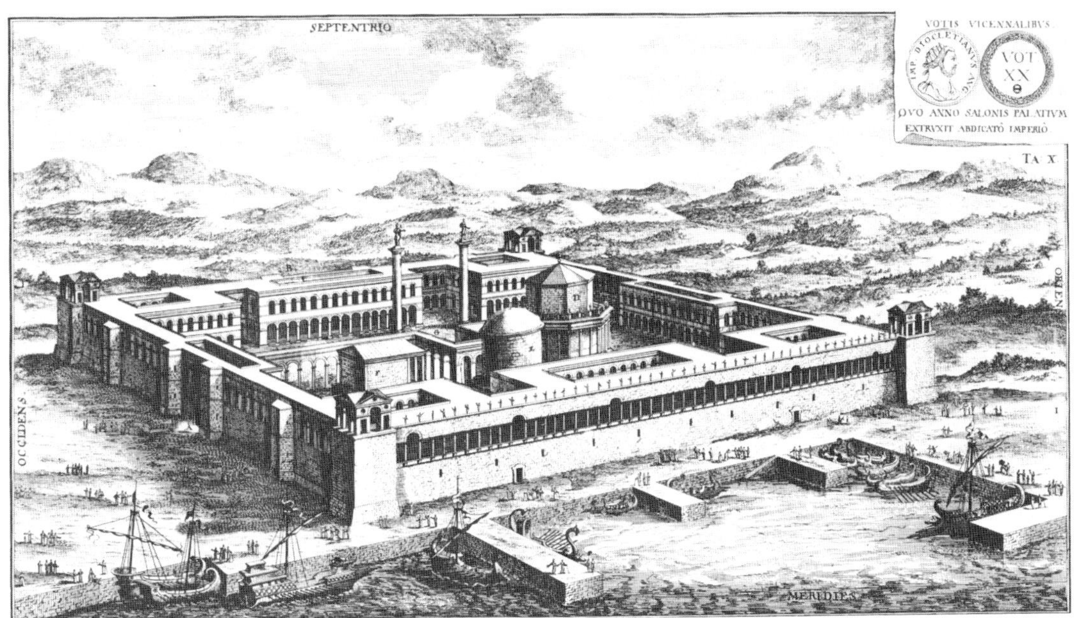

160 Fischer von Erlach, Diocletian's Palace, Spalato, 1721.

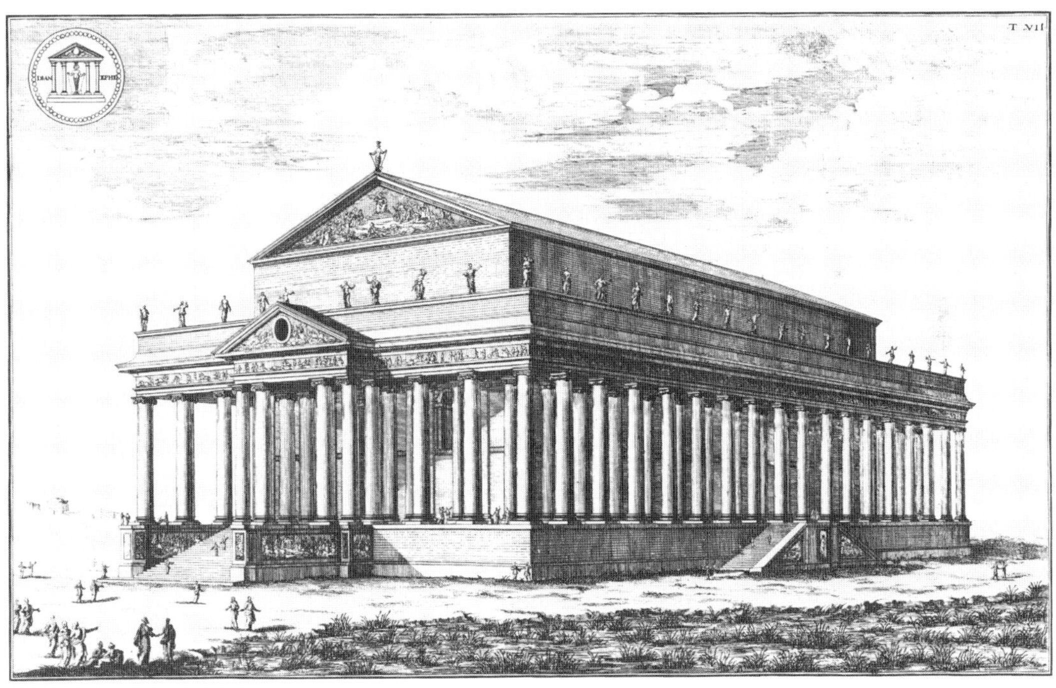

161 Fischer, Temple of Diana, Ephesus.

162 Fischer, Ruins of Palmyra.

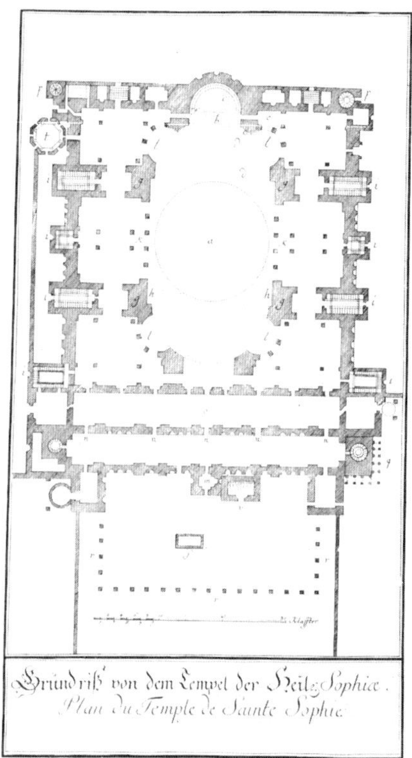

163 Fischer, Santa Sophia, Constantinople (Istanbul).

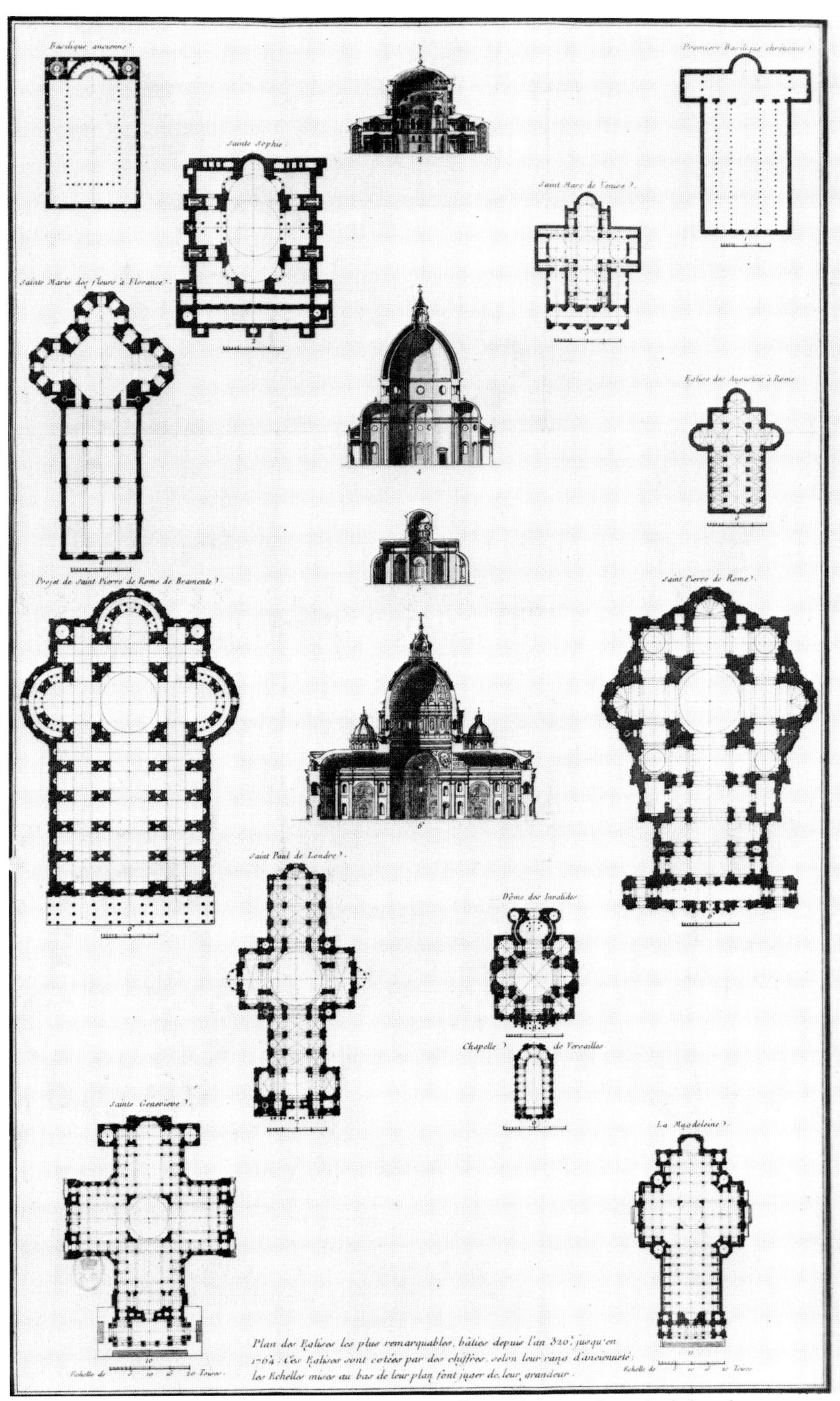

164 J.-D. Le Roy, "Plans of the Most Remarkable Churches Built from A.D. 326 to 1764. These churches are numbered according to their age; the scales below the plans are meant to measure their relative size," engraved by Neufforge, 1764.

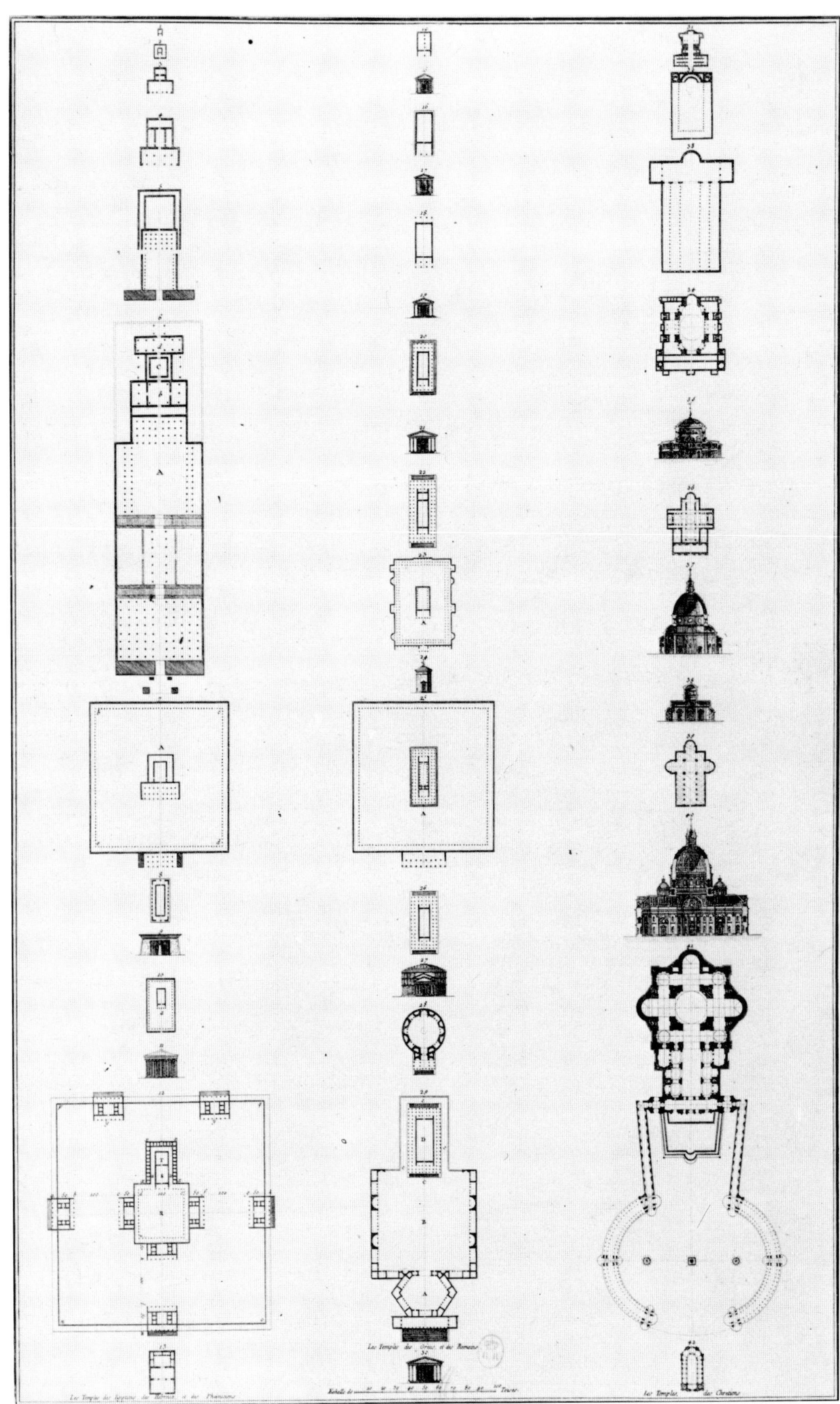

165 J.-D. Le Roy, *left,* temples of the Egyptians, Hebrews, and Phoenicians; *center,* of the Greeks and Romans; and *right,* of the Christians.

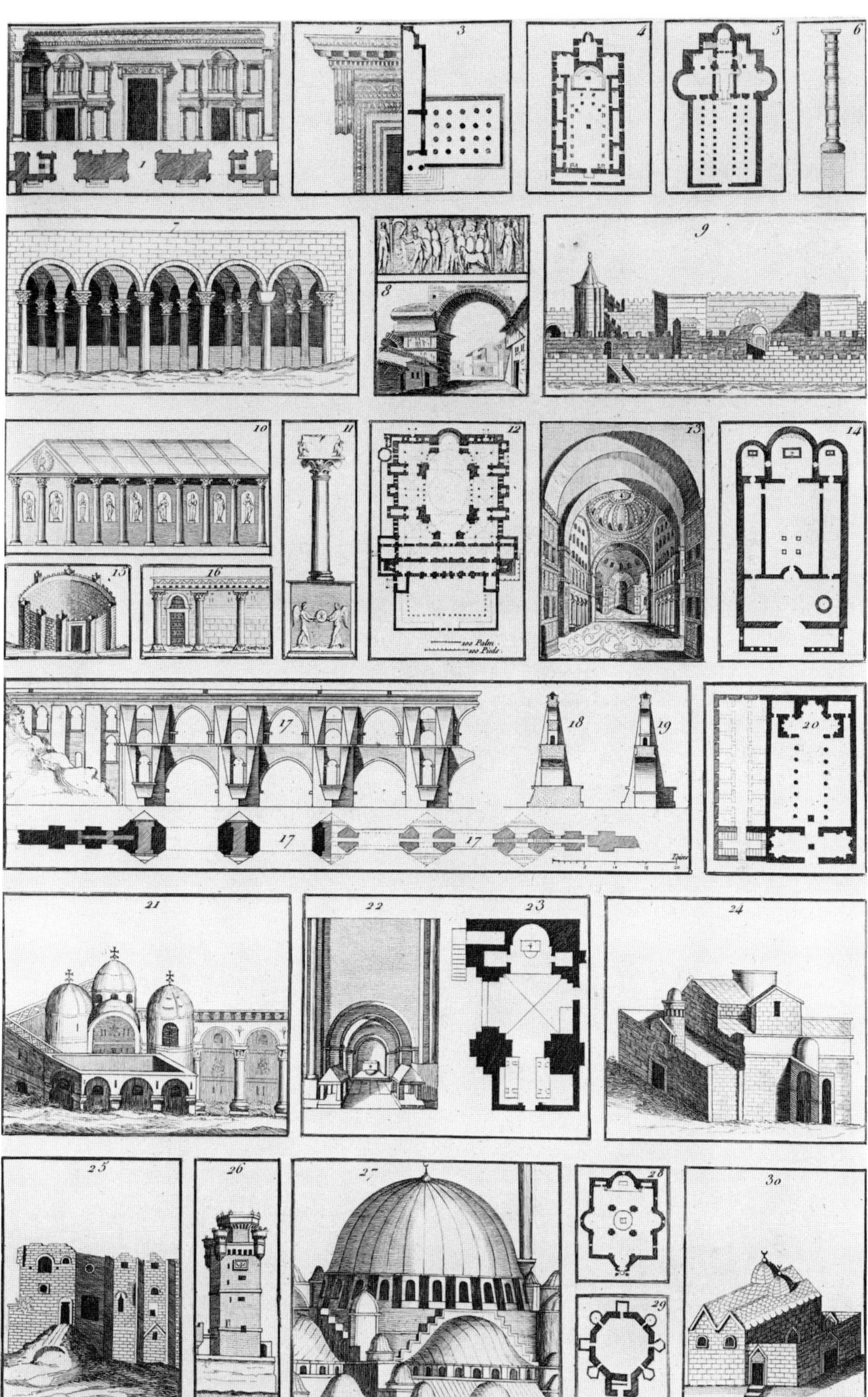

166 Séroux d'Agincourt, "General Catalogue of the Decadence of Architecture in the East."

167 Séroux d'Agincourt, "The Architecture of Sweden, before and during the Introduction in That Country of the Gothic Style, in the Thirteenth Century."

168 Séroux d'Agincourt, "Interior View of a Courtyard of Diocletian's Palace at Spalato, Third Century."

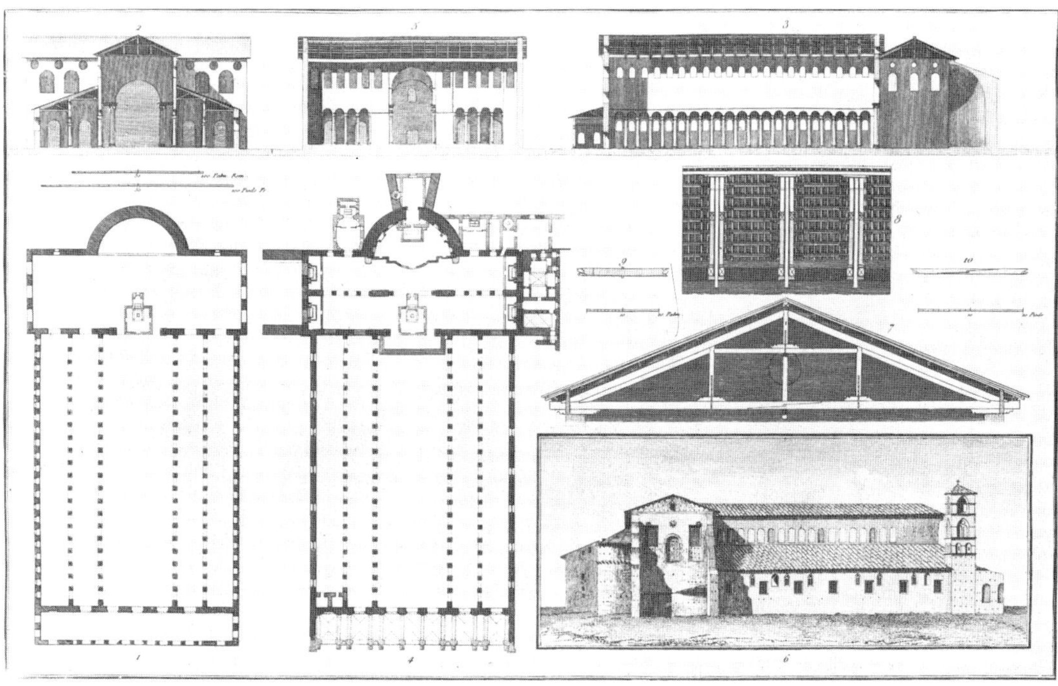

169 Séroux d'Agincourt, "Church of St. Paul Outside the Walls of Rome (*S. Paolo fuori le mure*) in Its Various States Since Constantine Founded It in the Fourth Century, Until the Present."

170 Séroux d'Agincourt, "S. Clementino, Rome, the Best-Conserved Model of the Arrangement of the Primitive Churches of the Fifth Century."

171 Séroux d'Agincourt, "Catalogue of the Most Famous Catacombs, Both Pagan and Christian."

172 Séroux d'Agincourt, interior view of a Roman catacomb.

173 Séroux d'Agincourt, interior view of an Etruscan catacomb in Tarquinia, near Corneto.

obscure the complicity of the Revolution in its vandalism, Grégoire denounced a veritable *complot vandale,* judiciously waiting until after the 10 Thermidor to name Robespierre and Hébert among those who had conspired to burn everything from the Porte Saint-Denis to the Bibliothèque nationale.[23]

More practical initiatives were taken by members of the Commission des arts: Vicq d'Azyr wrote a comprehensive brochure on the proper handling and conservation of national collections; David Le Roy proposed structural repairs to Amiens, Saint-Denis, and Chartres; Léon Dufourny called for each Department to conduct a methodical survey of its historical monuments.[5] By the end of 1794, the Commission was even congratulating itself on having saved a number of buildings from demolition, among which were the château of Chantilly and the Porte Saint-Denis.[25]

The transformation of this gradual movement towards a spirit of conservation into the creation of a national museum of monuments was, however, largely accidental, a result of the enthusiasm of Alexandre Lenoir, a young painter who had been assigned in 1791 as overseer of the *dépôt* for marble sculpture in the former convent of the Petits-Augustins.[26] Lenoir, who conceived his role to be more guardian than storekeeper, began almost immediately to take an active part in the saving of works of art, using his authority to have endangered monuments transported to the Petits-Augustins. Sculptures by Michelangelo and paintings by Raphael and Tintoretto were found in gardens and attics; tombs were protected from mutilation; and in a dramatic gesture that he never tired of retelling, Lenoir rescued sculptures from the royal tombs at Saint-Denis, where in April 1793 they had been used as building materials for the erection of a symbolic mountain in honor of Marat and Le Peletier.[27] It was, ironically enough in light of the order for the demolition of these latter monuments, the Minister of the Interior who ordered Lenoir to open his *dépôt* to the public in August of the same year, on the occasion of a festival to celebrate ratification of the Constitution.[28]

By September 1794, as many of the tomb sculptures as could be saved from Saint-Denis were installed in Lenoir's convent. He prepared a preliminary catalogue of his monuments and intermittently began to open the site to the public. Already, in July 1794, he had announced plans for the reerection of the tomb of François I and, with the cessation of the Terror, he had felt confident enough to petition the Comité d'instruction publique with his developed idea of a museum.[29] The Director of Public Instruction, Ginguené, accepted the proposal on October 21, 1795; it was ratified by the Minister of the Interior, Bénézech, on April 8, 1796; and Lenoir's collection was soon thereafter incorporated as a Musée d'antiquités et monuments français, a branch of the national museum, under the authority of the Louvre.[30] Following Lenoir's own suggestion, Bénézech instructed him to "arrange the objects in a suitable way, above all following a chronological order," so as to distinguish his *dépôt* from the others, which were without "system or plan."[31] Four years later, Lenoir published the first volumes of a comprehensive catalogue, which described the collection of more than five hundred pieces of sculpture and architectural decoration methodically and in the order of display, one synonymous with the other (plate 135).[32]

The convent of the Petits-Augustins, in the spaces of which Lenoir organized his museum, was, although Lenoir paid little attention to the fact, itself a historical monument of some importance.[33] Founded by Queen Marguerite de Valois in 1609, and built between 1615 and 1640, it was indeed a late example of Lenoir's favorite architectural style, the French Renaissance.[34] Arranged around a central cloister, the buildings—the church, with its sacristy and side chapel "des Louanges," the chapter house, refectory, and kitchens—were simple and unpretentious. As a whole, the group formed a typical monastic cluster, with gardens backing onto the refectory wing.

For Lenoir, however, the convent merely served as a convenient framework for his new museum. Between 1796 and 1800, Lenoir rebuilt each room, from the chapel to the refectory and kitchens, according to his own designs and those of architects like the younger Peyre, for the purpose of exhibiting fragments of French history from the "Tomb of Clovis" to the sculpture of late-eighteenth-century artists.[35] Following Winckelmann, whose overriding influence he acknowledged in his epigraph to the museum's guide, Lenoir divided history into epochs. He took the century as his basic unit, organizing his collection so that the visitor would proceed from room to room as from century to century (plate 136).[36] Tombs, sculptures, decorative fragments, paintings, furniture, and architectural elements were in this way "restored" to their proper place in history, and the more so as Lenoir undertook to endow each room with the look or style of its epoch, "the character, the exact physiognomy of the century that it should represent." Where possible, he used fragments of surviving windows, doors, and ceiling decorations to give added authenticity.[37]

In the former church of the convent, an introductory room (plate 137) that encyclopedically displayed objects representing every century, provided a "survey" of "the infancy of art among the Goths, its progress under Louis XII, its perfection under François I, and the origin of its decadence under Louis XIV . . . ; finally one will trace step by step, with the monuments of our own age, the restoration of the antique style in our country by the public lessons of Joseph-Marie Vien."[38] In a side chapel, the old Chapelle des Louanges (1608–1613), stood the tomb of François I, epitomizing the perfection of French Renaissance art.

From there the visitor moved to the first of the historical rooms, properly speaking, the thirteenth-century room, built in the old sacristy (plate 138). It was perhaps the most complete of Lenoir's fictional restorations.

> One sees the low vaults, groined and sprinkled with stars on a blue background, carried by simple pillars, roughly decorated: these vaults terminate in rosettes of the period . . . ; from them hang sepulchral lamps. The doors and windows, of ogival forms, are constructed from the debris of a monument of the Middle Ages, ruined by malefactors, the remains of which I collected at Saint Denis. . . . Above the doors is the following inscription in Gothic characters: "The state of the arts in the thirteenth century."[39]

Napoleon, whose ignorance of architectural history was a match even for Lenoir's, was reported to have said, on entering this room, "Lenoir, you transport me to Syria."[40]

The total effect of this first room, designed as a kind of initiation into history, was dark and gloomy. To inspire the visitor with awe, Lenoir, a Freemason preoccupied with the nature and history of ritual, used all the techniques outlined by Burke in his discussion of the sublime.[41] Such an effect was, according to Lenoir, also historically accurate; he noted that the older the monument, the darker its interior.

> The somber light that illumines this room is, again, an imitation of the epoch, of the magic by means of which those petrified with fear and superstition were maintained in a state of perpetual enfeeblement.[42]

Thus the visitor, as he passed from room to room, was to be made aware that "the closer one comes to centuries similar to our own, the more the light increases in public monuments, as if the sight of the sun was only suitable for an enlightened man," a literal evocation of progress.[43]

From these somber beginnings, the route through the museum circled the cloister of the convent, passing through rooms dedicated to each century, from the fourteenth to the eighteenth. The fourteenth-century room, "built with some debris taken from Sainte-Chapelle in Paris," displayed monuments from an age dominated, in Lenoir's eyes, by the "Asian" tastes of Louis IX[44] (plate 139). Following the myth of Saracenic origins, Lenoir understood the ogival arch to have been an imitation of the eastern styles observed by masons during the Crusades. Similarly, he interpreted the carvings of beasts on tombs as so many allegorical symbols: tigers, lions, and serpents were survivals of the cult of Bacchus; other symbols were descendants of the zodiacs of Persia or Egyptian hieroglyphs.[45]

The fifteenth-century room attempted to demonstrate "the art, taste, luxury, and brilliance of the age"; its ceiling, windows, and details were copied from the tomb of Louis XII, which was the centerpiece. This room's columns were taken from the church of St. Pierre at Chartres, its decorative motifs from the Château de Gaillon; its vaults were finished in brilliant violet and blue.[46]

The sixteenth century, in which "architecture developed rapidly" under Philibert de l'Orme and the "reign" of François I, was represented by details copied by Peyre from Lescot, Bullant, and de l'Orme (plate 140).[47] The showpiece of the sixteenth-century room, the tomb of the sculptor Jean Goujon, was fabricated by Lenoir out of pieces of Goujon's own works. Here, also, were exhibited the Michelangelo statues Lenoir had found in 1793, which originally stood in the courtyard of Bullant's Château d'Ecouën.[48] Lenoir neglected no attribute that would exhibit the Renaissance as the highest epoch of French architecture; the ceilings were covered with arabesques and heraldic devices symbolizing, according to Lenoir's personal program, Religion, the Nation, Honor, Friendship, and Love.

The seventeenth-century room was again designed by Peyre in a suitable style: its doorways, wrote Lenoir, "showed in their composition a character of nobility and simplicity that matched the whole room perfectly."[49]

Finally, the eighteenth-century room, demonstrating the beginnings of the decadence of art and its recent renewal, displayed a series of statues from a bust of Louis XV by Lemoine to a bust of Winckelmann by Deseine, the apogee of the entire exhibition.

In each of these rooms, despite Lenoir's frequent protestations that "everything has been executed according to notes taken from the actual monuments of the time and after the proper authorities," his theatrical virtuosity generally overcame his historical accuracy.[50] As he admitted, "the whole shows the effects that can be produced in decoration with old details skillfully applied."[51] Outside, in the courtyards and gardens of the convent, the theatrical effects were even more striking, as Lenoir, this time with the help of Percier, attempted to encircle the museum with a sequence of spaces that would complement the interior route and act as a frame for the larger pieces of found architecture.[52] The entry court (plates 141–143) served as the backdrop to the portico of the Château d'Anet by Philibert de l'Orme, which in turn acted as the facade of the introductory room (plates 144–145). The portico was flanked by two smaller porches, also from Anet. A semicircular arcade facing the portico completed the space and established the axis of entry. A second courtyard, which housed the remains of the Château de Gaillon (plates 146–147), was to be surrounded by galleries made of columns taken from the former home of the Cardinal d'Amboise, to be entered through the celebrated Arc de Gaillon. Lenoir and Percier projected a third courtyard decorated with "Arab" or Gothic arches, so that one might move from the sixteenth century (Anet) to the fifteenth (Gaillon) and, from there, to the thirteenth, or vice versa (plate 148).[53]

Joining this planned sequence of exterior courts to the interior route was a large, picturesque garden named the Elysée (plate 149). The visitor's view of the Elysée was, indeed, to have been framed by the three introductory courts.[54] In this garden were scattered, as if in arcadia, a number of freestanding monuments, almost all designed by Lenoir and constructed from old fragments: tombs of Descartes, Molière, La Fontaine, Turenne, Boileau, Mabillon and Montfaucon, the antiquarians of Saint Maur, and, as the major attraction, a tomb of Abelard and Héloise fabricated from Gothic and modern pieces and containing what was left of their remains after Lenoir himself had donated the skull of Héloise to the sculptor, to ensure the verisimilitude of her bust, and had given a number of bones to friends and patrons.[55] This historical cemetery would, Lenoir hoped, provide a fitting end to his trajectory through the centuries.

The entire establishment was thereby conceived as a didactic exercise, a kind of monumental book, the articulation of one space to the next, self-consciously designed as a passage through different "chapters." Lenoir was sensitive to every visual clue that would stimulate the visitor's interest and movement. The porticoes in the entry court and their visual extension toward the Elysée were intended to "give movement to the whole . . . architecture and form a very agreeable point of view."[56] This first space, Lenoir noted, "serves as a *preface* to our Museum," the starting point of the book. From there, "if one considers the chronology of past centuries like a book open for instruction, in which one reads the march of events," the rooms followed one another naturally, a spatial narrative transparent to its historical model.[57]

The museum in this way fulfilled the double aim of political representation and public instruction. Politically, it was "established with enough splendor and magnificence to speak to all eyes"; educationally, it became "a learned school and an encyclopedia where the young will find, word by word, all the degrees of imperfection, perfection, and decadence."[58] It was significant that the overall form of this narrative, shaped by the centralized and enclosed plan of the former convent, was topologically if not geometrically circular. Here Lenoir seemed to have returned to a version of Boullée's centralized, static typology, but with a crucial difference, intimating a new turn in historical sensibility: whereas Boullée's museum culminated in the microcosmic central dome, Lenoir's line of movement circulated endlessly about an empty center. In this circulation pattern, with its attendant moments of rest and reverie, a generation of younger romantics, as the historian Michelet attested, found "for the first time . . . the true order of the ages." They saw in "this ardent, curious, fearful search, from room to room, from age to age," less the decadence and imperfections measured by Lenoir than the absolute relativity of every age and style, the exhibition of the law of historical change.[59] It was, perhaps, this reason above all others that caused Quatremère de Quincy to fight so relentlessly for the museum's closure.[60]

THE DECLINE AND FALL OF ARCHITECTURE

STYLE AND EPOCH IN GIBBON AND SEROUX D'AGINCOURT

Oh, too happy Winckelmann! Having rapidly traced the development of art among different peoples . . . you have stopped at this brilliant epoch in Greece in order to fix our studies and pleasures in that place, with so much interest . . . . Led by the same desire, and almost by the same circumstances in relation to modern art, I hope, in the enterprise that I have undertaken, to continue this history, the first part of which has been completed by Winckelmann, in order to be of similar use to those who profess the arts, but by an opposite and doubtless less agreeable route: Wincklemann has shown them what they should imitate; I will show them what they should avoid.

J.-B.-L.-G. Séroux d'Agincourt, *Histoire de l'art par les monuments,* 1811[1]

WINCKELMANN'S *HISTORY OF ART* inspired the German and French neoclassicists; later, many romantics shared his empathy for formal qualities; but historians quickly found his philosophical and aesthetic generalizations too sweeping, his antiquarian knowledge too limited. The rediscovery of Greece reduced the value of his climatic and moral theories, and, gradually, most of his canonical statues were proved to belong to much later periods of art than he had imagined. His effect lasted, however, in the unspoken challenge he left to future historians to complete his story to the present and to continue his attempt, however flawed, to ally aesthetics to history. It was this project that became, not more than ten years after Winckelmann's death, the self-consciously assumed burden of the antiquarian and amateur of the arts Séroux d'Agincourt.[2]

Concluding a two-year period of travel—in England, the Low Countries, Germany, and Italy—this rich *fermier-général* and collector of antiquities decided (somewhere between Bologna and Rome) to devote the rest of his life to writing the history of art after Constantine, to picking up "the thread abandoned by Winckelmann," and, in the words of his friend and biographer La Salle, to fulfilling "the grand but difficult idea of recovering, following, and fixing the history of the arts amid the aberrations brought in the wake of the distress of the

Roman Empire, the invasion of the barbarians, the translation of the Imperial seat to Constantinople, the mixture of Asiatic taste, and, finally, the fusion of genres carried to the North by the Goths and to the South by the Arabs."[3] It is for this latter concern, the piecing together of one of the first histories of the Gothic period, that Séroux has been remembered, and also criticized. The publication of his six-volume work was held up by the Revolution, and another generation, intellectually formed by Chateaubriand and his contemporaries, found little interest in Séroux's essentially classical and negative assessment of the Gothic style. But, as recent research has demonstrated, the true importance of Séroux's *History* lies not in the period of its publication (1810–1823, for the most part posthumous) but in the period of its gestation, in his long residence in Rome from 1779 to his death in 1814, when Séroux indefatigably recorded, corresponded throughout Europe, and, especially, employed generations of young *pensionnaires* at the French Academy to meticulously record monuments from every epoch.[4]

In a sense, these students were his educational force; by 1790, they had been trained in the observation of historical monuments that were not classical, from the Byzantine churches of Ravenna to the works of the best Renaissance architects. Thus Séroux sent Dufourny, Norry, Legrand, and Molinos to verify the measurements of the Temple of Malatesta at Rimini; Legrand and Molinos measured S. Andrea at Mantua; Bellissard drew Sicilian tombs; Dufourny recorded the smaller churches of the Veneto; and Pâris contributed information on the restoration of the cathedral of Orléans.[5] Others who worked less frequently for Séroux included Rondelet, Le Magne, Percier, Deseine, Desprez, Vaudoyer, Delannoy, Guyot, Renard, Lemonnier, Marreux, Michaut, Cassas, and Dubut.[6] The subsequent interests and careers of Legrand and Dufourny alone testify to the lasting impact of Séroux on his collaborators: Legrand wrote the first historical biography of Piranesi and contributed a long historical text to Durand's *Recueil et Parallèle;* Dufourny spent a considerable part of his life after the Revolution directing the publication of Séroux's own *History.*

If the fourteen volumes of drawings (now in the Vatican) used in the preparation of its plates bear witness to an attention to detail and a quest for fidelity often betrayed by the small scale of the engravings themselves, the text of the work also deserves more credit than it has received from historiographers impatient with its apparently unredeemable classicism.[7] After Winckelmann, the text represents the first attempt, and a not entirely unsuccessful one, to apply the criteria he had established and to bring together philosophic vision and antiquarian knowledge in the context of a rigorous examination of monuments themselves; hence the title, *The History of Art through Its Monuments from Its Decadence in the Fourth Century to Its Renewal in the Sixteenth.* Séroux was quite explicit about this combined aim. First, he drew up what he called a *Tableau historique,* sketching the political and institutional history of the twelve centuries from Constantine to Leo X, outlining the "general causes of the state of the arts . . . what makes them in turn be born and flourish, decay and disappear, then be reborn and flourish again."[8] This was followed by separate histories of the three arts—architecture, sculpture, and painting—comprised of some 375 plates, in all depicting 1,400 monuments of every epoch, accompanied by an analytical table identifying each illustration and its sources. This was completed by a series of three "Historical Discourses" following the order of the plates, expanding on their aesthetic content and significance. For Séroux, these essays were the culmination and justification of his work.

> I arrive, finally, at what I can call the aesthetic part of my work, that in which the history of monuments should be transformed into the history of art. What I have presented to this point could be compared to an immense Museum, where the principal productions of the three arts, during a long series of centuries, offer themselves to the gaze, classified and described in an order at the same time systematic and chronological. What must be done now in order to draw from such a spectacle the fertile results it is destined to produce, the useful lessons that are to be found concealed therein? To lead the spectators in some way to confront the mass of the facts that constitute this material history and to point out to them its order and sequence; to stop them for a longer time before those that present more interest and to study them, in isolation or in groups, according to all the relationships I willingly call technical; to determine, finally, the special character and their reciprocal influences, fixing at once their relative and their absolute value; that is what should complete a history of art as I have conceived it.[9]

In this grand scheme of a history, a "museum" of monuments and an aesthetic discourse, Séroux proposed to go beyond Winckelmann in a number of ways. First, in the preparation of the history itself, he was furnished, as Winckelmann was not, with a model that, as he recorded, guided his work from beginning to end: Gibbon's *Decline and Fall of the Roman Empire*, published between 1776 and 1788. In the conception of Séroux's *History*, and in its execution, the influence of Gibbon's text was incalculable: it was the first scholarly treatment of the period between the age of Trajan and the Renaissance, undertaken with the same sense of decay that pervaded his own understanding of post-Roman greatness, as Francis Haskell has noted.[10] Second, Séroux's intellectual preparation for the work in Paris had been extraordinarily broad: as a young cavalry officer, then a rich *fermier-général,* he had cultivated a variety of interests and friendships in the period before 1788.[11] Studying natural history with Bernard de Jussieu and botany with Rousseau, he was friendly with Buffon and d'Aubenton; at the salon of Mme Geoffrin he met Marmontel, La Harpe, Morellet, and Suard; he was received by Voltaire at Ferney. His avid interest in collecting antiquities and works of art brought him into contact with such scholars as the Comte de Caylus, who guided his acquisitions, and Mariette and Blondel d'Azincourt, and such painters as Boucher, Fragonard, Vien, and Robert. Soufflot supported Séroux's emerging curiosity with respect to medieval architecture. On his visit to England in 1777, he was entertained by Horace Walpole at Strawberry Hill, who in turn introduced him to scholars of the English Middle Ages.[12] And in Rome, Séroux was equally at home in the company of figures such as Goethe, Stendhal, and Chateaubriand as he was with artists like Canova, diplomats like Choiseul-Gouffier, and travelers like Cassas. His self-education, then, bypassed or overcame the division that Gibbon abhorred, between the philosophe and the antiquarian.

Present throughout the *Tableau historique* was Séroux's acknowledged debt to Gibbon, who was, he says, "constantly devoted to the march of history." Gibbon guided him as he "tried to discern, among the general causes of decline, those that were particularly tied to art." Séroux's work traced the causes of the decadence of art from the reigns of Commodus and Caracalla to the end of the thirteenth century, noted its renaissance from the age of Dante to that of Alberti, and affirmed its renewal with Bramante and Michelangelo at the beginning of the sixteenth century.[13] Not only did Séroux frequently cite Gibbon, especially as a source for the history and character of the barbarian invasions, but he frequently paraphrased and sometimes countered *The Decline and Fall,* as in Séroux's spirited defense of the influence of Christianity on the arts in Rome.[14] It was Gibbon, too, who provided the principle of chronology that always, wrote Séroux, "forms the knots in the endless thread it suspends above our heads."[15]

Gibbon's influence, however, is equally present in what Séroux claimed to be his own expertise, his aesthetic and cultural judgments of the monuments of antiquity and the Middle Ages. For if *The Decline and Fall* paid little attention to the arts of painting and sculpture, and only slightly more to philosophy and literature, it was filled with detailed descriptions and comments on buildings, from the evocation of the public works of the emperors in the first volume to the meditation on the ruins of Rome in the last. Francis Haskell has pointed to Gibbon's general interest in the arts on the evidence of his travel journal; but his attention to architecture, the most social and political art, was even more developed, as it was informed by the antiquarianism of the Comte de Caylus and Gibbon's direct observation.[16] His notebook of the trip from Geneva to Rome in 1764 recorded this double interest: the triumphal arch of Susa, "a bold and unconstrained architecture"; the churches, streets, monuments, and squares of Turin; the cathedral of Milan, "one of the greatest and last efforts of Gothic architecture," where "one remarks an air of oldness common to Gothic buildings, which evokes only an idea of ruin and weakness, where the unity of antique proportions at once inspires that of strength and solidity"; the Charterhouse of Pavia; the palaces and the cathedral of Genoa, with its facade "of a very bad Gothic"; the different monuments of Florence and the cathedral, with its dome, "grand, simple, and sublime."[17]

In each case, Gibbon assessed and delineated the building for its artistic and historical value; he consulted and judged the available authorities; architecture, in fact, emerges as a principal concern of his journal. When translated to the narrative of *The Decline and Fall,* this passion for monuments not only afforded an illustrative device with which to punctuate the chronicles of political and diplomatic activity, but it also emerged as an integral part of the history, the monuments being treated for the first time by a historian-antiquarian as worthy of more than topographical note. Gibbon exempted architecture from the general censorship he exercised over the arts, for reasons he makes explicit in the first volume.

Among the innumerable monuments of architecture constructed by the Romans, how many have escaped the notice of history, how few have resisted the ravages of time and barbarism! And yet even the majestic ruins that are still scattered over Italy and the provinces would be sufficient to prove that those countries were once the seat of a polite and powerful empire. Their greatness alone, or their beauty, might deserve our attention: but they are rendered more interesting by two important circumstances which connect the agreeable history of the arts with the more useful history of human manners. Many of those works were erected at private expense, and almost all were intended for public benefit.[18]

Throughout the succeeding volumes Gibbon used this criterion, the connection made by patronage between the agreeable and the useful, in order to select monuments for meticulous examination, often according to the most recent measurements provided by travelers and architects, as illustrations of aesthetic and moral judgment and as representative of specific moments in the culture of decline. The first volume included discussions of the buildings of Hadrian, of the rich Athenian Herodes Atticus, of the works of Trajan, all testifying to a "liberal spirit of public magnificence"; these he contrasted with the low, circular wooden huts of the Germans, wretchedly destitute of "the useful and agreeable arts of life," as a prelude to the fall of the one at the hands of the other.[19] He used the Goths' burning of the Temple of Diana at Ephesus as an example of the incomprehension of the "rude savages of the Baltic" and as an opportunity to depict the dimensions and decoration of one of the wonders of the world.[20] The siege of Palmyra and its sack by Aurelius led Gibbon to reflect that "it is easier to destroy than to restore. The seat of commerce, of arts and of Zenobia, gradually sunk into an obscure town, a trifling fortress, and at length a miserable village. The present citizens of Palmyra . . . have erected their mud cottages within the spacious court of a magnificent temple."[21] And if these ruins attested to the triumph of barbarism, Gibbon also found in the architecture of the late Empire itself evidence of that "slow and secret poison" that from within was sapping "the vitals of the Empire." Despite excitement over the recent rediscovery of Diocletian's Palace at Spalato, based on Adam's publication of 1763, Gibbon noted that "there is reason to suspect that the elegance of [Adam's] designs and engraving has somewhat flattered the objects," and instead concluded that the architecture was marked by "imperfections, very repugnant to our modern notions of taste and conveniency"; he cited the Italian antiquarian the abbate Fortis as testimony that "the awful ruins of Spalato are not less expressive of the decline of the arts than of the greatness of the Roman Empire at the time."[22] Such observations continue throughout the following volumes—the building of Constantinople, Ravenna, Santa Sophia (which takes up several pages of details and measures), and finally Rome itself, as seen in the present.

Séroux echoed these observations, and he seems to have provided on one level an illustrated commentary to Gibbon. But in his complete acceptance of historical-antiquarian methods, Séroux retained a strong intellectual allegiance to the philosophes; he cited Montesquieu as his second mentor, equal to Gibbon, "one who has considered the great political phenomenon [of the decline] from a general point of view," and he often mentioned his debt to Buffon.[23] For Séroux, Montesquieu and Buffon provided a systematic and comparative structure for the otherwise seamless chronology of events. Montesquieu supported the separate treatment of the arts "because of the difference in climate, mores, religion, and government, whose influence is strong and inevitable," and perhaps provided a model for the systematic treatment of styles.[24] Buffon's influence on Séroux stemmed from their personal contact and, therefore, was more direct; it concerned the division of history into different periods. From Vasari and Winckelmann, Séroux adopted the thesis of a tripartite division in artistic periods—from invention to decadence, from decadence to renewal, from renewal to the present—and within the second period, which was his major concern, he similarly distinguished ages of decline, renaissance, and renewal. But it was Buffon who suggested that a more particular kind of periodization be articulated for each national or regional art.

> Buffon, that man of genius who, with the eye of an eagle, has distinguished among the grand epochs of nature, allowed me, a few days before my departure for Italy, to question him on the subject of the researches I was about to undertake there, telling me that art also has its great epochs.[25]

On this advice Séroux outlined the epochs of English Gothic and of the development of architecture in the east, from its origins to the Crusades, understanding that the chronology and nature of stylistic change differ from region to region.

The intellectual and scholarly debts of the *History* are easily seen; Séroux was scrupulous in noting and commenting on his sources, and the sheer body of literature he assimilated to write the two volumes of his text and to verify the sources of the plates alone qualified him as one of the foremost cultural historians of the late eighteenth century. In long excursuses he critically assessed, for example, previous accounts of the Roman catacombs from antiquity to the present, both those published and those in manuscript; he also described the reception of the Gothic style in relation to the use of the word "Gothic" in the various European countries. Such evident erudition has indeed obscured Séroux's own contribution to the history of art, that is, his insistence on the visual recording and representation of evidence that, in the last analysis, could be assessed only by the eyes: "the products of the arts, children of design, architecture, sculpture, and painting, consist in objects perceived by the sight . . . and thus their effect reaches the soul only through this sense; from which it results that one should only write or study their history with their different productions before one's eyes . . . ."[26] Monuments, stated Séroux, adapting a current analogy, "speak to the eyes by themselves," and it was for this reason that he counted the preparation of the plates as the better part of his work.

> What the historians of the fine arts have been willing enough to say, I wish to *show*. . . . Here, it is, above all, the monuments that should

> speak; I have charged myself, in some way, only to write under their dictation, all the more to explain or comment on their language.[27]

While this emphasis on the *discours graphique* might recall Diderot's claim in the prospectus to the *Encyclopédie* that "a glance at the object or its representation says more about it than a page of discourse," Séroux was referring the study of architecture not simply to its representation, but to its own nature as a visual language, a theme he found in the more general and philosophical theory of the fine arts of Quatremère de Quincy (whose work in the *Encyclopédie méthodique* he admired without wishing to emulate) and in the tradition of antiquarian iconology.[28]

Séroux's plates, like those of the *Encyclopédie*, have a particular system of representation, but one more complex than that of the simple vignette above an analytical display of parts. Séroux's plates are of three different kinds. First, there are those that present a kind of panorama of a field by means of the juxtaposition of many small-scale images, mingling plans, elevations, sections, and perspectival views. In this category would be the first plate, which summarizes "architecture in its state of perfection among the Greeks and Romans," showing, among others, vignettes of the Parthenon, the Maison Carrée at Nimes, and the Pantheon (plate 150); the virtue of this plate, noted Séroux, is that it reveals "at a glance" the major characteristics of the best antique styles. Other such "portmanteau" plates present "the general picture of the decadence of art in the east," which, in a small scale, moves from an image of the Temple of the Sun at Palmyra to the triumphal arch at Salonika.

> It is thus by bringing together the monuments of the different countries of the Orient, which have between them no very close chronological link, and which do not even offer a complete series illustrating the degradation of the style, that I can show to the reader, rapidly and in a single glance, the state of art in Greece and Asia Minor.[29]

Economy, rapidity, and a general impression are the gains from this system; the losses are only calculable when the minute engraved images are compared with the detailed and large-scale, measured drawings from which they are taken. More successful, "systematic" plates include the summary, at the end of the series, of all conceivable theories about the origins of the Gothic arch, in fifty-five separate vignettes on a single page (plate 151), as well as comparative plates of facades, vaults, architraves, domes, columns, capitals, bases, and techniques of construction that take in the entire period of the history (plates 152–4). Séroux planned the final plate of "Architecture," the "Summary and general catalogue of the buildings that constitute the history of the decadence of architecture," as a "summary of summaries" (plate 155).

A second kind of plate is also quasi-systematic, but refers to a particular building type or a stylistic system, for example, the Gothic (plate 156) or the Renaissance (also see plate 157). Third, and more rare, a single monument is illustrated in detail on a single plate (plate 158); such is the case, for example, with Notre-Dame of Paris (plate 159).

The systematic and comparative plate was, of course, not new in the field of architecture; Séroux had many precedents to work from besides the more general model of the *Encyclopédie* and its own predecessors. In 1721, Fischer von Erlach had compared facades derived from representations on coins and the entrances to rock temples; many of the plates in his *Entwurf einer historischen Architektur* were quasi-systematic in the same way (plates 160,161,162,163).[30] Later in the century, the architect Meissonnier had drawn up a comparison of the "most considerable" buildings of history from Egypt to the present, including an Egyptian obelisk, restorations of the eight types of temples described by Vitruvius, two versions of the Pantheon, three Roman monuments reconstructed by Palladio, two Chinese pagodas, three Gothic structures (the cathedrals of Rouen and Strasbourg and the tower of Malines), one Byzantine church (Santa Sophia), two baroque churches (including Sant Ivo), and six modern, domed churches, from Saint Peter's to Saint Paul's, ending with Fischer's Karlskirche in Vienna.[31] These were drawn in elevation, all to different scales, and arranged more according to compositional than to historical rule (Saint Peter's taking up the center of the plate, the vertical axis occupied by the obelisk at the top, Saint Paul's at the bottom, and the Gothic, Chinese, and Byzantine buildings arranged around the periphery).

Julien-David Le Roy, the antiquarian-architect to whom Séroux owed much, assayed a more systematic approach in his *Histoire de la disposition et des formes différentes que les chrétiens ont donné à leurs temples,* published in 1764.[32] Here a single plate (plate 164) displayed the "plans of the most remarkable churches built from A.D. 326 to 1764"; in plan and elevation, to different scales, it presented eleven examples, from Santa Sophia to Saint Peter's and Sainte-Geneviève. Such a format would, as Werner Szambien has pointed out in his detailed study of the genre, hardly have distinguished Le Roy from earlier exponents, notably Meissonnier, or even Fischer von Erlach, if it had not been for his redesigned version, published in the second edition of *Les Ruines des plus beaux monuments de la Grèce* (1770), where his approach was more systematic.[33] He arranged the temples in three groups, displayed chronologically from top to bottom of the page, in three parallel lines; their number was increased, and, most important, while retaining a mixture of elevations and sections, all the plans were drawn to the same scale, making the plate truly comparative, a *parallèle* in the terminology of the eighteenth century (plate 165).

Le Roy divided his examples into what he regarded as the three generic religions and their corresponding religious types: those of the Egyptians, Hebrews, and Phoenicians; those of the Greeks and the Romans; and those of the Christians. He referred each group back to an origin: the primitive hut for the Egyptians, the first temple for the Greeks and Romans, and the catacombs for the Christians. Le Roy made his intentions explicit:

> The table we present here of the changes in the form of Temples among the different peoples will only present general descriptions with few details. If they had been more extended, they would only have broken the chain that we have undertaken to follow, which shows us the progress achieved by men in the art of planning. . . . An illustration, however small, will furnish, at first glance, a more distinct idea of them than the clearest discourse. This is what has persuaded me to engrave this series of temples in the order most suitable to demonstrate their different degrees of growth and perfection.[34]

Here, then, was Séroux's most telling model: systematic and comparative among peoples and epochs, didactic and progressive in example and chronological representation, inclusive of all historical periods, and, finally, presented to the same scale throughout, Le Roy's tableau was both more historical and more exemplary than those building-type parallels developed in the last years of the century by Pierre Patte, Victor Louis, Dumont (all concerned with theaters), and, of course, Durand, whose publication of 1799–1801 was, as its title indicated, a mixture of the collection and the parallel arranged according to a typology of programs for the convenience of design students.

The number of plates Séroux allocated to each epoch of his study demonstrated the overwhelming importance he gave to reconstructing the history of the decline: after an initial plate, which gave the reader a last and fleeting glimpse of the splendors of antique architecture, he dedicated thirty-three to delineating the forms of the decadence to the beginning of the Middle Ages (e.g., plate 166), and fourteen to exploring the Gothic (e.g., plate 167); he devoted only thirteen plates to the Renaissance and Renewal, before his final series of twelve comparative plates. It was the "fatal period," bequeathed to him by Winckelmann, that engaged Séroux's attention despite himself, causing him to map and chart with care that "immense desert, where nothing could be seen but disfigured objects, scattered fragments."[35]

The decline began, for Séroux as for Gibbon, with the corrupt regimes of Commodus and Caracalla; the causes were both internal and external, from the gradual introduction of "effeminate luxury" into Rome and the insidious effects of the assimilation of different peoples and customs, to the exhaustion of the Empire under barbarian attacks. Echoing Gibbon in his essay "On the Triumphs of the Romans," written in Rome in 1764, Séroux drew the salutary contrast between the early triumphs of Paulus Emilius, where statues and noble trophies inspired the Romans "with an equal love for virtue and the fine arts," and the luxurious pomps of Aurelius and Diocletian, which satisfied only curiosity and pride.[36] With the introduction of animal combats into the arena, Roman artists even lost sight of the human beauties that had sustained the art of Greece.

Thus the second plate illustrated architectural examples of the first decadence: monuments of Septimus Serverus, Diocletian, and Constantine. As Francis Haskell has noted, Séroux derived his commentary on Diocletian from Gibbon's own negative judgment; but Séroux went further, specifying the aspects of the architecture that marked its decay.[37] The facade of the Baths of Diocletian manifested "the most bizarre and licentious style," with useless columns heaped on top of each other, badly proportioned pedestals, interrupted cornices, broken pediments. At Spalato, all the monuments showed the same "license," columns supporting arches, entablatures broken by arches, a superabundance of ornaments, "*bizarreries* that announced the contempt of antique principles and the forgetting of true beauty" (plate 168).

> It is thus evident that one must place the corruption of art before Constantine. The vices we have remarked on in the constructions of Spalato leave no doubt in this regard. This building presents dissonances of every kind, a discordant mixture of columns in granite, porphyry, and marble, columns whose shaft is in one material and base

> and capital in another, and, finally, bas-reliefs whose subjects announce a choice made without judgment or taste.[38]

After this, architecture, used up by the pagans, had to retreat into the catacombs to rebuild its forms according to the elements of the new religion: chapels, oratories, and altars. The rules of a new style were worked out in the asylums and tombs of the early Christians: "the character of the architecture in the religious monuments of the catacombs determined that of the Christians above ground when Christianity began to enjoy a full liberty."[39] Séroux seems to have found it symbolically satisfying that the germs of a new art were born out of the haunts of death.

He went on to trace the rise of Christian architecture, in the Eastern empire as much as in Italy. He depicted as accurately as possible the churches of Ravenna, from the tomb of Galla Placida to San Vitale; of Rome, from S. Paolo fuori le mure (plate 169) to S. Clementino (plate 170); and of Constantinople, from the first Christian temples to Santa Sophia. All exhibited the decline in varying degrees. San Paolo took its ornaments literally from the debris of antiquity; its columns were spaced too widely and supported semicircular arches, while its capitals and bases were mixed indiscriminately; San Vitale, emulating Santa Sophia, recovered "neither the simple and grand ordering of the antique temples of Greece and Rome, nor that of the basilicas of the preceding age"; Santa Sophia, despite its evident magnificence, summarized all the vices:

> . . . columns, heavy or thin, without entablature, deprived of all proportions in bases as in capitals, sometimes coupled, sometimes linked two by two in the middle, false doors everywhere, forms without purpose, entire parts of buildings without accord either among themselves or with the whole.[40]

Taking his cue from Winckelmann, Séroux called this the style of "imitation" in the epochs of Eastern art, following the perfection attained under Greek influence and preceding the Mohammedan era.

From these mixed antecedents, "out of the heart of ignorance and from the ill-assorted mixture of forms and ornaments of every kind, was finally born a new and extraordinary manner of building." Characterized by the ogive or pointed arch, this style could not, Séroux thought, be dignified by the term *order*—it obeyed no fixed and invariable principles—but it should be understood instead as a *system:* the "Gothic System."[41] In a long chapter in his "Historical Discourse on Architecture," Séroux examined the previous uses of the word Gothic, providing a concise history of attitudes toward the style before 1780, and tried to establish the origin, character, and proper limits of the style. He explored its origins in one of the more omnibus plates, with fifty-five possible derivations for the pointed arch, as put forward by architects and historians from the Renaissance to the eighteenth century, including the cave, the *allée* of trees, Laugier's hut, variations on Vitruvius from Galiani, Etruscan tombs, Eastern obelisks, mosques and palaces, Indian temples, Moorish tents, Turkish baths, Arab ships (turned upside down), and antique arches. Séroux confessed that as "a simple historian of the vicissitudes of architecture," he must avoid any grand conclusions of the kind offered by Quatremère de Quincy; he simply allowed this plate to speak for heterogeneity, with an inclination against the Arab or Saracenic influence that was favored by historians from Wren to Lenoir.[42]

On the character of Gothic, Séroux was more definite; it rested absolutely on the pointed arch. He traced what he claimed was its first appearance in Italy, in the abbey of Subiaco, south of Rome, and gave examples of the Gothic in France, where his selection of Notre-Dame over Amiens, Beauvais, Chartres, and Orléans was justified by its national importance; in England, where he found in Ely Cathedral an exposition of the different styles of Gothic from Norman times to the fifteenth century (the dean of Ely supplied him with drawings by a talented niece); and in Germany.[43] He was hardly less flattering on the merits of the style than on its predecessors: it was, despite an evident monumentality and grandeur, "blameworthy": "frequently ignoring proportions, with faults in symmetry and unity, an excessive variety of forms without propriety and without analogy among themselves, [it] fatigues the eye and exhausts the attention." It was, moreover, "one of the sources of the errors, *bizarreries,* and individual beauties that covered Europe for so long a period."[44] Séroux spoke as an irredentist classicist, in terms that had hardly changed since Alberti.

And yet, between the lines of his commentary, we can detect the emergence of a different sensibility, one marked by his friendship with Horace Walpole and his exposure to English scholarship and appreciation, a sensibility he shared with a number of late-eighteenth-century ideologues of his generation, notably the Comte de Volney and Alexandre Lenoir. This was an openness to the sublime aspects of the Gothic, a style that, in Walpole's words, quoted by Séroux, "'infused such sentiments of romantic devotion' in the medieval congregation and eighteenth-century visitor alike": its ability, as James Bentham put it, "to affect the imagination with pleasure and delight at the same time," or, as Strutt concluded, its "elegance agreeing perfectly with the romantic taste and genius of our ancestors."[45] Séroux had read Strutt's assessment of Westminster, "the awefull reverence and gloomy grandeur of that venerable pile," and knew of Pope's comparison of Shakespeare to the Gothic—a style at the same time sublime and barbarous. Occasionally, he allowed himself to speak in the same vein, as when he found in Canterbury and York, "these cathedrals without ornaments, great religious solitude," which he attributed to the cult of simplicity and severity of Anglicanism, leading in architecture to an "involuntary thrill that surprises the sense and disposes the soul to contemplation and respect."[46]

Such an aesthetics of the sublime was, however, too bound to the forces of nature for Séroux to consider it a valid constituent of high architecture, and it is only in buildings that more closely approached the nonarchitectural and, thereby, the truly natural that he was able to explore this sentiment fully. In a poetic passage marked by his reading of Delille's *Imagination* and in his friendship with the painter Robert, Séroux anticipated, or at least paralleled, those "meditations" on the ruins of civilization that, from Volney's *Ruines* of 1790 to Chateaubriand's *Génie du Christianisme* of 1802, marked a preromantic stance. Having recounted his terror on being lost underground for more than an hour—an experience, as he noted, in the grand tradition of Montfaucon and Robert, and a departure from the scholarly tone of his resume of sources for the catacombs (plates 171,172,173)—Séroux paused for reflection:

> After these testimonials of veneration given by men who themselves merit divine honors, after the touching descriptions they have made of the catacombs, should I venture to express the sentiments I have so often felt while perusing these celebrated monuments alone beneath these shadowy vaults, where no plant, bird, or animal affords the image of life, when I have found myself seated among so many tombs built above my head or hollowed out beneath my feet, or when I have measured these tortuous paths by the glimmer of a torch? . . . At first a vague disquiet took possession of me; my imagination found itself overwhelmed by the multitude of ideas presented by religion, history, and philosophy at the same time; then the profound silence that surrounded me reestablished calm in my spirit; a reverie then carried me away; and I tasted a repose almost similar to that of the thousands of dead who have slept in these cemeteries through fifteen centuries.[47]

Even this passage, with its undertones of stock soliloquy, stops well before romanticism, and Séroux himself lived to abhor the new taste, warning his last generation of helpers, with whom he seemed to have little rapport, "that it would be dangerous to push the study [of the Middle Ages] too far," and speaking disparagingly of the "enthusiasm of certain modern schools."[48] The mysticism of Humbert de Superville, who drew some of the final plates, had little in common with the rationalism of the classical antiquary.

Forced to remain in exile in Rome during the Revolutionary period, Séroux was able to see his work to publication by the efforts of the faithful Dufourny, who, as Quatremère recorded, had himself assembled "an immense collection of ornaments, moldings, decorative motifs, bas-reliefs," one whose knowledge of history allowed him to succeed David Le Roy as professor of architecture.[49] Séroux was thus only to follow, at a distance, the development of a peculiarly "revolutionary" sensibility toward French antiquities, one preparatory of later romanticism but in itself distinct and internally consistent as it searched to define ways of evaluating the remains of the *régime féodale,* both monuments to and signs of oppression, subject to all the fury of a well-recognized and -supported "revolutionary vandalism," and all that was left of the true history of France as a nation.

In a footnote, Séroux paid tribute to two figures in this continuing debate: Aubin-Louis Millin, who in 1790, had presented the first volume of his *Antiquités nationales* to the National Assembly, but later had withdrawn from political activity, and Alexandre Lenoir, the young painter who, also in 1790, had been appointed the caretaker of the *dépôt* established to collect any debris worth saving from the pillaged châteaux, monasteries, and palaces of the Old Regime. These two, as well as others whom Séroux noted, had begun the long work of developing a French architectural history, with respect to which "one must comb the history of our provinces and towns, stopping at descriptions of monasteries and churches, and join to this work engravings and particular researches on the chronology of styles."[50] At his death in 1814, Séroux still had been unable to visit Lenoir's Musée des monuments français, itself conceived in a classical spirit according to the premises of Winckelmann, yet which, like Séroux's *Histoire,* did much to collect and to popularize the remnants of the decline.

NOTES

INTRODUCTION

1. For Kaufmann's contribution, see Meyer Schapiro's essay, "The New Viennese School," *Art Bulletin* (1936), and, especially, Gilbert Erouart, "Situation d'Emil Kaufmann," in Emil Kaufmann, *Trois Architectes Révolutionnaires: Boullée, Ledoux, Lequeu,* ed. Gilbert Erouart and Georges Teyssot (Paris, 1978), 5–11. This contains a good bibliography of Kaufmann's major works (30–33). Kaufmann's first essay on the problem of late-eighteenth-century style was "Die Architekturtheorie der französische Klassik und des Klassizismus," *Repertorium für Kunstwissenschaft* 64 (1924): 197–237, written in 1920. This was followed by "Architektonische Entwürfe aus der französischen Revolution," *Zeitschrift für bildende Kunst* 63 (1929-1930): 38–46; "Die Stadt des Architekten Ledoux," *Kunstwissenschaftliche Forschungen* 2 (1933): 131-160; "Klassizismus als Tendenz und als Epoche," *Kritische Berichte* (1933), 204–214; *Von Ledoux bis Le Corbusier: Ursprung und Entwicklung des autonomen Architektur* (Vienna and Leipzig, 1933–1934); "Three Revolutionary Architects: Boullée, Ledoux and Lequeu," *Transactions of the American Philosophical Society,* New Series 42/43 (Philadelphia, 1952); and *Architecture in the Age of Reason: Baroque and Postbaroque in England, Italy and France* (Cambridge, Mass., 1955).

2. Beginning with J.M. Pérouse de Montclos, *Etienne-Louis Boullée, 1728-1799* (Paris, 1969), monographs have been written about most of the important architects of the late eighteenth century. Among others, see M. Gallet, *Claude-Nicolas Ledoux, 1736-1806* (Paris, 1980); D. Rabreau, Monique Mosser, et al., *Charles De Wailly, peintre architecte dans l'Europe des lumières* (Paris, 1979); G. Erouart, *Jean-Laurent Legeay, un Piranésien français dans l'Europe des lumières* (Paris, 1982); W. Szambien, *Jean-Nicolas-Louis Durand, 1760-1834* (Paris, 1984); M. Gallet and Jörg Garms, *Germain Boffrand, 1667-1754* (Paris, 1986); M. Mosser et al., *Alexandre-Théodore Brongniart, 1739-1813* (Paris, 1986). Joseph Rykwert, *The First Moderns: The Architects of the Eighteenth Century* (Cambridge, 1980), and Alan Braham, *The Architecture of the French Enlightenment* (London, 1979), assess the period as a whole from two distinct points of view, the former in the context of intellectual and cultural history, the latter with a scrupulous avoidance of ideas in favor of a history of buildings.

3. See, for example, B. Fortier et al., *La politique de l'espace parisien à la fin de l'Ancien Régime* (Paris, 1975); André Chastel et al., *Système de l'architecture urbaine: le quartier des Halles* (Paris, 1977); Françoise Fichet, *La théorie de l'architecture à l'âge classique, essai d'anthologie critique* (Brussels, 1979); M.K. Deming, *La Halle au Blé de Paris, 1762-1813* (Paris, 1984).

4. Among numerous studies following the pioneer work of Arnaldo Momigliano, Lionel Gossman, *Medievalism and the Ideologies of the Enlightenment: The World and Work of La Curne de Sainte-Palaye* (Baltimore, 1968), is a seminal work.

1. Charles Batteux, *Les Beaux-arts réduits à un même principe,* 2d ed. (Paris, 1776), 24–26. This passage was inserted in the second edition of Batteux's treatise, originally published in 1746, no doubt as a response to the debates over the origins of architecture that had occurred since 1750.
2. For a discussion, with translated passages, of ideas of primitivism in antiquity, see A.O. Lovejoy and G. Boas, *Primitivism and Related Ideas in Antiquity,* vol. 1 of *A Documentary History of Primitivism and Related Ideas* (Baltimore, 1935). Erwin Panofsky looks at the Renaissance manifestation of this complex tradition in "The Early History of Man in Two Cycles of Paintings by Piero di Cosimo," *Studies in Iconology* (Oxford, 1939), 33–67.
3. Claude Perrault tried to provide convincing illustrations to Vitruvius's description of primitive huts, noting that "the description of the building of huts is difficult enough to understand, both from the obscurity of the terms and the faults of the text," *Les dix livres d'architecture de Vitruve* (Paris, 1673), bk. 2, chap. 1.
4. Vitruvius, *De Architectura Libri decem,* vol. 2, 1. The translation provided by Lovejoy and Boas is worth quoting at length: "In the olden days men were born like wild beasts in woods and caves and groves, and they kept alive by eating raw food. Somewhere, meanwhile, the close-grown trees, tossed by storms and winds, and rubbing their branches together, caught fire. Terrified by the flames, those who were near the spot fled. When the storm subsided, they drew near, and, since they noticed how pleasant to their bodies was the warmth of the fire, they laid on wood; and thus keeping it alive, they brought up some of their fellows, and, indicating the fire with gestures, they showed them the use which they might make of it. When in this meeting of men sounds were breathed forth with differing intensity, they made customary by daily use these chance syllables. Then, giving names to things more frequently used, they began to speak because of this fortuitous event, and so they held conversation among themselves. Since, therefore, from the discovery of fire a beginning of human association was made, and of union and intercourse; and since many now came together in one place, being endowed by nature with a gift beyond that of the other animals, so that they walked, not looking down, but erect, and saw the magnificence of the universe and the stars, and, moreover, did easily with their fingers whatever they wished; some in that society began to make roofs of leaves, others to dig out caves under the hills; some, imitating the nests and constructions of the swallows, made places, into which they might go, out of mud and twigs. Finding, then, other shelters and inventing new things by their power of thought, they built in time better dwellings." Lovejoy and Boas, *Primitivism,* 375. The long history of the reception and transformation of this text and its successive descriptions of the houses of the Colchians in the Crimea, the Phrygians in northwest Turkey, and others, is traced by Joseph Rykwert in *On Adam's House in Paradise: The Idea of the Primitive Hut in Architectural History* (New York, 1972); Rykwert finds echoes of Lucretius, Posidonius, and "stoic doctrine tinged by peripatetic empiricism," in Vitruvius's eclectic formulation (110).
5. Joseph-François Lafitau, *Moeurs des sauvages américains comparées aux moeurs des premiers temps* (Paris, 1724), vol. 1, 3. Lafitau, a Jesuit missionary, was born in Bordeaux in 1681; he visited Canada and studied the lives and customs of its Indian tribes between 1712 and 1719. The best critical edition of the *Moeurs des sauvages* is the translation by William N. Fenton and Elizabeth L. Moore, eds., *Customs of the American Indians Compared with the Customs of Primitive Times* (Toronto, 1974). For a full biography, see Joseph-François Lafitau, *Moeurs des sauvages américains,* ed. Edna Hindie Lemay (Paris, 1983).
6. Lafitau, *Moeurs* (1724), vol. 1, 2–3. An analysis of this frontispiece looking at its implications for the methodology of ethnology is given in Pierre Vidal-Naquet, "Les jeunes: Le cru, l'enfant grec et le cuit," in J. Le Goff, P.Nora, eds., *Nouveaux objets,* vol. 3 of *Faire de l'histoire* (Paris, 1974), 137–168; also on method, see Michel de Certeau, "Writing versus Time: History and Anthropology in the Works of Lafitau," *Yale French Studies* 59 (1980): 37–64. See also, for general treatments of Lafitau, Michèle Duchet, "Discours ethnologique et discours historique: le texte de Lafitau," *Studies on Voltaire and the Eighteenth Century* 92 (1976): 607–623; Edna Lemay, "Histoire de l'antiquité et découverte du nouveau monde chez deux auteurs du XVIIIe siècle," *Studies on Voltaire and the Eighteenth Century* 93 (1976): 1313–1328.
7. Lafitau, *Moeurs* (1724), vol. 1, 3.
8. Vidal-Naquet, "Les jeunes," 139.

9. Marcel Detienne, *L'invention de la mythologie* (Paris, 1981), 21. The whole first chapter is devoted to the study of myth in the eighteenth and nineteenth centuries.
10. Lafitau, *Moeurs* (1724), vol. 2, 5.
11. Ibid., 6.
12. Ibid., 7.
13. Ibid., 7–8.
14. Ibid., 8.
15. Ibid., "Cabanes Iroquois," 10 et seq.
16. Ibid., vol. 1, 137.
17. Ibid., 146.
18. Ibid., 158.
19. Ibid., 167–8.
20. Ibid., plate 4, "Origine et progrès de l'idolatrie."
21. Ibid., vol. 2, 3.
22. Ibid.
23. Ibid., 5.
24. Voltaire, *Essai sur les moeurs,* in *Oeuvres complètes* (Paris, 1878), vol. 11, 18.
25. Marquis de Sade, *Justine* (New York: Grove Press, 1974), 544.
26. Lafitau, *Moeurs* (1724), vol 1, i.
27. Ibid., ii.
28. The jurist Samuel Pufendorf's *Le droit de la nature et des gens,* 2d. ed. (Amsterdam, 1712), was a favorite source for Rousseau; Antoine-Yves Goguet, a lawyer to the Parlement of Paris, wrote *De l'origine des lois, des arts et des sciences, et de leurs progrès chez les anciens peuples* (The Hague, 1758), which assessed the veracity of ancient accounts against modern observations—his history of primitive architecture was the most complete study of Vitruvius and his predecessors in the eighteenth century (bk. 3, chap. 3); Cornélius De Pauw's *Recherches philosophiques sur les Américains* (Berlin, 1768–1769), and *Recherches philosophiques sur les Egyptiens et les Chinois* (Berlin, 1773), provided a comprehensive summary of previous travelers' accounts and, incidentally, furnished much of Quatremère de Quincy's historical learning.
29. The full title was, *The Life and Strange Surprizing Adventures of Robinson Crusoe of York, Mariner: in an un-inhabited Island on the Coast of America, near the mouth of the Great River of the Oroonoque; Having been cast on Shore by Shipwreck, wherein all the Men perished but himself. With An Account how he was at last as strangely deliver'd by Pyrates* (London, 1719).
30. Henry Wotton, *The Elements of Architecture* (London, 1624).
31. Defoe, *The Life and Adventures of Robinson Crusoe,* ed. Angus Ross (London, 1965), 76.
32. Wotton, *Elements,* 4.
33. Defoe, *Robinson Crusoe,* 76–78.
34. Vitruvius, *The Ten Books of Architecture,* trans. M. H. Morgan (Cambridge, Mass., 1916), 39.
35. Wotton, 4.
36. Robert Morris, *Rural Architecture* (London, 1750), 12.
37. It is perhaps significant that the captured mutineers were, at the end of the narrative, "conveyed . . . to the cave, as to a prison; and it was indeed a dismal place, especially to men in their condition." Defoe, *Robinson Crusoe* (1965), 266.
38. Jean-Jacques Rousseau, *Emile ou de l'éducation* (1762) (Paris: Garnier-Flammarion, 1966), 239–240: "This book will be the first my Emile will read; for a long time it will be the whole of his library."
39. Jean-Jacques Rousseau, *Discours sur les sciences et les arts* (1750), in *Oeuvres Complètes,* vol. 3 (Paris: Bibliothèque de la Pléiade, 1966), 22.

40. Jean-Jacques Rousseau, *Discours sur l'origine de l'inégalité* (1755), in *Oeuvres complètes,* vol. 3, 167. The best analysis of Rousseau's system of stadial social development is in Michèle Duchet, *Anthropologie et histoire au siècle des lumières* (Paris, 1971), 264–313.
41. Ibid.
42. Ibid., 171.
43. Jean-Jacques Rousseau, *Du Contrat social* (1762), in *Oeuvres complètes,* vol. 3, 427
44. Jean-Jacques Rousseau, *Essai sur l'origine des langues* (Paris: A. Belin, 1817), 525.
45. Etienne Bonnot de Condillac, *La Langue des calculs,* in Georges Le Roy, ed., *Oeuvres philosophoques de Condillac* (Paris 1947–1951), quoted in I.F. Knight, *The Geometric Spirit: The Abbé de Condillac and the French Enlightenment* (New Haven, 1968), 144.
46. Jean le Rond d'Alembert, *Discours préliminaire de l'Encyclopédie'* (1750) (Paris: Editions Gonthier, 1965), 19.
47. For a succinct account of the theories of origin in the *Encyclopédie,* see René Hubert, *Les sciences sociales dans l'Encyclopédie'* (Lille, 1923). Hubert distinguishes between traditionalist theories, which based the order of society on the will of the creator and received law, and naturalist theories, which saw society as a result of the extension of the family (a kind of biological determinism), as caused by a natural instinct for sociability (that is, based on innate "sympathies"), as a direct outcome of the operation of personal interest (either divisive, according to Diderot, or unifying, as d'Alembert held), or, finally, as formed by the principle of a social contract. All naturalist concepts held society to be a fundamentally natural phenomenon, shaped in response to need or *besoin.*
48. See Hans Aarsleff, "The Tradition of Condillac: The Problem of the Origin of Language in the Eighteenth Century," in *From Locke to Saussure* (Minneapolis, 1982), 146–209. This

is by far the best study of the intellectual history of linguistic theory in the modern period.

49. Condillac, *La Langue des calculs,* in Knight, *Geometric Spirit,* 144. See Aarsleff, "Tradition of Condillac," and Knight, *Geometric Spirit,* for extended discussions of the importance of Condillac's language origin theories. For a comparison of different theories of language origin in the mid-eighteenth century, see Hubert, *Sciences sociales,* ch. 8. E.M. Hine, *A Critical Study of Condillac's "Traité des systèmes"* (The Hague, 1979), 167–182, analyzes the relation of the *Essai* to Condillac's later works and his treatment of the arts.

50. Condillac, *Traité des systèmes* (The Hague, 1749), ch. 7, deals with the different arts; the *Essai* traces the origins of the arts and the sciences to the same source as language, 80–82. See Hine, *Condillac's "Traité des systèmes,"* and Knight, *The Geometric Spirit.*

51. Condillac, "Essai sur l'origine" in *Oeuvres philosophiques,* vol. 1, 80.

52. Condillac, *Traité des systèmes,* 215.

53. Marc-Antoine Laugier, *Essai sur l'architecture* (Paris, 1753). For a complete analysis of the *Essai,* as well as of its reception, see the monograph by Wolfgang Herrmann, *Laugier and Eighteenth Century French Theory* (London, 1962).

54. Laugier, *Essai sur l'architecture,* 2d ed. (Paris, 1755), 8.

55. Rousseau, *Discours sur les sciences et les arts,* 22.

56. Laugier, *Essai sur l'architecture,* 2d ed., 9.

57. Ibid.

58. Condillac, *Essai sur l'origine des connaissances humaines* (1746), ed. Charles Porset (Paris: éditions Galilée, 1973); Abbé Charles Batteux, *Les Beaux-arts.*

59. Laugier, *Essai sur l'architecture,* 2d ed., 8.

60. Ibid., 10.

61. Ibid., 11.

62. Ibid., 56.

63. Ibid., 57.

64. Batteux, *Les Beaux-arts.* For Batteux, architecture was at once useful and beautiful, submitted to the two determinants of need or *besoin,* which included all the practical and social requirements of solidity and commodity, and pleasure, or *agrément,* which depended on the arts of beauty. Unlike the true crafts, architecture could not be held to the single criterion of necessity; unlike the fine arts, it could not simply please the eyes or ears. More like rhetoric, another mixed art, it formed a third category that might be defined as an art of convenience or comfort, or *commodité* (27). In Batteux's view, the hierarchy thus formed—arts of necessity, arts of commodity, fine arts—was natural and might be deduced from an examination of origins: the arts were invented first by need; some were polished and developed according to increasing standards of comfort; others were raised by the progress of taste into arts of pure pleasure: "When the necessary and the comfortable had been provided for, there was only one step left to arrive at pleasure, which is a third order of need" (27). The relations of each art with nature likewise followed this ascending order: the arts of necessity "use nature as it is, uniquely for use and service"; the arts of commodity use nature while "polishing it for service and pleasure"; the fine arts do not "use" nature at all—they only "imitate it, each according to its manner" (28). Batteux thus resolved his initial problem, which was "to reduce the fine arts to a single principle" by the technique of exclusion: only those arts that imitated nature were fine arts; ergo, the single principle of the fine arts was that of imitation. The endless arguments over the hierarchies of the different arts and their particular relations to social and individual status are well summarized in Paul O. Kristeller, *Renaissance Thought and the Arts* (Princeton, 1965), especially chap. 9.

65. D'Alembert, *Discours,* 49.

66. Charles-Alexandre Guillaumot, *Remarques sur un livre intitulé, "Observations sur l'architecture" de M. l'abbé Laugier* (Paris, 1768).

67. Jean-Louis Viel de Saint-Maux, *Lettres sur l'architecture des Anciens et celles des Modernes* (Paris, 1787), "Septième lettre," 54.

68. C.M. Delagardette, *Règles des cinq ordres d'architecture de Vignole* (Paris, 1786), plate 3.

69. Delagardette, *Règles des cinq ordres,* 2d ed. (Paris, 1797), 15.

1. Jacques-François Blondel, *Cours d'architecture* (Paris, 1771), vol. 2, 398–399.
2. The best account of the precedents, methods, and circumstances of Diderot's "Description des arts et métiers" for the *Encyclopédie* is in Jacques Proust, *Diderot et l'"Encyclopédie'* (Paris, 1967). The *Encyclopédie, ou dictionnaire raisonné des sciences, des arts et des métiers, par une société de gens de lettres,* edited by Denis Diderot and Jean le Rond d'Alembert, appeared between 1751 and 1765.
3. Proust, *Diderot et l'"Encyclopédie,'* 196 et seq.
4. Blondel, *Cours d'architecture,* vol. 2, 398 et seq.
5. The plates of the *Encyclopédie,* edited by Diderot, appeared in eleven volumes between 1762 and 1772. Many of the illustrations of the *arts et métiers* were based on engravings and drawings already prepared for the Académie royale des sciences after 1699, a project of documentation renewed under the editorship of Réaumur between 1762 and 1772; hence the denunciation of Diderot's "plagiarism" by Pierre Patte, who had engraved some of the Académie's plates. See Jacques Proust, "La Documentation technique de Diderot dans l'*Encyclopédie,*" *Revue de l'histoire littéraire* (July–September, 1957), 335–352; Georges Huard, "Les Planches de l'*Encyclopédie* et celles de la *Description des arts et métiers* de l'Académie des sciences," *Revue de l'histoire sociale* (July–December, 1951), 238–249. The collection of studies by Bertrand Gille, Huard, and others in *L'"Encyclopédie' et les progrès des sciences et des techniques* (Paris, 1952), is also useful.
6. Denis Diderot, "Encyclopédie," in *Oeuvres complètes* (Paris, 1875–1879), ed. Assezat et Tourneux, vol. 14, 495.
7. See *Encyclopédie, Planches,* vol. 5, 52.
8. The essay by Roland Barthes, "Les Planches de l'*Encyclopédie,*" in *Le Degré zéro de l'écriture suivi de Nouveaux Essais critiques* (Paris, 1972), 89–105, is an elegant analysis of the graphic discourse of the *Encyclopédie;* published first in 1964 under the title, "Image, raison, déraison," as an introduction to *L'Univers de l'"Encyclopédie'* (Paris, 1964), the article influenced Jacques Proust's examination of "L'image du peuple au travail dans les planches de l'*Encyclopédie,*" in *Images du Peuple au dix-huitième siècle,* Colloque d'Aix-en-Provence 1969 (Paris, 1973), 66–85. Barthes notes, "One cannot imagine a more simple idea of technique. An almost naive simplicity, a kind of golden legend of artisanry (because there is in these plates no trace of social ills): the *Encyclopédie* confounds the simple, the elementary, the essential, and the causal. The Encyclopedic technique is simple because it is reduced to a space of two terms: the causal trajectory, which goes from the material to the object. Also, all the plates that are concerned with some technical operation (of transformation) mobilize an aesthetic of nudity: large empty rooms, well-lit, where man and his labor coexist alone: a space without parasites, with bare walls, cleared tables ["*tables rases*"]; the simple here is nothing more than the vital. . . " (92).
9. "Hongroyeur, l'Opération de mettre au suif et Plan de l'étuve," in *Planches,* vol. 7, 3.
10. "Tireur d'or," in *Planches,* vol. 10, 157; "Tourneur, atelier," 175; "Marchande de Modes," in *Supplément,* 162; "Bouchonnier," vol. 2, 65; "Tapissier," vol. 9, 198–199.
11. "Marine, Forge des ancres," in *Planches,* vol. 7, 135–136, 141, 143–147.
12. "Tapisserie de Haute Lisse des Gobelins," in *Planches,* vol. 9, 231–232; "Teinture des Gobelins," vol. 10, 1–4, 11, 13–16, 19.
13. See, for example, the series of plates depicting the art of military movements in formation, *Planches,* vol. 1, 230 et seq.
14. Diderot, "Prospectus" to the *Encyclopédie,* in *Oeuvres complètes,* vol. 13, 142.
15. J. A. Naigeon, in his *Mémoires historiques et philosophiques sur la vie et les ouvrages de Diderot* (Paris, 1821), 50, stated that Diderot had small models of machines like the stocking-loom made for him, and he used them in trying to draw the various parts of the process.
16. Diderot, "Prospectus," 142.
17. Ibid., 143.
18. Diderot, "Art," in *Oeuvres complètes,* vol. 8, 368.
19. "Verrerie en bois, Plan général d'une grande verrerie en plats," in *Planches,* vol. 10, 297–298; "Verrerie en bois," 267–268; "Verrerie en bouteilles," 324–329.
20. For example, the illustrations of the village blacksmith at work, "Maréchal ferrant et opérant," in *Planches,* vol. 7, 58–60, and "Maréchal grossier," 66–67 (plates 17–18); the more "exotic" *métiers,* such as the cotton fields in America, include palm trees, strange birds, vegetation, and detailed pictures of slaves at work (*Planches,* vol. 1, 34).
21. "Verrerie en bois, Grande verrerie en vitres ou en plats," *Planches,* vol. 10, 294.

22. Diderot, "Art," 368.
23. In the *Encyclopédie* plate, the high, purely conical "Verrerie angloise" was joined to a workshop of conventional architecture, thus heightening the contrast between industrial form and traditional building ("Verrerie angloise," in *Planches,* vol. 10, 331–333).
24. Diderot's aesthetic theories of the "hieroglyphs" suitable to each of the arts are analyzed in James Doolittle, "Hieroglyph and Emblem in Diderot's *Lettre sur les Sourds et Muets,*" *Diderot Studies* (Syracuse, 1952): 148–167.
25. Diderot, "Additions pour servir d'éclairissemens à quelques endroits de la *Lettre sur les sourds et muets*"; P.H. Meyer, *Diderot Studies* 7 (Geneva, 1965): 98.
26. Jacques-François Blondel, *Architecture française,* vol. 2 (Paris, 1752), 97 et seq. See also "Plan de l'hostel social des Gobelins, fait par Sébastien le Clerc fils, 1691," *Société de l'Histoire de Paris, Mémoires* 19 (Paris, 1892): 288 et seq.
27. Blondel, *Architecture,* vol. 2, 97 et seq..
28. A good survey of existing *manufactures royales* from the seventeenth and eighteenth centuries is Maurice Daumas, *L'Archéologie industrielle en France* (Paris, 1980), although the lack of footnotes and documentary references reduces its usefulness.
29. "Papetterie, Vue des bâtimens de la manufacture de l'Anglée près Montargis," in *Planches,* vol. 5, 234–236.
30. See Bertrand Gille, "L'*Encyclopédie,* dictionnaire technique," in *L'"Encyclopédie' et le progrès des Sciences,* 187–214. The editors of the *Encyclopédie* have often been accused of not taking full account of new technologies already known in Britain. Proust, in *Diderot et l'"Encyclopédie',* agrees, but points out that in most respects the contributors do precisely what is asked of them, providing a balanced account of the state of the art around 1750 in France.
31. The architect Germain Boffrand constructed hand-powered pumps at the prison of Bicêtre in 1733; although they never functioned as intended, the work continued to usefully occupy the prisoners. See Michel Foucault, *Histoire de la folie à l'âge classique* (Paris, 1975), 81. A full account of Boffrand's institutional architecture is given by N. S. F. Garnot, "Germain Boffrand et l'Hôpital Général, in M. Gallet and Jörg Garms, *Germain Boffrand,* 143–160.
32. Jean-Rodolphe Perronet contributed the article "Pompe à feu," in *Encyclopédie,* vol. 6, as well as describing the manufacture of pins for the fourth volume of plates. Ling's activities are described in Charles Ballot, "La Révolution technique et les débuts de la grande exploitation dans la métallurgie française: l'introduction de la fonte au coke en France et la fondation du Creusot," *Revue d'histoire économique et sociale* (1912), 34 et seq.
33. The best account of French industrial development in the eighteenth century is Pierre Léon, "La réponse de l'industrie" and "L'élan industriel et commercial," in Ernst Labrousse et al., eds., *Histoire économique et sociale de la France,* vol. 2, *Des derniers temps de l'âge seigneurial aux préludes de l'âge industriel (1660-1789)* (Paris, 1970). For the glass industry, see Warren C. Scoville, *Capitalism and French Glassmaking, 1640-1789* (Berkeley, 1950). For the iron industry, see Bertrand Gille, *Les origines de la grande industrie métallurgique en France* (Paris, 1947). P. M. Bondois, "Le développement de la verrerie française au XVIIIe siècle," *Revue d'histoire économique et sociale* 23 (1936–1937): 237–261, is still useful. A good regional case study is Pierre Léon, *La Naissance de la grande industrie en Dauphiné (fin du XVIIe siècle—1869)* (Paris, 1954)
34. Scoville, *Capitalism and Glassmaking,* 45.
35. A detailed description of Buffon's forges at Montbard as they stand today is included in Serge Benoît, "Les Forges de Buffon," *Monuments Historiques* 107 (1980): 53–64. The grand staircase leading to the forge, on which visitors stood to survey the work in progress, might well have inspired Ledoux's staircase in the director's house at Chaux.
36. Although based entirely on a study of British sources, the best analytical summary of the social problems of management is Sidney Pollard, *The Genesis of Modern Management* (London, 1969).
37. "Manufacture," in *Encyclopédie;* this article is unsigned, and Proust believes that it is not by Diderot. In the octavo edition of the *Encyclopédie méthodique,* ed. Pellet (Paris, 1780), it is noted as by Diderot.
38. "Manufacture," in *Encyclopédie méthodique,* vol. 20 (Paris, 1780), 1003 et seq.
39. Ibid., 1005.
40. Ibid.
41. Ibid., 1006.
42. Michel Foucault, in *Surveiller et punir* (Paris, 1975), establishes this discourse as culminating in the panopticon principle of Jeremy Bentham, supported by disciplinary techniques in school and in the army; his conclusions have been debated, challenged, and extended by Michelle Perrot et al., *L'impossible prison* (Paris, 1980).
43. A typical set of regulations was published by Daniel Ligou, "Un règlement de manufacture à la fin du XVIIIe siècle," *Revue d'histoire économique et sociale,* 31 (1953): 273–275; this document, drawn up for a wool factory in the

department of Lot in 1770, orders the workers to remain within their own shops on penalty of fine, forbids them the cabaret "dans les heures de retraites," and sets punishments for all infractions of behavior on the job. Similar regulations pertained for all royal *manufactures*. See also Emile Levasseur, *Histoire des classes ouvrières et de l'industrie en France avant 1789* (Paris, 1901).

1. Claude-Nicolas Ledoux, *L'Architecture considérée sous le rapport de l'art, des moeurs et de la législation* (Paris, 1804), 122. The most comprehensive treatment of the life and work of Ledoux is Michel Gallet, *Claude-Nicolas Ledoux, 1736-1806* (Paris, 1980); the bibliography, chronology, documentary appendix, and list of works are indispensable and subsume most previous scholarship.

2. A letter from de Maupeou and the abbé Terray to Trudaine de Montigny, September 20, 1771, confirmed Ledoux as adjunct to Perronet; this was no doubt in recompense for his work for Madame du Barry at the Pavilion of Louveciennes, opened with a magnificent fête in the presence of Louis XV on September 2 the same year. Ledoux, however, took the job seriously and turned it into the commission that not only cemented his reputation but gave him a foundation for imaginary projects for the rest of his life. See Gallet, *Ledoux*, 266.

3. The increasing technical and economic role of the *inspecteurs des manufactures* is described in Léon, "Réponse de l'industrie," and detailed in F. Bacquié, "Les inspecteurs des manufactures sous l'Ancien Régime (1660–1791)," in J. Habyem, ed., *Mémoires et documents pour servir à l'histoire du commerce en France* (Toulouse, 1927). Daniel Trudaine (1703–1769), Trudaine de Montigny's father, had served as intendant of commerce since 1749; he was a friend of Perronet and founder, with him, of the Ecole de Ponts et Chaussées, supporting the development and completion of the highway and river network conceived by Colbert. Trudaine de Montigny (1733–1777) was a friend of Diderot and translator of Lessing, as well as an accomplished scientist, working with Lavoisier and conducting experiments in the proper evaporation procedures for salt. He succeeded his father in 1767. His concern for the regulation of manufacturing is discussed in P. Boissonnade, "Trois Mémoires relatifs à l'amélioration des manufactures de France sous l'administration de Trudaine (1754)," in *Revue d'histoire économique et sociale* 7 (1916): 56–86.

4. The best account of the technical difficulties confronted in building the saltworks is Pierre Lacroix, *La Saline d'Arc-et-Senans et les techniques de canalisation en bois* (Lons-le-Saunier, 1970). A description of the saltworks of Franche-Comté containing useful plans can be found in Guy Nicot, "Les Salines d'Arc-et-Senans," *Monuments historiques* 2 (1978): 33–48. The chronology of Ledoux's designs and of the building campaign is established by the account given in the survey of 1782, conducted by the then director of the saltworks, Jean Dorval, in the *Rendue* of 1782 (Archives Départementales du Jura, 8J 502). Ledoux's semicircular plan made its first appearance in October 1774, but the details of each building were not prepared until June of the next year; the director's house was not designed until the middle of 1776.

5. Accounts of these *salines* are detailed in numerous *mémoires* and books. The most useful are: Pierre Boyé, *Les Salines et le sel en Lorraine au XVIIIe siècle* (Nancy, 1901); Max Prinet, *L'Industrie du sel en Franche-Comté avant la conquête française* (Besançon, 1900); Paul Baud, "Une industrie d'état sous l'Ancien régime: L'exploitation des salines de Tarantaise," *Revue d'histoire économique et sociale* (1936), 149 et seq. A systematic account of the managerial structure of the *saline* of Salins is given in H. Dubois, "L'activité de la saunerie de Salins au XVe siècle d'après le compte de 1459," in *Le Moyen Age* (1964), 419–471.

6. The article "Salines" in the *Encyclopédie*, vol. 14 (1765), 544–569, was prepared by C. G. Fenouillot de Falbaire de Quingey (1727–1800), son of the former administrator of Salins and protégé of Daniel Trudaine. A playwright and poet, he campaigned strongly against Ledoux, whose saltworks he described in a "Supplément à l'article des salines de Franche-Comté, Saline de Chaux," in *Oeuvres de M. de Falbaire de Quingey* (Paris, 1787), 352–358. See Lacroix, *Saline d'Arc-et-Senans*, 91–92.

7. Described in L. Mazoyer, "Exploitation forestière et conflits sociaux en Franche-Comté à la fin de l'Ancien Régime," *Annales E.S.C.* 4 (1932): 339 et seq., and S. Monniot, "Le rôle de la forêt dans la vie des populations Franc-comtoises de la conquête française à la Révolution, 1674–1789," *Revue d'Histoire Moderne* (Sept.–Dec. 1937), 449 et seq.

8. Trudaine de Montigny had been sent by his father to Besançon in 1760 to investigate the complaints of local farmers and cheese producers against the poor quality of the salt produced at Montmorot; he conducted public experiments and made detailed recommendations as to improvements in technique. Trudaine de Montigny, "Mémoire sur les salines de Franche-Comté" (April 21, 1762), in *Mémoires de l'Académie royale des sciences* (Paris, 1764), 102 et seq.

9. The *Ferme générale* also administered the production of salt subject to the oversight of the intendancy of Commerce; the company became one of Ledoux's staunchest patrons, employing him to build the new tax wall around Paris after 1784. An excellent account of the financial and cultural activities of the *fermiers* is in Yves Durand, *Les Fermiers généraux au XVIIIe siècle* (Paris, 1971).

10. David Le Roy, *Les ruines des plus beaux monuments de la Grèce,* was published in 1758. Ledoux's first biographer, Jacques Cellérier, mentioned Le Roy as one of the architect's major teachers and influences (Cellérier, *Notice rapide sur la vie et les ouvrages de Claude-Nicolas Ledoux* [Paris, 1806]).

11. Ledoux, *L'Architecture,* 40.

12. Ibid., 68.

13. Ibid., 66.

14. Ibid., 67.

15. Ibid.

16. Ibid.

17. Ibid., 67–68.

18. These different functions followed a program for the new saltworks that had been detailed in the contract between the entrepreneur Jean Roux Monclar, and the *Ferme générale,* March 12, 1774 (Traité pour la construction d'une saline en Franche-Comté, Archives nationales, G1, 93).

19. Here, perhaps, the tendency to ascribe panoptical aspirations to all radial plans in the late eighteenth century should be modified. Too quickly dismissing the symbolic role of architecture in favor of an instrumental reading of plans, Michel Foucault concludes that the Saline de Chaux represents a "perfect" disciplinary apparatus that would "allow for a single gaze to see everything constantly. A single point would be at once a source of light illuminating all things and a place of convergence for everything that should be known, a perfect eye from which nothing could escape and towards which all gazes are turned" (*Surveiller et punir, 176*).

20. See Pierre Patte, *Essai sur l'architecture théâtrale* (Paris, 1782), and "Plan du théâtre trouvé dans la ville souterraine d'Herculanum," *Encyclopédie, Planches,* 10, 24. Perrault's restoration remains closest to Ledoux's transposition (Claude Perrault, *Les dix livres de Vitruve* [Paris, 1673]).

21. The ubiquitous nature of Masonic imagery in the 1770s and the affiliation of many architects to the growing lodge membership made the reference unambiguous; de Lacoré, intendant of Franche-Comté, for whom this engraving was prepared, was a prominent Mason in Besançon. See below, Chapter 6.

22. Ledoux, *L'Architecture, 77.*

23. Ibid., 109.

24. Ibid., 111.

25. The *saline* of Montmorot, near Lons-le-Saunier, received much attention in the 1760s as the newest saltworks of the region. Built by a pupil of Perronet, Jean Querret (1703-1788), engineer-in-chief of Franche-Comté, its buildings, especially the evaporating sheds, were planned according to the latest wisdom; most spectacular were the three "graduation buildings," long, open structures filled with bundles of thorn twigs over which the brine was trickled in order to evaporate it partially before it reached the boiling pans, thus conserving fuel. The Saline de Chaux had only one of these, 1,500 feet long, although its radial position with respect to the factory seems to indicate Ledoux's plan for more as needed (The archives of Montmorot in A.D. Jura, series 8J and C).

26. Ledoux, *L'Architecture,* 116.

27. Ibid.

28. *Rendue,* 1782, AD Jura, 8J 502.

29. Pierre-François Nicolas, *Mémoire sur les salines de la République* (Nancy, 1793), 30.

30. See Gille, *Les origines de la Grande Industrie.*

31. Querret's activity is described in Léon Four, *Le long des routes de Franche-Comté au XVIIIe siècle* (Besançon, 1939). His assistant, the engineer Philippe Bertrand, developed a regional plan for the development of the rivers, canals, and roads of the province (107). See Pierre Pinon et al., *Un canal...des Canaux...* (Paris, 1986), 343.

32. See Gallet, *Ledoux,* 15 et seq.

33. *Annales de l'Architecture et des Arts,* 36 (November, 1806): 591 et seq.

34. Ledoux's imitation is all the more striking considering that no other major *recueil* of architectural projects had adopted this arrangement on the page.

35. Ledoux, *L'Architecture,* 72.

36. Ibid., 74.

37. Ledoux describes this factory as standing next to a house belonging to a financier who had invested in its construction: "What you see at the bottom of the garden and along the banks of the river that meanders through the meadow is a printed-cloth works. This immense plain is for the bleaching of the cloth. . . . On one side you see a chemical laboratory for the colors, vats for the dyeing and boiling, the drafting room, the workshops of the engravers, the cylinder for the calender [or polishing machine], immense storehouses, *ateliers* for the painting. A long stretch of the river has been diverted to drive all the machines necessary for the work" (Ledoux, *L'Architecture,* 111). A playful reference to this source of wealth, Ledoux designed the financier's house in the form of a cylinder, sign of mobile capital, but also of the calenders.

38. The best study of the foundation and development of Le Creusot is Christian Devillers and Bernard Huet, *Le Creusot, Naissance et développement d'une ville industrielle, 1782-1914* (Seyssel, 1981). See also Ballot, "La Révolution technique." The career of Pierre Touffaire is dealt with in A. Reyne (Bertrand Gille), "Un constructeur d'usines métallurgiques au XVIIIe siècle: Pierre Touffaire," in *Revue d'histoire de la Sidérurgie* (1965). Louis Daubenton noted, "This establishment is one of the wonders of the world. . . . Almost impassable mountains are leveled daily to make way for these buildings, as curious as they are useful" (Ballot, "La Révolution," 55). See also Jean Chevalier, *Le Creusot, berceau de la grande industrie française* (Paris, 1946), as well as many of the contemporary descriptions, such as the anonymous *Mémoire sur la fonderie et les forges royales établies près Montcenis en Bourgogne pour fondre la mine de fer et affiner la fonte avec du charbon de terre par le moyen des machines à feu et sur la verrerie royale construite au même lieu* (1786), and La Métherie, "Mémoire sur la fonderie et les forges royales établies à Montcenis," *Journal de Physique,* vol. 30 (1787). The work of Pierre Touffaire's engineer-assistant, Barthélémy Jeanson, a student of Soufflot and project architect for the works at Montcenis, is discussed in Pierre Saddy, "Un élève de Soufflot: Barthélémy Jeanson, architecte-ingénieur, 1760–1820," in *Soufflot et l'architecture des lumières: Les Cahiers de la Recherche Architecturale,* supplement to nos. 6–7 (Oct. 1980), 192–203. A link with Ledoux's circle is established by the role of Perronet in the selection of Touffaire as architect, 1776–1782 (202, n.23).

39. Devillers, *Le Creusot, Naissance et développement,* 1832.

40. Ledoux, *L'Architecture,* 240.

41. Ibid.

42. Ibid., 235–239.

43. A description of this "civilization of the forest," more or less unchanged since the Middle Ages, is given in M. Devèze, *La vie de la forêt française au XVIe* siècle (Paris, 1961); the most comprehensive study of rural *métiers* in the eighteenth century is André J. Bourde, *Agronomie et Agronomes en France au XVIIIe siècle* (Paris, 1967), especially vol. 1, 143 et seq. See also Eugène Tarlé, *L'industrie dans les campagnes en France à la fin de l'Ancien Régime* (Paris, 1910).

44. *Encyclopédie, Planches,* vol. 1, 55.

45. See Desiré Monnier, *Souvenirs d'un octogenaire de province* (Lons-le-Saunier, 1871). Monnier was a collector of folklore and an amateur anthropologist of the customs of Franche-Comté.

46. Ibid., 219.

47. Ledoux, *L'Architecture,* 209.

48. Ibid.

49. Ibid., 198.

50. In England, the forms of kilns were also adopted for rural houses and lodges.

51. Léon Vandoyer, *Le Magasin Pittoresque* 20 (1852): 388 et seq.

1. Comte de Mirabeau, *Observation d'un voyageur anglais sur la maison de force appellée Bicêtre* (1788), 4.

2. There are many recent studies of the poor in eighteenth-century France, on a national and local level, and the question of the poor-law administration; the foundation work is still the monumental study by Camille Bloch, *L'Assistance et l'Etat en France à la veille de la Révolution (généralitées de Paris, Rouen, Alençon, Orléans, Châlons, Soissons, Amiens), 1764-1789* (Paris, 1908). The best overall view of poverty in the Old Regime is Olwen H. Hufton, *The Poor of Eighteenth-Century France, 1750-1789* (Oxford, 1974); this has inspired several excellent but more specific studies, notably, Colin Jones, *Charity and 'bienfaisance': the treatment of the poor in the Montpellier Region, 1740-1815* (Cambridge, 1982), and, for the later period, Alan Forrest, *The French Revolution and the Poor* (New York, 1981).

3. See Bloch, *L'Assistance et l'Etat en France*, introduction.

4. The history of the eighteenth-century medical profession and its practices has received much attention in the last twenty years. The most useful general studies are J. P. Peter, "Malades et maladies au XVIIIe siècle," *Annales E.S.C.* 4 (1967): 711–751; "Médecins, médecine et société en France aux XVIIIe et XIXe siècles," *Annales E.S.C.* 32 (1977); J. P. Goubert, *Malades et médecins en Bretagne* (Paris, 1974). R. Taton, ed., *Enseignement et diffusion des sciences en France au XVIIIe siècle* (Paris, 1964), provides a good introduction to the educational institutions that informed medical practice, especially the essay by Pierre Huard, "L'enseignement médico-chirurgical," 175–229. Michel Foucault, *Histoire de la folie à l'âge classique* (Paris, 1975), vol. 2, and his *Naissance de la Clinique* (Paris, 1963), remain the most ambitious and comprehensive studies of the intersection of ideology and practice. Despite the specific criticism of many social historians, whose aims and methods are entirely at odds with Foucault's global and epistemological approach, these two works, precisely because of their emphasis on the artificial boundaries drawn by separate disciplines and their categorical interpretation of a "discourse" conducted at many levels and in different media, are evocative for the historian of spatial order.

5. See Hufton, *The Poor of France*, part 1, and, for a detailed study of the urban distribution of poverty in Paris, the excellent article by C. Romon, "Le monde des pauvres à Paris au XVIIIe siècle," *Annales E.S.C.* 37 (1982): 729–763, which contains maps of the housing of the poor and the location of beggars in the streets.

6. See Foucault, *Histoire de la folie*, ch. 2; Hufton, *The Poor of France*, part 2, ch. 5.

7. The Edict of 1724 set the tone for poor-law administration for most of the century: dividing the poor into *valid* and *invalid*, it instructed the former to find work or present themselves at the nearest hospital; the latter were, forcibly if necessary, to be interned and given work. See Hufton, *The Poor of France*, 155–156.

8. The act of 1762, which permitted certain rural industries to function outside the control of the guilds, was largely a recognition of an existing state of affairs. See E. Tarlé, *L'Industrie dans les campagnes en France à la fin de l'Ancien Régime* (Paris, 1910).

9. See Hufton, *The Poor of France*.

10. Diderot, "Hôpital," in *Oeuvres complètes*, vol. 15, 140.

11. Abbé Nicolas Baudeau, *Idées d'un citoyen sur les devoirs et les droits d'un vrai pauvre* (Paris, 1765), 29. Baudeau (1730–1792), an economist, founded the journal *Ephémérides du citoyen* in 1765 to combat the physiocrats; he later converted to the physiocratic position and engaged Mirabeau and Du Pont de Nemours as journalist collaborators. Exiled to Auvergne in 1776 for criticizing the government's finances, he remained silent until 1785. During the Revolution, Baudeau was sick and confined to one of his hated institutions; he ended his life symbolically enough by throwing himself from the window of a *maison de santé* in Auvergne.

12. Ibid., 44–45. An anonymous pamphlet, *Des Hospices* (Paris, 1784), Bibliothèque Nationale Imprimés Rp6477, made a similar connection between "a comfortable, healthy, well-administered hospital" and the influence of natural surroundings: "the sight of a rural place, of a tree, the least image of grass, is capable of giving life; such is the power of nature over our senses. It is not always doctors who cure" (9).

13. This was not the first fire to cause alarm about the state of the Hôtel-Dieu; in 1737 and again in 1748, fires had sparked a discussion about the condition of the old buildings, and in 1749 Le Jeune had published a scheme for a new hospital on the Ile des Cygnes ("Mémoire de M. Le Jeune, ancien vicaire de Saint-Laurent sur le projet d'un Hôtel-Dieu dans l'Ile des Cygnes," reported in *Mercure de France,* 1748). Le Jeune, like other designers of large institutions, was attacked for what F. Carré characterized as a building where "the air [would be] soon corrupted in these enormous masses, too confined and too high, where the poor and the sick are piled up, suffocated, infected, by the lack of space." Carré compared such false luxury to an epidemic that would lead to never-ending repairs and enlargements. In its place Carré suggested a single, narrow building with large windows. See Rondonneau de la Motte, *Essai historique sur l'Hôtel-Dieu de Paris* (Paris, 1787), 178–183. This latter essay is a useful, contemporary account of the hospital reform movement before the Revolution; it was favorably reviewed in *Mercure de France* 28 (July 1787): 79–80.

14. The research for this chapter was completed before the publication of what is the best summary of the hospital debate, with analytical essays on the profession and the architectural projects, as well as a selection of documents and bibliography: Michel Foucault, Bruno Fortier et al., *Les Machines à guérir (aux origines de l'hôpital moderne)* (Brussels, 1979). This is a partial republication of an equally useful and innovative study: B. Barret-Kriegel et al., *La Politique de l'espace parisien à la fin de l'Ancien Régime* (Paris: CORDA, 1975). A good general history of the hospital as a building type is J. D. Thompson and G. Goldin, *The Hospital: A Social and Architectural History* (New Haven and London, 1975). Colin Jones and Michael Sonensher, "The Social Functions of the Hospital in Eighteenth-Century France: The Case of the Hôtel-Dieu of Nimes," *French Historical Studies,* 13 (1983): 172–214, offers a less biased account of conditions in hospitals outside Paris.

15. See Foucault et al., *Machines à guérir,* 145–159, for a selection of documents illustrating this debate.

16. The Hospital Saint-Louis was built under Henry IV in 1607 by Claude Villefaux, on plans by the architect Claude de Châtillon; it was illustrated in detail by Jacques Tenon in his *Mémoires sur les Hôpitaux de Paris* (Paris, 1788), plates 3–5, 60–68.

17. See Jean-François Garnier, "Soufflot et Mâcon: la Charité, l'Hôtel-Dieu," in *Soufflot et l'architecture des lumières* (Oct. 1980), 142–151.

18. Soufflot's building campaign for the Hôtel-Dieu is described in detail in Daniel Ternois, "L'Hôtel-Dieu de Lyons," in D. Ternois and M. F. Perez, *L'Oeuvre de Soufflot à Lyons: études et documents* (Lyons, 1982), 43–76. Soufflot began work on the project in 1739; the first stone was laid in 1741; and the building was complete, save for the central dome, by 1754. Arguments were made for the necessity of the dome for ventilation of the new wards, and the completed hospital was inaugurated in 1764. The healthy effects of the high central space, which drew off the infected air, were noted by contemporary commentators.

19. Blondel, *Cours d'architecture* (Paris, 1771), vol. 2, 337 et seq. The essay on hospitals is accompanied by a criticism of existing buildings and a plea for government attention to the plight of the poor; here we may see the ideological roots of Ledoux's own sentiments toward poverty. Blondel envisaged a system of small, neighborhood hospitals, feeding a large, central institution. Ever the teacher, Blondel also saw the need for specialized teaching hospitals. The most elaborate project along these traditional lines was drawn by Neufforge in "Hôtel ou Hôpital de malades," in *Suite du supplément au recueil élémentaire d'architecture* (Paris, 1780).

20. Cited in B. Barret-Kriegel, "Instances et séquences de la médicalisation de l'espace urbain," in Fortier et al., *La politique de l'espace parisien,* 179–181.

21. Pierre Panseron, *Mémoire relatif à un plan d'Hôtel-Dieu pour Paris* (Paris, 1773), 15.

22. Ibid., 15 et seq.

23. Diderot, "Hôtel-Dieu," in *Oeuvres complètes,* vol. 15, 140.

24. C. H. Piarron de Chamousset, "Vues d'un citoyen" (Paris, 1757), in *Oeuvres complètes* (Paris, 1783), vol. 1, 42–46. De Chamousset (1717–1773) was a celebrated philanthropist, praised by Rousseau and Voltaire. He organized a hospital in his own house and another by the barrière de Sèvres, where he paid doctors to give free treatment to over one hundred poor patients each day. In 1761, he was named intendant-general of military hospitals. He wrote numerous *mémoires* on his model hospice, on military hospitals, and on mutual insurance associations. See F. Martin Ginouvier, *Un philanthrope méconnu du XVIIIe siècle: Piarron de Chamousset* (Paris, 1905).

25. De Chamousset, "Vues d'un citoyen," 42.

26. Claude Chevalier, *Dissertation physico-médicale sur les causes de plusieurs maladies dangereuses et sur les propriétés d'un liqueur purgative et vulnéraire qui est une pharmacopée presqu'universelle* (Paris, 1758), 215. Dr. Chevalier, who, like de Chamousset, set up a private hospital in an old château, no doubt administered his patent *pharmakon* daily.

27. For a succinct discussion of the debates over the nature and behavior of the air, see Richard Etlin, "L'Air dans l'urbanisme des lumières," *Dix-huitième siècle* 9 (1977): 123–124.

28. Léopold de Genneté, *Purification de l'air*

croupissant dans les hôpitaux, les prisons et les vaisseaux de mer (Nancy, 1767), 9. Genneté was a prolific inventor, specializing in chimneys, flues, and ventilators, as well as a student of the circulation of air in mines and of the flow patterns of rivers.

29. Duhamel de Monceau, *Moyens de conserver le santé aux équipages des vaisseaux avec la manière de purifier l'air des salles des Hôpitaux* (Paris, 1759), 216 et seq. The ventilator designed by Stephen Hales and installed in Newgate Prison was widely discussed; see Robin Evans, *The Fabrication of Virtue: English Prison Architecture, 1750-1840* (Cambridge, 1980), and Stephen Hales, *A Description of Ventilators* (London, 1743).

30. Reported in the *Journal Encyclopédique* (September, 1781); the prize was won by a Doctor Raft from Lyons.

31. For Lavoisier's experiments on the composition of the air, see Etlin, "L'Air dans l'urbanisme des lumières."

32. Antoine Petit, *Mémoire sur la meilleure manière de construire un hôpital de malades* (Paris, 1774). According to contemporaries, Petit (1722–1794) was "one of the most celebrated doctors of his age." Born in Orléans, he studied surgery, anatomy, and medicine in Paris, becoming *docteur-régent* at the university in 1746. In 1760, he was admitted to the Académie des sciences, and eight years later he was appointed to the chair of anatomy at the Jardin du Roi, where he lectured to overflowing crowds. On his retirement in 1775, he was replaced by his most celebrated student, Vicq d'Azyr. Diderot corresponded with him on the subject of physiognomies and bodily changes in relation to particular trades (Diderot, *Oeuvres complètes,* vol. 11, 239–249). Petit was the author of part of the article "Homme" in vol. 8 of the *Encyclopédie,* 530.

33. Petit, *Mémoire sur la meilleure manière,* 1–2.

34. Ibid., 5–6.

35. Ibid., 8.

36. "Verrerie Angloise, coupe sur la largeur," in *Encyclopédie, Planches,* vol. 10, 333.

37. Petit, *Mémoire sur la meilleure manière,* 14.

38. Perier, *Mémoires sur la machine de Marly* (Paris, 1810), 33: "I needed no outside help, neither any engineer nor architect, when I built the foundry of Le Creusot," quoted in Pierre Saddy, "Un élève de Soufflot: Barthélémy Jeanson, architecte-ingénieur, 1760–1820," in *Soufflot et l'architecture des lumières,* 33.

39. Petit, *Mémoire sur meilleure manière,* 9.

40. Jean-Baptiste Le Roy, *Précis d'un ouvrage sur les hôpitaux, dans lequel on expose les principaux résultats des observations de physique et de médecine qu'on doit avoir en vue dans la construction de ces édifices, avec un projet d'hôpital disposé d'après ces principes* (1773, 1777), in *Mémoires de l'Académie des sciences, 1787* (Paris, 1789), 585–601. Le Roy (d. 1800) was prevented from publicizing his plans by the edict that suppressed all schemes for a new Hôtel-Dieu "in the public interest." See Louis S. Greenbaum, "Tempest in the Academy: J. B. Le Roy, The Paris Academy of Sciences and the Project of a New Hôtel-Dieu," *Archives internationales d'histoire des sciences,* 24 (1974): 122–140.

41. Le Roy, *Précis d'un ouvrage, 10.*

42. Ibid., 14.

43. Ibid.

44. Charles-François Viel, *Principes de l'ordonnance et de la construction des bâtiments; notions sur divers édifices publics et particuliers* (Paris, 1812), quoted in Foucault et al., *Machines à guérir,* 150–154.

45. Ibid., 154.

46. Hugues Maret, "Mémoires sur la construction d'un Hôpital, dans lequel on détermine quel est le meilleur moyen à employer pour entretenir dans les infirmeries un air pur et salubre," in *Nouveaux Mémoires de l'Académie de Dijon, 1782* (Dijon, 1783), 25–68. Maret (1726–1785) came from a family of surgeons and specialized in the treatment of plagues and infectious diseases. He wrote the articles "Bains," "Cimetières," and "Dépôts laiteux" for the *Encyclopédie,* collaborated with Guyton de Morveau on the *Eléments de chimie, théorique et pratique* (Dijon, 1773), and, just before he died fighting an epidemic in Franche-Comté, he was appointed editor of the volumes on Pharmacy for the *Encyclopédie méthodique.* His correspondence with doctors and scientists throughout Europe was widely known and admired; thus his article on the forms of ventilation, in the *Journal de Paris* of April 10, 1780, attracted the notice of Soufflot, who replied with a sketch plan of a ward block that would answer Maret's specifications. Soufflot's written reply to Maret was published in the *Journal de Paris* of June 21, 1780; the architect died August 29 the same year.

47. Maret, "Mémoires sur la construction d'un Hôpital," 34.

48. Ibid., 45.

49. Ibid.

50. Jacques Soufflot to Maret, April 21, 1780 and June 21, 1780.

51. Tenon to the members of the Faculty of Medicine at Edinburgh University, August 27, 1788, quoted in Foucault et al., *Machines à guérir,* 147.

52. Diderot, "Hôpital," 140.

53. Bernard Poyet and Claude Philibert Coquéau, *Mémoire sur la nécessité de transférer et reconstruire l'Hôtel-Dieu de Paris suivi d'un projet de translation de cet Hôpital, proposé par le Mon-*

sieur Poyet, arch. et contrôleur des bâtiments de la ville (Paris, 1785); C. P. Coquéau, *Essai sur l'établissement des hôpitaux dans les grandes villes* (Paris, 1787). Poyet (1742–1824), a student of Charles De Wailly, studied in Italy between 1769 and 1775, became architect to the Duc d'Orléans, and, in 1785, was appointed controller of works for Paris. In 1786, he was admitted to the Académie d'architecture and, in 1790, he was appointed architect to the city of Paris. His project for the Hôtel-Dieu was the first of many grand public schemes that included monuments and theaters. Coquéau (1755–1794) was an artist, musician, and architect employed by Poyet after 1784; he became architect to the Baron de Breteuil in 1785, worked with Poyet again after 1789, and was sent to the scaffold for Girondin sympathies on the 8 Thermidor.

54. Charles De Wailly, *Projet d'utilité et d'embellissement pour la ville de Paris qui s'accorde avec les projets déjà arrêtés par le gouvernement* (Paris, 1788).

55. Poyet and Coquéau, *Mémoire sur l'Hôtel-Dieu*, 32.

56. Petit had already outlined the theory in *Mémoire sur la meilleure manière*, 5.

57. Poyet and Coquéau, *Mémoire sur la Hôtel-Dieu*, 35.

58. Ibid., 38.

59. Ibid., 27.

60. Ibid., 27.

61. Coquéau, *Supplément au mémoire*, 38.

62. Poyet and Coquéau, *Mémoire sur l'Hôtel-Dieu*, 38.

63. Ibid., 34.

64. Coquéau, *Supplément au mémoire*, 52.

65. Legrand and Landon, *Annales de Musée*, 2 (1805): 62.

66. The commission included de Lassone, Daubenton, Tenon, Bailly, Lavoisier, La Place, Coulomb, d'Arcet; see Louis S. Greenbaum, "Jean Sylvain Bailly, the Baron de Breteuil and the Four New Hospitals of Paris," *Clio Medica* 8 (1973): 261–284.

67. De Lassone et al., *Rapport des commissaires chargés par l'Académie de l'examen du projet d'un nouvel Hôtel-Dieu (extrait des registres de l'Académie royale des sciences, 22 Nov. 1786)* (Paris, 1787), 5.

68. Jacques-René Tenon (1724–1816), the son of a surgeon, studied anatomy and botany in Paris; he was named surgeon to the army in 1744 and returned to Paris as first surgeon to the Salpêtrière, where he taught and experimented in inoculation. He was admitted to the Académie des sciences in 1759. His papers, conserved in the Bibliothèque Nationale, Nouvelles acquisitions, 22136–7, 22742–52, 11357–68, are a little explored mine of information, with notes on every aspect of hospital reform; see P. Huard, "Les papiers de J. Tenon (1724–1816)," in *Compte rendu du XIXe congrès international d'histoire de la médecine* (Basel, 1964)

69. De Lassone et al., *Rapport des commissaires*, 5 et seq.

70. Ibid., 21.

71. Ibid., 57 et seq.

72. Ibid.

73. Ibid.

74. See Foucault et al., *Machines à guérir*, 71.

75. See J.-R. Tenon, *Mémoires sur les hôpitaux de Paris* (Paris, 1788); the collected notes for this work are in B.N. Nouvelles acquisitions, 22137, folio 237. Tenon, despite his severe criticisms of traditional architects and his initial response to Poyet, later employed Poyet to draw up his own scheme: "Equipped with these givens, I tried to apply them to a hospital that would replace the Hôtel-Dieu; I drew on paper the plan of a hospice, that of a lying-in hospital, and that of a hospital of contagious diseases. I submitted my plans to the scrutiny of my colleagues; it was then necessary to invest them with the grace of design in order to make them public: a talented and honest man, whose name will be remembered in the history of our hospitals as in that of our fine arts, M. Poyet wanted to render me this service, adapting my dispositions of buildings, understanding them, and welcoming them, giving them, finally, that character of architecture that gives them value."

76. See Louis S. Greenbaum, "Health-Care and Hospital Building in Eighteenth-Century France: Reform Proposals of Du Pont de Nemours and Condorcet," *Studies in Voltaire and the Eighteenth Century* 152 (1976): 895–930.

77. Du Pont de Nemours, *Idées sur les secours à donner aux pauvres malades dans une grande ville* (Philadelphia and Paris, 1786). Pierre Samuel Du Pont de Nemours (1739–1814) was a physiocrat, follower of Quesnay and Mirabeau, and editor of Baudeau's *Ephémérides* after 1786.

78. Ibid., 10 et seq.

79. Ibid., 44.

80. Mallet du Pin, "Review of Coquéau and Poyet's *Mémoire*," *Mercure de France*, February 11, 1786, 54–68.

81. Ibid., 59.

82. A. Tzonis and L. Lefaivre, "Un Mémoire sur les hôpitaux de Condorcet," *Dix-huitième siècle* 9 (1977).

83. See Coquéau, *Essai sur des hôpitaux*, 20 et seq., for a detailed rebuttal of Du Pont.

84. Foucault, *Naissance de la Clinique*, ch. 2. "Gradually, in this young city entirely dedicated to the happiness of possessing health, the face of the doctor would fade, leaving a faint trace in men's memories of a time of kings and wealth, in which they were sick, impoverished slaves. All this was so much daydreaming, the dream of a festive city, inhabited by an open-air mankind, in which youth would be naked and age know no winter, the familiar symbol of ancient arcadias, to which has been added the more recent theme of a nature encompassing the earliest forms of truth—all these values were soon to fade." (*The Birth of the Clinic* [New York, 1973], 34.)

85. Audin-Rouvière, *Essai sur la topographie-physique et médicale de Paris* (Paris, 1794).

86. Nicolas-Marie Clavareau (1757–1816) completed the new facade for the Hôtel-Dieu in 1803; his buildings for the hospitals at Arras were completed only in 1838.

87. Clavareau, *Mémoire sur les Hôpitaux civils de Paris* (Paris, 1805), 21.

88. Marc-Antoine Laugier, *Essai sur l'architecture,* 2d ed. (Paris, 1755), 170.

89. Clavareau, *Mémoire sur les Hôpitaux,* 112. He placed a statue of Aesculapius over the door and decorated the interior with the god's attributes.

1. Jacques-Pierre Brissot de Warville, *Théorie des lois criminelles* (Paris, 1781), vol. 1, 162.
2. See Michel Foucault, *Surveiller et punir: naissance de la prison* (Paris, 1975), for the most comprehensive study of this discourse. The literary myths and figures of imprisonment are elegantly posed in Victor Brombert, *La Prison romantique* (Paris, 1975), 11–50.
3. For Mirabeau, the Bicêtre and the Bastille were the most powerful symbols, the one of the state of the poor and thus of the nation, the other of despotism in the raw.
4. Philippe Roger, "*Delenda est* . . . les lumières françaises et la prison," *Lectures* 12 (June, 1983): 95–114, is an excellent essay on the absence of the prison in late-eighteenth-century practice and its presence in literary debates.
5. See B.N. Nouvelles acquisitions, 22137, *Papiers de Tenon*, vol. 284, Extrait des registres de l'académie royale des sciences, March 14, 1780.
6. Ibid.
7. Ibid.
8. Tenon described his visits of inspection of February 8, 1780, in ibid., 302–303.
9. Ibid., 357.
10. Ibid.
11. Ibid.
12. For a full discussion of Boullée's involvement with rebuilding the Hôtel de Force, see Pérouse de Montclos, *Etienne-Louis Boullée* (Paris, 1969), 136–140.
13. John Howard first visited the prisons and hospitals of Paris in April 1775; he was able to gain access to the Bicêtre (with its underground cells "dark and beyond imagination, horrid and dreadful"), the Petit Châtelet, Fort l'Evêque, the Conciergerie, the Abbaye, but not the Bastille or Vincennes. His book *The State of the Prisons in England and Wales with Preliminary Observations from Accounts of Some Foreign Prisons* was published in London in 1787, followed two years later by a long *Appendix on the State of the Prisons,* in which he translated an anonymous pamphlet describing the "horror" of the Bastille. See H. Dixon, *John Howard and the Prison-World of Europe* (London, 1850); D. L. Howard, *John Howard: Prison Reformer* (London, 1958).
14. For Brissot, see the still sound biography by Eloise Ellery, *Brissot de Warville: A Study in the History of the French Revolution* (Boston and New York, 1915); for a less idealistic reading, see Robert Darnton, "A Spy in Grub Street," ch. 2 in *The Literary Underground of the the Old Regime* (Cambridge, Mass., 1982). Brissot, imprisoned briefly in the Bastille in 1784, was executed as a Girondin in October 1793.
15. Brissot, *Théories des lois criminelles,* vol. 1, 98.
16. Ibid.
17. Ibid., 164.
18. Jeremy Bentham, *A View of the Hard Labour Bill,* March 28, 1778, in Bowring, ed., *Works,* vol. 4, 5 et seq.
19. Ibid., 10.
20. Ibid.
21. Ibid., 32.
22. Ibid.
23. Ibid.
24. Brissot, *Théorie des lois criminelles,* vol. 1, 184.
25. Ibid.
26. Michel Foucault, *Histoire de la folie,* 448–449.
27. Brissot, *Théorie des lois criminelles,* vol. 1, 184 et seq.
28. Blondel, *Cours d'architecture,* vol. 2, 626–627.
29. J.C. Delafosse, "Project for a prison," Cooper-Hewitt Museum, New York.
30. François Cuvilliés, "Prison criminel," in *Ecole de l'architecture bavaroise* (Munich and Paris, 1769–1776); Daubanton, Project of 1775, B.N. Estampes.
31. Jacques Gondouin, *Description des écoles de chirurgie* (Paris, 1780).
32. For a complete list of Ledoux's projects and drawings for the Palais de Justice and Prisons of Aix, see Jean-Jacques Gloton and Serge Conard, *Aix-en-Provence dans l'oeuvre de Claude-Nicolas Ledoux,* in *Monuments et Mémoires publiés par l'Académie des Inscriptions et Belles-Lettres* 65 (Vendôme, 1983): 55–150.
33. Charles Blanc, *Grammaire des Arts du Dessin* (Paris, 1867), 96.
34. Etienne-Louis Boullée, *Architecture: Essai sur l'art,* ed. J.M. Pérouse de Montclos (Paris, 1968), 113–114.
35. Ibid., 113.
36. See *Les Fêtes de la Révolution* (Clermont-Ferrand: Musée Bargoin, 1974), 33, plate 58.
37. Ibid.
38. François Doublet, *Rapport sur l'état actuel des prisons de Paris* (Paris, 1791).
39. Pierre Giraud, *Plans et description historique des prisons et maisons d'arrêt . . .* (Paris, n.d. [1805]).
40. J.-N.-L. Durand, *Nouveau précis des leçons d'architecture données à l'Ecole Impériale polytechnique* (Paris, 1813), 98.

41. A. Détournelle, Review of *Précis de leçons*, in *Journal des Arts*, 414 (30 Germinal an XIII [April 19, 1805]): 121–126, quoted in W. Szambien, *Jean-Nicolas-Louis Durand* (Paris, 1984), 178.

42. Louis-Pierre Baltard, *Architectnographie des prisons* (Paris, 1829), 17. See the excellent summary of 19th-century developments, Bruno Foucart, "Architecture carcérale et architectes fonctionnalistes en France au XIXe siècle," *Revue de L'Art* 32 (1976): 37–56.

43. Peter Brooks, *The Melodramatic Imagination* (New Haven and London, 1976).

44. Baltard, *Architectnographie*, 17.

THE ARCHITECTURE OF THE LODGES

1. This study of the spatial forms of Freemasonry and its related cults in the eighteenth century naturally relies on the social and institutional histories of the societies for its understanding of the conditions of their existence. Several excellent works have been published recently that begin to situate the Freemasons more firmly in the cultural and social development of prerevolutionary France, supplanting older "conspiracy theories" and mystical "searches for origins." The best general histories of the order are Pierre Chevallier, *Histoire de la Franc-Maçonnerie française,* vol. 1, *1725–1799* (Paris: Fayard, 1974); Carlo Francovich, *Storia della Massoneria in Italia* (Florence: La Nuova Italia, 1974), for its clear exposition of the English origins of continental Masonry; and D. Knoop and G. P. Jones, *The Genesis of Freemasonry* (Manchester, 1957). Frances Yates devotes an excellent chapter to early Freemasonry in *The Rosicrucian Enlightenment* (London, 1972). Also invaluable is the list of members of the Parisian lodges under the Grand Orient between 1773 and 1789, compiled by Alain le Bihan in *Francs-Maçons Parisiens du Grand Orient de France* (Paris: Bibliothèque Nationale, 1966). For a comprehensive review of all historical studies through 1964, the most useful work is D. Ligou, "La Franc-Maçonnerie française au XVIIIe siècle (Position des problèmes et état des questions)," *L'Information Historique* 3 (May-June 1964): 98–110. See also D. Ligou et al., *Histoire des Francs-Maçons en France* (Toulouse, 1981), for the most recent assessment of the history and culture of the order.

2. Laurent Bordelon, *La Coterie des Anti-Façonniers* (Paris, 1716), quoted in Arthur Dinaux, *Les Sociétés badines, bachiques, littéraires et chantantes* (Paris, 1867), vol. 1, 37. Bordelon's satirical fantasy of a society of anti-formalists rolling in their sphere-shaped lodge indicates the extent to which in 1716 societies were already assuming identities according to specific forms. The comparison with Ledoux's spherical "lodge" for the agricultural guards of Maupertuis (c.1784) is amusing.

3. The conditions of bourgeois sociability are meticulously discussed by Maurice Agulhon in his *Pénitents et Francs-Maçons de l'ancienne Provence* (Paris: Fayard, 1968). This work is primarily concerned with provincial life during the Old Regime, circles, clubs, and confraternities, as well as the survival or transformation of one form in another: "not many societies, but the group life" (212).

4. See Agulhon, *Pénitents et Francs-Maçons,* 68. The trade confraternities of the fifteenth century through the seventeenth century "had a chapel, either isolated or in a parish church, that was both place of worship and place of assembly." The early-eighteenth-century eating societies, loath to imperil their newly-found middle estate by using the popular cabarets, established homes of their own. Dinaux, in *Les Sociétés badines,* vol. 2, 16, notes that the order of Medusa, formed by maritime officers in Marseilles and Toulon around 1684, "assembled to hold their chapters in hospices named Manses, established in different parts of the realm; these chapters were held at table."

5. The Fendeurs, probably one of the oldest Masonic societies of "adoption," were apparently formed by the Chevalier Beauchaine, a master of the Grand Lodge, in 1747. For their first meeting, he appropriated a vast estate to the north of Paris at la Nouvelle-France. An imitation of the ancient orders of *compagnonnage* among the foresters and *charbonniers* of the Jura, the order developed its rituals according to "rustic" forms. See *O ∴ ou Histoire de la fondation du Grand Orient de France* (Paris, 1812), 361 et seq., and J. Brengues, *La Franc-Maçonnerie du bois* (Paris, 1973).

6. The Chambrées of Provence, descendants of earlier meetings of scholars, are described in Agulhon, *Pénitents et Francs-Maçons,* 241–243.

7. According to James Anderson, *The Constitutions of the Free-Masons* (London, 1723), 51, "a LODGE is a Place where Masons assemble and work: Hence that Assembly, or duly organiz'd Society of Masons, is call'd a LODGE, and every Brother ought to belong to one. . . . It is either particular or general, and will best be understood by attending it."

8. Jérôme de Lalande (1732–1807), member of the Académie des sciences and Professor of Astronomy at the Collège de France from 1762, was orator of the Grand Orient as well as a founder and venerable of the "philosophic" lodge of Les Neuf Soeurs from 1776. The opening ceremony of the quarters of the Grand Orient is described in a circular published by the Orient in June 1774, *Grand Orient of France, Miscellaneous documents and papers* (Paris, 1773–1777), piece 5, 1–4.

9. The article "Asyle" in the *Encyclopédie,* vol. 1 (Paris, 1751), defines asylum as "a sanctuary or place of refuge sheltering a criminal who retires therein." Not yet tainted with overtones of medical confinement for the insane (a connotation that was not fixed until the first years of the nineteenth century), the word was used ubiquitously in literature and philosophy throughout the eighteenth century. Masonic lodges were generally termed "asylums of friendship" or of "virtue." Rousseau called the retreat of Julie and Wolmar, in *La Nouvelle Héloise* (1759), "an inviolable asylum of confidence, friendship, and liberty" *(Oeuvres Complètes* [Paris: Bibliothèque de la Pléïade, 1961], vol. 2, 544); the abbé Delille, in his poem "Les Jardins" (1784), used the word indiscriminately for woods, gardens, clearings—any space adopted for refuge.

10. As described in Emile Lesueur, *La Franc-Maçonnerie Artésienne au XVIIIe siècle* (Paris, 1914), 173.

11. De Lalande wrote the article "Francs-Maçons" for the *Encyclopédie, Supplément* (Paris, 1777), which was published in a slightly fuller version by the Grand Orient, in *Etat du G .˙. O .˙. de France*, vol. 1, part 2 (Paris, 1777), 86: "The society or order of Freemasons is the bringing together of chosen peoples who join themselves together by the obligation to love each other like brothers, to aid each other in need, and, above all, to protect with an inviolable silence whatever has to do with their order. The way Freemasons recognize one another in whatever country they might be is a part of their secret; this is a way of rallying together, even amidst those who are strangers to them and whom they call profane."

12. Charles-François Dupuis, "Initiation, initié," in *Encyclopédie méthodique: Antiquités, Mythologie* (Paris, 1790), vol. 3, 269.

13. Voltaire, *Essai sur les Moeurs*, in *Oeuvres complètes*, vol. 12, 64–65.

14. *Constitutions*, 1–48; this Masonic "history of architecture" was in fact a compilation of accounts of the history of the craft from manuscripts dating from around 1360. These are discussed in D. Knoop, "Pure Ancient Masonry," *Ars Quatuor Coronatorum* 53 (1940): 4 et seq., republished in Knoop, Jones, and Hamer, *Early Masonic Catechisms* (London, 1943). The 1723 *Constitutions* was first translated into French in 1736 (Jean Kuenen, The Hague) and again in 1742 (de la Tierce, Frankfurt).

15. This account of the formation of the early Parisian lodges is largely drawn from Pierre Chevallier, *Les Ducs sous l'Acacia, ou Les premiers pas de la Franc-Maçonnerie française 1725–1743* (Paris, 1964), chaps. 1–3.

16. See Chevallier, *Franc-Maçonnerie française*.

17. Leclerc de Douay to Chancellor d'Agnesseau, May 2, 1744, quoted in *Essai historique sur les Francs-Maçons d'Orléans, 1740–1886*, by "U.P." (1887), 3.

18. Minutes of M. Aubert, commissioner of the Châtelet (Paris), May 24, 1744, in Pierre Chevallier, *La Première Profanation du Temple Maçonnique, ou Louis XV et la Fraternité* (Paris, 1968), 182. Chevallier published these police reports in full (180–191). The inventories of items seized are an invaluable source for the reconstruction of mid-century rituals.

19. Ibid., 183.

20. The "Carmick MS" is published in facsimile in *Ars Quatuor Coronatorum* 22 (1909): 95–115.

21. See the survey article by E. H. Dring, "The Evolution and Development of the Tracing or Lodge Board," *Ars Quatuor Coronatorum* 29 (1914): 243–275. In the "Mason's Confession" of about 1727 (published in *Scots Magazine*, March 1755), there is an interesting reference to the checkered pavement often depicted both in floor-drawings and in illustrations of lodges: "What's the square pavement for? For the Master Mason to draw his ground draughts on."

22. Louis Travenol (pseud. Léonard Gabenon), *Catéchisme des Francs-Maçons* ("Jérusalem" and Limoges, 1744). Travenol published the designs of the floor-drawings for the Apprentice-Companion's Lodge (a combined drawing for the use of both grades) and of the Master's Lodge. In a second edition of this work, *La Désolation des Entrepreneurs Modernes du Temple de Jérusalem, ou Nouveau Catéchisme des Francs-Maçons* (1747), he published revised versions of these two drawings. The most interesting addition was the facade of the temple, set in true perspective beyond the two columns. The anonymous author of the exposure *L'Ordre des Francs-Maçons Trahi* (Amsterdam, 1745), reprinted Travenol's first versions, labeling them "inexact," supplementing them with two new drawings, called "true plans."

23. Abbé Gabriel-Louis Pérau, "Le Secret des Francs-Maçons" (1742), included in *L'Ordre des Francs-Maçons Trahi*, 50. A carefully annotated collection of the major exposures, translated into English, has been published by the Quatuor Coronati Lodge: Harry Carr, ed., *The Early French Exposures* (London, 1971).

24. Abbé Larudan, *Les Francs-Maçons Ecrasés* (Amsterdam, 1747). Larudan, pseudonym of Arnaud de Pomponne, outdid all previous exposures in the elaborate detail of his floor-drawings. He illustrated five drawings: for the admission of a serving brother, an apprentice, a companion, a master, and the higher degree of architect, or Scottish Mason.

25. "Reception d'un Frey Maçon" (Paris, 1737), in Carr, ed., *Early French Exposures,* 8.
26. Pérau, "Secret des Francs-Maçons," 3–6; he mentions the orders of liberty, Medusa, the grape (Arles), the Trancardins, and drinking (in lower Languedoc, c.1703), as well as many English coteries and clubs. In some provincial towns, where the Masons took over the forms and functions of earlier trade corporations, like the Lodge of Fidélité at Hesdin, or Perfect Union of Montreuil, the feasts were held on the same days as the major religious festivals; the annual banquets of the lodges of Constance and Amitié in Arras were virtual replicas of the corporative fêtes of St. John. See Lesueur, *Franc-Maçonnerie Artésienne,* 75.

27. Martin Couret de Villeneuve, *L'Ecole des Francs-Maçons* ("Jérusalem," 1748), 127–129.
28. Pérau, "Secret des Francs-Maçons," 35.
29. Abbé Laugier, "Prédicateur du Roi," quoted in Abbé Grandidier, *Essais Historiques et Topographiques sur l'Eglise Cathédrale de Strasbourg,* vol. 2 (Strasbourg, 1782), 417. The Masonic poem attributed to Laugier was a response to the papal bulls of 1738 and 1751; I am indebted to Professor Joseph Rykwert for drawing my attention to this isolated piece of evidence linking Laugier with Freemasonry. The letter within which this poem was quoted (attributed to Grandidier by eighteenth-century Masonic historians) was first published in 1779, in the *Journal de Monsieur* (January), 75–85, and in the *Journal de Nancy* (1779), 118–124 and 139–148. It contained a general argument for the evolution of speculative from operative Masonry in the context of the builders of Strasbourg; this has also been studied by contemporary scholars: see P. Frankl and E. Panofsky, "The Secret of the Medieval Masons," *Art Bulletin* (March 1945).
30. Travenol, *La Désolation des Entrepreneurs,* describes this horseshoe-shaped table; that of the lodge Amitié at Arras was also of this form, the paradigmatic figure of brotherhood.
31. The drinking songs of the Masons are a delight to read and an important source of imagery; this refrain comes from the Apprentices' Song, in a collection published by the brothers Villeneuve of Orléans in 1748, *Recueil de Poésies Maçonnes* ("Jérusalem").
32. "Lettre et discours d'un maçon libre," quoted in Robert Mauzi, *L'Idée du Bonheur dans la Littérature et la Pensée française au* XVIIIe *siècle* (Paris, 1965), 612. Mauzi characterizes Masonry as realizing "the alliance between repose, pleasure, and virtue. Everything being identified with morality, it constitutes an art of living, equally far from asceticism and debauch."
33. Jean-Jacques Rousseau, *Essai sur l'Origine des Langues* (Paris: A. Belin, 1817), 523: "They gathered around a common hearth; they made feasts and danced; the sweet ties of custom imperceptibly drew man to his fellows; and on this rustic hearth burned the sacred fire that carried the first sentiment of humanity to the depth of all hearts."
34. Lettre écrite par un maçon à un de ses amis en province (1764), quoted in Mauzi, *L'Idée du Bonheur,* 611.
35. See Lesueur, *Franc-Maçonnerie Artésienne.*
36. *Les Francs-Maçons Ecrasés,* 127.
37. These drawings were published for the first time in Monique Mosser et al., *Charles De Wailly,* 23–33.
38. "Livre d'Architecture de la R .·. L .·. de l'Amitié," quoted in Lesueur, *Franc-Maçonnerie Artésienne,* 176.
39. Jean-Pierre Louis de Béyerlé, "Concerning the Locale of the Lodge," in *Essai de la Franc-Maçonnerie* ("Latomopolis," 1784), ii, 178. He divided his subject into "distribution" and "decoration" and described as a type form the plan generally in use from the 1740s, with much elaboration of the organization of the archives.
40. Ibid. Béyerlé stated that a lodge room 28 feet wide should be 54 feet long; that of Amitié was 21 feet wide and 33 feet long; the Grand Orient of Paris was divided into two parts, 21 feet by 51 feet, and 21 feet by 27 feet; the Grand Lodge of London (1776) was 43 feet by 100 feet. For a discussion of the "Solomonic" tradition, see A. Horne, *King Solomon's Temple in the Masonic Tradition* (Whitstable, Kent, 1972).
41. Villeneuve, *L'Ecole des Francs-Maçons,* 13. In the "Discourse on Friendship" (32), the analogy is made clear:

> Let us build, according to their models, buildings that astonish by their magnificence, where all the orders of architecture are resplendent: that is to say, let us form our hearts following all the virtues.

42. Jean-Baptiste Willermoz to the Duke of Brunswick (1780), quoted in Gustave Bord, *La Franc-Maçonnerie en France des origines à 1815* (Paris, 1908), vol. 1, 40. Willermoz (1730–1824) was continuously developing Masonic mysticisms throughout his life; his theories, half occultist, half alchemical, were linked to the "Templar" movement.
43. See Wolfgang Herrmann, "Unknown Designs for the 'Temple of Jerusalem' by Claude Perrault," in *Essays in the History of Architecture Presented to Rudolf Wittkower* (London, 1967), and Frank E. Manuel, *Isaac Newton, Historian* (Cambridge, Massachusetts, 1963), 161–165.
44. Mosser et al., *Charles De Wailly,* 32.

45. *Constitutions* (1723), 1–2.
46. Villeneuve, *L'Ecole des Francs-Maçons,* 3.
47. Abbé Laugier, *Essai sur l'Architecture* (Paris, 1753). Wolfgang Herrmann, in *Laugier and Eighteenth-Century Theory* (London, 1962), notes the paradigmatic form of the chapel at Versailles as strongly influencing Laugier's views on church architecture; in his later article, "Designs for the 'Temple of Jerusalem,'" he draws a relation between this chapel and the reconstruction of the Temple of Jerusalem along lines suggested by Villalpanda and Perrault. In this context, it must be assumed that Laugier was concerned with both the primitive (natural) and the civilized (revealed) paradigms of Masonic architectural theory. Although the connections need to be elaborated in more detail, with an accurate reading of Masonic texts, this confrontation between models, so to speak, is also characteristic of mid-century Freemasonic history. See, for example, Villeneuve, "Discours abrégé sur l'origine de la Maçonnerie," in *L'Ecole des Francs-Maçons,* 1–22,
48. Béyerlé, *Essai de la Franc-Maçonnerie.*
49. This estimate is based on the lists published by Alain le Bihan, supplemented by archival sources in the Bibliothèque Nationale. See Jacques Brengues and Monique Mosser, "Le monde maçonnique des lumières," in D. Ligou et al., *Histoire des Francs-Maçons,* 97–158.
50. J. B. de Puisieux, *Eléments et traité de géométrie* (Paris, 1765).
51. "Grand Orient de France, Planche à tracer générale de l'Installation" (June 1773); Pierre Chevallier has established the date of installation as October 22, 1773.
52. The administrative procedures and finances are noted in several circulars of the Grand Orient. At the Assembly of January 31, 1774, Pierre Poncet was asked to search for a property; he presented his plan for renovating the old Jesuit Novitiate in the rue Pot-au-fer, faubourg Saint Germain, on March 7. On August 12, the Grand Orient was installed. Lalande's inaugural speech has already been noted. See *Miscellaneous Documents of the Grand Orient* (January 1775), piece 6, 14, which notes that "the Temple is still without decoration, and the few pieces of necessary furniture are rented at high cost."
53. This detailed description of the completed lodge was published in *Etat du G .˙. O .˙. de France* (Paris 1777), vol. 1, part 4, 7 et seq. and 35–36. In vol. 1, part 1, there is a remarkable description of the lodge festivities at the Orient of Bordeaux on the arrival of the Duc de Chartres, February 1776. The whole facade of the lodge, 88 feet long, "was decorated with a magnificent illumination of Gothic architecture. Eight twisted columns carried an entablature of lights, allowing the sight of obelisks in the spaces between" (67).
54. F.-M. Grimm, Diderot, et al., *Correspondance littéraire, philosophique et critique* [1778], ed. M. Tourneux (Paris, 1877–1882). A general account of this philosophical lodge is given in Louis Amiable, *Une Loge Maçonnique d'avant 1789: la R .˙. L .˙. les Neuf Soeurs* (Paris, 1897). The abbé Delille, Bernard Poyet, Houdon, and Greuze were all members of this lodge.
55. Grimm et al., *Correspondance Littéraire,* 188.
56. See Auguste Viatte, "Le Préromantisme," in *Les Sources occultes du Romantisme* (Paris, 1965), vol. 1. At the turn of the century, Lavater distinguished some seven types of "pious assemblies"—magico-religious, mystico-religious, theosophico-religious, visionary, etc.
57. See Chevallier, *Franc-Maçonnerie française,* 87. "Scottish rites" introduced thirty-three grades into the canon; these were most clearly set out, and their symbolism explained, in de l'Aulnaye, *Thuileur des trente-trois degrés de l'Ecossisme du rit ancien, dit accepté* (Paris, 1813). The book's fourteen plates are useful.
58. The magisterial work by René le Forestier, *La Franc-Maçonnerie Templière et Occultiste aux XVIIIe et XIXe siècles* (Paris, 1970), is the best guide through the labyrinths of the "intellectual" and philosophic history of these cults.
59. See Robert Darnton, *Mesmerism and the End of the Enlightenment in France* (New York, 1970).
60. See Marc Haven, *Le maître inconnu: Cagliostro* (Lyons, 1964).
61. Court de Gébelin, *Monde Primitif considéré dans l'Histoire civile, religieuse, et allégorique du Calendrier ou Almanach* (Paris, 1774–1776), vol. 4, 320. De Gébelin (1719–1784) paraphrased Themistios's "On the Soul," taken from Plutarch. Also see G. E. Mylonas, *Eleusis and the Eleusinian Mysteries* (Princeton, 1961), which characterizes this description of initiation as essentially Orphic in origin and not part of the original mysteries of Eleusis. The spatial hermeneutics of Eleusis are explored in K. Kerenyi, *Eleusis: Archetypal Image of Mother and Daughter* (New York, 1967). The adoption of the so-called mysteries into the rites of the brotherhoods had a respectable history of its own: on September 21, 1645, the Compagnons du devoir in Paris were condemned by the Faculty of Theology for having introduced into their initiation ceremonies for apprenticeship a seeming parody of religious forms—administering baptism with rites "common to the mysteries of

Eleusis." See Dinaux, *Sociétés Badines*, vol. 1, 229.

62. Jean Terrasson, *Séthos, ou vie tirée des monuments anecdotes de l'ancienne Egypte* (Paris, 1731). This extraordinarily influential work was translated into English in 1731 and into German in 1737; it was reprinted in Paris in 1767. Emanuel Schikaneder, in 1791, used it for the libretto of Mozart's *Magic Flute;* Cagliostro based his "Egyptian Rite" of 1775 on its descriptions of Séthos's initiations; and many of the fantasies of Jean-Jacques Lequeu were derived from its pages.

63. Willermoz (in part), "Instruction secrète des Grands Profés," in Le Forestier, *Franc-Maçonnerie Templière*, 1026. Edited by Antoine Faivre, this document presents the fully developed theories of Willermoz on the temple and its emblems. See also, for a clear and reasoned account of mystical Masonry, Alice Joly, *Un Mystique Lyonnais et les secrèts de la Franc-Maçonnerie* (Macon, 1938).

64. Antoine-Chrysostome Quatremère de Quincy, *De L'Architecture Egyptienne considérée dans son origine, ses principes, et son goût* (1785; Paris, 1803). First partially published in the *Encyclopédie méthodique* of 1800, this article was Quatremère's prize essay for the Académie des Inscriptions of 1785. It contains an extended discussion of the virtues of Greek architecture over Egyptian and of the type of the temple, the primitive hut. Quatremère (1775–1849) was a member of the Parisian lodge Thalie from 1782 to 1786.

65. See especially Lequeu, "Vertical Section of the Cellars of the Gothic House," in *Architecture Civile* (Paris, 1779–1825; unpub.), plate 156, in the Cabinet d'Estampes, Bibliothèque Nationale. Plate 158, the "Temple of Divination at the Northern End of the Elysian Fields," and Plate 164, "Porch or Vestibule That Serves as an Entry to the Subterranean Places and the Dwelling of Pluto," are also connected to *Séthos*. The problem of Lequeu, inadequately explored in the "rationalist" explanations of Emil Kaufmann, has recently been reopened by the researches of Jacques Guillerme (who noted the *Séthos* connection) and of Philippe Duboy, *Periodo Ipotetico* 8–9 (Venice, 1974): 122–144.

66. See the abbé Delille's poem "Les Jardins" of 1784 and Robert Mauzi's analysis of its spatial and literary antecedents in "Delille, peintre, philosophe, et poète dans les Jardins," in *Delille est-il mort?* (Paris: Clermont-Ferrand, 1967).

67. See, for example, the Marquis René de Girardin, *De la composition des paysages* (1775; Paris, 1777). De Girardin was the last patron of Rousseau, who, according to a chronicler, "raised his children according to *Emile* [and] designed his gardens at Ermenonville according to *La Nouvelle Héloïse.*"

68. See Marc Haven, *Le maître inconnu: Cagliostro*, 97.

69. For a detailed description of this ritual, see *O∴ ou Histoire de la fondation du Grand Orient de France*, 244 et seq.; the rite called for four rooms, the first or "parvis," the porch, the temple or tribunal, and the final retreat. The instruments to be used in the ceremony were elaborate: a machine to imitate thunder, three other machines to make lightning flashes, a wide pan with lighted coals, a vase full of water, another with petrified earth, an intricate spiral staircase with marked levels and a trap door on the last step, three sticks, censers, thirty candles, and chalk. This last was to describe a microcosmic figure on the floor of the lodge within which the candidate was ritually transported through the traumas of "birth," "hell chaos and death," and, finally, "life."

70. The Désert de Retz was designed by François Barbier between 1771 and 1782 for the eccentric François-Racine de Monville, also a patron of Boullée. Carmontelle designed the "landscape of illusions" for the Duc de Chartres at Monceau, 1773–1778. Jubert, Comte de Bouville, was a member of the lodge La Candeur from 1777.

71. Published in J. C. Krafft and N. Ransonette, *Recueil d'Architecture Civile* (Paris, 1812), plates 37–39, showing the house leveled to its foundations (or built only to this level) before the Revolution.

72. The documentation on the estate of Maupertuis is scanty: A. de Laborde illustrated some of the *fabriques* in his *Description des Nouveaux Jardins de France* (Paris, 1808); C. Rivière published Ledoux's drawings of the ideal village in *Un village de Brie au XVIIIe siècle: Maupertuis* (Paris, 1939). There exists an inventory of the *fabriques*, made in 1795 on Montesquiou's emigration, that mentions a "round tower, serving as the base of a temple dedicated to the arts," a Chinese house built on piles, the Mausoleum of Admiral Coligny, and a "subterranean grotto in rusticated stone . . . surmounted by a facade in the form of a pyramid." The construction of this grotto, which still exists, was estimated in 1781, and the park and *fabriques* developed from 1782 to 1787. This Inventaire des fabriques (21 Prairial an III) is now in private hands. See, for Brongniart's part in the design of these *fabriques*, M. Mosser et al., *Alexandre-Théodore Brongniart, 1739-1813* (Paris, 1986), 267–272.

73. This account is quoted in full in J. W. Oliver, *The Life of William Beckford* (London, 1932), 172–181. The letter was purportedly written from Paris in 1784 to Louisa Pitt-

Rivers, William's sister-in-law and lifelong passion. It was apparently much worked over and elaborated throughout Beckford's life, and often recounted to friends; Oliver is willing to accept its general accuracy, but Guy Chapman, in *Beckford* (London, 1937), thinks it "almost certainly a pure romance." The circumstantial details are all accurate, however, particularly those relating to Ledoux, and it is difficult to see how Beckford would have known of the architect's work with such intimacy without having met him in the context described. Boyd Alexander, *England's Wealthiest Son* (London, 1962), and André Parreaux, *William Beckford* (Paris, 1960), both attest to Beckford's occultist friends and mesmeric dabbling. It should be noted that the celebrated scene-painter Jacques Loutherbourg (1740–1812), the scenic director of Drury Lane from 1771, was a reputed adept and friend of Cagliostro; it was Loutherbourg who provided the sets for Beckford's notorious "Egyptian" party at Fonthill in 1781.

74. The setting described by Beckford, "a vast space entirely occupied by wood-piles, some of enormous dimensions and very lofty, others with thatched roofs acutely pointed these innumerable accumulations of timber cloven and uncloven," could as well denote the ritual forest of the Hewers as that of the Eveillés; this latter sect, a branch of the Illuminés of Bavaria, was noted by the author of *O . . ou Histoire de la fondation du Grand Orient de France,* 225 et seq. "The locale ought to be vast," he wrote, "containing long corridors, cellars, and garden—a country house in an isolated place, but not far from the city; a garden of many acres, wild and uncultivated for receptions." An article by F. J. W. Crowe, "The Fendeurs or 'Hewers,'" *Ars Quatuor Coronatorum* 22 (1929), outlines the regulations of 1788, the "Instruction des Fendeurs."

75. William Beckford, *Vathek*, ed. Roger Lonsdale (London: O.U.P., 1970); this novel was written in French in 1782 and published first in that language in 1786–1787. The Oriental scenes, particularly that of the hospice, or *caravansérail,* seem to have influenced Ledoux. Over the doorway of the hospice was the inscription, "This is the asylum of pilgrims, the refuge of travelers, and the depository of secrets from all parts of the world" (54).

76. See the evocative article by B. Baczko, "Lumières et Utopie," *Annales E.S.C.* (March-April, 1971).

77. Ledoux, *L'Architecture.* Of the many interpretations and descriptions of this ideal city and its monuments, by far the most serious and useful is Mona Ozouf, "L'image de la ville chez Claude-Nicolas Ledoux," in *Annales E.S.C.* (November–December, 1966).

78. Ledoux, "Prospectus" to *L'Architecture* (Paris, 1802), 20.

79. Ledoux, *L'Architecture,* 3.

80. Ibid., 118.

81. Abbé Desmonceaux, *De la bienfaisance nationale* (Paris, 1789), 14; quoted in Michel Foucault, *Histoire de la Folie,* 379: "These compulsory asylums form retreats as useful as they are necessary."

82. Fourier's perceptive essay on Freemasonry, considered as the possible germ of his new society, was first published as an appendix to his *Théorie des Quatre Mouvements* (Lyons, 1808), 195–202. His own relation to the quasi-Masonic mystical cults of Lyons has yet to be clarified; Fourier's first publisher was Pierre Ballanche, a leading mystic of postrevolutionary Lyons. The way in which Fourier was led to define his personal vision of sociability in general, from his knowledge of the clubs and circles of Besançon and Lyons, as well as of Paris, is at present unclear; but a study of his architectural and social propositions within the development of the conceived and lived forms of bourgeois associational life will perhaps move them from the realm of "utopia" into that half-world of "idealized existence" so typical of the primitive forms of political organization.

1. Diderot, "Libertinage," *Oeuvres,* vol. 15, 510.
2. See Roland Barthes, *Sade, Fourier, Loyola* (Paris, 1971), especially 7–16.
3. D. A. F. de Sade, *Monsieur le 6, Lettres inédites,* ed. Georges Daumas (Paris, 1964), 22.
4. See Gilbert Lély, *Vie du Marquis de Sade,* in *Oeuvres complètes* (Paris: Au cercle du livre précieux, 1962), vols. 1 and 2.
5. Lély, *Vie du Marquis de Sade,* vol. 2, 352–389. On October 25, 1792, the Section des Piques appointed de Sade a commissioner to the administrative assembly on hospitals. Three days later, de Sade read his *Observations* to the assembly, outlining a reform program (Ibid., 353–354). Later, he was to visit and report on conditions in hospitals, prisons, and asylums for the same body. His interest and expertise had been developed much earlier, when on his travels in Italy he had met a Dr. Giuseppe Iberti in Rome. Iberti, in exile for his dubious medical interest in sexuality, published his own *Observations générales sur les hôpitaux* with plans for a model establishment drawn up in 1788 by Delannoy, sometime student of the Académie in Rome.
6. De Sade, *Voyage d'Italie* (Paris, 1967), 360. In other notes, de Sade sharply contrasted such voluntary self-imprisonment with that "horrible principle of tyranny" invented "to make the wretched person suffer more . . . by leaving him to rot in prison instead of putting him to death" (*Le Carillon de Vincennes* [Paris, 1953], 21). In the more conventionally utopian romance, *Aline et Valcour* (Paris, 1956), 269, he repeated eighteenth-century commonplaces criticizing prisons as "those pestiferous cesspools."
7. De Sade, *La Nouvelle Justine ou les malheurs de la vertu,* in *Oeuvres complètes* (Paris, 1963), vol. 6, 354–355. See also Jean-Jacques Brochier, "La circularité de l'espace," in *Le Marquis de Sade* (Paris: Centre Aixois d'études et de recherches sur le dix-huitième siècle, 1968).
8. De Sade, *Les 120 jours de Sodome,* in *Oeuvres complètes* (Paris, 1964), vol. 13, 44.
9. Ibid., 44.
10. Ibid., 48.
11. Ibid., 433.
12. De Sade, *Histoire de Juliette ou les prospérités du vice,* in *Oeuvres complètes,* vol. 8, 401 et seq. The elaborate description of the "lodge" and statutes of the Societé des Amis du crime was a direct parody of contemporary Masonic practices.
13. De Sade considered himself a playwright first and foremost; he organized plays, tableaux-vivants, and other, more directly pornographic performances in the Château d'Evry (1764) and at La Coste (1765); he worked ceaselessly to have his plays publicly performed during the Revolution and ended, as is well known, organizing the inmates of Charenton in spectacles and plays. See Lély, *Vie du Marquis de Sade,* vol. 2, 56 et seq., and Dr. L. J. Ramon, "Notes sur M. de Sade," in *Marquis de Sade, Cahiers personnels (1803-1804),* published by Lély (Paris, 1953), app. 2.
14. Barthes, "L'espace du langage," in *Sade, Fourier, Loyola,* 150–152. This "theater" should be compared to other theaters of the period, notably that built by Ledoux for Mlle. Guimard, *première danseuse* of the Opéra.
15. For the Maison de plaisir, see Ledoux, *L'Architecture,* ed. D. Ramée (Paris, 1847), plates 238–239; for the Oikéma, see Ledoux, *L'Architecture,* 199–204 and plates 103–104.
16. Lély, *Vie du Marquis de Sade,* vol. 2, 607–608 and plate 46.
17. Charles Fourier to his mother, January 8, 1790, in Ch. Pellarin, *Charles Fourier, sa vie et sa théorie* (Paris, 1843), 2.
18. Charles Fourier, *Traité de l'Association Domestique-Agricole* (Paris, 1822) (including "Sommaire" of 1823), 1433. On the Hôtel Thélusson, Fourier noted, "for the rest, as an indication of the falsification of taste, it is enough to say that the mercantile demolition of the charming Hôtel Thélusson has found its apologists" (1418).
19. Archives Nationales, 10AS (Archives Sociétaires), art. 23, pièce 18, cote supplémentaire; plans. This folder contains a number of sketches and plans by Fourier, which I have classified as follows:
I. *Hôtels* and plans for dwellings. (c.1790–1808)
a. Plans of *hôtels* (single sheet, plan on each side).
b. Three plans of *hôtels* (folded sheet).
c. Four plans of *hôtels* (folded sheet).
d. Four plans of *hôtels* (sheet folded in four).
e. Postcard: elevation with mansard (window grid on reverse).
f. Postcard: elevation without mansard (plan on reverse).
g. Postcard: two elevations (two elevations on reverse).
h. Stairway plan.
i. Stairway plan with note: "Dénouement de

toutes les utopies, ancienne et moderne."
II. Plans for Besançon (c.1826–1828)
a. "Plan d'extension et correction de Polygone de Besançon," brochure printed by L. Gauthier, Besançon, no date; seven examples, many annotated by Fourier.
b. Outlines of fortifications; six tracings.
c. Notes for printed brochure (a) with detailed annotation.
d. Sketch for brochure with annotation.
e. Notes on street alignment.
f. Place des Casernes, tracing of existing layout with modifications.
g. Plans and sketches of proposed embellishments; thirteen sheets.
III. Plans for the Tourbillon or Phalanstère (c.1804–1820)
a. Section and plan of the gallery street.
b. Aerial perspective sketch of Phalanstère. Tower of Order.
c. Plan of Tourbillon, inscribed within circle.
d. Ideal gridded plan: "Quatre lymbes."
e. Ideal gridded plan: "Quatre lymbes."
f. Gridded plan.

20. Fourier to the municipality of Bordeaux, Marseilles, 20 frimaire, an V (December 10, 1796), A.N. 10AS, art. 15, pièce 18, cote suppl. 152. The competition for the site of the Château Trompette was announced in 1796; see Courteault, *Bordeaux, cité classique* (Paris, 1932), 176–179, and L. Hautecoeur, *Histoire de l'architecture classique en France* (Paris, 1953), vol. 5, 139.

21. Fourier to Just Muiron, July 13, 1819, in Pellarin, *Charles Fourier.*

22. A.N. 10AS, art. 6, cahier 38, 6. Fourier was scornful of the talents of professional architects speaking of "les architectes servilement révérencieux pour l'antiquité" (*Traité de l'Association,* 1418). In a manuscript note entitled "Materiel de Paris, lésine et mauvais goûts dans les constructions nouvelles," he called architecture *une science vierge* (10AS, art. 15, cahier 6–7). Elsewhere, he organized the historical styles of architecture into a harmonic series to correspond to his general theory of groups (10AS, art. 12, cahier 7).

23. Probably written between 1803 and 1808, this *mémoire,* "Formation d'une Phalange [that is, Tourbillon] d'Attraction," was published in *Publication des Manuscrits de Charles Fourier* (Paris: Librairie phalanstèrienne, 1851), 80 et seq.

24. A.N. 10AS, art. 23, pièce 18 (my classification IIb, see note 19 above). With its considerable overdrawing, overlays, and cuts, this plan seems to have been worked on for a long time in response to Fourier's changing concepts of the Phalanstère.

25. Charles Fourier, *Théorie des Quatre Mouvements* (Lyons, 1808; Paris, 1966), 118.

26. Ibid., 119.

27. *Publication des Manuscrits,* 87.

28. Charles Fourier, *Le nouveau monde amoureux* (Paris, 1967).

29. *Publication des Manuscrits,* 103.

30. Ibid.

31. This is, of course, the basis of the resemblance between Fourier and Jean-Jacques Lequeu: both delighted in a solitary, closeted revolt; both drew up endless lists of objects and their desired classifications; both displaced their erotic fantasies, the one into the realm of sociological numerology, the other into the play of representation. It is significant that Fourier, the nonarchitect, worked almost entirely in plan; Lequeu, the architect, worked almost without exception in elevation.

32. A.N. 10AS, art. 19., pièce 268. Note of Fourier on Condé-sur-Vesgres. He accused the architect of having deliberately intended to abort the building campaign. Aided by the deputy Baudet-Dulary in 1832, Fourier, together with Muiron, Considerant, Abel Transon, and Jules Lechevalier, tried to establish a "Colonie sociétaire" at Condé, Seine-et-Oise. See 10AS, art. 19, pièces 3–268.

33. Jean-Jacques Lequeu, note on the back of a letter from de Barante, Secretary-General of the Ministry of the Interior, August 12, 1815, Donation of Lequeu, Archives Estampes, B.N. N. 571, published (as "Lettre de de Barante") in Phillippe Duboy "Lo sguardo di Orfeo," *Il Piccolo Hans* 10 (Bari, April–June 1976): 153.

34. See Robert Darnton, *The Literary Underground of the Old Regime* (Cambridge, Mass., 1982), esp. chaps. 1–3; this work has furnished many of the insights that I have here attributed to the study of a member of the Grub Street of architecture.

35. The literature on Lequeu is scarce and notoriously unreliable, often participating in the plays intiated by Lequeu with more gusto than historical accuracy. Following Emil Kaufmann's study, in *Three Revolutionary Architects* (Philadelphia, 1952), the best essays are by Jacques Guillerme: "Lequeu et l'invention du mauvais goût," *Gazette des Beaux Arts* (September 1965), 153–166, and "Thèmes, partis et formes chez l'architecte Lequeu," *Vie Médicale* 47 (1966): 67–82; Philippe Duboy, who has made the study of Lequeu a focus of his research, has published invaluable documents in "G. G. LeOmaggio a Raymond Roussel a Marcel Duchamp: Ready-Made rettificato," *Periodo Ipotetico* 8/9 (December 1974): 122–144, and in "Lo sguardo di Orfeo." Duboy's monograph on Lequeu, *Lequeu: An Architectural Enigma* (Cambridge, Mass., 1986), will be published soon.

36. Deschamps to Lequeu's father, August 19, 1778, in Jean-Jacques Lequeu, *Architecture Civile,* B.N. Estampes Ha80–Ha80c.
37. See "Etat des ouvrages de Mr Lequeu Architecte, donnés par lui à la Bibliothèque du Roi en Juillet 1825," B.N. Estampes, Archives, 1809–1826, published by Duboy in "G.G.Le"
38. Ernst Kris, "Die Charakterköpfe des Franz Xaver Messerschmidt," *Jahrbuch der Kunsthistorischen Sammlungen in Wien* (Vienna, 1932), and "A Psychotic Sculptor of the Eighteenth Century," *Psychoanalytic Explorations in Art* (New York, 1952), 128–150; for a more detailed assessment of Messerschmidt and a more balanced view of his supposed madness, see Maria Pötzl-Malikova, *Franz-Xaver Messerschmidt* (Vienna, 1982).
39. Guillerme, "Lequeu et l'invention du mauvais goût," 154.
40. His donation to the Bibliothèque royale included a "Lettre sur le savonnage qu'on pourroit appeller savonnement de Paris, Adressée aux mères de famille," Paris, An II, B.N. Estampes, Lh 34.
41. Kris, "A Psychotic Sculptor," 150.
42. Ibid., 138.
43. Lequeu, *Architecture Civile,* vol. 1, certificate attached to frontispiece, appointing Lequeu "dessinateur de la première classe," 13 Thermidor, An I (July 27, 1792), signed by Rondelet for the Commission des Travaux Publics.
44. The following account of Lequeu's career is drawn from his autobiographical summary attached to page 3 of *Architecture Civile* and addressed to the Minister of the Interior some time after 1802.
45. "Plans et décorations intérieures de l'hôtel Montholon, boulevard Montmartre, élévé par J. J. Lequeu sous la direction de Soufflot le Romain," B.N. Estampes, Ve 92, Fol.
46. Lequeu, *Architecture,* vol. 2, includes drawings for a casino, dated 1786, for a Madame de Meulenae(u)r; a "Temple de la Nature," or belvedere, for Mr. Q***, lawyer of Romainville; a garden design for a "jardin chinois-français," for M. Jeaumaire of Bourglibre; and a plan, elevations, and sections for the Temple de Silence or Maison de Campagne "près Promort, Boulogne-sur-Seine," overlooking Meudon and Saint Cloud, for the Comte de Bouville. Lequeu recorded a visit to Italy with de Bouville, probably before 1786. A "Jubert, Comte de Bouville" was a member of the lodge La Candeur in Paris between 1777 and 1780. J. C. Krafft published Lequeu's designs in his *Recueil d'Architecture Civile* (Paris, 1812): the casino for madame Meulenaur, plates 55–60; the Temple de Silence, plates 37–39.
47. Lequeu, *Architecture,* vol. 1, reverse of page 4; copy of diploma naming him *adjoint associé* of the Académie royale des Sciences, Belles-lettres et Arts de Rouen, November 26, 1786.
48. Lequeu, *Architecture,* vol. 1, 3, resumé of life.
49. Letter from de Barante; see note 33.
50. Phillippe Duboy, "Lo sguardo di Orfeo," 157–8.
51. Lequeu, *Architecture,* vol. 1, 78.
52. "Etat des ouvrages," note 37.
53. Lequeu, *Architecture,* vol. 1, 73, attachment. This text was first cited in F. Benoit, *L'Art Français sous la Révolution et l'Empire* (Paris, 1897), 252.
54. Donation de Lequeu, B.N. Estampes, Archives 1631–1914, vol. 1809–1826, Ye1, published in Duboy, "Lo sguardo di Orfeo," 143–156.
55. Diderot, "Lubrique, Lubricité," in *Oeuvres,* vol. 16, 5.
56. Duboy, "Les signatures de Lequeu," an unpublished *mémoire* delivered at Bordeaux, April 8, 1974, in "Jean-Jacques Lequeu(x): 'Le véritable bonheur est dans les campagnes,'" 8.
57. Lequeu, *Architecture,* vol. 4, 5.
58. Ibid., vol. 1, Frontispiece.
59. Diderot, *Oeuvres,* vol. 15, 43.
60. Lequeu, *Architecture,* vol. 1, 33, fig. 100.
61. The best analysis of Lavater's work and influence is in Graeme Tytler, *Physiognomy in the European Novel* (Princeton, 1982), 35–81. Lavater's *Physiognomische Fragmente* were published in Leipzig between 1775 and 1778 in four volumes and were translated into French almost immediately as *Essai sur la physionomie destiné à faire connoistre l'homme et à le faire aimer* (Paris and Le Hague, 1781–1803).
62. See John Graham, *Lavater's Essays on Physiognomy* (Bern, 1979), 15–33.
63. Lequeu, *Architecture,* vol. 4, 15–19; see Guillerme, "Lequeu et l'invention du mauvais goût."
64. Lavater, *Physiognomische Fragmente* (Leipzig, 1775–78), vol. 4, 39, quoted in Tytler, *Physiognomy,* 65.
65. Note of Lequeu on physiognomy published by Duboy, "G.G. Le," 129–30.
66. "Physionomie," in *Encyclopédie,* wrongly attributed to Diderot, in *Oeuvres,* vol. 16, 292. See J. Proust, "Diderot et la physiognomie," *Cahiers de l'Association internationale des études françaises* (1961), 317–329.
67. Self-portrait of Lequeu, in Duboy, "Lo sguardo di Orfeo," fig. 15.
68. Duboy, "G.G.Le," figs. 8–9.
69. Lequeu, *Architecture,* vol. 4.
70. Jacques-François Blondel, *Cours d'Architecture* (Paris, 1771–1777), vol. 1, plates X, XI, XII.

71. See, especially, Nicholas Le Camus de Mézières, *Le Génie de l'Architecture* (Paris, 1780), 2–3.
72. Ledoux, *Architecture,* 119.
73. Emil Kaufmann, *Three Revolutionary Architects.*
74. Roland Barthes, *Arcimboldo* (Milan, 1978), reprinted in *L'Obvie et l'obtus* (Paris, 1982), 126.
75. Ibid., 128.
76. Ibid., 127.
77. Diderot, *Oeuvres,* vol. 16, 5.

1. Comte de Caylus, *Recueil d'Antiquités égyptiennes, étrusques, grecques et romaines* (Paris, 1752), vol. 1, vi–vii.
2. Ibid., ix.
3. Johann Joachim Winckelmann, *History of Ancient Art,* trans. Henry Lodge (Boston, 1872), vol. 1, 150, a translation of *Geschichte der Kunst des Altertums* (1764). I have used this translation for convenience, but I have modified it where necessary. Two French translations have been published, *Histoire de l'art de l'antiquité,* trans. M. Huber (Leipzig, 1781), and *Histoire de l'art chez les anciens* (Paris, 1802–1803).
4. See, for example, Friedrich Meinecke, *Die Entstehung des Historismus* (Berlin, 1936).
5. See Arnaldo Momigliano, "Ancient History and the Antiquarian," *Studies in Historiography* (London, 1966), 20–24.
6. Bernard de Montfaucon and Jean Mabillon, Benedictine monks from the abbey of Saint Germain-des-Prés, joined meticulous scholarship with an omnivorous pleasure in collecting; see Arnaldo Momigliano, "Mabillon's Italian Disciples," in *Essays in Ancient and Modern Historiography* (Oxford, 1977). For a comprehensive account of the contribution of Francesco Bianchini, see Werner Oechslin, "Storia e archeologia prima del Piranesi: nota su Francesco Bianchini," in *Piranesi nei luoghi di Piranesi* (Rome, 1979).
7. Winckelmann, *History of Ancient Art,* vol. 1, 154.
8. The nature of the "Description" as a set-piece that develops in words the emotional and intellectual criteria for understanding a work experienced as an object, has been analyzed by Karl Justi: "the new descriptions [after 1757] are not objective as those in the natural sciences, where the author uses an exhaustive terminology in an effort to be adequate to his subject matter. Merely from these descriptions, one could hardly form images of the statues. But such a description is a conversion of the impression, received by the mind in a moment of sacred contemplation, into a series of images and concepts, just as the artist gradually converts his creative intuition into plastic reality." (Karl Justi, *Winckelmann und seine Zeitgenossen* [1872], vol. 1, 45 et seq., quoted in Max Dessoir, *Aesthetics and Theory of Art* [1906; Detroit, 1970], 407.)
9. See Francis Haskel and Nicolas Penny, *Taste and the Antique* (New Haven, 1980), 102.
10. Walter Pater, "Winckelmann," *Westminster Review* (Jan. 1867), 94; republished in *The Renaissance* (London, 1873).
11. See Barbara Maria Stafford, "Beauty of the Invisible: Winckelmann and the Aesthetics of Imperceptibility," *Zeitschrift für Kunstgeschichte* (1981), 65–78. Winckelmann's aesthetics have suffered in retelling by generations of art historians who wished to see him as a starting point, but not as a sophisticated one. The reductive and often mechanical sculptors of later neoclassicism, notably Thorvaldsen, have contributed to this image of a "frozen" past. Pater was more acute when he juxtaposed to his essay on Winckelmann a conclusion summarizing his own understanding of the relation between outer physical life—its "perpetual motion" of passage, waste, repair, modification, and process—and the "inner world of thought and feeling"—the whirlpool, the flood, the race of the stream. "How," he asks, almost paraphrasing Winckelmann, "shall we pass most swiftly from point to point, and be present always at the focus where the greatest number of vital forces unite in their purest energy?" (Pater, "Conclusion" to *The Renaissance* [omitted in the 2d ed.], drawn from "Poems by William Morris," *Westminster Review* 90 [Nov. 1868]: 311.) Pater's Hegelianism and neo-Hellenism are studied in Anthony Ward, *Walter Pater—The Idea in Nature* (London, 1966).
12. Winckelmann, *Recueil de différentes pièces sur les arts* (Paris, 1786), 33, a translation of *Gedanken über die Nachahmung der griechischen Werke in der Malerei und Bildhauerkunst* (Dresden, 1755).
13. Winckelmann, *History of Ancient Art,* vol. 3, 177.
14. Ibid., 189–196.
15. Ibid., 196.
16. See Jean Seznec, *Essais sur Diderot et l'antiquité* (Oxford, 1957), 85 et seq.
17. Winckelmann, "Observations sur l'architecture de l'ancien temple de Girgenti en Sicilie," in *Oeuvres* (Paris, 1803), vol. 2, 655 et seq., a translation of *Anmerkungen über die Baukunst der alten Tempel zu Girgenti in Sizilien* (1759); Winckelmann, "Observations sur l'architecture des anciens," in *Oeuvres,* vol. 2, 526 et seq., a translation of *Anmerkungen über die Baukunst der Alten* (1761).
18. Winckelmann, "Observations...de l'ancien temple de Girgenti," 655.
19. Ibid.
20. Ibid., 658.
21. Ibid., 659.

22. Ibid., 676.
23. Winckelmann, "Observations sur l'architecture des anciens," 526.
24. Ibid., 526–533.
25. Ibid., 543.
26. Ibid., 557.
27. Ibid., 559.
28. Ibid., 559–560.
29. Ibid., 627.
30. Ibid.
31. Ibid., 627–628.
32. Winckelmann, "Réflexions sur l'imitation des artistes Grecs dans la peinture et la sculpture," in *Recueil de différentes pièces,* 33.
33. Winckelmann, "Observations sur l'architecture des anciens," 629. Winckelmann returned to this theme in *History of Ancient Art,* vol. 3, 233 and 339, n. 5.
34. Ibid. Winckelmann cites the example of the temples of Palmyra, from the evidence of Robert Wood, *The Ruins of Palmyra* (London, 1753), 15, as evidence for this decadent style.
35. Ibid., 651.
36. Winckelmann, *History of Ancient Art,* vol. 2, 22.
37. Ibid., 44.
38. Ibid., vol. 4, 159–188.
39. Ibid., 254.
40. Ibid., 282.
41. Ibid., 283.
42. Ibid., 285.
43. Ibid., 292.
44. Ibid., vol. 3, 34.

1. Antoine Court de Gébelin, *Monde primitif, analysé et comparé avec le monde moderne* (Paris, 1787), vol. 8, 33. There has been little study of this antiquarian, champion of Protestant rights in the area of Toulouse, supporter of the Physiocrats, member of lodges (Les Neuf Soeurs, 1778–1781, and Les Amis Réunis, 1778–1784), and official historian of the Masonic order. See J. Cabrière, *Court de Gébelin* (Paris, 1899), and Paul Schmidt, *Court de Gébelin à Paris, 1763–1784* (Paris, 1908), for his Protestant activism; see also F. Baldensperger, "Court de Gébelin et l'importance de son *Monde primitif,*" in *Mélanges offerts à Edmond Huguet* (Paris, 1940), 315–330. Gerard Gennette, *Mimologiques* (Paris, 1976), 119–148, assesses de Gébelin's theory of writing.

2. Rousseau, *L'Origine des langues,* 505.

3. Ibid., 503.

4. Condillac drew from William Warburton, *Divine Legation of Moses Demonstrated from the Principles of a Deist* (London, 1738), an extract of which was published in translation as *Essai sur les hieroglyphes des Egyptiens,* trans. Léonard des Malpeines (Paris, 1761).

5. Warburton, *Divine Legation,* bk. 4, sec. 4, 23 et seq.

6. Rousseau engaged Condillac first in the *Discours sur l'origine de l'inégalité,* where the digression on language origin forms a part of the account of the rise of man from savagery to civilization, and then in the posthumously published *Essai sur l'origine des langues.* The best treatment of his social and moral arguments is still that of Jean Starobinski, "Rousseau et la recherche des origines" and "Rousseau et l'origine des langues," in *Jean-Jacques Rousseau, La transparence et l'obstacle suivi de Sept essais sur Rousseau* (Paris, 1971), 319–329, 356–379.

7. Rousseau, *L'Origine des langues,* 501: "Even though the languages of gesture and of voice are equally natural, the first is nevertheless easier and depends less on conventions."

8. Ibid., 502.

9. Rousseau, *Emile,* bk. 4, 422–423.

10. Rousseau, *Discours sur les sciences,* 8.

11. Voltaire, "De la langue des Egyptiens et de leurs symboles," in *Essai sur les moeurs,* in *Oeuvres complètes* (Paris: Garnier, 1878), vol. 11, 63–64.

12. Momigliano, "Ancient History," 17.

13. Jacob Spon, *Voyage d'Italie, de Dalmatie, de Grèce et du Levant* (Lyons, 1678), the record of his travels with Sir George Wheler, the botanist; four years earlier, he had published *Recherche des antiquités et curiosités de la ville de Lyons;* Bernard Montfaucon, *Antiquité expliquée par les images* (Paris, 1718–1724). In the Preface, Montfaucon states, "By this term 'antiquity,' I mean only what can be seen by the eye and what can be represented in images" (vi). As Momigliano noted in 1950, "The history of the attempts to create a scientific iconography from . . . Jacob Spon, passing through . . . Montfaucon, is still to be written." This is still largely true, and especially with regard to the origins of architectural history, which owes so much to this antiquarian tradition.

14. Comte de Caylus, *Recueil d'antiquités égyptiennes, étrusques, grecques et romaines* (Paris, 1752–1767). See Seznec, *Essais sur Diderot,* 86–96, and S. Rocheblave, *Essai sur le Comte de Caylus: l'homme, l'artiste, l'antiquaire* (Paris, 1889).

15. Court de Gébelin, *Monde primitif,* vol. 1, 4.

16. Ibid., vol. 8, 32.

17. Jean-Louis Viel de Saint-Maux, *Lettres sur l'architecture des Anciens et celle des Modernes* (Paris, 1787). The only studies of Viel are the note of J. M. Pérouse de Montclos, "Charles-François Viel, Architecte de l'Hôpital général et Jean-Louis Viel de Saint-Maux, Architecte, peintre, et avocat au Parlement de Paris," *Bulletin de la Société de l'Histoire de l'Art Français* (1966), 257–269, which finally separated the two writers and architects, but shed little light on Viel; and the recent article by Jean-Rémy Mantion, "La solution symbolique, Les *Lettres sur l'architecture* de Viel de Saint-Maux (1787)," *Urbi* 9 (Brussels, 1984): 46–58, which sketches the theory and attempts incorrectly to relate Viel's notion of symbolism to that of Hegel.

18. Among other *mémoires,* Viel wrote a *Dissertation sur les cornes antiques et modernes, ouvrage philosophique* (Paris, 1785), and *Observations philosophiques sur l'usage d'exposer les ouvrages de peinture et de sculpture* (Paris, 1785). He was recorded as a member of the Academy of Marseilles in 1762, protected by the marquis de Paulmy, a member of the lodges La Minerve (1777) and Les Neuf Soeurs (1779), where his date of birth was noted as 1736. (Alain le Bihan, *Francs-maçons parisiens du Grand Orient de France* [Paris, 1966], 478.) A lost essay on the "origin of painting and language" is also mentioned in Viel's footnotes.

19. Viel, *Lettres,* lettre 1, 14.
20. Ibid., 16.
21. Ibid., 17.
22. Ibid.
23. Ibid., vol. 2, 8.
24. Ibid., 9–10.
25. A partial list would include Guillaume-Joseph Grelot, *Relation nouvelle d'un voyage de Constantinople* (Paris, 1680) (still used by Gibbon and Séroux d'Agincourt in the 1770s); *Voyages de Richard Pococke . . . en Orient, dans l'Egypte, l'Arabie, la Palestine, la Syrie, le Thrace, etc.* (Paris, 1772–1773), translated from the English edition of 1743–1745; *Journal du voyage du chevalier Chardin en Perse et aux Indes Orientales* (London, 1686) (with several editions to 1735); Robert Wood's and James Dawkins's descriptions of Palmyra and Balbec (*The Ruins of Palmyra* [London, 1753] and *The Ruins of Balbec* [London, 1757]), translated in 1753 and 1757, respectively, probably by the abbé Barthélémy; Frederick Norden, *Voyage d'Egypte et de Nubie* (Copenhagen, 1755); Cornelius de Bruin, *Voyage au Levant* (Delft, 1700), from the Dutch edition of 1698, reprinted with his *Voyages . . . par la Muscovie, en Perse et aux Indes Orientales* (Paris, 1725); Engelbert Kaempfer, *Histoire naturelle, civile et ecclésiastique de l'Empire du Japon* (The Hague, 1732), from the earlier German edition. Travel accounts after 1760 have been excellently surveyed by Barbara Maria Stafford, *Voyage into Substance, Art, Science, Nature, and the Illustrated Travel Account, 1760-1840* (Cambridge, Mass., 1984).
26. Viel, *Lettres,* vol. 3, 22–25.
27. Ibid., vol. 4, 17 et seq.
28. Ibid., vol. 3, 5.
29. See Michel de Certeau, "Writing Versus Time," 37–64.
30. Legrand et Landon, *Annales du Musée* 2 (1801): 123–128.
31. *Mercure de France* (September 24, 1785), 179 et seq.
32. Viel, *Lettres,* lettre 7, 47.
33. Ibid., 59.
34. Ibid., 58: "M. LeJai [*sic*], Architect to the King of Prussia, was astonished when he returned to Paris to see that his students had scattered columns everywhere. This was all well and good, he said, in the designs for decorations or fireworks that I gave them to copy. . . . This artist, full of talent, could find no occupation in Paris, no amateur who would find him a place, nor any student, despite the number he had created, who would pay him a visit." Viel noted that one of Legeay's drawings resembled the decorations of Ledoux's gate to the Hotel d'Uzés, another mark against Ledoux.
35. Quatremère de Quincy, "Allégorie," in *Encyclopédie méthodique: Architecture* (Paris, 1788), vol. 1.

1. Quatremère de Quincy, "Type," in *Encyclopédie méthodique: Architecture* (Paris, 1788–1825), vol. 3, 543.
2. Abel Boyer, "Type," in *Dictionnaire royal anglo-français* (Amsterdam, 1727).
3. François Marie Arouet de Voltaire, "Miracles typiques," in *Questions sur miracles,* quoted in Robert, *Dictionnaire* (Paris, 1966), vol. 6, 705–706: "I call typical those miracles that are evidently the type, the symbol of some moral truth." Isaac Newton's studies of biblical history, which included a sketched "restoration" of the Temple of Solomon, are discussed in Frank E. Manuel, *Isaac Newton, Historian* (Cambridge, Mass., 1963). Newton's comments on the "Language of the Prophets" are included in *Sir Isaac Newton: Theological Manuscripts,* ed. H. McLachlan (Liverpool, 1950), 119–126.
4. Jean-Louis Viel de Saint-Maux, *Lettres sur l'architecture,* lettre 1, 17.
5. *Le Grand vocabulaire français* (Paris, 1773), vol. 29.
6. Voltaire, quoted in *Le Petit Robert* (Paris, 1973), 84.
7. Diderot, "Grec," in *Encyclopédie,* supplément (1777), quoted in Robert, *Dictionnaire,* vol. 6, 706
8. See J. Seznec, *Essais sur Diderot et l'antiquité* (Oxford, 1957), 23–42, for a detailed discussion of Diderot's concept of antique beauty with respect to Winckelmann.
9. For the Freemasonic connection, see Martin Couret de Villeneuve, *L'Ecole des Francs-Maçons* ("Jérusalem," 1748).
10. Ribart de Chamoust, *L'Ordre français trouvé dans la Nature* (Paris, 1783).
11. Ibid., 2.
12. Ibid.
13. Ibid.
14. Ibid., 3–4.
15. Ibid., 5.
16. Ibid., 6–7.
17. See Monique Mosser, "Monsieur de Marigny et les jardins: projets inédits de fabriques pour Menars," in *Bulletin de la Société de l'Histoire de l'Art Français* (1973), 269–293.
18. Quatremère de Quincy, *De l'Architecture égyptienne, considérée dans son origine, ses principes et son goût, et comparée sous les même rapports à l'architecture grecque* (Paris, 1803).
19. Ibid., 205.
20. Ibid., 229.
21. Ibid., 204.
22. Quatremère de Quincy, *Encyclopédie méthodique: Architecture* (Paris, 1788), vol. 1. This, the only volume to appear before the Revolution, comprised terms from "Abajour" to "Coloris des Fleurs." Volume 2, Part 1 ("Colossal" to "Escalier") was published in 1801, Volume 2, Part 2 ("Escalier" to "Mutules") in 1820, and the final volume ("Nacelle" to "Zotheca") in 1825. All three volumes were drastically revised and shortened to form the two-volume *Dictionnaire historique d'architecture* (1832). The history of the *Encyclopédie* under the general editorship of Charles-Joseph Panckoucke has been detailed in Robert Darnton, *The Business of Enlightenment* (Cambridge, Mass., 1979). For information about Quatremère's editorial role, the only sources are still two studies by René Schneider, *Quatremère de Quincy et son intervention dans les arts (1788–1830)* (Paris, 1910), and *L'Esthétique classique chez Quatremère de Quincy (1805–1823)* (Paris, 1910). An annotated selection of articles from the *Encyclopédie méthodique: Architecture,* with excellent introductions by Georges Teyssot and Valeria Farinati, has been published in Quatremère de Quincy, *Dizionario Storico di Architettura* (Venice: Marsilio, 1985).
23. Quatremère de Quincy, "Cabane," in *Encyclopédie méthodique* (Paris, 1788), vol. 1.
24. Quatremère de Quincy, "Architecture" and "Caractère," in *Encyclopédie méthodique,* vol. 1.
25. Quatremère de Quincy, "Type," in *Encyclopédie Méthodique.*
26. For the classical concept of the Idea, see Edwin Panofsky, *Idea: A Concept in Art Theory* (1924; New York, 1968). The transformation of classical ideas of imitation in Quatremère has been analyzed in Jean-Claude Lebensztejn, "De l'imitation dans les beaux-arts," *Critique* (January 1982), 3–21, and in Georges Teyssot, "Mimesis dell'Architettura," in Quatremère de Quincy, *Dizionario storico di architettura,* 7–42.
27. B. Lafaye, *Dictionnaire des synonymes* (Paris, 1857), 780, notes that, "*Model* belongs to common language, but not *type.*"
28. Quatremère de Quincy, "Type."
29. Ibid.
30. Ibid.
31. Quatremère de Quincy, *Le Jupiter Olympien* (Paris, 1814), 214.
32. Quatremère de Quincy, "Architecture."
33. Quatremère de Quincy, "Type."
34. See Joseph Rykwert, *The First Moderns* (Cambridge, Mass., 1980), 316–317, for a discussion of Lodoli's functionalist chair. M.

Brusatin, in *Venezia nel Settecento* (Turin, 1979), proposes the affinity with David's "Brutus" chair.

35. Quatremère de Quincy, "Type."

36. Jacques-François Blondel, *Cours d'architecture* (Paris, 1772), vol. 2, 229 et seq.

37. Quatremère de Quincy, "Caractère," 477.

38. See Michel Foucault, *Les Mots et les Choses* (Paris, 1966), 150–158.

39. Quatremère de Quincy, "Caractère," 477.

40. Ibid., 480 et seq.

41. Ibid., 490.

42. Ibid., 492.

43. Ibid., 494.

44. Ibid., 495.

45. Ibid., 496.

46. See P. Frankl, *The Gothic: Literary Sources and Interpretations Through Eight Centuries* (Princeton, 1960).

47. Quatremère de Quincy, "Caractère," 498.

48. Ibid.

49. Ibid., 502.

50. Ibid., 506.

51. Ibid., 509 et seq. The quasi-historical novel, *Voyage du jeune Anacharsis en Grèce,* by the antiquarian Jean-Jacques Barthélémy, was published in 1788. Based on an encyclopedic knowledge of ancient texts, it rapidly became the most popular of guides to the world of the fourth century B.C.

52. Ibid., 512: "When a form [the circle] is as rigorously ordered by need and the nature of things . . . it becomes the essential motif and the *type* of the building."

53. Ibid., 515.

54. Ibid., 516.

55. Abbé Pluche, *Histoire du Ciel* (Paris, 1748), vol. 2, 427.

56. De Beauzée, "Allégorie," in *Encyclopédie méthodique: Belles-Lettres,* vol. 1, 119 et seq.

57. Ibid., 126.

58. Quatremère de Quincy, "Allégorie," in *Encyclopédie méthodique: Architecture,* vol. 1, 31–32.

59. Quatremère de Quincy, "Décoration," in *Encyclopédie méthodique,* vol. 2, part 1, 179 et seq.

60. Quatremère de Quincy, "Barrière," in *Encyclopédie méthodique,* vol. 1, 214–216.

61. Quatremère de Quincy, "Catania," in *Encyclopédie méthodique,* vol. 1, 557.

62. Quatremère de Quincy, "Athènes," in *Encyclopédie méthodique,* vol. 1, 156.

63. Quatremère de Quincy, *Le Jupiter Olympien* (Paris, 1814).

64. Quatremère de Quincy, "Restaurer," "Restitution," and "Ruines," in *Encyclopédie méthodique,* vol. 3, 286–288, 312–314.

65. Quatremère de Quincy, "Ruines," 314.

1. Armand-Guy Kersaint, *Discours sur les monuments publics prononcé au conseil du département de Paris, le 15 décembre 1791* (Paris, 1792), 71; Kersaint, a deputy for Paris, proposed his own solution to the formation of a national museum by moving the Bibliothèque Nationale to the Louvre and building a museum on the rue de Richelieu in its stead. See Louis Courajod, *Alexandre Lenoir, son journal et le Musée des monuments français* (Paris, 1878–1887), vol. 1, xix et seq., for a summary of proposals to establish a museum in the Louvre.

2. Thiéry, in his *Guide des amateurs et des étrangers à Paris* (Paris, 1787), vol. 1, 375, spoke of the idea of a "Museum, a school, where genius should be warmed by the fire of great men immortalized in their works!"

3. See Jean-Marie Pérouse de Montclos, *Etienne-Louis Boullée, 1728–1799* (Paris, 1969), 163–164. The program of 1779 is quoted in full, together with illustrations of the four prize-winning designs by Gisors, Delannoy, Barbie, and Durand, in Szambien, *Jean-Nicolas-Louis Durand,* 31 and Plates 29–33.

4. For a general discussion of the development of the museum as a building type, see Nikolaus Pevsner, *A History of Building Types* (Princeton, 1976), 111–139.

5. See Courajod, *Alexandre Lenoir,* vol. 1, xxx et seq.

6. In this sense, a "museum" of prize-winning designs for the Prix de Rome; Boullée himself projected such a didactic display, first for the Académie and then, after 1793, for the newly founded Institut.

7. Boullée, *Architecture,* 40.

8. Ledoux's "Précis" of 1800 is published in H. Ottomeyer, "Autobiographies d'architectes parisiens, 1759–1811," *Bulletin de la Société de l'histoire de Paris, 1971* (Paris, 1974), 180–181; for Durand, see Szambien, *J.-N.-L. Durand.*

9. Jacques-Guillaume Legrand, *Histoire générale de l'architecture* (Paris, 1809), 7.

10. Ibid., 18.

11. Ibid.

12. Louis-François Cassas (1756–1827), a student of the painter Vien, specialized in the recording of ruins and monuments around the Mediterranean. His voyages with Saint-Non under the patronage of the Duc de Choiseul-Gouffier were published in *Voyage pittoresque de la Syrie, de la Phoenicie, de la Palestine et de la Basse-Egypte* (Paris, 1799); *Voyage pittoresque et historique de l'Istrie et de la Dalmatie* (Paris, 1802); and *Grandes vues pittoresques des principaux sites et monuments de la Grèce, de la Sicile et de sept collines de Rome* (Paris, 1813). His assembled collection of models—a realization of the comparative method of Le Roy, Legrand, and Durand—included eight Egyptian examples, three Indian, two Persian, thirty Greek, two Etruscan, one Cyclopean, two Celtic-Druidic, twenty-three Roman, and three Byzantine, reflecting his classicist disposition. They were exhibited in 1806 with a catalogue by Legrand. See H. Boucher, "Louis-François Cassas," *Gazette des Beaux-Arts* 2 (1926): 27–53, 209–230; D. Poulot, "Modelli d'architettura—La nascita del museo di archittettura in Francia," *Lotus International* 35 (1982): 32–35.

13. J.-G. Legrand, *Collection des chefs-d'oeuvre de l'architecture de différents peuples, exécutés en modèles sous la direction de L.-F. Cassas* (Paris, 1806), v.

14. Ibid., xviii.

15. Alexandre Lenoir, *Musée des monuments français, ou description historique et chronologique des statues en marbre et en bronze, bas-reliefs et tombeaux des hommes et des femmes célèbres pour servir à l'histoire de France et à celle de l'art* (Paris, 1800), vol. 1, 50–51.

16. The discussion of Revolutionary vandalism has generally been conducted in openly partisan terms; the best recent study is by Daniel Hermant, "Destructions et vandalisme pendant la Révolution française," *Annales E.S.C.* 33 (1978): 703–719.

17. Abbé Henri Grégoire, *Second rapport sur le vandalisme* (Paris, 1794), 6. Grégoire, Bishop of Blois and deputy to the Convention for Loir-et-Cher, was a member of the Comité d'instruction publique, which had oversight of the Commission des arts; his three *mémoires* addressed to the Convention established the discussion of "vandalism" in political and cultural terms. See Grégoire, *Instruction publique—Rapport sur les destructions opérées par le vandalisme et sur les moyens de le réprimer* (Paris, 1794), and *Troisième rapport sur le vandalisme* (Paris, 1795). See also Hermant, "Destructions," 709–711, and Pierre Marot, "L'abbé Grégoire et le vandalisme révolutionnaire," *Revue de l'Art* 49 (1980): 36–39.

18. Administration du département de police de Paris, A.N. M. 666, dossier S, quoted in Hermant, "Destructions," 711.

19. See Courajod, *Alexandre Lenoir,* vol. 1, xix.

20. See Christopher M. Greene, "Alexandre Lenoir and the Musée des Monuments Français During the French Revolution," *French Historical Studies,* vol. 12, no. 2 (Fall

1981): 200–222; and L. Tuetey, ed., *Procès-verbaux de la Commission temporaire des arts* (Paris, 1912–1917), vii et seq.
21. Greene, "Alexandre Lenoir," 201.
22. Hermant, "Destructions," 706–711.
23. Ibid., 709.
24. Tuetey, *Procès-verbaux,* vol. 1, xviii-xxiii and 107 et seq.
25. Ibid., xxii.
26. The fundamental works on Lenoir are Courajod, *Alexandre Lenoir;* Greene, "Alexandre Lenoir"; Bruno Foucart, "La fortune critique d'Alexandre Lenoir et du premier Musée des monuments français," *L'Information d'histoire de l'art 14,* 5 (1969): 223–232, which summarizes the recent literature; also, S. Mellon, "Alexandre Lenoir: the Museum Versus the Revolution," *Proceedings of the Consortium of Revolutionary Europe* 9 (1979): 75–88. Lenoir (1762–1839) was a painter, a student of Doyen, and as an amateur antiquarian, a friend of the scholar Leblond.
27. Lenoir, *Musée,* vol. 1, 4; Courajod, *Alexandre Lenoir,* vol. 1, xci.
28. Courajod, *Alexandre Lenoir,* vol. 1, clxiii.
29. Lenoir, *Musée,* vols. 1 and 2.
30. Ibid.
31. Ibid.
32. Ibid.
33. There are few descriptions of the original state of the convent buildings. Suzanne Thouronde, "Le Couvent des Petits-Augustins," *Information d'histoire d'art* (October 1964), summarizes the remaining evidence and attempts a hypothetical reconstruction of the convent.
34. Lenoir himself took little care either to preserve any of the existing fabric or to record its state before his reconstruction.
35. For a detailed chronology of this process, see Courajod, *Alexandre Lenoir,* vol. 1. Antoine-Marie Peyre (1770–1843) was the son of Marie-Joseph Peyre, friend and collaborator of Charles De Wailly on the design of the Théâtre français (Odéon) from 1767. After studying with De Wailly, Peyre fils began working with Lenoir in 1795. His association with De Wailly explains the theatrical milieu of the museum.
36. Lenoir quoted at length from Winckelmann, *History of Ancient Art,* in *Musée,* vol. 1, note 1, stressing the analogy between post-Revolutionary France and Periclean Athens in terms of cultural progress.
37. Lenoir, *Musée,* vol. 1, 6.
38. Ibid., 7.
39. Ibid., 180 et seq. The "debris" from Saint Denis was, as Lenoir admitted, from the twelfth century; it was accordingly "refashioned following the taste of the architecture regenerated by the Arabs."
40. Lenoir, *Musée,* vol. 3, 8, note 1.
41. Lenoir's later study, *La franc-maçonnerie rendue à sa véritable origine, ou l'antiquité de la franc-maçonnerie prouvée par l'explication des mystères anciens et modernes* (Paris, 1814), summarized the course of lectures he gave to the Mère Loge Ecossaise in 1811 and made the comparison between initiation and the aesthetics of the sublime.
42. Lenoir, *Musée,* vol. 1, 181.
43. Ibid.
44. Lenoir, *Musée,* vol. 2, 46 et seq.
45. Ibid., vol. 2, 61–62.
46. Ibid., vol. 2, 110.
47. Ibid., vol. 3, 36 et seq.
48. Ibid.
49. Ibid., vol. 5, 151.
50. Ibid., vol. 2, 114.
51. Ibid.
52. These projected courtyards, designed by Percier but never completed, were illustrated and described in detail in Lenoir, *Musée,* vol. 4, 51–60, plates 1 and 2 (160–165).
53. Lenoir, *Musée,* vol. 4, 59.
54. Ibid., vol. 1, 19.
55. See Greene, "Alexandre Lenoir," 216. Lenoir seems to have indulged in the somewhat necrophiliac hobby of collecting parts of the exhumed bodies from the tombs he restored; these he distributed as gifts to his friends; portions of Héloise were still being given away in 1831.
56. Lenoir, *Musée,* vol. 4, 51.
57. Ibid.
58. Ibid., vol. 1, 50–51.
59. Jules Michelet, *Ma Jeunesse* (Paris, 6th ed., 1884), 45.
60. For a summary of Quatremère's eventually successful campaign for closure of the Museum, see René Schneider, "Un ennemi du Musée des Monuments Français, Chrysostome Quatremère de Quincy," *Gazette des Beaux-Arts 2,* 4 (1909): 353–370; and Michael Greenhaigh, "Quatremère de Quincy as a popular Archeologist," *Gazette des Beaux-Arts 71* 6 (April 1968): 249–256.

1. Jean-Baptiste-Louis-Georges Séroux d'Agincourt, "Discours Préliminaire," in *Histoire de l'art par les monuments depuis sa décadence au IVe siècle jusqu'à son renouvellement au XVIe* (Paris, 1811–1823), vol. 1, iv.

2. Séroux d'Agincourt (1730–1816) has received little attention from historians. The only biographical source remains the "Notice sur la vie et les Travaux," contributed to the *Histoire* by La Salle, a friend of the family. A. Cipriani, "Una proposta per Séroux d'Agincourt; la Storia dell'Architettura," *Storia dell'arte* 11 (1971): 211–261, listed for the first time the original drawings for the *Histoire* in the Vatican Archives, but provided little new information. The best summary of his work to date is Henri Loyrette, "Séroux d'Agincourt et les origines de l'histoire de l'art médiéval," *Revue de l'Art* 48 (1980): 40–56. Séroux's earlier career in Paris as a *fermier-général* is treated in Yves Durand, *Les fermiers généraux au XVIIIe siècle* (Paris, 1971), 518–520.

3. La Salle, "Notice."

4. See Henri Loyrette, "Séroux d'Agincourt."

5. Séroux was scrupulous in giving credit to these collaborators; many of them are listed in "Architecture," in *Histoire,* vol. 1, 37; in "Description des planches," in *Histoire,* vol. 3, most of the drawings are attributed by name.

6. Loyrette, in "Séroux d'Agincourt," published the correspondence with the architect Delannoy, who provided drawings of Notre-Dame between 1787 and 1789.

7. The preparatory drawings for these engravings are conserved in fourteen volumes in the Vatican Library, Rome; those at Vat.Lat., 9839, I and II; Vols. 9844 and 9855 are concerned with architecture.

8. Séroux, "Preface," in *Histoire,* vol. 1, i.

9. Ibid., iii.

10. Francis Haskell, "Gibbon and the History of Art," *Daedalus* 105, no. 3 (Summer 1976): 217–229. Haskell was the first to note the strong influence of Gibbon on Séroux.

11. La Salle, "Notice."

12. Séroux, *Histoire,* vol. 1, 69.

13. Séroux, "Tableau Historique," in *Histoire,* vol. 1, 5.

14. Ibid., 9.

15. Séroux, "Discours préliminaire," in *Histoire,* v.

16. Haskell, "Gibbon."

17. Gibbon's Journey from Geneva to Rome—His Journal from 20 April to 2 October 1764, ed. Georges A. Bonnard (London, 1961). Susa is mentioned on page 9; Turin, 12 et seq.; Milan, 45 et seq.; Pavia, 59 et seq.; Genoa, 67 et seq.; Florence, 119 et seq.

18. Edward Gibbon, *The History of the Decline and Fall of the Roman Empire* (London, 1776–1778; New York: Modern Library, n.d.), 39.

19. Ibid., 191.

20. Ibid., 233. Gibbon compared the Temple of Ephesus to Saint Peter's, Rome, "that sublime production of modern architecture . . . ; the boldest artists of antiquity would have been startled at the proposal of raising in the air a dome of the size and proportions of the Pantheon."

21. Ibid., 268.

22. Ibid., 338 et seq.

23. Séroux, "Tableau Historique," in *Histoire,* vol. 1, 5.

24. Séroux, "Architecture," in *Histoire,* vol. 1, 1.

25. Ibid., 48. Buffon had published his "Des époques de la nature" in 1778 as a supplement to his *Histoire naturelle;* it included a theoretical discussion of world history. He spoke of the "monuments" of nature, "the order of time indicated by the facts and by the monuments," and he compared to civil history the six "spaces of time" or epochs in the "succession of the first ages of nature"; the civil history was more precise in its limits and dates (Buffon, *Histoire naturelle,* ed. Jean Varloot [Paris, 1984], 241 et seq.).

26. Séroux, *Histoire,* vol. 1, i.

27. Ibid.

28. Diderot, "Prospectus," in d'Alembert, *Discours préliminaire de l'Encyclopédie* (Paris: Editions Gonthier, 1966), 140.

29. Séroux, "Architecture," in *Histoire,* vol. 1, 46.

30. Fischer von Erlach, *Entwurf einer historischen Architektur* (Vienna, 1721), plates 46, 77. For a detailed study of Fischer's sources, see George Kunoth, *Die Historische Architektur Fischer von Erlach* (Dusseldorf, 1956).

31. See Werner Szambien, *J.-N.-L. Durand, 1760–1834* (Paris, 1984), 27–30 and plates 21–25, for a fuller discussion of the genre of comparative history in the eighteenth century. The engraving by Meissonnier is bound in with Dumont, *Détails des plus intéressantes parties d'architecture de la basilique Saint-Pierre* (Paris, 1763), copy in the Bibliothèque nationale, Paris.

32. J.-D. Le Roy, "Plan des Eglises les plus remarquables bâties depuis l'an 326 jusqu'à an 1764," in *Histoire de la disposition et des formes différentes que les chrétiens ont donné à leurs tem-*

ples depuis le règne de Constantin le Grand jusqu'à nous (Paris, 1764), 88–89, engraved by Neufforge. This plate is discussed in Richard Etlin, "Grandeur et décadence d'un modèle: l'église Sainte-Geneviève et les changements de valeur ésthétique au XVIIIe siècle," in *Soufflot et l'Architecture des lumières, 26–38.*
33. Le Roy, *Les ruines des plus beaux monuments de la Grèce considérées du côté de l'architecture,* 2d. ed (Paris, 1770); this is the second and revised edition of the work first published in 1758.
34. Ibid., vol. 1, viii–ix, a text that repeats the introduction to the comparative plate of 1764 almost word for word.
35. Séroux, "Discours préliminaire," in *Histoire,* vol. 1, ii.
36. Edward Gibbon, "On the Triumphs of the Romans" (November 1764), in *Miscellaneous Works* (London, 1814), vol. 4, 359–394.
37. See Haskell, "Gibbon"
38. Séroux, "Architecture," in *Histoire,* vol. 1, 11.
39. Ibid., 25.
40. Ibid., 48.
41. Ibid., 55.
42. Ibid., plate 46. The different theories of the origin of Gothic architecture are summarized in Paul Frankl, *The Gothic: Literary Sources and Interpretations through Eight Centuries* (Princeton, 1960), 512–513.
43. Frankl, *The Gothic,* 513, points out that the monastery Scholastica at Subiaco has since been dated much later, c. 1200 A.D. and, further, that Séroux presented the French Gothic cathedrals in incorrect chronological order.
44. Séroux, *Histoire,* vol. 1, 61.
45. Ibid., 69. Séroux quotes from Horace Walpole, *Anecdotes of Painting in England* (London, 1762), chap. 5, and James Bentham, *History of the Antiquities of Ely* (London, 1771), among other, numerous contemporary histories of the Gothic in England.
46. Ibid., 68.
47. Ibid., 21.
48. Séroux, "Peinture," in *Histoire,* vol. 2, 131.
49. Quatremère de Quincy, *Recueil de notices historiques lues dans les séances publiques de l'Académie Royale des Beaux-Arts à l'Institut* (Paris, 1834), vol. 1, 240.
50. Séroux, "Architecture," in *Histoire,* vol. 1, 66.

ILLUSTRATION CREDITS

1. C. Perrault, *Les dix livres d'architecture de Vitruve* (Paris, 1684), plate V.
2–8. J.-F. Lafitau, *Moeurs des sauvages américains* (Paris, 1724).
9. M.-A. Laugier, *Essai sur l'architecture,* 2nd edition (Paris, 1755), Frontispiece.
10. J.-J. Rousseau, *Discours sur l'origine de l'inégalité* (Paris, 1755), Frontispiece.
11. C. Delagardette, *Règles des cinq ordres d'architecture de Vignole* (Paris, 1786), plate 3.
12–19,21–23,26,44. *Encyclopédie, Planches,* 1751–1765.
20. I. Ware, *A Complete Body of Architecture* (London, 1768), plate 5.
24. Courtesy David Apter.
25,27,29–31,33–35,39–44,46–49,68–69,96–98. C.-N. Ledoux, *L'Architecture considéreé sous le rapport de l'art des moeurs et de la législation* (Paris, 1804).
28. J. Bentham, *Outline of a Work Entitled "Pauper Management Improved"* (London, 1797).
36. E. A. Ancelon, "Recherches historiques et archéologiques sur les salines d'Amelécourt et de Château-Salins," *Mémoires de la Société d'archéologie de Lorraine* (1880).
50. P. Panseron, *Mémoire rélatif à un plan d'Hôtel-Dieu pour Paris* (Paris, 1773).
51–52. A. Petit, *Mémoire sur la meilleure manière de construire un hôpital des malades* (Paris, 1774).
54–55. J.-B. Le Roy, *Précis d'un ouvrage sur les hôpitaux* (Paris, 1787).
56. H. Maret, *Mémoires sur la construction d'un hôpital* (Dijon, 1783).
57–59. B. Poyet, *Mémoire sur la nécessité de transférer et reconstruire l'Hôtel-Dieu de Paris* (Paris, 1785).
60. J. R. Tenon, *Mémoires sur les hôpitaux de Paris* (Paris, 1788).
61. *Mémoires de l'Académie royale des sciences* (1786).
62,70a. J.-N.-L. Durand, *Recueil et parallèle des édifices en tous genres* (Paris, 1799–1801).
63–65. N. M. Clavareau, *Mémoire sur les Hôpitaux civils de Paris* (Paris, 1805).
66. Courtesy Cooper-Hewitt Museum, New York.
67. J. Gondouin, *Description des écoles de chirurgie* (Paris, 1780).
70. J.-N.- L. Durand, *Nouveau précis des leçons d'architecture données à l'Ecole Impériale polytechnique* (Paris, 1813).
71. G.-L. Pérau, *L'Ordre des francs-maçons trahis* (1742).
72–74. Abbé Larudan, *Les Francs-maçons écrasés* (1741).
76. *Oppositions* 8.
77. Courtesy Ecole Nationale Supérieure des Beaux-Arts, Paris.
79,131–133. A.-C. Quatremère de Quincy, *De l'Architecture égyptienne* (Paris, 1803).
80–84,86–88,107–125. Courtesy Bibliothèque nationale, Cabinet d'estampes.
85. M. Haven, *Le maitre inconnu. Cagliostro* (Lyons, 1964).
89–90. A. de Laborde, *Description des nouveaux jardins de France* (Paris, 1808).
91a. Anonymous, *Athenée des Francs-maçons* (Paris, 1808).
95. Ramon Alejandro, in Roland Barthes, *Sade, Fourier, Loyola* (Paris, 1971).
99. G. Lély, *Vie du Marquis de Sade* (Paris, 1962).
101–106. Courtesy Archives nationales, Paris.
126,165. J.-D. Le Roy, *Les ruines des plus beaux monuments de la Grèce* (Paris, 1758,1770).
127–130. Ribart de Chaumoust, *L'Ordre françois* (Paris, 1783).
134. A.-C. Quatremère de Quincy, *Le Jupiter Olympien* (Paris, 1814).
135–140,149. J. E. Biet, *Souvenirs du Musée des monuments français* (Paris, 1821).
141–148. A. Lenoir, *Musée des monuments français* (Paris, 1800).
150–159,166–173. J.-B. Séroux d'Agincourt, *Histoire de l'Art, Architecture* (Paris, 1823).
160–163. Fischer von Erlach, *Entwurf einer historischen Architektur* (Vienna, 1721).
164. J.-D. Le Roy, *Histoire de la disposition* (Paris, 1764).

INDEX

The Writing of the Walls was designed by Eric R. Kuhne of Eric R. Kuhne and Associates of New York. The jacket uses Stoneface, type designed by Eric Kuhne, based on stone inscriptions by Leon Battista Alberti. The book type, Caslon, was composed at Princeton Architectural Press using troff publishing software and set by House of Equations in Newton, NJ. The paper is Mohawk Superfine, which is acid-free, alum-free, and rosin-free and will not yellow; the binding is Smyth-sewn, to insure permanence. The binding cloth is Holliston Payko and conforms to ANSI and library standards.